Linn's

Who's Who on U.S. Stamps

By Richard Louis Thomas

Published by *Linn's Stamp News*, the largest and most informative stamp newspaper in the world. *Linn's* is owned by Amos Press, 911 Vandemark Road, Sidney, Ohio 45365. Amos Press also publishes *Scott Stamp Monthly* and the Scott line of catalogs.

033021

Introduction

By Donna O'Keefe

Who's Who on U.S. Stamps contains biographies of nearly every person ever portrayed on a U.S. postage stamp — a complete reference on the many personalities featured on U.S. stamps. The exceptions are some of those who are portrayed on the American Bicentennial issues, Scott 1686, 1687, and 1691-94. Lieutenant Thomas Grosvenor (Scott 1361) also continues to elude the author. Of course, stamps such as the Army and Navy issues, which feature anonymous faces, are also excluded.

Since the U.S. Postal Service was formed in 1971, replacing the U.S. Post Office Department, the United States has issued an increasing number of stamps portraying individuals who are largely unknown to the general public, as well as to stamp collectors.

Unfamiliar faces peer from the stamps included in such series as the Great Americans and Black Heritage. For the most part, these stamps contain no descriptive information to help the collector — or the user — know who the honored person is or why the person is honored on the stamp.

In *Who's Who on U.S. Stamps*, author Richard Thomas provides biographical information not only for the unfamiliar faces shown on the stamps in these recent series but for nearly every person who has ever appeared on a U.S. stamp, from 1847 through 1990. From the most easily identified U.S. personalities (George Washington and Benjamin Franklin) to the most obscure (such as Chief Shadoo and Hollow Horn Bear), a brief biography tells who the person is and why he or she deserved to be honored with a stamp.

The book is arranged alphabetically, from Abigail Adams to "Babe" Didrikson Zaharias. Although many of these individuals have appeared on more than one stamp, only one stamp is pictured with each biography. A listing of all stamps portraying the individuals is included in an appendix together with their Scott catalog numbers. Topical collectors will find a handy topical index in the appendix.

Who's Who on U.S. Stamps will serve as an entertaining reference not only to stamp collectors but also to students and casual readers. The book had its roots in a series of articles Thomas created for *Linn's Stamp News*.

Appreciation

I am most grateful to Michael Laurence, Donna O'Keefe and Elaine Durnin Boughner for showing initial interest in my compendium of people on U.S. stamps and accepting it in late 1987 for weekly publication in *Linn's Stamp News* as a regular feature entitled Who's Who on U.S. Stamps.

My sincere thanks to Linn's staff writers Wayne Youngblood, Michael Schreiber and especially Laura Hardy and Jill Bable for week after week polishing my articles into publishable form and to Donna O'Keefe for her intense editing in the final analysis.

Closer to home, I am forever indebted to the grand man of philately, F. Burton Sellers, for laboriously exposing my manuscripts to the philatelic editors and especially for encouraging me to keep working on and adding to my mini-biographies.

And I shan't overlook my wife Virginia's constant efforts to correct my misspellings and typos and for her suggestions, recommendations and keen judgment on nearly every sketch.

Also I render my thanks to Arthur A. Streng, Gordon R. Nielson and L. George Hooper of our Westminster Village Stamp Club, whose constant hazing kept me within bounds.

I am also much obliged to the many *Linn's* readers who sent me their kudos and "tomatoes," beginning with the first appearance of my column in the November 30, 1987 issue, suggesting excellent additions and corrections. To all, I willingly and humbly replied.

They are: Warren H. Moore, Thomas Desha, Raymond A. Brubacher, Gene Babow, Donald M. Hosmer, J.W. Paisley, J. Walter Allen, Conrad P. Mook, Earle M. Boyes, Eric J. Kovacs, Sanford Solarz, Jack Graham, David H. Stoltenberg, Tom Engle, John Peebles, Dan Ringo, Dr. E.G. Chuinard, Kathleen Wolsiffer, Todd Ronnei, Charles Wonderlin, John A. Weyl, the Reverend Harry C. Green, Judson May, Helen Holloway, Walter J. Walzer, Arthur A. Delaney, Lancelot Bell, Ed Weinberg, Roger S. Krischke, Rudy M. Gross, Philip G. Collins, Harvey Timberlake, John M. Cunningham, M.W. Scott, Douglas J. Cutler, William Robert Cory, George Saqqal, Sebastian Sofiano, Robert Barron, Ronnell B. Townsend, Brigadier General Jack Capps (Retired), and especially Paul A. Cristenson, Betty Taussig, Jim Holmes, Amanda Dortch, Donald B. Stevens and Joseph H. Boatwright.

To this list, I must add Robert H. Thomas, my brother, and Asa Hanamoto, my good friend, who goaded me to persevere.

Richard L. Thomas

Abigail Adams

Scott 2146
Born: November 11, 1744 (old style), Weymouth, Massachusetts
Died: October 28, 1818, Quincy, Massachusetts

Abigail was the wife of John Adams, the second president of the United States, and mother of John Quincy Adams, the sixth U.S. president.

In 1764, she married John Adams when he was a young Boston lawyer. During the 1770s and 1780s, John was away in Philadelphia with the Continental Congress and on various diplomatic missions in Europe.

During this time, Abigail managed affairs at home, educated the children and cared for her husband's large correspondence. She also wrote letters in which she expressed her views on public matters, especially independence from England, and America's relationship with France.

She made certain her son John Quincy, at age 8, personally witnessed the Battle of Bunker Hill. She also had him experience diplomacy first-hand by allowing him to travel with his father on missions to Europe.

After the War of Independence, Abigail went to Paris and London to be with her husband, who was a foreign minister in Europe.

She worked with him while he was vice president, and kept busy at the new nation's capital and at her home in Braintree (now Quincy), Massachusetts. The Adams were the first couple to live in the White House.

Abigail was one of the first women in the United States to advocate strongly that women were equal, not inferior, to men. She provided her daughter, Abigail, with a broad education. She also opposed slavery.

Abigail and Thomas Jefferson had a great admiration for one another. Even after her husband and Jefferson split politically in the 1790s, she continued a friendly correspondence with Jefferson until her death.

Of the many first ladies of the White House, Abigail Adams is remembered for the steadfastness of her principles, her diligence and her hard work.

Abigail Adams is shown on a 1985 22¢ commemorative stamp.

1

John Adams

Scott 2216b
Born: October 30, 1735, Braintree (now Quincy), Massachusetts
Died: July 4, 1826, Quincy, Massachusetts

John Adams was the second president of the United States and the father of John Quincy Adams, the sixth president. He graduated from Harvard College in 1755, initially wanting to be a teacher, After teaching school for a short time, he studied law in the office of James Putnam in Worcester, Massachusetts. He began to practice law in 1758. In 1764 he married Abigail Smith. He was a leader in the movement for independence from Great Britain, and opposed the Stamp Act, which taxed newspapers, legal papers and other items. Adams was a member of the First and Second Continental Congress and was one of the negotiators when peace with England was signed.

Perhaps his greatest diplomatic achievement was traveling to the Netherlands, where he obtained recognition of the United States as a sovereign power. He also received a loan of $1.4 million for the United States. In 1785 he was envoy to England. In 1778 he was the United States' commissioner to France. He returned to the United States in 1788 to serve as the vice president under George Washington. He served with Washington for two terms.

Adams was a Federalist. He was elected president of the United States in 1796, despite attempts by Alexander Hamilton to prevent him from doing so. During his term in office, Adams prevented war with France. The enactment of the Alien and Sedition Acts, which he directed against foreigners and critics of governmental policies, resulted in a split between Adams and Hamilton. Hamilton criticized the Adams administration, which ultimately resulted in the election of Thomas Jefferson as the nation's next president.

After serving as president, Adams retired to his home in Quincy, Massachusetts. He died on July 4, 1826, the 50th anniversary of the Declaration of Independence and the same day on which Thomas Jefferson died.

John Adams is pictured on a 1986 22¢ Presidential stamp.

John Quincy Adams

Scott 2216f
Born: July 11, 1767, Braintree (now Quincy), Massachusetts
Died: February 23, 1848, Washington, D.C.

John Quincy Adams served as the sixth president of the United States. He was the son of John Adams, the second president of the United States, and Abigail Smith Adams. When he was eight years old, Adams was taken by his mother to witness the Battle of Bunker Hill. She sent him at age 11 and again at age 16 to Europe with his father to learn about diplomatic missions. He graduated in 1787 from Harvard College and began to practice law. In 1797 Adams and Louisa Catherine Johnson, the daughter of an American consul general, were married. From 1794 to 1801, he was involved in several diplomatic assignments. In 1801 he returned to Boston. Adams was elected to the U.S. Senate in 1803. He was a Federalist, but often voted with the Democratic-Republicans. When Congress passed the Embargo Act in 1807, Adams broke with his party completely. He supported the embargo, while they wanted to trade with the British.

President James Madison persuaded him to accept a position in 1809 as minister of Russia. From mid-1814 to early 1815, he served as one of the American commissioners who negotiated the Treaty of Ghent with the British, ending the War of 1812. He was appointed minister to Great Britain. He began discussions that led to improved relations along the Canadian border. In 1817 Monroe appointed him secretary of state. He aided in the acquisition of Florida from Spain, as well as in drafting the Monroe Doctrine.

In 1824 Adams was supported by Henry Clay for the presidency, which he won over Andrew Jackson. His unwillingness to succumb to party politics resulted in his loss for re-election. Andrew Jackson succeeded Adams, who returned to Washington in 1830 as a member of the House of Representatives. He became a leader in the fight against slavery.

Adams died in the Speaker's room in Congress as the result of a paralytic stroke. He is pictured on a 1986 22¢ Presidential stamp.

Jane Addams

Scott 878
Born: September 6, 1860, Cedarville, Illinois
Died: May 21, 1935, Chicago, Illinois

Jane Addams was the daughter of well-to-do parents. She graduated from Rockford Seminary in 1881. She traveled to Europe as the culmination of her college education. While visiting in Europe, she was impressed by Toynbee Hall in England and also by its social reform movements. Addams decided to dedicate her life to helping people in need. With her college classmate Ellen Gates Starr, she founded Hull House in the slums of Chicago.

Hull House became a famous settlement house and grew rapidly. The house was a center for many social workers who were bent on reform, and desired to learn and work in that vocation. Addams was a leader in her field at the time and was instrumental in encouraging immigrants to become Americanized. She also advocated progressive education in the schools. In addition, she wanted the vote for women and was in favor of prohibition. She pressed for better housing, playgrounds for children, and more open spaces and parks in the cities.

Addams became the president of the International Congress of Women. In 1914, as an avowed pacifist, she became the chairman of the Woman's Peace Party. She campaigned in Europe and America for ending the war through mediation. The flurry of war sentiment in 1917, when the United States entered World War I, resulted in many people denouncing her. Nevertheless, in 1931 she was awarded the Nobel Peace Prize, along with Nicholas Murray Butler.

Always an advocate for social reform, she wrote more than 400 articles and 10 books, including *Twenty Years in Hull House*. From Hull House radiated reform for the betterment of mankind. Although her hopes for the betterment of mankind were idealistic and many of her goals were unattainable, Addams remained practical, always active and never discouraged.

She is depicted on a 1940 10¢ Famous Americans stamp issued in honor of famous American scientists.

Louisa May Alcott

Scott 862
Born: November 29, 1832, Germantown, Pennsylvania
Died: March 6, 1888, Boston, Massachusetts

Louisa May Alcott moved to Boston with her parents when she was a child. She grew up and remained in the Boston-Concord area for the rest of her life. Her father, Bronson Alcott, was an American transcendentalist philosopher, educator and author. Louisa received most of her early education from him. He also directed the Concord School of Philosophy, located on his farm in Concord, which he called Orchard House. Later in life, Louisa was given guidance and instruction by the well-known writers Henry David Thoreau and Ralph Waldo Emerson. Both spent much time at the Alcott's farm house as guests and fellow philosophers.

In 1854 Louisa wrote a collection of stories called *Flower Fables*. Her first book stemmed from the fairy stories she made up to tell her students. In addition to teaching, she also worked as a seamstress and a household servant to support her family. The Alcotts spent many years in poverty because Louisa's father invested in many idealistic projects that failed.

In 1860 Louisa sent her poems and short stories to the *Atlanta Monthly* for regular publication. In 1862, during the Civil War, she served as a nurse in the Union Army. She wrote frequent letters home to her family. In 1863 her letters were published in her first successful book, *Hospital Sketches*.

In 1867 she edited *Merry's Museum*, a magazine for young girls. In 1868 she published the first volume of *Little Women*. The second volume was published in 1869. *Little Women* is a semi-autobiographical account. It is an episodic-type fiction of a family named March, who live in a small town in New England. It tells about teenagers growing up. They were much different from today's youth. The author's "little women" devised ways to entertain themselves that included skating parties and dances, creating a newspaper, conducting their own post office, and writing and performing plays.

In 1871 she published *Little Men*. In addition to writing, Alcott worked to gain voting rights for women and was active in the temperance movement.

Louisa May Alcott appears on a 1940 5¢ Famous American Authors commemorative stamp.

Ethan Allen

Scott 1071
Born: January 10, 1738, Litchfield, Connecticut
Died: February 12, 1789, Burlington, Vermont

Ethan Allen was an ambitious and intelligent young man. His early education was halted when his father died in 1755, and he had to help support the family. Allen served in the French and Indian War in 1757. Afterward he was able, with his brothers, to obtain a large amount of the New Hampshire Grants, now Vermont.

However, New York disputed the grants. To harass the New Yorkers and keep control of the region, the Allen brothers organized the Green Mountain Boys. Ethan was such a nuisance that New York put a price of $750 on his head. He petitioned help from the king, but the Revolutionary War prevented help from coming.

In 1775 the Connecticut Assembly petitioned Allen and his boys to capture Fort Ticonderoga. Together with Colonel Benedict Arnold and his Massachusetts militia, Ethan Allen and the Green Mountain Boys easily captured the fort on May 10, 1775, and gained control of Lake Champlain.

Allen then attempted to take Montreal. Since Congress needed men in the Army, the New York Assembly was counseled to pay the Green Mountain Boys regular Army pay. The boys joined General Philip Schuyler's forces. Along with Colonel John Brown and his militia, Allen was to make secret missions into Canada. Brown somehow didn't arrive, and Allen was promptly captured and taken prisoner on September 25, 1775. Nearly three years later, he was released in a prisoner exchange on May 6, 1778.

Allen was given the honorary rank of colonel in the Continental Army, but he did not serve in the militia. Instead, he returned to his Vermont affairs to protect his land interests. He petitioned the Continental Congress for Vermont's statehood. After that failed, he tried to get help from his former captors to annex Vermont to Canada.

Allen retired to Burlington, Vermont, and died February 12, 1789. Two years later, Vermont was admitted to the Union as the 14th state.

The 1955 Fort Ticonderoga issue shows a map of the fort, artillery and Allen. The 3¢ stamp honors the bicentennial of the fort.

Susan Brownell Anthony

Scott 784
Born: February 15, 1820, Adams, Massachusetts
Died: March 13, 1906, Rochester, New York

Susan B. Anthony's name is synonymous with the woman suffrage movement and the 19th Amendment to the Constitution of the United States. Anthony campaigned for women's rights for more than 50 years against continual opposition.

She grew up in western New York. Her parents were staunch Quakers whose home near the city of Rochester was the meeting place for reformers.

Elizabeth Cady Stanton, a leader of the women's rights movement, especially influenced Anthony. Even at the young age of 13, Anthony believed the country would be in hopeless condition until women were on an equal basis with men.

Anthony initially crusaded for temperance. In 1852, when she and other women workers were not allowed to speak at a temperance rally in Albany, New York, she formed the Women's State Temperance Society of New York.

She advocated that women must have the right to control their own property, be able to have guardianship of their children in case of divorce, and receive an education equal to the education that men receive.

Before and during the Civil War, Anthony and Stanton supported abolitionism, but broke away from those who had been involved in the abolitionist movement because these people had little interest in woman suffrage. In 1869, Anthony and Stanton formed the National Woman Suffrage Association and worked for a woman suffrage amendment to the constitution.

Anthony served as president of the National American Woman Suffrage Association from 1892 to 1900. In 1904, she established the International Woman Suffrage Alliance with Carrie Chapman Catt, another supporter of the suffrage movement.

In 1920, 14 years after Anthony's death, the 19th Amendment to the Constitution became law and gave women the right to vote.

Susan Brownell Anthony appears on a 1936 3¢ stamp.

Edwin H. Armstrong

Scott 2056
Born: December 18, 1890, New York, New York
Died: February 1, 1954, New York, New York

Edwin Howard Armstrong was a pioneer in radio technology. He invented the frequency modulation (FM) technique for radio communication. When Armstrong was 17 years old, he put together his own radio station. At that time, radio was a new field. He studied at Columbia University in 1909. In 1913, he received his degree in electrical engineering and worked with Professor M.I. Pupin as an assistant professor. In 1934, he became a full professor of electrical engineering.

Even before Armstrong received his engineering degree at Columbia, he developed the regenerative (feedback) circuit in 1912. During World War I, he investigated signaling methods for the United States Army.

However, in 1919, he got into difficulties with Lee De Forest over the invention of his feedback circuit, which resulted in a 12-year-long lawsuit. Armstrong lost his case to De Forest. Because of this suit and other litigations, he donated $50,000 to Columbia University toward the study of how law courts are able to decide complex technical questions.

In 1918, Armstrong invented the superheterodyne circuit, which is the basic component of modern (AM) radio receivers. He worked on FM for many years, starting as early as 1925. Although he received a patent on FM in 1933, it was not perfected until four years later.

He invented the multiplexing system used for broadcasting more than one program on the same frequency. On the New Jersey Palisades, he built his own broadcasting station. In addition, Armstrong developed stereophonic broadcasting.

He was awarded the Medal of Merit in 1947 for his World War II contributions. Despondent over FCC litigations, patent problems and finances, he took his own life in 1954.

Armstrong and his frequency modulator are depicted on a 1983 20¢ American Inventors stamp.

Henry Harley 'Hap' Arnold

Scott 2192
Born: June 25, 1886, Gladwyne, Pennsylvania
Died: January 15, 1950, Sonoma, California

Henry "Hap" Arnold was a flier. Four years after he graduated from West Point Military Academy in 1908, he was transferred to Dayton, Ohio, to take flying instructions under Wilbur and Orville Wright. He flew an early Wright biplane on a 30-mile reconnaissance flight in 1912, for which he won the first Clarence H. Mackay trophy. In 1935, he commanded a squadron of 10 bombers from Washington, D.C., to Fairbanks, Alaska. This round trip of 18,000 miles also won Arnold the Clarence H. Mackay trophy.

During World War I, Lieutenant Arnold was assigned to the Signal Corps in Panama. He commanded the seventh Aero Squadron, an aviation defense unit, from 1917 to 1918. His next assignment, after a few months overseas, was as an Air Service Department officer in San Francisco, from 1919 to 1922. Arnold was convinced early that future wars would be fought primarily from the air and only secondarily from the ground and sea. The decisive factor in war would be loads of large bombs dropped from many airplanes.

Arnold became deputy chief of air in 1940. In March 1942, he was appointed commanding general of the Army Air Force and, as such, a member of the joint chiefs of staff. He was appointed in 1943 to the rank of full general, the first in the Air Force. Along with Eisenhower, Marshall and MacArthur, he was promoted to the rank of five-star general. In addition to being the commander of the entire U.S. Air Force, he established the 20th Air Force Command in 1944 and remained its commander until the end of the war.

General Arnold retired as head of the United States Air Force on January 24, 1946 and was succeeded by General Carl A. Spaatz. He died four years later at age 63.

He is shown on a 1988 65¢ Great Americans stamp.

Chester Alan Arthur

Scott 2218c
Born: October 5, 1830, Fairfield, Vermont
Died: November 18, 1886, New York, New York

Chester Arthur was the 21st president of the United States. His father came to the United States from Northern Ireland. At age 15, Arthur entered Union College in Schenectady, New York, and graduated in 1848. He studied law while earning his living as a teacher at North Pownal, Vermont, and as the principal of the Cahoes, New York, Academy. In 1854 he became a partner in the law firm of Culver and Parker in New York. He won a case in 1855 that established the rights of blacks to ride on any streetcar in the city.

Arthur married Ellen Lewis Herndon on October 25, 1859. She died a year before he took office as president. His youngest sister, Mary McElroy, served as first lady. Arthur began his political career after joining the Republican party and becoming New York State's engineer-in-chief under Governor Edwin D. Morgan. After the Civil War began in 1861, Arthur was appointed the state's assistant quartermaster for the New York militia. He advanced to quartermaster general in 1862. In 1863 he returned to law practice. He became an associate of Senator Roscoe Conkling of New York, leader of the New York Republican organization. President Ulysses S. Grant in 1871 appointed Arthur collector of the New York Customs House. In this position, Arthur gave jobs to hundreds of Republicans, and averaged $40,000 a year from percentages of fines during President Grant's administration.

Arthur's practices were investigated when Rutherford B. Hayes took office. In 1878 Arthur was removed from his position. He ran with Garfield as vice president in 1881 and won. On July 2 of that year, he became president when Garfield was assassinated. A year after he took office, he learned that he was dying of a kidney disease known as Bright's disease. He chose not to run for re-election. He returned to New York City after leaving the presidency. He died two years later of a cerebral hemorrhage. Arthur is pictured on a 22¢ stamp, part of the 1986 Presidential sheetlets.

John James Audubon

Scott 874
Born: April 26, 1785, Les Cayes, Santo Domingo (now Haiti)
Died: January 27, 1851, Minnie's Land, New York, New York

John James Audubon's father, Jean, was a French sea captain. His mother, Jeanne Rabine, was a Breton peasant woman. James was their illegitimate son. His mother died a few months after his birth. During his early childhood, he was taken to Nantes, France, where he was legally adopted in 1794 by his father. He was baptized Jean Jacques Fougere Audubon in 1800, but his legal name in France was Jean Rabine. His father sent him to live on an estate called Mill Grove near Philadelphia. He spent time there drawing birds. He returned to France in 1805 to study ornithology. He went back to America in 1806, and worked with Benjamin Bakewell, a merchant. He also opened a store in Louisville, Kentucky, with Ferdinand Rozier, who came with him from France.

Audubon married Bakewell's niece, Lucy Bakewell, in 1808. Rozier conducted their business, while Audubon traveled through the countryside looking for birds. His business career ended in 1819 when he was jailed for debt. He entered a plea of bankruptcy to gain his freedom. For half a year, Audubon drew chalk portraits and taught art in Louisville. He also worked for a few months for a taxidermist in a museum in Cincinnati.

In 1820 Audubon went down the Ohio and Mississippi rivers to paint birds in their natural surroundings. Lucy joined him in 1821. In 1826, Audubon, who was unable to find an American publisher for his collection of paintings, sailed with his family to England and Scotland. His *Birds of America* was engraved and published. It contained 87 parts with 435 life-sized colored engravings made from his watercolors.

He returned to the United States in 1839, and published American editions of his bird paintings. His eyesight failed, along with his mental capacities. He made his last collecting trip, along the Missouri River in 1843.

His sons Victor and John completed his later editions in 1850.

John James Audubon is pictured here on a 1940 1¢ Scientists stamp.

Stephen Fuller Austin

Scott 776
Born: November 3, 1793, Austinville, Virginia
Died: December 27, 1836, Waterloo, Texas

The capital of Texas, once called Waterloo, was renamed in 1839 for Stephen Fuller Austin. He was the eldest son of Moses Austin, who planned the first American colony in Texas, and Maria Brown. When Austin was 5 years old, his parents moved from Virginia to Missouri. He went to school at Colchester Academy in Connecticut and Transylvania University in Lexington. He returned to his home in Missouri, where he worked with his father in manufacturing and lead mining. He also worked as a land speculator and trader. From 1814 to 1820, he served as a territorial legislator, and an officer in the militia.

In 1821, when Texas was a Spanish province, Moses Austin received a grant to settle 300 American families on the Brazos River. When he died that same year, Stephen inherited the grant. In December, Stephen settled a colony along the Gulf of Mexico between the Brazos and Colorado rivers, directly south of Houston. Later, 750 more families settled there. Austin managed the affairs of the colony wisely. He organized defenses against hostile Indians. He also made two trips to Mexico City, one in 1822 and the other in 1833 to settle problems between the Anglo-Americans and the Mexican government.

A Mexican revolution resulted in a convention in 1832 and 1833 concerning the independence of Coahiula, the state to which Texas had joined in 1824. President Antonio Lopez de Santa Anna denied statehood, but repealed the anti-immigration decree of 1830. Austin was sent to prison, although he never received a trial, because he tried to annex Texas to the United States. He returned to Texas from Mexico in 1835.

Upon his return, Austin took command of the Texan army, which had been formed to fight for freedom from Mexico. The Texas Revolution followed. Texas became a republic in 1836. Austin ran for president of the republic, but lost to Sam Houston, who appointed him secretary of state. Austin was serving the new republic in this capacity when, at age 43, he died.

Stephen Fuller Austin appears with Sam Houston on a 1936 3¢ Texas Centennial stamp.

Vasco Nunez de Balboa

Scott 397
Born: circa 1475, Jerez de los Caballeros, Spain
Died: January 1519, Acla, (north coast) Panama

In 1501, Vasco Nunez de Balboa joined Rodrigo de Bastidas on a Spanish expedition to South America. The party explored the north coast of the continent, including an area along the Gulf of Uraba in what is now Colombia. With too few people in the party to attempt a settlement, the expedition sailed in 1502 to the island of Hispaniola. Balboa tried raising pigs there, but he failed and ended in debt. To escape those whom he owed, he hid in a barrel on a ship heading for a new colony on the mainland of South America.

When he arrived, the ship's leader, Alonso de Ojeda, had gone. The colony was in chaos. Balboa helped remove the colony to Darien, Panama, where he became acting governor. He called it Santa Maria de la Antigua del Darien.

In 1511 Balboa heard about a sea on the other side of the Isthmus of Panama from the Indians. They also told him stories about gold and other wealth. To please King Ferdinand of Spain in an attempt to claim the title of governor of Darien, Balboa led an expedition of about 90 soldiers and a large number of Indians down the Darien coast across the isthmus until he reached an elevated plateau. On September 26, 1513, Balboa climbed a mountain and saw the Pacific Ocean. The Spaniards found gold and pearls on the Pacific coast. Balboa believed these treasures would help him earn the title of permanent governor of Darien.

Before the news of Balboa's expedition reached Spain, Ferdinand appointed Pedro Areas Davila, called Pedrarias, to take over the governorship of the settlement. Hatred between the two governors flared. The Spanish government tried to make peace between them, even giving Pedrarias' daughter to Balboa in marriage. In 1518, the governor falsely accused Balboa of treason and called him before the authorities. He was tried, convicted and beheaded on the public square of Acla in January 1517.

Vasco Nunez de Balboa appears on a 1913 1¢ stamp.

Abraham Baldwin

Scott 1850
Born: November 22, 1754, North Guilford, Connecticut
Died: March 4, 1807, Washington, D.C.

Abraham Baldwin was a leader. His father was a hard-working blacksmith who was able to send his son to college. In 1772 young Baldwin graduated from Yale College. In 1775 he was licensed as a minister. He taught at Yale College from 1775 to 1779. He then became a chaplain for the Continental Army.

After the war, Baldwin studied law and was admitted to the bar. He practiced law in Georgia, where he worked to establish Franklin College. It is the oldest college of the University of Georgia and the first state-supported college in the United States. Franklin College was officially charted in 1785.

From 1786 to 1801, Baldwin was the first president and trustee of the newly chartered college. He used his knowledge of Yale College as a basis for the curriculum, but with much less theological emphasis.

Baldwin was on the committee that selected the site for the buildings. He chose an acquaintance from Yale, whom he knew was well-qualified, to be his successor. Baldwin then served as chairman of the board of trustees, a position he held until his death.

He took an active part in politics. He was a delegate to the Confederation Congress in 1785 and was a representative from Georgia in the Constitutional Convention in 1787. Despite his theological background and his early life in Connecticut, he defended slavery as being necessary for the economic development of Georgia and the South in general.

He was elected to the House of Representatives of the First Congress under the Constitution and then to the Senate in 1799. During the sessions of the Seventh Congress, he was president pro tempore. In 1787, he was one of the signers of the United States Constitution.

Baldwin is shown on a 1985 7¢ stamp in the Great Americans issue.

Benjamin Banneker

Scott 1804
Born: November 9, 1731, Ellicott, Maryland
Died: 1806, Baltimore County, Maryland

Benjamin Banneker was a brilliant young man with an inquisitive mind. His father was a slave, but his mother was a free black woman. Banneker was free and was able to attend the local school. Early in his schooling, he showed an unusual talent for mathematics, but his interests ranged from bees and locusts to the stars in the heavens. Banneker read all the books he could borrow from friendly white neighbors. He built a wooden clock that kept accurate time for many years to come.

Banneker was a member of the surveying team appointed by Thomas Jefferson in 1790 to lay out the plans for the city of Washington and the District of Columbia. Once the site for the capital was chosen, Jefferson selected Pierre Charles L'Enfant as the chief planner and architect for the project. But the high-handed opportunist was dismissed in 1792 for insubordination and for forging ahead without orders. L'Enfant took off with all the detailed maps and plans, but all was not lost. Banneker was able to accurately reconstruct the plans from memory. His was probably a more sensible plan than L'Enfant's grand baroque one, which was reminiscent of Versailles or Paris. L'Enfant intended the District of Columbia and the city of Washington to be the capital of a vast empire, with the federal house and the residential palace having commanding views in all directions.

In 1791 Banneker published an almanac illustrating the results of his observations and calculations of astronomy. He sent a copy to Thomas Jefferson, along with a letter defending the rights and equality of Negroes. Jefferson was sufficiently impressed by the almanac to send a copy to the French Academy of Sciences. Banneker continued to publish his almanac, which appeared regularly, until 1802.

A 1979 15¢ stamp in the Black Heritage issue depicts Banneker.

Francois de Barbe-Marbois

Scott 1020
Born: January 3, 1745, Metz, France
Died: January 14, 1837, Paris, France

Francois de Barbe-Marbois was a French diplomat assigned to the United States as a consul general after he had served as a diplomat in Germany. He was sent to Santo Domingo as an administrative official in 1786 and returned in 1789 to France, where he served the revolutionaries. He was arrested twice, and in 1797 he was exiled to French Guiana as a royalist. Barbe-Marbois was liberated by Napoleon, who sent him to Oleron in 1799. He was appointed director and then minister of the treasury. It was in 1803 that he negotiated the Louisiana Purchase for Napoleon.

In April 1803 President Thomas Jefferson sent James Monroe to France as the foreign minister to both France and Spain. Even as early as the mid-1700s, New Orleans was an important port for shipping goods to foreign countries and to the East Coast of America. Grain and goods from Kentucky and Tennessee could be sent down the Ohio and Mississippi rivers to New Orleans. In 1795 the Spanish intendant suddenly revoked the duty-free rights. Kentucky and Tennessee were ready to go to war with Spain, and the situation was driving America to an alliance with Britain. Napoleon selected Barbe-Marbois to handle negotiations. Napoleon said, "I renounce Louisiana. It is not only New Orleans that I cede; it is the whole colony without reserve."

On April 30, 1803, Livingston and Monroe bargained. During that financial convention, France finally gave up the entire 800,000 square miles of territory for $11,250,000, and thereby doubled the extent of the United States. The purchase opened up a vast amount of land for westward expansion. Napoleon obtained a better deal than he had expected.

Francois de Barbe-Marbois was made a peer of France (1814), minister of justice (1815-16) and marquis (1816) by Louis XVIII. He is pictured on the 1953 3¢ Louisiana Purchase issue with Livingston and Monroe.

16

John Barry

Scott 790
Born: 1745, Tacumshane, County Wexford, Ireland
Died: September 13, 1803, Philadelphia, Pennsylvania

John Barry went to sea as a young man and later became a shipmaster in Philadelphia. At the start of the Revolutionary War, the Continental Congress commissioned him one of the first captains in the Navy. On April 17, 1776, as commander of the brigantine *Lexington*, he sailed into Chesapeake Bay and captured the British sloop *Edward*. Later in 1776, Barry directed four small boats into the Delaware River near Philadelphia, raided British ships and seized quantities of supplies as his prize. On the day after Christmas 1776, he led a volunteer company in the Army artillery at the Battle of Trenton.

Back in the Navy in 1780, he commanded the frigate *Alliance* until the end of the war. After the Battle of Yorktown, Barry was commissioned to deliver the Marquis de Lafayette home to France on the *Alliance*. His final cruise on the *Alliance* was in 1782. His last engagement in the war was March 10, 1783, in the Gulf of Florida with the British frigate *Sybil*.

In 1794, the United States Navy was organized with John Barry as senior captain and in command of the flagship *United States*. A naval war was fought with France from 1798 to 1800, and Barry commanded all the ships fighting on the West Indies waters. At the end of the war, John Adams commissioned Barry to sail the *United States* to France. Through stormy waters, Barry safely delivered the diplomatic envoys who negotiated peace.

In 1801 Thomas Jefferson reduced the size of the United States Navy, but retained Barry to command ships intended to quell the Barbary pirates on the Mediterranean Sea in 1802. But Barry was too ill to carry out that assignment.

During his many years on the high seas, Barry taught seamanship to Stephen Decatur and many others who captained the ships of the early U.S. Navy. Known as the Father of the Navy, he is shown on the 1936 1¢ Navy issue with John Paul Jones.

Ethel Barrymore

Scott 2012
Born: August 15, 1879, Philadelphia, Pennsylvania
Died: June 18, 1959, Los Angeles, California

American dramatist Ethel Barrymore was the daughter of the Shakespearean actor Maurice Barrymore and actress Georgiana Emma Drew Barrymore. Her father, Maurice Barrymore, was born Herbert Blythe in Agra, India. He gained fame as a boxer while studying law at Oxford University. He won the Queensberry Cup in 1874, the year he began an acting career, appearing in a London revival of *London Assurance*. He adopted the name Barrymore, which became the stage name of the entire Blythe family. This included his wife Georgianna; their three children, Lionel, Ethel, and John; and John's two children, Diana and John Barrymore Jr. John Drew, Ethel's mother's brother, was a leading matinee idol of his time. He lived from 1853 to 1927. Ethel's grandfather and grandmother, John and Louisa Lane Drew, were also actors and managers, and launched the careers of Lionel and Ethel. Grandfather John Drew was a charter member of the Players Club, which he helped found on December 31, 1888, at 16 Gramercy Park, New York City.

Ethel made her stage debut in New York City in 1896 in *Rosemary* with her celebrated uncle, John Drew. In 1900 she starred in the New York production *Captain Jinks of the Horse Marines*, for which she won an award as the outstanding young actress of the United States.

From 1922 to 1926, she was active in Shakespearean performances. In 1928 she inaugurated the opening of the Ethel Barrymore Theater in New York City, acting her role in the celebrated performance *The Kingdom of God*.

Her successes that followed include such classics as *The Corn is Green* and *Embezzled Heaven*. Of her many motion pictures performances, *None but the Lonely Heart*, in which she starred in 1944, is one of the notable classics of motion picture's illustrious history.

Ethel Barrymore appears with her two brothers, Lionel and John, on a 1982 20¢ Performing Arts stamp.

John Sidney Barrymore

Scott 2012
Born: February 15, 1882, Philadelphia, Pennsylvania
Died: May 29, 1942, Los Angeles, California

John Sidney Barrymore was the youngest of three children of Maurice (Herbert Blythe) and Georgiana Drew Barrymore. He, like his older brother, Lionel, had a flare for art and worked as an illustrator for two New York City newspapers. His first exposure to the world of the stage was in 1903 in Chicago in the play *Magda*. He had a more important role in 1905 in New York City in a play called *The Dictator*, in which he toured the United States, England and Australia.

In 1910 in John Galsworth's *Justice*, Barrymore performed his first important role. In 1917 he teamed up with his brother Lionel in *Peter Ibbetson* and again in 1919 in *The Jest*. In 1920 he demonstrated his genius for Shakespearean theater in the title role of *Richard III*. As Hamlet, in 1922, he was regarded as the greatest Shakespearean interpreter of the day.

He left the legitimate stage the following year for a future in motion-picture films. His film successes included such classics as *Dr. Jekyll and Mr. Hyde*, *Beau Brummell*, *The Sea Beast* and *Don Juan*. In 1939 he returned to the stage in an inferior play, *My Dear Children*, which was based loosely on the Barrymore family. Later successes came again in the films including *Moby Dick*, *Grand Hotel*, *Twentieth Century*, and *Romeo and Juliet*.

During the last years of his life, he became a popular radio actor. He showed a flair for writing and published a book, *Confessions of an Actor*.

John Barrymore married three times. His first wife was Katherine Corri Harris. With Michael Stange, his second wife, he had a daughter, Diana Barrymore. His second wife wrote *Too Much, Too Soon*, concerning her bout with alcoholism. John Barrymore Jr. was born in 1932, the son of the elder Barrymore's third wife, Dolores Costello.

John Barrymore appears with his brother, Lionel, and sister, Ethel, on a 1982 20¢ Performing Arts stamp.

Lionel Barrymore

Scott 2012
Born: April 28, 1878, Philadelphia, Pennsylvania
Died: November 15, 1954, Los Angeles, California

American dramatist Lionel Barrymore was the eldest son of Maurice (Herbert Blythe) and Georgiana Emma Drew Barrymore. In the stage production of *The Rivals*, in 1893, Lionel, at age 15, performed his first acting role along with his celebrated grandmother, Louisa Lane Drew, who played the role of Mrs. Malaprop.

Lionel actually wanted to be a painter. Some of his etchings were published and many prints were made. In keeping with family tradition, he remained a stage performer, something for which he had innate talent. This talent was first noted when he performed the role of the organ grinder in *The Mummy and the Hummingbird*, this time with his uncle, John Drew, in 1898. Ten years later, his stage performances in *Peter Ibbetson*, *The Jest*, and *Macbeth* established him as a solid member of the thespian dynasty of the Drews and Barrymores.

In 1915 he played opposite Mary Pickford in the silent film *The New York Hat*. Although this was his introduction to movies, it was in sound films that he found his greatest successes. He won an Academy Award for *A Free Soul* in 1931. All three Barrymores appeared in *Rasputin and the Empress* in 1933.

On the radio at Christmastime, beginning in 1934, his voice thrilled listeners with his interpretation of Ebenezer Scrooge in Charles Dickens' *A Christmas Carol*.

Severe hip fractures in later life forced him to perform from a wheelchair on stage and in films. He wrote *Mr. Cantonwine: A Moral Tale* in 1953, which was a successful novel.

Lionel Barrymore appears with his brother, John, and sister, Ethel, on a 1982 20¢ Performing Arts stamp.

Frederic Auguste Bartholdi

F. A. Bartholdi, Statue of Liberty Sculptor

Scott 2147
Born: April 2, 1834, Colmar, Alsace
Died: October 4, 1904, Paris, France

Frederic Auguste Bartholdi's claim to fame is twofold. In 1880 he completed the gigantic sculpture in the red-rock hill that towers above the city of Belfort, France.

The sculpture is titled *The Lion of Belfort* and honors the city's defense against the Prussians in the Franco-Prussian War of 1850-71.

His second and better-known colossus is in New York Harbor and is titled *Liberty Enlightening the World*. The statue was a gift from France following the terrible Civil War and was sent to America in 1885. The huge sculpture was originally conceived by the French historian Edward de Laboulaye as a way of celebrating the common principles of liberty and equality held by both France and the United States. Situated on an island in the harbor, it sits on a pedestal furnished by a fund-raising effort in the United States. The little island was called Bedloe's Island, but was renamed Liberty Island in 1956. Bartholdi's great creation of the stately lady with the torch is now known as the Statue of Liberty.

It took Bartholdi 10 years to create his titanic statue. It was made of copper, and the sheets had to be hand-hammered into shape. These sheets of copper were then fastened over a framework of four huge steel supports. After the statue was completed, it was again taken apart into its separate sections. The sections were shipped to the United States and pieced back together again, where it has stood for more than 100 years. President Grover Cleveland originally dedicated the statue on October 28, 1886. More than 100 years of salty sea breezes and acrid smog ruined the statue's copper plates. President Ronald Reagan commissioned Lee Iacocca in 1983 to raise funds for her restoration.

On July 4, 1986, the repaired and refinished Lady Liberty was unveiled again with fabulous fanfare and a fantastic display of fireworks.

Bartholdi is portrayed on a 22¢ stamp issued in 1985.

Clara Barton

Scott 967
Born: December 25, 1821, North Oxford, Massachusetts
Died: April 12, 1912, Glen Echo, Maryland.

Clara Barton, called the Angel of the Battlefield, was founder of the American Red Cross. She earned her nickname by distributing supplies for the relief of wounded soldiers during the Civil War. When the war was over, she went to Washington, D.C., and established a bureau of records to aid in the search for missing men. The bureau identified and marked the graves of more than 12,000 soldiers in the National Cemetery at Andersonville, Georgia.

During the Franco-Prussian War, she helped organize hospitals for wounded soldiers. In 1871, Barton supervised the distribution of relief to the poor in Strassburg and Paris. Strassburg was part of Germany at that time. The German emperor decorated Barton with the Iron Cross for her services. The Red Cross was organized in Geneva, Switzerland, in 1864.

In 1873 Barton returned to the United States and began to organize the U.S. branch of the International Red Cross. She also attempted to bring the United States into the Treaty of Geneva. Her efforts were successful in 1882. Since then, America has abided by the Geneva Convention.

Barton was honored for her endeavors by being selected the first president of the American Red Cross. She was president until 1904. She represented the United States at all the International Red Cross conferences — Geneva in 1884, Karlsruhe in 1887, Rome in 1892, Vienna in 1897 and St. Petersburg (Leningrad) in 1903.

Barton extended the services of the Red Cross beyond the battlefield with an American amendment to the constitution of the Red Cross. This amendment provided for aid and assistance in times of crises such as earthquakes, cyclones, floods, famine and pestilence. She headed the American Red Cross until she resigned in 1904, when Congress called for its reincorporation.

The 1948 3¢ Clara Barton issue depicts the humanitarian, along with the words "Founder of the American Red Cross."

Alexander Graham Bell

Scott 893
Born: March 3, 1847, Edinburgh, Scotland
Died: August 2, 1922, Baddeck, Nova Scotia

Alexander Graham Bell received his early education from his mother, Elisa Grace Symonds Bell. She was a fine portrait painter and an accomplished musician. Bell went to high school in Edinburgh, Scotland. After his graduation from there, he spent a year in London with his grandfather, Alexander Bell, who was a well-known lecturer and speech teacher. After teaching for a short time in Elgin, Scotland, and Bath, England, the younger Bell joined his father, Alexander Melville Bell, who had since moved to London to continue his father's work. Alexander Graham devoted his time to teaching deaf-born children to speak. During this time, the deaths of Alexander's two brothers from tuberculosis and his demanding schedule took their toll on young Alexander's health. His mournful father left the unhealthy city of London for a country home near Brantford, Ontario, Canada, where Alexander Graham regained his robust health.

When Bell was 24, he taught his father's method of visible speech to instructors of the deaf in Boston. This method consisted of a code of symbols that indicated the position of the throat, tongue and lips in making sounds. From 1873 to 1877, he taught vocal physiology at Boston University. He met Mabel Hubbard, who became his wife in 1877. Deaf from scarlet fever at age four, she encouraged him to work on inventions to aid hearing.

In 1874 he received a patent for sending multiple messages simultaneously over the same telegraph wire. In 1875 he accidentally produced electric sound of speech for a split second. He reasoned that if varying sound of the human voice could be transmitted by varying intensities of electrical current, speech also could be transmitted. He exhibited his invention in the centennial exposition in Philadelphia in June 1876. At the end of the year, at age 29, his basic telephone patent was granted. Although Bell is remembered for inventing the telephone, he also was interested in flying, gave many years of service to the deaf and produced other communication devices.

Alexander Graham Bell is portrayed on a 1940 10¢ Famous American Inventors stamp.

Mary McLeod Bethune

Scott 2137
Born: July 10, 1875, Mayesville, South Carolina
Died: May 18, 1955, Daytona Beach, Florida

Mary McLeod Bethune's parents were former Negro slaves. Mary was able to receive an education at the Moody Bible Institute in Chicago, from which she graduated in 1895. Thereafter, she was a teacher in the southern mission schools until 1903. She founded the Daytona Normal and Industrial Institute for Girls in Daytona Beach, Florida, in 1904. For nearly 20 years, she was the headmaster of this school. In 1923 the school merged with the Cookman Institute. The newly organized institution was known as Bethune-Cookman College. Bethune was the president of the college until 1942.

In 1935 she founded the National Council for Negro Women. She also directed the Division of Negro Affairs of the National Youth Administration from 1936 to 1944.

During World War II, Bethune was appointed special assistant to the secretary of war, Henry L. Stimson, to aid in the selection of officer candidates for the Women's Army Corps (WAC). The WAAC, Women's Army Auxiliary Corps, was created in May 1942. Oveta Culp Hobby was the first director. On September 1, 1943, the WAC was established by Congress. Officers were required to have a college degree, and all WACs had to be high school graduates. As an educator, Bethune was well-qualified for her assignment. She also served as a special adviser on minority affairs to President Franklin D. Roosevelt, as vice president of the National Association for the Advancement of Colored People and as a special consultant on interracial affairs at the San Francisco Conference of the United Nations Organization in 1945, working with Eleanor Roosevelt.

Bethune-Cookman College today has an enrollment of more than 1,700 students. It is a private Methodist co-educational school. Bethune received many honors and awards. She is shown on the 1985 22¢ Black Heritage issue.

Emily P. Bissell

Emily Bissell
Crusader Against Tuberculosis
USA 15c

Scott 1823
Born: May 31, 1861, Wilmington, Delaware
Died: March 8, 1948, Wilmington, Delaware

During the last years of the 18th century, an American doctor, Edward L. Trudeau, discovered he had tuberculosis. He rested and recovered. This experience offered hope to tuberculosis victims, and many sanitariums were opened. In 1904 the American Lung Association was organized. Dr. Trudeau was its president. The red double-barred cross was chosen as its emblem.

Einter Holboell opened a similar clinic in Denmark. To raise money, he devised the idea of selling Christmas seals. He obtained permission from King Christian of Sweden and Iceland. Other countries joined the seals campaign. In 1904 Jacob Riis, a Danish-American writer, wrote about the seals. But it was not until 1907 that Dr. Joseph Wales of Delaware, who ran a tuberculosis treatment center and needed funds, studied Riis' articles and decided to use seals to finance his clinic.

Dr. Wales called upon his cousin, Emily Bissell. Her achievements included the first free kindergarten, first children's playground, the first better-babies demonstration, the first Boy's Brigade (Boy Scouts), and first gymnasium for boys in Delaware. She assisted with Delaware's first child labor commission, organized the Delaware Children's Bureau, lobbied to limit the working hours of women in industry, and established the Delaware Chapter of the American Red Cross. She was an excellent choice to promote Christmas seals. The first effort did not sell well, so she went to Philadelphia and persuaded writer Leigh Mitchell Hodges of *The North American* newspaper to publicize her project. E.A. Van Valkenburg, editor-in-chief, lent his support. Other organizations joined in. Dr. Wales received 10 times what he needed. Today, Christmas seals help finance the fight against all lung diseases.

Bissell designed the first Christmas seal (Scott WX1). She is portrayed on a 15¢ stamp issued in 1980.

Hugo Lafayette Black

Scott 2172
Born: February 27, 1886, Harlan, Alabama
Died: September 25, 1971, Bethesda, Maryland

Hugo Lafayette Black was an associate justice of the Supreme Court appointed by President Franklin D. Roosevelt. Black's mother was the local postmaster. His older brother was a physician, who persuaded Hugo to enter the Birmingham Medical College. After a year there, he entered the Alabama Law School. He graduated in 1906 and was admitted that same year to the Alabama bar. He started his law practice in Ashland, Alabama, but later moved to Birmingham. Black won a case involving a black convict who had been kept at work 15 days longer than his sentence had stated. Black's eloquence in pleading the case so impressed the circuit court judge that Black was appointed Birmingham's police judge in 1910. He held the post for nearly two years. In 1914 Black was elected to the office of prosecuting attorney of Jefferson County, Alabama.

Black served in World War I as a captain in the field artillery. Afterward, he returned to his law practice.

In 1923 he accepted a life membership in the Ku Klux Klan but resigned two years later. The following year, he ran for and was elected to the U.S. Senate in 1932. A month after his confirmation as Supreme Court justice his involvement in the Ku Klux Klan experience was publicized. Although many people demanded that he resign, he remained on the Supreme Court. Two years later, he sided with contralto Marian Anderson, who had been refused permission to sing at Washington, D.C., in the Constitution Hall of the Daughters of the American Revolution.

In the 1944 case, Korematsu versus United States, Black upheld the right of the military to evacuate Japanese-American citizens from the West Coast after the attack on Pearl Harbor. He served on the Supreme Court for more than 30 years, strongly supporting government protection of civil rights.

Hugo Lafayette Black appears on a 1986 5¢ dark olive green Great Americans stamp.

Elizabeth Blackwell

Scott 1399
Born: February 3, 1821, Bristol, England
Died: May 31, 1910, Hastings, England

When Elizabeth Blackwell was 11 years old, her family emigrated to the United States from their home in Bristol, England. Her parents, Samuel and Hannah Blackwell, settled first in New York City, then later moved to Cincinnati. When her father died, it was up to Elizabeth to support her family. She taught school for several years, and when she was free to do so, she decided to become a physician. Unfortunately, she was denied admittance to medical schools in Philadelphia and New York City, so she studied privately until 1847.

Blackwell was finally admitted to the Geneva Medical School in Geneva, New York, and graduated in 1849. She did post-graduate studies in London at St. Bartholomew's Hospital and also studied in Paris. Once again she was denied a position when she tried to practice medicine in a hospital or clinic in the United States. She opened her own dispensary in New York City in 1853 and staffed it entirely with women. The dispensary later became known as the New York Infirmary.

Blackwell used her clinic as a training school for nurses who were to serve in the Union Army during the Civil War. She was assisted in the endeavor by Clara Barton of Oxford, Massachusetts, and Louise Lee Schuyler.

In 1865, she opened the Women's Medical College of the New York Infirmary. She likewise helped establish a medical school in London. It was called the London School of Medicine for Women.

The adoption of the Geneva Convention in 1864 created a necessity for better nursing in Europe. In America this same movement was furthered by Elizabeth Blackwell, in order to keep up with the advancements in Europe. Blackwell was instrumental in advancing medical training for women in both Europe and America.

She is honored as America's first woman physician on the 1974 18¢ regular issue.

27

Montgomery Blair

Scott C66
Born: May 10, 1813, Franklin County, Kentucky
Died: July 27, 1883, Silver Spring, Maryland

Montgomery Blair was postmaster general under Abraham Lincoln. In 1863 he assembled the first International Postal Conference in Paris, France, which led to the establishment of the Universal Postal Union on October 9, 1874. Since 1947 the UPU has been a specialized agency of the United Nations. The objectives of the organization are to facilitate reciprocal exchange of correspondence with uniform procedures by all its members, to help governments to modernize and to speed up mailing procedures. Montgomery Blair's father, Francis Preston Blair (1791-1876), was a journalist and politician who was quite influential during the presidency of Andrew Jackson. He edited the *Globe* in Washington, D.C., and also published the *Congressional Globe*. Montgomery's brother, Francis Preston Blair Jr. (1821-75), was a soldier and politician.

The Blairs were well-known in Washington, D.C., and were well-to-do. In 1836 they purchased the Lovell home, which is located directly across the street from the White House and is now known as the Blair House. The house was acquired by the government in 1942. It is often used as a guest house for the presidential mansion and as the president's home, when the White House is not available for use.

Blair was educated at West Point and Transylvania University. He practiced law in Missouri and Maryland. He opposed slavery and served as an attorney for Dred Scott in 1857. Blair was a conservative Republican. After Lincoln's death, he supported Andrew Johnson. He rejoined the Democratic party and was Samuel Tilden's counsel in 1876.

A 1963 15¢ airmail issue honors Blair and the 100th anniversary of the first International Postal Conference.

Simon Bolivar

Scott 1110
Born: July 24, 1783, Caracas, Venezuela
Died: December 17, 1830, near Santa Marta, Colombia

El Liberador (the liberator), as Simon Bolivar was called, probably learned his early lessons about being a soldier and statesman while in Paris. In France, he witnessed the rise of Napoleon in 1801 after the French Revolution. Before going to France, however, he had private tutors as a child and studied in Madrid, Spain. He was married in Madrid in 1802 and returned to his hometown of Caracas. Early the next year, his bride died of yellow fever, and he returned to Europe.

On December 2, 1804, he attended Napoleon's coronation. Bolivar was dedicated to the emancipation of South America. In 1808 France invaded Spain. Spanish America was in a crisis. Bolivar and others saw their chance to fight for independence of Venezuela, although many remained loyal to Ferdinand VII. In 1810 Bolivar joined patriots who seized Caracas and proclaimed independence from Spain. The Spanish viceroy was ousted, and Bolivar was chosen to go to London to plead with Britain for help to protect Venezuela from France. Bolivar met Francisco de Miranda, a Venezuelan patriot. Together they returned to Caracas in December 1810. Six months later, they formed a Venezuelan Congress and declared independence.

Bolivar became the governor of Puerto Cabello, but royalist Monteverde, aided by an earthquake, defeated Bolivar, who then fled to Cartagena in New Granada, now Colombia. He wrote the *Cartagen Memorial*, which roused people to independence.

With help from New Grenada, Bolivar invaded Caracas in 1813. He was declared their liberator. In 1814 he was forced out, and in 1815 he fled to Jamaica. He went to Haiti, where President Tetion helped him. He tried again in April 1816 to take Venezuela, but failed. He failed again in December. He fought a slow overland fight in 1817 and 1818. In July 1819 he succeeded in joining Santander to defeat the enemy. Later that year he became the first president of Colombia. By December 1824, Peru was secured and North Peru, now Bolivia, was independent in 1825. Bolivar wrote its constitution.

Simon Bolivar appears on a 1958 4¢ Champion of Liberty stamp.

Daniel Boone

Scott 904
Born: November 2, 1734, near Reading, Pennsylvania
Died: September 26, 1820, St. Charles County, Missouri

Daniel Boone was known as an explorer, Indian fighter, county militia officer and surveyor. He had no formal education. He learned to read and write from his Quaker parents, Squire and Sara Morgan Boone, and learned enough mathematics to become a surveyor. He was good at hunting and trapping in the woods, but he also helped his father at farming, weaving and blacksmithing. In 1750 the family moved to the North Fork of the Yadkin River, south of Winston-Salem, North Carolina. Boone went with the South Carolina troops and their English leader General Edward Braddock Duquesne in 1755. He escaped on his horse from a devastating raid by the Indians and the French. The following year, he married Rebecca Bryan, a neighbor girl.

In 1767 he explored as far as eastern Kentucky. Beginning in 1769, he spent two years traveling through the Cumberland Gap to Station Camp Creek, where he encountered the Shawnee Indians. In 1773 he and his family headed for Kentucky and reached Clinch River, where they settled. With 30 men, he laid out the Wilderness Road and settled Boonesborough, which was south of present-day Lexington.

The Shawnee Indians captured Boone and 30 of his men in 1778. He raced 160 miles back to Boonesborough, where he thwarted an Indian attack on his settlers. He served in the Kentucky militia, and was captured and released by the British. He was in the Battle of Blue Lick in 1782.

After the revolution, he moved westward to Marysville, Kentucky, then to the junction of the Ohio and Kanawa rivers at Point Pleasant. In 1799, he moved to Missouri to join his son. He obtained 850 acres of land in 1814 and sold most of it to pay debts. He died at age 86 while visiting his son Nathan.

Daniel Boone is pictured with three frontiersmen on a 1942 3¢ stamp.

William Jennings Bryan

Scott 2195
Born: March 19, 1860, Salem, Illinois
Died: July 26, 1925, Dayton, Tennessee

William Jennings Bryan was a noted orator and statesman. He championed the common man on the street, the factory worker and the farmer in the field. Three times he ran for the presidency of the United States, and three times he was defeated. Much of what he put forth as his campaign policies have since become law.

Bryan graduated in 1881 from Illinois College in Jacksonville, Illinois. He spent two years at the Union College of Law in Chicago, where he received his law degree. He returned to Jacksonville to practice law. In 1887 he moved to the Republican state of Nebraska. In 1890 he was the second Nebraska Democrat to be elected to Congress. He was re-elected in 1892.

He sought the nomination for the Senate seat in 1893 and 1895. He campaigned strongly for free coinage of silver, a tariff reform and an income tax. In 1896, at the Democratic National Convention in Chicago, he was the candidate of four different parties for the presidency. Despite this, he was defeated by William McKinley.

In 1900 he campaigned again, favoring anti-imperialism, but again lost to McKinley. When Bryan ran in 1908, he lost to William H. Taft.

After helping Woodrow Wilson to power in 1912, he was appointed secretary of state. He aided in Latin American diplomacy and was an advocate of peace.

He resigned in 1915, after the German sinking of the *Lusitania*, because he believed that Wilson's strong protest against the act could involve the United States in World War I.

Bryan was instrumental in the adoption of the 18th and 19th Amendments to the Constitution. An anti-evolutionist, he stumped with the Chautauqua circuits, mostly about religious topics. He wrote three books about his political experiences. He counseled on the famous Scopes trial, which he won. He died in Dayton, Tennessee, while recuperating from the trial.

William Jennings Bryan is shown on a $2 1986 Great Americans stamp.

James Buchanan

Scott 2217f
Born: April 23, 1791, Cove Gap (near Mercersburg), Pennsylvania
Died: June 1, 1868, Wheatland (near Lancaster), Pennsylvania

James Buchanan grew up on a frontier trading post, Stony Batter, near Mercersberg, Pennsylvania. His father had emigrated from County Donegal, Ireland, in 1783. Buchanan attended Dickinson College in Carlisle, Pennsylvania, and graduated an honor student in 1809. He served in the War of 1812, studied law, and was admitted to the Pennsylvania bar in 1813. He practiced law in Lancaster, Pennsylvania, and simultaneously served as a Federalist to the Pennsylvania assembly. An unhappy love affair with Ann Coleman, who committed suicide during their engagement, probably was the reason Buchanan never married after she died. The only bachelor president, Buchanan had his niece, Harriet Lane, serve as hostess of the White House.

Buchanan served five terms in the House of Representatives, from 1821 to 1831. In 1824 he supported Andrew Jackson for the presidency, but John Quincy Adams defeated Jackson. When Jackson won the next election in 1834, Buchanan was elected to the Senate. As minister to Russia from 1832 to 1834, he negotiated the first trade treaty between the United States and Russia. President Polk named Buchanan secretary of state in 1845. While in that position, Buchanan settled the Oregon dispute. He returned to Wheatland, Pennsylvania, near Lancaster, to plan his campaign for the 1852 presidential elections, but Franklin Pierce won. Buchanan became minister to Britain. He ran against John Fremont and Millard Fillmore in 1856 and won the presidency. In 1861 Kansas was admitted as a free state. Buchanan did not run for re-election, but he supported Southern Democrat John Breckinridge. The Northern Democrats supported Stephen Douglas. Republican Abraham Lincoln was elected president. Buchanan supported the Union and Lincoln's policies, then retired to his home in Wheatland.

James Buchanan is shown on a 22¢ stamp, part of the Presidential sheetlets issued for the Ameripex international stamp show in 1986.

Pearl Sydenstricker Walsh Buck

Scott 1848
Born: June 26, 1892, Hillsboro, West Virginia
Died: March 6, 1973, Danby, Vermont

Pearl S. Buck was the daughter of Presbyterian missionaries. She spent most of her life in China. When she was an infant, she was taken to Chinkian, China. During her early school years, she was tutored in Shanghai by Chinese teachers. At age 16, she attended Randolph-Macon Woman's College in Lynchburg, Virginia, where she graduated in 1914.

She returned to China where, in 1917, she married John L. Buck, an agriculturalist who was working as a missionary. She wrote the novel *East Wind: West Wind* in 1930 while she was teaching at Nanking. Her first fiction, *A Chinese Woman Speaks*, appeared in *Asia Magazine* in 1926. In 1931 she published *The Good Earth*. It was widely accepted, and appeared in 30 languages. It won the Pulitzer Prize in 1932.

Buck was a member of the Presbyterian Board of Foreign Missions, but she resigned in 1933, after publishing an article that was critical of foreign missionary personnel. In 1934 she returned to the United States and divorced John Buck. She married Richard J. Walsh, her publisher, the following year. Prior to her last marriage, she wrote and published *Sons*, *A House Divided*, and sequels to *The Good Earth*. The novels were published as a trilogy, titled *The House of Earth*.

In 1936 she published *The Exile* and *The Fighting Angel*, which were biographies of her mother and father, respectively. She also wrote short stories, children's stories and nonfiction.

In 1938 she was awarded the Nobel Prize for Literature. In 1949 she founded the Welcome House to provide for the children of Asian mothers and U.S. servicemen. In 1964 she founded the Pearl S. Buck Foundation in Philadelphia for Amerasian youth.

Pearl S. Buck appears on a 1983 5¢ Great Americans stamp.

Ralph Johnson Bunche

Scott 1860
Born: August 7, 1904, Detroit, Michigan
Died: December 9, 1971, New York, New York

As mediator between Israel and the Arab nations in the 1949 Palestine conflict, Ralph Bunche received the 1950 Nobel Peace Prize. He was the first black to do so.

His grandparents had been slaves. He worked his way through college and graduated from the University of California in 1927 summa cum laude. Bunche was a fine basketball player, and his team won the championship three times. He attended Harvard for his master of arts degree in 1928, joined the faculty of Harvard and received his doctor of philosophy degree in 1934. He studied in England and South Africa for his post-doctoral work. His subject was political science and government. He was the chief assistant to Bunnar Myrdal, the well-known Swedish sociologist, from 1938 to 1940.

During World War II, Bunche served in the Office of Strategic Services as a specialist on colonial areas and peoples. He joined the State Department in 1944.

At the request of the United Nation's secretary general, Trygve Lie, Bunche was granted leave from the State Department to organize and direct the United Nations trusteeship division. In 1947 he was appointed to the United Nations Palestine Commission. After the assassination of Count Folke Bernadotte, Bunche became the chief mediator.

He was appointed professor of government at Harvard University in October 1950, but resigned in 1952 to give his full time to the United Nations. He became the U.N. undersecretary in 1954 after he had been the U.N. undersecretary for special political affairs from 1950 to 1954.

He was a member of the board of overseers of Harvard University and was on the board of directors of the National Association for the Advancement of Colored People. In addition, he was president of the American Political Science Association.

Bunche is honored on the 1982 20¢ Great Americans issue.

Luther Burbank

Scott 876
Born: March 7, 1849, Lancaster, Massachusetts
Died: April 11, 1926, Santa Rosa, California

Luther Burbank was a farm boy who, early in his life, took notice of plants and animals and observed that no two were exactly alike. He attended school until he was 15 years old. He studied Charles Darwin's book, *Variations of Animals and Plants Under Domestication*. From his own observations of plants and animals on the farm, he understood and agreed with what Darwin wrote, mainly that species originate from a natural selection.

When Burbank was of age, he purchased a 17-acre plot of land near Lunenburg, Massachusetts, and planted potatoes. He examined every potato he raised and one day found 20 seeds in one potato seedball. He planted all the seeds, and 20 different plants grew. He culled out the four best plants. From this simple procedure he produced the world's best potato, known as the Burbank, or the Idaho, potato, which has been estimated to be worth more than $2 billion to the world's economy.

From the profits of his potato venture he moved to Santa Rosa, California, in 1875. On a four-acre plot, he established his home and a garden with a greenhouse, where he could continue with his work. Burbank also had an eight-acre plot nearby to raise plants on a larger scale. He developed hybridization and thereby modified the heredity of plants. He thus was able to produce offspring of superior varieties and variations.

He developed more than 800 new varieties of fruit trees, ornamental trees, flowers, vegetables, grains, grasses and forage plants. He even developed a cactus that had no stickers. He grew 30,000 new varieties of plums just to find one special variety. "I shall be content, he said, "if because of me, there shall be better fruits and fairer flowers." But Burbank never understood the genetic principles involved in his work, as we do today.

Burbank is pictured on a 1940 3¢ Famous Americans issue.

John Burgoyne

Surrender at Saratoga 1777 by Trumbull

US Bicentennial 13 cents

Scott 1728
Born: 1722, London, England
Died: August 4, 1792, London, England

Dashing and debonair, but usually on the defensive, describes John Burgoyne, a British army officer and playwright. After finishing his studies at Westminster School in 1740, he joined the British army. He eloped in 1743 with the daughter of the 11th Earl of Derby. To avoid overextended debts, the Burgoynes fled to France. He rejoined the army and served in Europe during the Seven Years War. Burgoyne was elected to Parliament in 1761 and made a name for himself in the investigation of the East India Company.

He was appointed a major general in 1772 and was sent to Boston in 1775. He saw the Battle of Bunker Hill, then returned to London.

In 1776, Burgoyne was named second in command to Sir Guy Carleton to invade New York from Canada. On Lake Champlain they captured Crown Point, but Burgoyne was dissatisfied with Carleton and returned to London. Burgoyne was convinced that he could invade New York from Canada more effectively and persuaded the king to let him do so. In June 1777, with 7,000 soldiers, he reoccupied Crown Point. He took Fort Ticonderoga July 6. Burgoyne's troops proceeded southward. Colonel Barry St. Leger was to bring reinforcements from the west, but he had been stopped by the Americans. General Howe's reinforcements from the south never appeared. Burgoyne was repulsed at Bemis Heights and Freeman's Farm and had to surrender to General Gates at Saratoga. This was the turning point of the war for the Americans.

Burgoyne returned to England to write plays. He had been castigated for his failures by every party in Parliament. Except for the title of general, he was deprived of all offices. After his wife died, he had seven illegitimate children by the opera singer Susan Caulfield. One of these children was Field Marshal Sir John Fox Burgoyne.

The 1977 13¢ American Bicentennial issue features the painting *Surrender of Burgoyne* by John Trumbull.

36

Richard Evelyn Byrd

Scott 2388
Born: October 25, 1888, Winchester, Virginia
Died: March 11, 1957, Boston, Massachusetts

Richard Byrd attended the Virginia Military Institute. He graduated from the U.S. Naval Academy in 1912. During World War I, he was trained as an aviator at Pensacola, Florida. From July to November 1918, he commanded the United States Air Force of Canada.

In preparation for the first transatlantic airplane flight in 1919, Byrd was in charge of navigation. He commanded the aviation unit of the U.S. Navy-MacMillan Arctic Expedition over Greenland and Ellesmere Island in 1925. With Floyd Bennett as co-pilot, Byrd made the first flight over the North Pole on May 9, 1926. With three others, he made a 42-hour non-stop flight from Roosevelt Field, Long Island, to France in 1927.

In 1928 he led his first expedition to Antarctica. On the Bay of Whales, Byrd established his base camp and called it Little America. He made his first flight over the South Pole on November 28, 1929, in the trimotored monoplane, *Floyd Bennett*, named after his co-pilot who had died the previous year. It was a 1,600-mile flight from Little America. By a special act of Congress, Byrd advanced to rear admiral.

In 1933 he returned to Little America. In the winter of 1934, he lived alone for five months at a weather station 123 miles south of the base camp. He described this experience in his book *Alone*.

President Franklin D. Roosevelt named him commander of the Antarctic development project, Operation Highjump, with 4,700 men, 13 ships, modern aircraft and tractors. Rear Admiral Richard Cruzen was project commander.

In 1955 and 1956, Byrd made his fifth and last trip to Antarctica to begin preparations for the 1957-1958 International Geophysical Year's Operation Deepfreeze. He again raised the American flag on the base camp at Little America. He died before the operation was carried out.

Richard Evelyn Byrd appears on a 1988 25¢ Antarctic Explorers stamp.

Antoine Laumet de la Mothe Cadillac

Scott 1000
Born: March 5, 1658, Les Laumets, Languedoc, France
Died: October 15, 1730, Castelsarrasin, Tarn-et-Garonne, Gascogne, France

In 1902 Henry Leland founded an automobile company in Detroit. He called the car he manufactured the Cadillac, named after the founder of Detroit, Antoine Laumet de la Mothe Cadillac. Detroit is the French word for a strait or sound, such as the narrow passageway of water that connects Lake Erie between Michigan and Ontario, Canada. The passageway is called the Detroit River. The fort that Cadillac established, now the city of Detroit, lies on the west bank of the river. Fort Detroit was originally called Fort Ponchetrain. It was a strategic point established to protect the western fur trade from Iroquois and French attacks and as a barrier against the invaders of the English traders from Fort Orange (Albany, New York).

Louis XIX, anxious to establish French feudalism in the New World, granted the island to Cadillac in 1688 as part of the Seigneuries of Doaquet.

Cadillac's real name was Antoine Laumet. He was the son of a village lawyer. Antoine Laumet changed his name to La Mothe and gave himself the title Sieur de Cadillac.

The people of Mount Desert Island, Maine, claim that Cadillac and his wife may have lived near Schooner Head one summer. Others believe they were at Otter Creek or east of Schoodic Point. Just west of Schooner Head and inland about two miles is Mount Cadillac, the highest coastal mountain north of Rio de Janeiro. Cadillac was a military man before he went to Canada in 1683. From 1694 to 1697, prior to the founding of Fort Detroit, he commanded the post at Michilimackinac.

Cadillac had returned to France in 1699 to arrange for his mission, even though the intendant, Jean Bochard de Champigny, and the Company of Canada were opposed to it. Fort Detroit was founded in 1701, and in 1704 Cadillac was appointed its commandant.

Ten years later Cadillac served as governor of Louisiana, until he was called to return to France in 1717. He opposed John Law's scheme for developing Louisiana. For this, Cadillac was thrown into the Bastille. He was released in 1718.

The 250th anniversary of the landing of Cadillac is commemorated on a 1951 stamp.

Chester Floyd Carlson

Scott 2180
Born: February 8, 1906, Seattle, Washington
Died: September 19, 1968, New York, New York

The name "Xerox" comes from the technical term xerography. It has become so commonplace that it is now a frequently used term meaning to make a quick copy of most anything on paper. This type of copy is made by the formation of a picture or copies of graphic material by the action of light on an electrically charged photoconductive insulating surface (sulfur-coated zinc). The latent image usually is developed with powders (lycopodium) that adhere only to the areas that remain electrically charged. The image formed by the powders sometimes is transferred to a sheet of paper. This method of dry imagery was so named by using the International Scientific Vocabulary terms xer plus graphy. From this term evolved the name of the Xerox Corporation of Rochester, New York, which was originally the Haloid Company.

Chester Carlson began working as a patent lawyer with the patent department of a New York electronics firm. Patent applications required multiple copies. Mimeographs, carbon copies and expensive photostats proved to be slow and clumsy. They were often blurred and inaccurate. Necessity being the mother of invention, Carlson created his photocopies in the kitchen of his Jackson Heights, New York, apartment. He used the knowledge he had gained as a high school amateur chemist in San Bernardino, California, and as a graduate of the California Institute of Technology. He studied law at night at the New York Law School, graduating in 1939, and passed the New York bar in 1940.

Carlson obtained a patent on his creation in 1940. He could not interest any company in his discovery until 1944, when the Battelle Memorial Institute of Columbus, Ohio, showed interest. In 1947 the Haloid (Xerox) Company developed a commercial photocopying machine. In 1959 the Xerox 914 machine was launched as a quick, clear and inexpensive method for all types of duplicated copies, creating a whole new industry.

Carlson became wealthy from royalties and gave away millions of dollars. More than 50 copying machine companies have entered the field.

Carlson was honored on a 1988 21¢ stamp in the Great Americans series.

Andrew Carnegie

Scott 1171
Born: November 25, 1835, Dunfermline, Scotland
Died: August 11, 1919, Lenox, Massachusetts

Andrew Carnegie, a steel manufacturer and philanthropist, first came to the United States when he was 13. His father, William, a hand-loom weaver in Scotland, moved with his wife and two sons after the power loom came into use and the 1848 depression struck. The younger Carnegie emigrated with his family to Allegheny, Pennsylvania, where his father sold the products of his loom door-to-door.

Andrew found work in a cotton factory, and then in a bobbin-making shop as a clerk. At night school, he studied bookkeeping. In 1850 he became a telegraph messenger boy in Pittsburgh. He learned to send and decipher telegraphic messages, and in two years, he was an operator. A year later he became a personal clerk and telegraph operator for Thomas A. Scott, the division superintendent of the Pennsylvania Railroad. Within six years, he was the division superintendent.

Scott had been placed in charge of military transportation early in the Civil War. Carnegie was his assistant and organized the eastern military telegraph and railroad service. Carnegie began investing in stock. His mother mortgaged the house for $500, and he invested the money in Adams Express Stock. A loan from the bank enabled him to acquire an eighth interest in a sleeping car and a bridge company.

He invested in the Superior Rail Mill and Blast Furnaces, the Union Iron Works, the Pittsburgh Locomotive Works and Pennsylvania oil fields. In 1865 he devoted most of his energies to the expanding iron industry. In 1873 he was one of the largest shareholders of the Pullman Company and an officer of the Pennsylvania Railroad. By 1877, Carnegie furnaces were feeding iron to the railroad industry. He acquired the Homestead plant. He sold out to J.P. Morgan and developed the United States Steel Company. Shrewdly he made millions, and in his later life gave it away just as judiciously.

A 4¢ stamp was issued in 1960 to honor Andrew Carnegie.

Rachel Louise Carson

Scott 1857
Born: May 27, 1907, Springdale, Pennsylvania
Died: April 14, 1964, Silver Spring, Maryland

As a young girl, Rachel Carson had a love and appreciation for the great outdoors. She seemed to sense that the environment had dangers to its survival lurking within it. Carson devoted her studies and her life's work to making the world aware of the dangers of spewing poisonous carbon monoxide and acid rain in the atmosphere, spreading poisonous herbicides in agriculture and forestry, and spraying poisonous insecticides over the cities, the fields and the orchards to destroy insect pests. She knew such practices were upsetting the balance of nature so that birds that fed on poisoned insects died or their eggs were so altered that they did not hatch.

Animals that fed on poisoned forage became sick or died. Poisons washed into the creeks and rivers and, finally, out into the sea where many fish were poisoned. Clams and shrimp could hardly survive and even the seaweed became altered and died. Instead of saving man's natural wealth, he was destroying it with his own manufactured poisons.

Come spring it might be that no birds would be alive to chirp and sing, and the fish that man ate or the vegetables he put on his table would contain poisons that would cause cancer or poison his blood. Thus, Carson wrote her book *Silent Spring* in 1962. The title tells it all.

Her other books, *Under the Sea* (1941), *The Sea Around Us* (1951) and *The Edge of the Sea* (1955), resulted from her experience as an aquatic biologist with the Bureau of Fisheries, from which she resigned in 1952 to research her now famous book, *Silent Spring*. From 1931 to 1936 she had been on the zoology staff at the University of Maryland, while studying at the Marine Laboratory in Woods Hole, Massachusetts. In 1952 she won several awards. In 1963 she was elected to the National Academy of Arts and Letters.

Carson is portrayed on the 1981 17¢ Great Americans issue.

Philip Carteret

Scott 1247
Born: 1639, Jersey, Channel Islands, England
Died: 1682, New Jersey

Philip Carteret was a personage of little moment who made his way into the history books by being the cousin of Sir George Carteret, who was the joint proprietor of New Jersey. Philip was elected, or rather selected, to act as the first governor of what was then called the Province of Nova Caesaria, or New Jersey. It was so called because Sir George Carteret had governed the Isle of Jersey from 1643 to 1651, and the province was named to honor him.

Charles II was restored to the throne in 1660, and he owed much to his friends and relatives. Because he hated the Dutch, Charles II decided to give to his brother James, the Duke of York, New Netherland and a good bit of its surrounding territory. Then he declared war on Holland.

He named Richard Nicolls his deputy, and with four frigates, Nicolls secured his prize. Peter Stuyvesant gave up the territory with just a whimper, and the young duke owned a large hunk of real estate to do with as he saw fit. Nicolls was made governor of the area, and he renamed it New York.

In 1664 he sliced off the lower part, called New Jersey, and gave it to his good friends Sir George Carteret and Lord John Berkeley. Sir George sent his cousin, Philip Carteret, to take over as its new governor in 1665. He also issued a most liberal grant of political privileges to the few hundred Dutchmen and English Puritans who had settled Woodbridge and Newark.

In 1674 Berkeley sold the southwestern part, his half-share of New Jersey, to two Quakers. Sir George died in 1680, and his widow promptly sold the northeastern half to William Penn and 11 associates for £3,400. Philip Carteret was forcibly carried to New York and imprisoned by the governor of New York, Sir Edmund Andros. The New York jury freed Philip of charges of illegal exercise of authority, and the Duke of York recalled Andros. Philip quietly retired from history.

He is shown on the 1964 5¢ New Jersey Tercentenary issue.

Enrico Caruso

Scott 2250
Born: February 25, 1873, Naples, Italy
Died: August 2, 1921, Naples, Italy

Enrico Caruso was an Italian operatic tenor, who, like the present-day Luciano Pavarotti, combined vocal superiority with superb acting ability to bring liveliness and entertainment to the opera stage. Even as a small boy he had an exceptionally beautiful singing voice. He studied voice with Vergine and Lombardi. He grew up in a home with 21 other children. The family was very poor. His father found work for him in a factory. Young Caruso's earnings helped support the large family. He worked his way up to book-keeper.

His mother, Anna Caruso, recognized the greatness of his voice and encouraged him. She saved to pay for Enrico's singing lessons. When he was only 15 years old, his mother died. This was one of the most heart-rendering experiences of his turbulent life; he loved his mother very much.

He sang in the church choir, and at fashionable watering places, and later with a touring company as the understudy tenor. One evening while enjoying a few drinks with his friends, Enrico was summoned to perform in place of the lead tenor. He ran all the way. Out of breath and a bit tipsy, he performed poorly. He was also accused of being a baritone. Caruso fell into financial difficulty with his tutor, Bergine, who demanded 25 percent of his earnings.

Despite difficulties and opposition, he studied and practiced hard on his own and worked his way to the top. He became famous when he sang with Dame Nellie Melba in *La Boheme* at Monte Carlo (1902). His London and New York debut was as the duke in *Rigoletto* at Covent Gardens and the Metropolitan (1903).

Addicted to cigarettes, he died of a lung disease at the young age of 48.

Caruso was honored in the Performing Arts series with a 22¢ stamp issued in 1987.

43

George Washington Carver

Scott 953
Born: July 12, 1861, Diamond Grove, Missouri
Died: January 5, 1943, Tuskegee, Alabama

Young George Washington Carver worked hard for his education. He devoted his knowledge to the betterment of mankind rather than using it to increase his own wealth. In 1892 he received his master of science degree from Iowa State College. He worked at the college as a botanist until 1896, when he was given the opportunity to teach under Booker T. Washington at the newly created department of agriculture at the Tuskegee Institute in Alabama. He spent the rest of his life at the institute as a chemurgist and agricultural experimenter. He devoted his efforts to discovering new uses for southern agricultural crops and for improving and diversifying the crops that were already being grown in abundance.

Planting cotton year after year was exhausting the soil. He persuaded the farmers to rotate their cotton crops with crops of peanuts and sweet potatoes to enrich the soil. From the peanut, he made cheese, milk, coffee, flour, ink, dyes, soap, wood stains and insulating board. In all, he discovered or devised more than 300 different products.

He discovered how to make synthetic marble from wood chips and shavings years before plastics became so common. He made flour, vinegar, molasses, rubber and other useful products from the sweet potato.

More importantly, he opened the way for other industries to devise useful products from commonly grown or abundantly available material. For example, he extracted rubber from the milk of the goldenrod. He worked with hybridization of cotton and with various kinds of fertilizers.

Henry Ford worked with Carver developing synthetic rubber. Thomas Edison offered him a job at a much increased pay, but he stayed on at the Tuskegee laboratory and even refused an increase in salary. He devoted his life savings to establishing the Carver Research Foundation (1940). The Carver Museum (established in 1941) is in Tuskegee.

George Washington Carver was honored in 1948 with a 3¢ stamp marking the fifth anniversary of his death.

Mary Cassatt

Scott 2182
Born: May 22, 1844, Allegheny City, Pennsylvania
Died: June 14, 1926, Chateau de Beaufresne, near Paris, France

When Mary Cassatt went to Paris with her parents (1851-1856), she visited the art museum and decided that when she returned home she would study the fine arts. She spent four years (1861-1865) at the Pennsylvania Academy of Fine Arts. She returned to Europe, and studied painting and art history while traveling in France, Italy, Spain and Belgium. She was most impressed by the paintings by Correggio in Italy and Rubens in Belgium.

She exhibited her work at the Paris Salon's annual art show. When Edgar Degas saw her painting *Portrait of Ida*, he invited her to exhibit her work at the impressionist painters' showings. She joined the impressionists in 1872 and exhibited her painting *The Cup of Tea* in their fourth show. The painting now hangs in the Metropolitan Museum of Art in New York City.

Cassatt worked hard for the next several years so that she could exhibit her paintings in the fifth, sixth, and eighth impressionist's showings. The Durand-Ruel Galleries in Paris showed her work in an exclusive showing in 1891, and again in 1893. Earlier, in 1882, she showed some changes in her style with the portrait of her mother, *Reading "Le Figaro."* She showed even more change in her style in the painting *Lady at the Tea Table*.

After that work, she leaned toward Japanese style, probably influenced by the great exhibition of Japanese art she viewed in Paris in 1890. She then made numerous prints (about 200) exhibiting the Japanese style.

She again changed her style in her painting *After the Bath* (1091), where she was influenced by the more colorful exhibits by the French paintings.

About 1900 Mary Cassatt's eyesight began to fail because of cataracts. Her style became formless. She gave up painting after 1914.

She was honored in the Great Americans series with a 1988 23¢ stamp.

Willa S. Cather

Scott 1487
Born: December 7, 1873, Back Creek Valley (near Winchester), Virginia
Died: April 24, 1947, New York, New York

When Willa Cather was a child, her family moved from Virginia to Webster County on a ranch near Red Cloud, Nebraska. After a year, the Cathers moved into the little frontier village. Willa learned firsthand, during her formative years from age 8 to 15, the difficult work required of the immigrant farmers and ranchers of that area. It was from these childhood experiences that Cather unconsciously gathered material for the short stories and novels she later wrote.

She obtained her basic education at home and later attended schools in Red Cloud and Nebraska's capital, Lincoln. She supported herself by writing drama criticism for the *Nebraska State Journal*. She attended the University of Nebraska in Lincoln, where she became interested in music and intellectual pursuits. She was especially fond of Latin.

At age 22, she moved to Pittsburgh, where she was on the editorial staff of *The Home Monthly*. Later, she taught Latin and English in the Pittsburgh high schools. She devoted more time to writing. Her collected stories, *The Troll Garden* (1905), was impressive enough to gain her a position as managing editor of the reform-minded *McClure's Magazine in New York City*. She gave up the editorial position in 1912 to devote her time to writing novels, mostly at the suggestion of Sarah Orne Jewell, a New England author.

Cather visited her brother, Douglass, in Arizona, then returned to Red Cloud to refresh her childhood memories. For the next 15 years, she and her future biographer, Edith Lewis, shared an apartment in Greenwich Village, where she wrote eight more novels. Her best-known writings are *O Pioneers!* (1913), *My Antonia* (1918), *A Lost Lady* (1933), *Death Comes to the Archbishop* (1927) and *Shadows on the Rock* (1931).

Cather was honored on an 8¢ stamp in the 1973 American Arts issue.

Carrie Chapman Catt

Scott 959
Born: January 9, 1859, Ripon, Wisconsin
Died: March 9, 1947, New Rochelle, New York

Carrie Chapman Catt spent her childhood and youth on the frontiers of Wisconsin and Iowa. She attended Iowa State College and graduated in 1880. Catt obtained the position of school administrator in Mason City, Iowa. In 1885 she married Leo Chapman, the editor of the local newspaper. Chapman died the next year.

Catt was remarried in 1890 to George Catt, a civil engineer, and the couple moved to New York City. Between her marriages, she became involved in the Iowa Woman Suffrage Organization and was soon nationally recognized for her work. In 1900 she followed Susan B. Anthony as the president of the National American Woman Suffrage Association. Because her second husband was ill, she was forced to resign the presidency. After his death in 1905, she returned to her work with the movement in New York. She again served as the president of the National American Woman Suffrage Association from 1915 to 1920.

Catt was a gifted speaker and an able administrator. She devised the Winning Plan, which emphasized working with both political parties on all levels, the net result being the ratification of the 19th Amendment to the Constitution.

The Anthony Amendment, as it was called, extended the right to vote in political matters to all women. She also founded the League of Women Voters of the United States in 1920, a non-partisan organization that promotes political responsibility through informed and active participation of citizens in government. Through the league's publications and meetings the public is made aware of political issues and candidates, and voters are given reliable information concerning voting laws, elections and the major issues.

Catt was also active in the world peace movement and founded the National Committee on the Cause and Cure of War. This became the Women's Action Committee for Victory and a Lasting Peace.

The 3¢ Progress of Women issue was released in 1948 to commemorate a century of progress of American women. Elizabeth Stanton, Carrie Chapman Catt and Lucretia Mott are pictured.

Octave Chanute

Scott C93
Born: February 18, 1832, Paris, France
Died: November 23, 1910, Chicago, Illinois

When Octave Chanute was six years old, in the fall of 1838, he emigrated to the United States. He became one of the most outstanding civil engineers in this country, but he gained fame also in the field of aeronautics. He wrote and published, in New York City, the book *Progress in Flying Machines* (1894), which outlined the most recent advancements up to that time. He told of the technical advancements of the aviation pioneers and followed Samuel P. Langley's book *Experiments in Aerodynamics* (1891).

Two years later (1896), the year Otto Lilienthal of Germany crashed fatally after making more than 2,000 successful glides, Chanute designed his famous stable biplane hang glider. He and his employee Augustus M. Herring began gliding from sand dunes along Lake Michigan. His glider had very fine rigging and proved to be the turning point in glider designing. This rigging system was utilized by the Wright Brothers, but Chanute also gave Orville and Wilbur Wright valuable advice and assistance, which helped them to put their flying machine in the air.

In 1903 Chanute lectured in Paris and encouraged European inventors to turn their attention to the field of flying devices. He spurred them on in their airplane production and design improvements.

Chanute was much involved in bridge building. As the railroad extended in all directions, more and more rivers were encountered. Travelers were impatient about having to transfer from car to ferryboat and back again as they went from place to place. Octave Chanute was chief engineer of the Erie Railroad in 1875 when his assistant George S. Morison accomplished a crossing of the Genesee River at Portage, New York, for the Erie Railroad by spanning the river with an iron bridge.

As an aeronautics engineer, Chanute also learned from the sparrow, especially the tail-down landing.

He was honored in 1979 with two 21¢ airmail stamps.

John Chapman (Johnny Appleseed)

Scott 1317
Born: September 26, 1774, Leominster, Massachusetts
Died: March 10, 1845, Allen County, Indiana

During the latter half of the 1800s, when migrants moved west from western Pennsylvania to Indiana they often followed the apple trees planted by John Chapman, who was known as Johnny Appleseed. Many of these apple trees provided seed for trees planted later. Marietta, Ohio, is today the center of one of the finest apple regions in the United States.

Johnny Appleseed sold or gave away many thousands of seedlings that were subsequently planted over a 100,000 square mile area of Ohio, Indiana and Illinois (from the Allegheny River to the St. Mary's River). Not only did he love to grow seedling apple trees, but he had a way with animals, even wild ones. He was eccentric, especially in his dress. He sometimes wore a tin plate on his head.

He was a frugal man. He saved the apple seeds from the pomace of cider presses. From his early apple orchards in Pennsylvania, he showed the way to others and thus contributed to American pomology. The name Johnny Appleseed is a catchy nickname. Through the years, some of the stories about him have become exaggerated.

In 1784 James Glen of Philadelphia formed a reading circle of Swedenborgianism, from the book written by Emanuel Swedenborg (1688-1772) titled *Heaven and Hell*, with descriptions of the spirit world. Chapman became interested in this religious philosophy. Until his death, he was an active missionary for Swedenborgianism.

Folktales portray him as an earnest frontiersman, an unselfish planter of apple trees and a simple man with the natural and spiritual mission of preparing the wilderness for the people moving westward. He has become the "patron saint" of American orcharding, floriculture and conservation.

He was commemorated in 1966 with a 5¢ stamp.

The Four Chaplains

Scott 956
Protestant Chaplain George L. Fox (Vermont)
Protestant Chaplain Clark V. Poling (Michigan)
Catholic Chaplain John P. Washington (New Jersey)
Jewish Chaplain Alexander D. Goode (Pennsylvania)
Died: February 3, 1943, at sea

Not much is known about the lives of the four chaplains who died February 3, 1943, on the *SS Dorchester*.

George Lansing Fox was the oldest of the four chaplains. He served in World War I with an ambulance company. Hours before the war ended, he was honored with the Purple Heart, the Silver Star, and the Croix de Guerre. Fox worked as an accountant, but received the call to the ministry. At age 34, he was ordained a Methodist minister. Six years later he returned to serve his country as a chaplain.

The Reverend Clark Poling was born into the ministry. Poling attended Yale Divinity School and was ordained in Schenectady, New York, where he served the First Dutch Reformed Church. He went to serve in World War II.

Father John P. Washington was the oldest child of a staunch Irish Catholic family of seven children who lived in Newark, New Jersey. He was ordained in 1937 and assigned to St. Stephen's Church in Arlington, New Jersey. He then applied for a commission in the service of his country.

Rabbi Alexander Goode's father, grandfather and great grandfather were rabbis. Goode was leading a temple in York, Pennsylvania, when Pearl Harbor precipitated U.S. involvement in World War II. He married Teresa Flax and took the ferry to Staten Island, where he boarded the *SS Dorchester*.

On January 23, 1943, the *Dorchester* joined a convoy bound for Greenland, with a crew of 130 merchant seaman and 23 U.S. Naval Armed Guard and 751 passengers. On February 3, 1943, a German submarine sunk the *Dorchester*. Records show that 675 people lost their lives. The four chaplains remained with the ship, helping people into lifeboats. Survivors say the four chaplains had linked arms together in prayer while the ship sank. They received the Purple Heart and Distinguished Service Cross posthumously.

On January 18, 1961, a special medal of heroism was awarded by vote of Congress. In 1951 President Harry Truman dedicated the Chapel of the Four Chaplains in Philadelphia. A 1948 3¢ stamp honors the four chaplains.

Claire Lee Chennault

Scott 2186
Born: September 6, 1893, Commerce, Texas
Died: July 27, 1958, New Orleans, Louisiana

Before World War I, Claire Chennault was a high school principal. He joined the Army during the war and in 1917 earned a commission in the Infantry Reserve. In 1919 he won his wings. These experiences and his studies of aerial tactics convinced him of the important role of airplanes in time of war. Chennault had been an associate of Brigadier General William "Billy" Mitchell during the days of the struggle for a strong U.S. Air Force. Chennault emphasized this in 1935 in his report, "The Role of Defensive Pursuit."

Because of a hearing problem, he was retired from the service in 1937. He went to China to act as air adviser to Chiang Kai-shek. He organized and commanded the American Volunteer Group (AVG), known as the Flying Tigers. These were men willing to fly missions against the Japanese.

Chiang Kai-shek appointed Chennault lieutenant colonel and placed him in command of all China's air activities. By December 20, 1941, his group consisted of 90 pilots and about 20 nearly obsolete P-40 planes. With their plane's snout painted with the Flying Tigers insignia, they made their first appearance when they shot down four Japanese bombers raiding Kunming near the Burma Road on December 20. On December 26, they shot down 108 Japanese bombers and fighter planes over Rangoon in Burma The success of the daring Flying Tigers, later the 14th Air Force, resulted on July 4, 1942, in Brigadier General Chennault being named commander of the U.S. China Air Task Force, under General "Vinegar Joe" Stilwell's command. Despite his differences with Stilwell, his force continued to create havoc along the routes from the north.

Chennault resigned his commission at the end of the war in 1945. In Taipei, Formosa (now Taiwan), he helped organize the Civil Air Transport, the Nationalists' Chinese Civil Airline, appropriately called CAT. Congress honored him by passing a bill promoting him to lieutenant general, retired, just a few days before his death. He was honored with a 1990 40¢ stamp, part of the Great Americans series.

51

Winston Leonard Spencer Churchill

Scott 1264
Born: November 30, 1874, Blenheim Palace, Oxfordshire, England
Died: January 24, 1965, London, England

Young "Winny" completed studies at Harrow School and graduated from Sandhurst, the Royal Military College, in 1895. He was appointed second lieutenant in the 4th Hussars. On leave from the army, he went to Cuba, where he reported for a London newspaper on the people's revolt against their Spanish ruler. In 1896 his regiment was sent to Bangalore, India. He stayed until 1897. Churchill was a direct descendant of the first duke of Marlborough, through his father, Lord Randolph Henry Churchill.

Churchill wrote *The River War* in 1899, while he was with the 21st Lancers on the Kitchner Nile expedition. He also worked for the London *Morning Post*. He was taken prisoner by the Boers, while reporting on the South African war. He escaped, becoming a hero. He was elected to the House of Commons. He became president of the board of trade in 1908, the year he married Clementine Hoziers. In 1910 he was appointed home secretary.

In 1911 he became first lord of the admiralty and had the navy mobilized for the war with Germany in 1914. After a naval failure in the Dardanelles, he came under political fire and was demoted. In 1916 he returned to the army and served in France. He commanded the 6th Royal Scots Fusiliers. In 1917 he was appointed minister of munitions. From 1919 to 1922, he was secretary of state for war and for air. As war secretary, he was charged with demobilization of the British army. In 1924 he returned to the House of Commons. In 1939 he was recalled as the first lord of the admiralty. On May 10, 1940, he became prime minister, first lord of the treasury and defense minister. He remained in these positions through World War II. From 1948 to 1953 his six-volume memoirs, *The Second World War*, were published. In them, he coined the phrase "Iron Curtain." In 1951 he was again prime minister. He resigned in 1955, but continued to sit in the House of Commons until 1964.

Sir Winston Leonard Spencer Churchill appears on a 1965 5¢ stamp.

George Rogers Clark

Scott 651
Born: November 19, 1752, near Charlottesville, Virginia
Died: February 13, 1818, Locust Valley, Kentucky

When George Rogers Clark was a young man, he was interested in surveying the frontier land. In 1772 he was active in platting and clearing the land for the new settlers in the Ohio Valley. He also acted as a scout when Lord Dunmore fought to protect the new settlers in Kentucky from the raiding Indians. Clark scouted for and guided the settlers into Transylvania, which included Kentucky and much of what is now Tennessee. In addition, he led a revolt against the proprietors, such as Judge Richard Hendersen and other wealthy North Carolinians, who had not only purchased the land illegally from the Cherokee Indians but were also exacting exorbitant rents for the land. Clark must have encountered Daniel Boone somewhere in his activities.

When the American Revolution broke out in 1775, the Indians intensified their harassment of the settlers in Kentucky. The Indians were goaded by the British out of Detroit, because Kentucky was the heart of the new westward settlement. Clark organized an attack on Kaskaskia, Cahokia (Illinois) and Vincennes (Indiana) in the summer of 1778, but the British recaptured Vincennes the following December. With 130 men, Clark retook Vincennes, thus paving the way for the United States to later acquire the Northwest Territory.

After the Revolution, Clark held an office allowing him to allocate land grants in Illinois. Former Continental General James Wilkinson falsely charged Clark of drunkenness, illegally raising troops, failing his campaigns and seizing property. History has exposed Wilkinson as a traitor paid by Spain to protect the Spanish interests. An ignorant Congress accepted Wilkinson's charges and demoted Clark.

Clark later planned a colony in Louisiana and Mississippi, and led a force to take Louisiana, but all was thwarted by the U.S. government. He retired to Louisville. He is honored on Scott 651, the 1929 2¢ George Rogers Clark issue. The stamp commemorates the 150th anniversary of the surrender of Fort Sackville to Clark.

Grenville Clark

Scott 1867
Born: November 5, 1882, New York, New York
Died: January 13, 1967, Dublin, New Hampshire

Grenville Clark was the author, along with L.B. Sohn, of *World Peace Through Law* (1958; third revision, 1966). He was also the leader in the movement for peace through world federalism. He instigated and directed the World War I Plattsburgh Plan, under which some 16,000 United States business and professional men were trained to be army officers at the Plattsburgh Barracks training camp in New York.

In 1915 the United States was not ready for war. Woodrow Wilson demanded that Germany make reparations for the sinking of the *Lusitania*. He denied the legality of a war zone. William J. Bryan, then secretary of state, looked upon this as a dangerous ultimatum, so he resigned his cabinet post. Bryan said that a ship carrying contraband to the Allies with passengers aboard to protect it from an attack was like putting women and children in front of an army.

After the sinking of the *Lusitania*, the United States began preparation for war. It was believed that the United States would eventually have to intervene on the side of France and England. Societies, such as Navy League, urged Congress to prepare for war, taking the position that only by being strong could neutrality be preserved. Wilson ignored their advice.

On the initiative of Grenville Clark, Theodore Roosevelt, Jr. and other New York business and professional men, General Leonard Wood and the War Department organized the first Plattsburgh training camp in the summer of 1915, paying for their own food, uniforms and travel expenses. By the following summer, the idea spread from the original 1,200 civilian volunteers to more than 16,000. At first Wilson refused to support the idea, but on November 4, 1915, he set forth his program of strong preparedness — to "keep out of war."

Grenville Clark is portrayed on a 39¢ stamp in the Great Americans series. The stamp was issued in 1985.

54

William Clark

Scott 1063
Born: August 1, 1770, Caroline County, Virginia
Died: September 1, 1838, St. Louis, Missouri

Young William Clark followed in the footsteps of his brother, George Rogers Clark, who was 18 years older than he. William, too, fought Indians in the wilderness as a militiaman and later as an officer of the 4th Sub-Legion. He lived near Louisville, Kentucky, and in 1796 left the military to be at home. Meriwether Lewis needed a partner to share the leadership of an overland expedition to the Pacific, and he chose William Clark for the job.

In the spring of 1804 following the settlement of the Louisiana Purchase, President Thomas Jefferson instructed Lewis and Clark to make a thorough study of the newly acquired land. They went up the Missouri River and spent the winter with the Mandan Indians in North Dakota. The following spring, with their Indian guide, Sacagawea, they headed west, crossing the Rocky Mountains and then rafted down the Columbia River to its mouth. They were the first white men to cross the western part of North America south of Canada. William, like his brother George, was skilled at map making, which was his special assignment on this famous expedition. For many years, Clark's maps and manuscripts were the most reliable sources of information on the lay of land that spread westward.

Clark was appointed superintendent of Indian affairs for the Louisiana Territory and served as a brigadier general. During the War of 1812, he kept peace among the Indians in the Upper Mississippi Valley. He was governor of the Missouri Territory from 1813 until 1821, the year Missouri became a state. That year he returned to being superintendent of Indian Affairs.

Clark's greatest contribution to his country was his life's work as a mediator between the settlers and the Indians. The expedition was his single most important contribution. He is portrayed, along with Lewis and Sacagawea, on a 1954 3¢ stamp issued to commemorate the Lewis and Clark expedition.

Henry Clay

Scott 1846
Born: April 12, 1777, Hanover County, Virginia
Died: June 29, 1852, Washington, D.C.

Henry Clay was the seventh child of a family of nine children. He grew up on a farm. His father, John Clay, had been a Baptist preacher but turned to farming to support his large family. His wife, Elizabeth Hudson Clay, was a hard-working, charming woman and a kindly mother. When Henry was just 4 years old his father died. Ten years later his mother married Captain Henry Watkins and moved to Richmond, then to Kentucky.

Henry stayed in Richmond, where he was deputy clerk in the high court of chancery. He was advised by Chancellor George Wythe to study law and was admitted to the bar in 1792. He moved to Lexington, Kentucky, a town of 1,600 people, where land suits were bountiful. In 1799 he married Lucretia Hart. By 1805 he had acquired much property.

Clay was a Jeffersonian-Republican by conviction and education. He was elected to the state legislature in 1803 and to the U.S. Senate in 1806 to fill an unexpired term. From 1807 until 1824, he served in the Senate and the House of Representatives, often as the speaker of the House. He was an active expansionist and a backer of the War of 1812. At its conclusion, he was one of the five members of the peace commission for the treaty of Ghent.

He sought the presidency in 1824, but lost the nomination. He backed John Quincy Adams, who appointed him secretary of state. He again sought the presidency in 1831 but lost to Andrew Jackson. Clay was nominated in 1844 but lost to James Polk. He sought the Whig nomination for a fourth time in 1848 but lost out to Zachary Taylor. He returned to the Senate in 1849.

Clay left his mark on many important political issues and historical events. He was an industrious political leader and an exceptionally wise statesman.

He is portrayed on several stamps, including the 3¢ Great Americans issue released in 1983.

Samuel Clemens (Mark Twain)

Scott 863
Born: November 30, 1835, Florida, Missouri
Died: April 21, 1910, Redding, Connecticut

Mark Twain was born Samuel Clemens in Florida, Missouri, but he grew up in Hannibal, a larger town on the Missouri River. His father was essentially a ne'er-do-well and died when Twain was 11 years old. His mother was energetic and ambitious. When his father died, Clemens vowed he would become a successful businessman, but most business ventures he entered into ended in bankruptcy and failure.

After working as a printer's apprentice, he boarded a riverboat for New Orleans, with the intention to go to South America to seek his fortune collecting cocoa along the Amazon River. While traveling down the Mississippi River, he changed his mind after meeting Horace Bixby, a well-known river pilot. He persuaded Bixby to let him sign on as a river pilot apprentice.

Those were the most fruitful years of his life, but the Civil War ended river traffic. After unsuccessfully mining for gold in Nevada, he left for San Francisco in 1864. He wrote short pieces for a newspaper, using the pen name Mark Twain, the river term for a depth of two fathoms of safe water.

In 1867 he took a cruise to Europe and the Holy Land. He said he went "to see dead men's graves" and wrote *The Innocents Abroad* in 1869 to tell the world. It was an immediate best seller. He published two more successful books, *The Adventures of Tom Sawyer* in 1876 and, in 1884, *The Adventures of Huckleberry Finn*. Between publishing these two books, he wrote several other books and many short stories.

In 1870 Twain married Olivia Langdon, who came from a wealthy New York family. They moved to Elmira, New York. He invested his money, and his wife's fortune, in such ventures as a typesetting machine, lightning rods and his own publishing company. All went sour. To recoup his losses, he went on an extensive speaking tour. Two of his daughters and his wife died, and his only daughter, Clara, married in October 1909. He died the following year, broken and exhausted.

Samuel Langhorne Clemens is depicted on a 1940 10¢ stamp .

Roberto Clemente

Scott 2097
Born: August 18, 1934, Carolina, Puerto Rico
Died: December 31, 1972, off the coast of San Juan, Puerto Rico

On the last day of December 1972, a cargo plane loaded with relief supplies taking off for Managua, Nicaragua, crashed into the sea. All the cargo was lost, all the passengers on board the plane perished. Roberto Clemente was one of the persons who lost their lives. He had instigated a relief drive and helped gather needed supplies destined for the impoverished victims of Nicaragua's capital city. Two days before Christmas, an earthquake that registered 6.25 on the Richter scale, leveled the city leaving an estimated 10,000 to 12,000 people dead, 15,000 others injured and more than 300,000 homeless.

Clemente, who had been described as "the complete baseball player," died at age 38. He was regarded as the best defensive right-fielder in the history of professional baseball.

He considered himself fortunate to be able to help his fellow man, but he would not consider himself a humanitarian. As a Puerto Rican first and foremost, he had spent 18 seasons in the United States as a major league baseball player with the Pittsburgh Pirates when he died. He was first drafted in 1954 by the Pittsburgh Pirates from the Brooklyn Dodgers farm team in Montreal.

On September 30, 1972, just three months before his death, he became the 11th major league player to get the magical 3,000 hits for a career total. In the 1960s he won four batting championships. He had a lifetime batting average of .318, the highest among the active baseball players at that time. He was chosen to play in the annual All-Star game 12 times. He was the National League's Most Valuable Player for the 1966 season. In 1971, when the Pittsburgh Pirates defeated the Baltimore Orioles in seven games of the World Series, Roberto Clemente was chosen the Most Valuable Player.

He is portrayed on a 20¢ stamp issued in 1984.

Stephen Grover Cleveland

Scott 2218d
Born: March 18, 1837, Caldwell, New Jersey
Died: June 24, 1908, Princeton, New Jersey

"It is as a strong man, a man of character, that Cleveland will live in history," wrote Allen Nevins, who has made a most exhaustive study of Grover Cleveland, the 22nd and 24th president of the United States. For more than 20 years after he was admitted to the New York bar in Buffalo in 1859, Cleveland practiced law and dabbled in politics as a Democrat. He was such an able mayor of Buffalo (1881) that his reform program won him the governorship of New York in 1882. In 1884 he won the Democratic nomination for U.S. president. James G. Blaine was the Republican candidate. With Mugwump (independent Republican) support, Cleveland won.

In 1886 he married 22-year-old Frances Folsom in the White House. This was the first White House wedding. Cleveland urged civil-service reform, fought the pension grab and the high tariff rates. He was renominated in 1888 but was defeated by Benjamin Harrison. In 1892 he was again elected president, defeating Harrison in his attempt for a second term.

A depression hit the country in 1893. Cleveland made himself unpopular with the free-silver supporters with his sound-money measures, and alienated the protectionists with his tariff policy. He was firm with his foreign policies concerning the rebels in Hawaii and Cuba. He persuaded Great Britain to back down in the Venezuela border dispute.

After his second term as president, he settled in Princeton, New Jersey, but remained a public figure, lecturing and involving himself in business affairs. He stood for honesty, economy and efficiency in government. His actions in office proved him to be one of America's greatest presidents. His terms in office proved to be the most distinguished between Abraham Lincoln and Theodore Roosevelt's and are held as an example by historians.

He is portrayed on a 22¢ stamp in the 1986 Presidential sheetlets issued for the Ameripex stamp show.

William Frederick 'Buffalo Bill' Cody

Scott 2178
Born: February 26, 1846, LeClair, Scott County, Iowa
Died: January 10, 1917, Denver, Colorado

William Cody's parents, Isaac and Mary Cody, built a four-room log cabin on a land tract west of LeClaire, Scott County, Iowa. Julie Melvina was born in the new cabin, as was William Frederick. Their first son, Samuel, was killed in a horse accident when he was 12 years old. In 1854 Isaac took his family to a cabin he had built on the Salt Creek Valley, filed his quarter-section claim at nearby Fort Leavenworth, Kansas, and went to work building a seven-room log house. In 1857 Isaac contracted pneumonia and died.

Young Will went to work for Russell, Majors and Waddell to accompany wagon trains on trips over the plains. For a time, he rode on the Pony Express. During the Civil War, he served well with the 7th Cavalry. In 1867-1868, Cody killed buffalo to feed the construction crew of the Kansas Pacific Railroad. From this, he earned the nickname "Buffalo Bill."

He was a messenger boy for General Philip H. Sheridan and became chief of scouts for the 5th U.S. Cavalry. Cody defeated the Cheyenne in 1869 at Summit Springs, Colorado. He killed Yellow Hand at Hat Creek, Wyoming.

Edward Zane Carroll Judson, whose pen name was Ned Buntline, glamorized the wild west and Cody in his dime novels. He referred to Cody as "Buffalo Bill," the daring scout and Indian fighter. Ned Buntline persuaded Cody to appear on the stage (1872). After a year, Cody left Buntline but continued acting for 11 years. He was the hero of 1,700 dime novels, some of which he wrote himself. Novelist Prentiss Ingraham wrote most of them.

At North Platte, Nebraska, on July 4, 1883, Cody organized his first Buffalo Bill's Wild West show, which was to continue for 30 years. His extravaganza made its greatest success at the Chicago World's Fair in 1893. He also took his show to Europe. From the Buffalo Bill Wild West came the rodeo. His show people were useful in making peace with the Indians, including the hostile Sioux in 1890-91.

Cody is portrayed on a 15¢ stamp in the Great Americans series. The stamp was released in 1988.

George Michael Cohan

Scott 1756
Born: July 3, 1878, Providence, Rhode Island
Died: November 5, 1942, New York, New York

If someone could be considered the father of musical comedy, the honor would have to go to George M. Cohan, a versatile performer in American theater. Cohan could sing, act and dance. He was a playwright, producer, director, actor and songwriter.

Despite all his talents, he is probably best remembered as the Yankee Doodle Dandy who was born on the Fourth of July. The stage was his school and his home.

Cohan made his first stage appearance with his vaudevillian parents at age nine. When he was 10 years old, he was one of the regulars in the family who billed itself as The Four Cohans. In addition to his parents, his sister was part of the act. Cohan took to the stage like a frog to a lily pond. By the time he was 13 years old, he was contributing songs and scripts to the family act.

He published *Why Did Nellie Leave Home?* when he was 16 years old. His first real hit, *I Guess I'll Have to Telegraph My Baby*, came when he was age 20. Cohan always wrote the words to his own tunes. *The Governor's Son* was his first musical comedy. Three years later, in 1904, he starred in *Little Johnny Jones*. That musical show was such a hit that it put musical comedy in the American scene, stealing the spotlight away from the foreign operettas.

Memorable songs from his plays are now considered classics. These include *Yankee Doodle Boy, Give My Regards to Broadway, You're a Grand Old Flag* and *Mary's a Grand Old Name*. Cohan wrote many plays, of which the best known is *Seven Keys to Baldpate*. This 1913 play was based on the novel by E.D. Biggers.

In addition, Cohan portrayed Franklin D. Roosevelt in the Rogers and Hart musical *I'd Rather be Right*. He also had a successful production company with Sam Harris.

Cohan is shown on the 15¢ Performing Arts stamp released in 1978.

Christopher Columbus

Scott 245
Born: probably in 1451, in or near Genoa, Italy
Died: May 20, 1506, Valladolid, Castilian Court Palace, Spain

In 1509 Christopher Columbus' body was removed to Seville, Spain. His remains were shipped to Santo Domingo (now Dominican Republic) and entombed in the cathedral. Columbus was Italian but spent his adult life in the service of Castile. However, he retained his Genoese citizenship.

Columbus' father was a master weaver and kept a wine shop. Christopher was educated at home. He worked with his father. To collect supplies of wool and wine, he sailed down the coast. The trips became longer, and he signed on as a deckhand. On one voyage, a French pirate ship sunk the ship Columbus was on. Columbus landed penniless in Logos, Portugal. He made his way to Lisbon to be with other Genoese who lived in that city. He learned to read and write and studied all aspects of seamanship. With his knowledge of navigation and hydrography, he made several voyages, and prospered.

In 1479 he married Filipa Perestrello e Moniz and went to Madeira to live. Their son, Diego, was born in 1480.

In the early 1480s, he made a voyage with the fleet of Diego d'Azambuja to the Gulf of Guinea. This voyage was the beginning of his urge for discovery. It took him eight years of supplication to acquire three ships and 90 men from Ferdinand and Isabella to prove his theory that the Earth was round. It was his correspondence with the Florentine physician and cosmographer Paolo Tosconelli that fired him to search for Asia (Cathay) by sailing west.

On his first voyage in 1492, he came to an island (probably Watling in the Bahamas). Bearing the royal standard of Castile, he took the island in the name of the king and queen, and named it San Salvador. He returned to Spain in the *Nina*. Three more voyages followed. Many of his people remained in the New World to colonize it. He never found his Cipango or Cathay. The landing of Columbus and his party was depicted on the 15¢ 1869 stamp.

Columbus is shown on the 1893 issues commemorating the Columbian Exposition in Chicago.

Henry T.P. Comstock

Scott 1130
Born: 1820, Trenton, Ontario, Canada
Died: September 27, 1870, Bozeman, Montana

Henry T.P. Comstock served in the Black Hawk War and the Patriot and Mexican wars, then prospected between 1856 and 1862. Comstock was called "Ole Pancake" by his friends, one of whom was James Fennimore. Fennimore was also called "Jim Finney" and "Ole Virginny." It was from the Fennimore's nickname that the town of Virginia City, Nevada, got its name. Virginia City was settled when the Comstock lode was discovered. Today it is a ghost town south of Reno.

In the spring of 1859, Comstock and Fennimore and other prospectors discovered a rich vein of silver in the Virginia Range. This lode, with many bonanzas, provided half the silver output of the United States up to 1886.

It produced not only silver but also gold, copper, lead, zinc, mercury, barite and tungsten. In 1873, the big bonanza was discovered, which was the richest silver strike in America. The famous Comstock lode brought in no less than $15 million worth of gold and silver in a single year.

Adventurers by the thousands headed in from the west, and greedy hopefuls came charging from the east. Carson City and Virginia City threw their wealth around in the middle of the arid desert, where water was as costly as the whiskey the miners and prospectors liberally consumed in the saloons.

In 1861 Nevada was made a territory by Congress. In 1864, just three years later, its population was large enough that it could be declared a state.

When most of the gold and silver ran out, the population decreased. Copper now is the main metal produced in Nevada. Along with the fast life of the prospectors came gambling, which has continued on in Nevada. It was the lucky strike by "Ole Pancake," "Ole Virginny" and other prospectors that hastened the settlement and early statehood of Nevada.

The 1959 Silver Centennial issue depicts Comstock at the Mount Davidson site. The 4¢ commemorative was issued in honor of the centenary of the discovery of silver at the Comstock lode.

James Cook

Scott 1732
Born: October 27, 1728, Marton-in-Cleveland, Yorkshire, England
Died: February 14, 1779, Kealakekua Bay, Hawaii

After a few years of elementary schooling, James Cook worked with a storekeeper. He began an apprenticeship with a ship-owners firm, the Walker Brothers, in 1746, at Whitby, a British shipbuilding port, where the ships for Cook's later voyages were constructed. He joined the British Navy in 1755. During the Seven Year's War with France, he gained experience in navigation and cartography. He played an important role in the capture of Quebec and mapped the St. Lawrence River. He became master of the flagship *Northumberland* and surveyed Newfoundland. He made an accurate calculation of the longitude of Newfoundland and predicted a solar eclipse in 1766.

The Royal Society was duly impressed. Cook was made first lieutenant of an expedition to Tahiti to observe the transit of Venus between the earth and the sun, and to seek new lands in the southern Pacific. He sailed on the *Endeavour* out of Plymouth on August 26, 1768, rounded Cape Horn to Tahiti, and dutifully observed Venus crossing the sun. He surveyed the unexplored east coast of Australia, claiming possession on August 23, 1770, in the name of King George III. He called the land New South Wales.

From 1772 to 1775, Cook sailed the *Resolution* along with Tobias Furneaux on the *Adventure*, searching for Antarctica. In January 1773, they crossed the Antarctic Circle. They became separated. Furneaux sailed west. Cook continued his Pacific Island discoveries.

In July 1776, he set out on the *Resolution*, joined by Charles Clerke in the *Discovery*. They discovered the Sandwich (Hawaiian) Islands and sailed the coast of North America. They returned to the Sandwich Islands. When Cook tried to investigate the theft of a boat, he was brutally slain by the islanders. His mutilated remains were recovered and sunk into the sea.

He is portrayed on a 13¢ stamp issued in 1978. The stamp is one of a pair issued to mark the 200th anniversary of his arrival in Hawaii and Alaska.

John Calvin Coolidge

Scott 2219b
Born: July 4, 1872, Plymouth Notch, Vermont
Died: January 5, 1933, Northampton, Massachusetts

Calvin Coolidge has often been described as an astute, reticent person. He earned the nickname "Silent Cal." He occupied the White House as the 30th president of the United States at a time of prosperity, turmoil and instability. To Coolidge one may apply the old adage "still water runs deep." He had an idealistic upbringing. He believed in a divine intelligence and that it was a God-given duty to render public service.

He graduated cum laude from Amherst College in Massachusetts in 1895. He went to Northampton, Massachusetts, in 1897 to practice law. Six years later he married Grace Anna Goodhue.

As a Republican, he began politics as mayor of Northampton, then served as state senator, and later lieutenant governor. In 1919 he was elected governor of Massachusetts. He used the state militia to end the Boston police strike in 1919. He telegrammed Samuel Gompers, president of the AFL: "There is no right to strike against the public safety by anybody, anywhere, any time."

He declined the nomination for the presidency in favor of Warren G. Harding. He served as Harding's vice president without flair or dash. He presided over the Senate quietly and unenthusiastically.

On the night of August 2, 1923, Harding died. At 2:47 a.m., Coolidge was sworn in as president by his father in his country home in rural Vermont. In 1924, he was elected for a second term. His major accomplishments were the reduction of the tax and debt, and the Kellogg-Brian Pact renouncing war. This pact did not hold up in the 1930s.

Following his retirement, his health declined. He died January 5, 1933.

Coolidge is portrayed on one of the stamps of the Presidents miniature sheets issued for the Ameripex international stamp show in 1986.

Gary (Frank James) Cooper

Scott 2447
Born: May 7, 1901, Helena, Montana
Died: May 13, 1961, Los Angeles, California

Some actors have gained fame for their renditions of long and expressive lines spoken on stage and screen, but Gary Cooper may have gained fame for the shortest — his "yup" and "nope." His words were spoken with an even expression, but in an authoritative masculine tone, nonetheless, with kindness. Cooper exemplified a strong and manly personality. He represented the man who respected the law and had no use for desperadoes or cheaters.

In the 1941 film based on Thomas J. Skeyhill's *Sergeant York, Last of the Long Hunters* (1930), he portrayed such a character, Sergeant Alvin Cullum York, World War I hero of the 82nd Infantry Division. His unselfish heroic character was again displayed in the 1952 film *High Noon*, with the late Grace Kelly. He received an Oscar for each of these two films.

He was born Frank James Cooper. He was the son of an English lawyer. His father had moved to Montana and later became an associate justice of the state supreme court. Young Cooper grew up in Helena. He was sent to England for his education and returned to America for further college training at Grinnell, Iowa. In 1924 he moved to Los Angeles to attend an art school. He helped support himself working in films, doing bit parts in Westerns.

By 1926, as Gary Cooper, he landed an important role in *The Winning of Barbara Worth*. His slightly British accent and cryptic way of speaking won him many roles in Westerns, war stories, swashbucklers and sophisticated comedies. In 1929 *The Virginian* was filmed, casting Cooper as the hero.

From 1927 to 1961, he acted in more than 80 films as the starring performer. Be it Ernest Hemingway's *Farewell to Arms* and *For Whom the Bell Tolls* or *The Adventure of Marco Polo*, *Wings*, P.C. Wren's *Beau Geste in the French Foreign Legion*, *Mr. Deeds Goes to Town* or *The Hanging Tree*, Cooper always seemed to be in complete control of his character.

His last movie was *The Naked Edge*, filmed in 1961. He died that year of cancer, a week after his 60th birthday.

He is portrayed on one of four 1990 25¢ Classic Film stamps.

James Fenimore Cooper

Scott 860
Born: September 15, 1789, Burlington, New Jersey
Died: September 14, 1851, Cooperstown, New York

James Fenimore Cooper was the son of Judge William and Elizabeth Fenimore Cooper. Judge Cooper was a representative to the fourth and fifth Congresses. He was a Federalist and had gained considerable wealth by acquiring and developing large tracts of native land. Judge Cooper founded frontier village of Coopers Town at the lower end of Lake Otsego in east-central New York state. He moved his family to the frontier village when James was about one year old.

As James grew up, he roamed unrestrained in the surrounding wilderness and took excessive pleasures at the expense of his father's wealth. He was ousted from Yale in his junior year for unbecoming levity incompatible with the principles of the school. He was sent to Europe as an ordinary deckhand to learn seamanship and discipline.

He returned to the United States in 1808 and received a warrant as a midshipman in the navy. Three years later he married Susan Augusta De Lancey and quit the navy. The couple lived in comfort and splendor, first at her place in Westchester. Later, they moved to the shores of Lake Otsego in Cooperstown. They returned to Westchester in 1817 when things went sour in Cooperstown.

To help his thinning pocketbook, he wrote novels. His first, *Precaution* (1820), was just a warm-up for *The Spy* (1821), which was widely accepted. His next book, *The Pioneers* (1828), was even more widely acclaimed. His Leatherstocking tales, *The Deerslayer* (1841), *The Last of the Mohicans*, *The Pathfinder* (1840), *The Pioneers*, and *The Prairie* (1827) became classics of American literature. They tell the adventures of the American forester-frontiersman Natty Bumppo and his Indian companion Chingachgook.

He also wrote action-packed sea adventures, romances with European settings, mysteries, a play and a trilogy.

Cooper was honored on a 1940 2¢ Famous Americans stamp.

67

Nicolaus Copernicus

Scott 1488
Born: February 19, 1473, Torun, Poland
Died: May 24, 1543, Frombork, Poland

Perhaps one of the most important prelates of the Catholic church was Nicolaus Copernicus, canon of the cathedral in Frombork (Frauenburg), Poland. He contributed greatly to the advancement of science and putting man on the right track of understanding the world and its relation to the entire universe. Yet, his works were not published until he lie on his deathbed in 1543, even though he dedicated his life's work to Pope Paul III and had submitted his treatise 13 years earlier. His treatise, *De revolutionibus orbium*, was banned by the Catholic Church for 300 years.

Copernicus studied mathematics, astronomy, law, and medicine at Krakow, Bologna and Padua, and received his doctorate at Ferrara University. Through the influence of his eminent prelate uncle, he was appointed canon of Frombork Cathedral in 1497. Not satisfied with the Ptolemaic astronomical system, as he had learned it, he set out to correct its erroneous assumptions — mainly that the Earth was the center of the universe and the sun and all the stars rotated around it.

In the 17th century, Galileo was persecuted for supporting Copernicus' heliocentric planetary theory. According to this theory, the sun — not the earth — is the center of the universe. Even Christopher Columbus had sailed in the wrong direction, hoping to find Cipango and Cathay (Japan and China). He and many others believed the Earth rotated and that it, and all the other fixed stars, circled around the sun. Balboa had seen the South Sea (1513), Magellan circumnavigated the globe (1521), Captain Cook's partner, Furneaux, circumnavigated the Earth from west to east (1773), and thousands navigated on the basic principle of astronomy set down by Copernicus.

Copernicus is portrayed on an 8¢ stamp issued in 1973 to mark the 500th anniversary of his birth.

Elizabeth Clarke Copley

Scott 1273
Born: 1770, Boston, Massachusetts
Died: 1866, Boston, Massachusetts

Elizabeth Copley was the eldest child of the famous painter John Singleton Copley. Copley spent some 21 years in Boston as a portrait painter, painting his subjects as they really were, not exaggerated and embellished as was the custom.

He had a very successful career in Boston, and even though Joshua Reynolds and Benjamin West urged him to come to Europe to work and study, he stayed on in his estate on Beacon Hill. In 1769 he married Susanna Farnham Clarke, daughter of a wealthy Bostonian.

Elizabeth was born in 1770. When the political situation became precarious in America, the Copley family left for Europe in the spring of 1774. John Copley was in Rome when the Revolutionary War began. He joined his family in London in 1775.

In 1800 Elizabeth married a widower, Gardiner Greene of Boston. She returned to the United States and lived on Pemberton Hill in Boston. After Greene's death in 1832, the land was sold and became Pemberton Square. Elizabeth bought a home on Beacon Hill, just a few houses from her childhood home.

Elizabeth was the subject of many of Copley's paintings. Perhaps the most famous is the *Copley Family*. A detail from this painting is reproduced on a 1965 5¢ stamp honoring John Copley. The detail portrays Elizabeth.

69

Francisco Vasquez de Coronado

Scott 898
Born: 1510, Salamanca, Spain
Died: September 22, 1554, Guadalajara, Mexico

Don Antonio de Mendoza sailed to the New World in 1535 to become the first viceroy of New Spain. He brought with him young Francisco Vasquez de Coronado. Mendoza gave him several assignments. Coronado married Dona Beatriz de Estada, the daughter of the colonial treasurer, and in 1738 was sent to Nueva Galicia as its governor. He sent Fray Marcos de Niza to look for the rumored Seven Golden Cities of Cibola in 1539.

Fray Marcos went to what is now Arizona and western New Mexico, and returned with a glowing report. This sparked hopes of great riches for New Spain. Don Mendoza appointed Coronado, leader of the expedition.

From the small village of Compostela (100 miles northwest of Guadalajara and 25 miles due south of Tepic) Coronado gathered a colorful band of 336 soldiers and several hundred Indian allies. They headed 350 miles northward to Caliacan. Coronado and a small group set off in advance. Through the gorge of Rio Sonora, up the Valle de Sonora toward the upper Gila, trudging through the wilderness of eastern Arizona, they finally came to the first of the cities of Cibola, a Zuni pueblo of Hawikuh. This was hardly a city of gold. Coronado pushed upward to the upper Rio Grande valley and spent the winter in Tiguex. Another group under Cardenas made its way to the Grand Canyon of the Colorado River and found some Hopi towns. Still no cities of gold were found.

Indians told of the Gran Quivira, a land rich in gold and silver. Coronado journeyed through Texas, across Oklahoma and into Kansas. He went onto the Llano Estacado (Staked Plain), but found no cities of gold. He returned in 1542 to report that the north had little to offer. He resumed his governorship of Neuva Galicia.

In 1546 he was accused of committing cruel acts against the Indians. He was found innocent of the charges.

A 3¢ stamp issued in 1940 commemorates the Coronado expedition.

Crazy Horse (Tashunca-Uitco)

Scott 1855
Born: 1840? Oglala Sioux country in the Northern Plains
Died: September 5, 1877, Fort Robinson, Nebraska

As the white man moved westward over the middle United States, he moved onto and over the Indian's sacred land. The white man invaded the land and the Indian tried to defend it. One of the greatest leaders of the Indians was Tashunca-Uitco, which best translates as "wild" or "unbroken horse." He was best known as Crazy Horse. He was a Sioux, and it was his leadership that made the Sioux a formidable Indian nation.

One of the first major conflicts between the Sioux and the white men was on August 19, 1854, at Grattan near Fort Laramie, Wyoming. Many Americans were massacred. In retaliation, the U.S. forces destroyed the Indian village near Ash Hollow, Nebraska. Crazy Horse was not involved in the fight but saw the bloody carnage afterward. He was so incensed by what he saw that his hatred and animosity for the white man turned his heart to flint.

During the Sand Creek Massacre (1864) and thereafter, Crazy Horse became a great Indian chief and warrior. On December 21, 1866, he led the Fetterman massacre and was a stirring figure at the Wagon-Box fight near Fort Phil Kearny, Wyoming, on August 21, 1867.

Surveying parties of the Northern Pacific Railroad were a favorite target for Crazy Horse and his band.

Along the Yellowstone River, Crazy Horse made two attacks on General George A. Custer's troops. He gathered more strength and defeated General George Crook on the Rosebud River on June 17, 1876. Then came "Custer's last stand," when Crazy Horse wiped out the American forces at Little Bighorn on June 25, 1876. Fearing mass retaliation, many Sioux fled. Crazy Horse fought on, but he could not defeat the United States single-handedly. He surrendered at Fort Robinson, Nebraska, on May 6, 1877. When he tried to escape on September 5, 1877, he was killed by a guard.

He is shown on a 13¢ Great Americans issue released in 1982.

David Crockett

Scott 1330
Born: August 17, 1786, near Greenville, Tennessee
Died: March 6, 1836, at the Alamo, San Antonio, Texas

Davy Crockett, "king of the wild frontier," had little formal education. He grew up on the Tennessee frontier. He farmed and herded cattle to Virginia. He scouted for Andrew Jackson in the Creek War of 1813-14. He married Mary "Polly" Finley in 1806. They had three children. Polly died in 1815, and Davy married Elizabeth Patton, a widow with two children.

Following the Creek War, he moved further inland in Tennessee and tried to farm. He was a sharpshooting hunter. Because of his homely oratorical style, was elected to the state legislature. He was elected to the House of Representatives in 1827 for two terms, and again in 1833. He traveled the northern cities to support the Whig party. His speeches brought him the reputation as a somewhat illiterate frontiersman and a "big bold b'ar-hunter." He was known as the "coonskin congressman."

Crockett was to be the answer to the Democrat's Andrew Jackson, but he was defeated for election to the House of Representatives in 1835. He accepted the defeat poorly and moved to Texas.

He supposedly wrote an autobiography, *A Narrative of the Life of David Crockett, of the State of Tennessee* (1834), which salted his legendary reputation. According to the *New-York Historical Society*, an observant Englishman visiting America noted that "everything here is Davy Crockett. He picked his teeth with a pitchfork — combed his hair with a rake — fanned himself with a hurricane, wore a cast-iron shirt, and drank nothing but creosote and aquafortis (nitric acid). . . He could whip his weight in wildcats — drink the Mississippi dry — shoot six cord of bear in one day — and, as his countrymen say of themselves, he could jump higher, dive deeper, and come up dryer than anyone else."

In 1836 Crockett was killed while trying to defend the Alamo in San Antonio, Texas, against Mexican troops.

He is featured along with scrub pine on a 5¢ American Folklore stamp issued in 1967.

Glenn Hammond Curtiss

Scott C100
Born: May 21, 1878, Hammondsport, New York
Died: July 23, 1930, Buffalo, New York

Perhaps Glenn Curtiss' most important contribution to aerodynamics is the invention of the aileron, the movable control surface on the trailing edge of the airplane wing that permits a plane to roll. With the aileron, it is possible to roll a plane 360 degrees without changing its flight path.

Curtiss began his working life as a bicycle mechanic. In 1902 he opened his own shop making motors for motorcycles. He designed and built a motor for the dirigible *California Arrow*. This resulted in a commission to build the motor for the U.S. Army's *Dirigible No. 1*. This led to building heavier-than-air craft. By 1908 he made the *June Bug*, flew it for one kilometer in the United States, and was awarded a trophy by *Scientific American*. In 1911 he built a seaplane with which he demonstrated takeoffs and landings on water in San Diego, California.

When World War I broke out, his factory was making military planes for England, Russia and the United States. The factory produced 5,000 training Curtiss "Jennies" and the NC-(Navy-Curtiss)-4, which in May 1919 made the first transatlantic flight. Curtiss designed the first land-sea plane with a retractable landing gear.

The Wright Brothers accomplished rolling by an awkward method of twisting or warping the wings. The first Curtiss aileron was independent of the wing. Curtiss then put it in the trailing edge of each wing. It proved to be simple and successful.

The Wright's challenged Curtiss' claim of independent invention, but when Curtiss received a patent on his aileron on December 5, 1911, the litigation concerning the flaps for lateral control of the flying machine was settled. The two companies merged after World War I.

Glenn Curtiss was honored on a 35¢ airmail stamp issued in 1980.

Harvey Williams Cushing

Scott 2188
Born: April 8, 1869, Cleveland, Ohio
Died: October 7, 1939, New Haven, Connecticut

Harvey Cushing graduated from Yale in 1891 and received his medical degree from Harvard in 1895. He was admitted to Johns Hopkins Hospital staff in 1896, where he specialized in neurology and surgery of the nervous system. His studies were not confined to the United States alone. He spent time in England, Switzerland and Italy, returning to make Johns Hopkins medical school's department of surgery his home base. He focused his attention on improving the results of surgery on the brain, which, at the time, was almost 100 percent fatal.

In 1910 he successfully removed a tumor from General Leonard Wood. He paid special attention to the pituitary gland, describing a condition now called Cushing's syndrome and ascribed by him to pituitary basophilism, which is called Cushing's disease. Cushing's law states that an increase in intracranial tension causes an increase in blood pressure. However, the blood pressure remains higher than the intracranial pressure, thus preventing the brain from being shut off from its blood supply.

The Cushing incision or "crossbow incision" was devised by Cushing for subtentorial craniotomies. In 1900 he introduced an operation of an excision of the semilunar ganglion, making his approach below the middle meningeal artery. In 1905 he successfully operated on an intracranial hemorrhage of a newborn child. In 1915 he also devised a method of establishing a cerebral hernia as a means of decompression in inaccessible brain tumors.

In 1906 he began his investigations of pituitary tumors, and in 1910 began experimental hypophysectomy. He successfully anastomosed the spinal accessory nerve and the facial nerves for the relief of facial paralysis. By 1932 he had devised techniques and improved operative procedures for brain tumors, reducing the mortality rate from nearly 100 percent to less than 10 percent.

Cushing is portrayed on a 45¢ stamp issued in 1988 as part of the Great Americans series.

74

Manasseh Cutler

Scott 795
Born: May 3, 1742, Killingly, Connecticut
Died: July 28, 1823, Ipswich Hamlet, Massachusetts

Manasseh Cutler was a lifetime pastor of the Congregational church in Ipswich Hamlet, Massachusetts, even though he was absent from his post on many occasions. He was ordained in 1771, six years after he graduated from Yale. He spent the intervening six years as a teacher, merchant and lawyer. Cutler was a chaplain with the Continental Army during the Revolution and was cited for unusual bravery.

To supplement his clerical duties, he studied and practiced medicine, and was knowledgeable of such broad subjects as botany, astronomy and microscopy. For 25 years, Cutler's home was used as a boarding school.

He saw the need for developing Ohio and suggested that Revolutionary War veterans be given the opportunity to settle on that land. With Rufus Putman, Winthrop Sargent and others, he formed the Ohio Company of Associates, hoping to get from Congress a land grant that encompassed 1.5 million acres of land north of the Ohio River.

Cutler went to New York to negotiate with Congress and was instrumental in steering Congress to pass the Ordinance of 1787.

With William Duer, the secretary of the board of the New York investors, Cutler formed the Scioto Company for a second grant of five million acres of land west of Ohio.

The Ohio Company sent out a party, led by General Putnam, into the new territory. At the mouth of the Muskingum River, they formed a community called Muskingum. It was later named Marietta, in honor of Marie Antoinette. Marietta became a thriving river town as the westward expansion developed.

Cutler served from 1801 to 1805 in the House of Representatives. Back in Ipswich Hamlet, he continued his duties as a minister and delved into various scientific pursuits.

Cutler is shown with Putnam and a map of the Northwest Territory on the 1937 3¢ Ordinance of 1787 Sesquicentennial issue.

Dante Alighieri

Scott 1268
Born: 1265, Florence, Italy
Died: September 14, 1321, Ravenna, Italy

Dante, of the old and respected Florentine family Alighieri, first met Beatrice Portinari in 1273, when he was eight and she was nine. He fell in love with her, an adoration that lasted throughout his lifetime. When Dante's poetry came to the forefront, Beatrice was immortalized in *Vita Nuova* and in the *Paradiso* of the *Divine Comedy*.

He had been active in the political and military life of Italy. His exile was the result of a ruthless internal conflict between the Blacks and the Whites, two opposing Guelph factions. Dante was one of six administrators of Florence. The Whites were the doves, and they governed in peace until Dante was about 30 years of age. The Blacks were the hawks and were allied to the pope. King Charles, with the Blacks, committed arson, murder and pillage to seize control of Florence. He charged Dante and others with political corruption and defiance against the pope. All the administrators were found guilty in absentia, stripped of their property and banished from the city.

Dante was joined by two of his children but not by his wife, the former Gemma di Manetto Donati, the daughter of a powerful and influential family in Florence. They had four children, but their marriage was more for the family's convenience and was not an entirely happy union.

After 1300, Dante wandered from Verona to Bologna, Lunigiana, Casentino, Paris and finally to Ravenna. His banishment from Florence and the early death of Beatrice in 1290 resulted in his ultimate literary masterpiece, the *Divine Comedy*.

The 1965 Dante issue marked the 700th anniversary of the poet's birth.

Virginia Dare

Scott 796
Born: August 18, 1587, Roanoke Island, Virginia
Died: Unknown

Virginia Dare was the daughter of Ananias and Eleanor White Dare and the granddaughter of John White. John White was a painter, cartographer and colonial official under Sir Walter Raleigh in the Chesapeake Bay regions from 1585 to 1590. On the first expedition sent out by Raleigh, which sailed from England April 9, 1585, in ships under the command of Sir Richard Grenville, White created paintings depicting the life of the Indians and of the flora and fauna of the coast from Florida to Virginia.

The entire first colony returned to England in 1586. Raleigh was intent upon establishing a colony in Virginia and selected White as governor of the second colony. The ships sailed May 8, 1587, with 117 people aboard, including White's daughter, Eleanor, and her husband Ananias Dare. Shortly after their arrival in Virginia, Eleanor gave birth to a baby girl. She was named Virginia after the colony. She was the first English child born in North America.

This landing was again at Roanoke Island because the commander was anxious to be on his way to do some privateering. In August 1587 the ships were dispatched to England to obtain supplies for the new colony. John White went along. Because of the war between England and Spain, the supply ships were delayed. They finally returned in 1590.

John White returned to Virginia only to find an inscription that seemed to indicate that the colonists were either all killed or had fled from hostile Indians and had taken refuge with the Croatan tribe. White returned to Ireland and died three years later in 1593.

One may speculate that if the Dare family was killed by the Indians, the infant Virginia may have been spared and reared by the natives. She is depicted on a 5¢ stamp issued in 1937.

Jefferson Davis

Scott 1408
Born: June 3, 1808, Christian County, Kentucky
Died: December 6, 1889, New Orleans, Louisiana

Jefferson Davis was the 10th and youngest child of Samuel and Jane Davis. When he was still a boy the Davis family moved from Kentucky to Wilkinson County, Mississippi. He went to a Dominican school in Kentucky and attended Transylvania College. He secured an appointment to West Point in 1824. A less-than-average student, he received more than the average number of demerits, but managed to graduate. Davis served on the frontier in the Northwest, where he met Sara Knox, the daughter of his commander, Colonel Zachary Taylor. After taking part in the Black Hawk War in 1832, he resigned his commission to marry Sara and manage Brierfield, a 1,000-acre plantation near Biloxi, Mississippi. Three months after their marriage, Sara died of malaria.

In 1843, Davis won the Democratic nomination for the Mississippi legislature. He campaigned for James Polk in 1844. The next year, he married Varina Howell, of a prominent Mississippi family, and also won the nomination to the House of Representatives. In 1846 Davis resigned to command the Mississippi Rifles in the Mexican War. He saw action at the Battle of Monterrey and at Buena Vista, where he was wounded. He was forced to return home.

He was appointed to the U.S. Senate in 1847. He believed that management of agriculture and menial services by black slaves was right and just. He became a sectionalist, and opposed the Compromise of 1850.

Davis campaigned for Pierce and was appointed secretary of war. He was again elected senator. He backed Breckinridge for the presidency, but when Lincoln was elected, Davis became active in organizing the Southern Confederacy. He was elected president of the Confederate States of America. Although he chose his generals wisely, the South could not stand against the powerful and industrialized North. The horrible events of the Civil War ended in 1865. Davis lived to the age of 81.

The 1970 Stone Mountain Memorial commemorative depicts Jefferson Davis, along with Robert E. Lee and Thomas J. "Stonewall" Jackson.

Stephen Decatur

Scott 791
Born: January 5, 1779, at Sinepuxent, near Berlin, Maryland
Died: March 22, 1820, Washington, D.C.

Sailing and international conflict came early to young Stephen Decatur. He was schooled in that direction. When he was born, his mother escaped from Philadelphia to avoid the British occupation. His father, Stephen Decatur (1752-1808), was a Navy captain during the war with France. He had been a Revolutionary War privateersman and a merchant ship master and owner. Sea salt was in the Decaturs' veins, and gunpowder in their brains.

In 1798 Stephen Decatur was appointed midshipman. He served in the Mediterranean from 1801 to 1805 during the Tripolitan war. When Jefferson became president, the United States was paying out one-fifth of its annual revenue in ransom to the Moslem states of Morocco, Algiers, Tunis and Tripoli, some $2 million, either for captured ships and prisoners or for permission to sail in the Mediterranean.

The pasha of Tripoli declared war on the United States in 1801 to extract even more money. Commodore Preble appeared off the coast of Tripoli in 1804 with a task force headed by the flagship USS *Constitution*. Before this happened the frigate *Philadelphia* had been grounded and captured. The pasha imprisoned Captain Bainbridge and his crew. Decatur, with the *Enterprise*, captured the Tripolitan ketch *Masstico*, sailed it into the harbor and set flame to the *Philadelphia*. In a subsequent hand-to-hand fight, Stephen's brother, James, was killed.

Decatur served on the court martial that found Captain James Barron guilty after the USS *Chesapeake* and HMS *Leopard* incident. In November 1815, serving on the Board of Navy Commissioners, he opposed the reinstatement of Captain James Barron. Barron challenged Decatur to a duel and mortally wounded him at Bladensburg, Maryland. Decatur died in Washington, D.C.

He is portrayed on the 2¢ stamp of the 1936-37 Navy issue, along with Thomas MacDonough.

George Dewey

Scott 793
Born: December 26, 1837, Montpelier, Vermont
Died: January 16, 1917, Washington, D.C.

George Dewey was the third officer of the U.S. Navy to be honored by Congress with the rank of admiral (March 2, 1899). Farragut was first (1866), and Porter second (1870). Dewey had risen in the ranks from first being commissioned lieutenant in 1861, after he had graduated from the U.S. Naval Academy in 1858. Before attending the Academy, he had studied at Norwich University, Norwich, Vermont. At the time Farragut was passing the ports below New Orleans (during the Civil War), Dewey served on the steam sloop *Mississippi*. He took part in the fighting below Donaldsonville, Louisiana in 1863. He served on the gunboat *Agawam* (1864-1865) with the North Atlantic blockading squadron and was involved in the attacks on Fort Fisher (1864 and 1865). He became lieutenant commander in 1865, commander in 1872 and commodore in 1896.

At his own request, he took sea duty and was sent to the Asiatic area (1897). While his fleet was in the South China Sea off Hong Kong, he received a cable containing information that the Spanish-American War had begun (1898). He sailed to Manila Bay with orders to destroy the Spanish fleet in the Philippine waters. Admiral Montojo and his Spanish fleet were completely overwhelmed May 1, 1898, and Dewey won without a single loss of man or ship. He was promoted to vice admiral. His fleet remained in the Philippines to maintain control after the capture of Manila.

Admiral Dewey returned home to a great acclamation in 1899 in New York, and was appointed to the Schurman Philippine Commission. In 1901 he acted as moderator to the court that inquired into the Sampson-Schley controversy concerning Schley's alleged insubordination to Rear Admiral William T. Sampson in the battle of Santiago de Cuba Harbor. Schley was found guilty, but no action was taken. Sampson received no recognition. Dewey was never retried.

He is portrayed, along with Sampson and Schley, on the 4¢ stamp in the 1936-37 Navy issue.

John Dewey

Scott 1291
Born: October 20, 1859, Burlington, Vermont
Died: June 1, 1952, New York, New York

John Dewey received his doctorate from the newly established Johns Hopkins University in Baltimore in 1884 with a dissertation on "The Psychology of Kant." Prior to this, he studied at the University of Vermont (graduated 1879), and taught for three years in Pennsylvania and Vermont. At the University of Vermont, he was inspired by Professor Torrey to pursue the field of psychology and philosophy. Upon receiving his doctorate, he was made assistant professor of philosophy at the University of Michigan.

In 1886 he married Alice Chipman. He served as department chairman from 1889 to 1894, then went to the University of Chicago, where he served as department chairman of philosophy, psychology and pedagogy (1894-1904). During this time, he was president of the American Psychological Association. He next accepted the chair of professor of philosophy at Columbia University, where he gained international repute as a leader in public affairs, and as an educator and writer.

He was president of the American Philosophical Association from 1905 to 1906. In 1915 he was the main force behind the establishment of the American Association of University Professors and served as its first president. He was a charter member of the Teacher's Union from 1916 until 1930. He resigned because of the union's strong leftist tendencies. In 1920 he helped form the American Civil Liberties Union.

He retired in 1930 and became involved in the People's Lobby in Washington and the League for Independent Political Action and the League for Industrial Democracy. Because he served on the commission of inquiry into charges against Leon Trotsky in the Moscow trials, he was unpopular with the communist party when Trotsky was determined innocent.

Dewey's wife died in 1927, and he married Roberta Grant in 1946.

John Dewey is shown on a 30¢ stamp issued in 1968 as part of the Prominent Americans series.

81

Emily Elizabeth Dickinson

Scott 1436
Born: December 10, 1830, Amherst, Massachusetts
Died: May 15, 1886, Amherst, Massachusetts

Emily Dickinson was called "the nun" of Amherst. A few years before the death of her father in 1874, she became a literary recluse. But she was not a nun in the true sense of the word because men did play a role in her life. Ben Newton, a law student in her father's office who gave Emily a book of Ralph Waldo Emerson's *Poems*, was never forgotten by Emily after his early death. When the Reverend Charles Wadsworth, the pastor of the Philadelphia church, whom she regarded highly, moved to California, she suffered an emotional crisis. She called these men her mentors. She leaned on the words of clergyman and essayist Thomas Wentworth Higginson of Cambridge, Massachusetts, for encouragement and advice. After Dickinson's father died, Judge Otis Lord counseled and consoled her. After Lord's wife died, the relationship between Lord and Dickinson developed romantically. They considered marriage, but he died.

Dickinson was the middle child of three in the family of Edward and Emily Dickinson. She grew up in the small town of Amherst, Massachusetts. The town was becoming a center of learning because it was the home of lexicographer Noah Webster, who founded Amherst Academy and was on the first board of trustees of Amherst College. The college was founded in 1821 by Dickinson's grandfather, Samuel F. Dickinson. Emily Dickinson studied six years at the academy and a year at Mount Holyoke Female Seminary.

Dickinson's voracious reading influenced her poetry, Shakespeare and the Bible being the most evident allusions. The New Thought philosophy emanating from Concord, and especially from Ralph Waldo Emerson, influenced her thoughts as well. Emerson was like a second father to her.

After her death, 1,750 of Dickinson's poems were discovered in her room by her sister Lavinia. The first volume was published in 1890. Few had been printed during her lifetime. Dickinson appears on a 1971 8¢ stamp.

Everett McKinley Dirkson

USA 15c
Everett Dirksen

Scott 1874
Born: January 4, 1896, Pekin, Illinois
Died: September 7, 1969, Washington, D.C.

"Ev" Dirkson's parents were German immigrants. As a young man, he worked at several small-business jobs, attended the University of Minnesota for three years, then joined the Army in World War I. Until 1926 he held a local office in his hometown. He ran for Congress in 1930 but was defeated. In 1932 he tried again for the House of Representatives and was successful. He served until 1948. He retired from politics for two years because of problems with his vision, which were corrected. In 1950 he campaigned for the Senate. He defeated the Democratic majority leader, Scott W. Lucas, and remained in the Senate for the next 19 years, until his death.

In 1952 Dirkson supported Senator Robert Taft for the Republican presidential nomination. Taft lost to General Dwight D. Eisenhower. Senator Dirkson was conservative and did not always agree with President Eisenhower, but when he was elected leader of the Republican minority in the Senate, he strongly supported the president.

In the Kennedy administration, he opposed the federal medical care program for the elderly, but supported the nuclear test ban treaty. He supported the U.N. bond issue in 1962. Though he was the Republican leader during the Democratic Johnson administration, he worked closely with Johnson on such programs as the Civil Rights Act (1964) and the Voting Rights Act (1965). He had at first opposed these issues.

He attempted to override two Supreme Court decisions by proposing constitutional amendments concerning prayers in public schools and allowing the apportionment of one house in a state legislature geographically. He supported Johnson's actions and goals in the Vietnam conflict, but disagreed with his offer of "negotiation without prior conditions."

Dirkson was honored with a 15¢ stamp issued in 1981.

Walter Elias Disney

Scott 1355
Born: December 5, 1901, Chicago, Illinois
Died: December 15, 1966, Los Angeles, California

Walt Disney and his brother Roy moved to Hollywood, California in 1928, after they had produced a few short advertising cartoons in Kansas City, Missouri. They made a series of film cartoons, *Alice in Cartoonland* and *Oswald the Rabbit*. Soon after came *Mickey Mouse* in two film series, which, when first offered in silent films, were not accepted. When Roy and Walt added sound to this feature and called it *Steamboat Willie* (1928), it became a worldwide success. *Steamboat Willie* was first shown in New York City at the Colony Theater.

In 1937 Disney's company produced its first full-length fairy-tale classic, *Snow White and the Seven Dwarfs*. In 1953 he produced *The Living Desert* and in 1954 *The Vanishing Prairie*, and other educational nature films of the *True Adventure* series. Then came *Fantasia, Pinocchio, Dumbo, Bambi, Cinderella, Alice in Wonderland, Peter Pan* and *Sleeping Beauty*. In 1964 came the classic musical fantasy, *Mary Poppins*.

Donald Duck and Pluto first made their appearance in Disney's *The Wise Little Hen — A Silly Symphony* cartoon that won an Oscar in 1943. The voice for Donald Duck, for nearly 50 years, was that of Clarence "Ducky" Nash.

For television, Disney produced "Davy Crockett," "Mickey Mouse Club," "Zorro" and "Walt Disney's Wonderful World of Color."

In 1955 he created the amusement park, Disneyland, in Anaheim, California. In 1965 the park attracted more than 50 million visitors. In 1966 two more projects were started — Disney World near Orlando, Florida, and in California, Mineral King, an all-year resort in the Sequoia National Forest.

Disney received honors and awards around the world. In all, he received a record 29 Academy Awards.

A 6¢ stamp paid tribute to Walt Disney in 1968.

Dorothea Lynde Dix

Scott 1844
Born: April 4, 1802, Hampden, Maine
Died: July 17, 1887, Trenton, New Jersey

Before Dorothea Dix became involved in bettering the treatment of the mentally ill and improving conditions for prisoners, she was a teacher. She began teaching at the young age of 14 in a Worcester, Massachusetts, school. In 1821 she opened a young ladies school in Boston and taught there until poor health made it too much for her. She retired from teaching and wrote children's books for the next six years.

Sometimes a certain incident in a young life will so impress the person that it will determine their entire life's work. At age 39, Dix was called to teach Sunday school classes in an East Cambridge, Massachusetts, house of correction. The conditions in that institution were horrible. The mentally ill were mingling freely with the prisoners. Dix visited other Massachusetts prisons, poorhouses and insane asylums, only to find similar conditions. Her shocking conclusions were summarized in 1843 in her Memorial to the Legislature of Massachusetts. The results of her studies were duly noted by the state officials, and soon thereafter the conditions in the institutions were considerably improved.

She was encouraged by the results of her efforts, and this became her crusade. She visited similar institutions in all the states east of the Rocky Mountains. Dix took her cause to Washington, D.C., hoping to secure land and support for the mentally ill. The bill was approved by Congress but vetoed by President Pierce in 1854. She was most disappointed, but continued her work. When the Civil War began, she was appointed superintendent of women nurses in the Union Army. In 1865 she returned to her crusade. Dix was directly and indirectly responsible for the founding or enlarging of 32 mental hospitals in America, Europe and Japan. She retired in 1881.

The 1983 1¢ Great American stamp honors Dorothea Lynde Dix for her social contributions.

Stephen Arnold Douglas

Scott 1115
Born: April 23, 1813, Brandon, Vermont
Died: June 3, 1861, Chicago, Illinois

Stephen Douglas' mark in history stems from the famous debates with Abraham Lincoln. He started early in life as a worker. First he apprenticed to a Vermont cabinetmaker. When he had served his time, he went to New York to attend the Canadaigua Academy. He moved west to Cleveland then on to St. Louis, then ventured to Jacksonville, Illinois, where he studied law. He was admitted to the bar at age 20.

Douglas was a Democrat. Within seven years (1841-1843), he was a member of the Illinois Supreme Court, and well on his way to climbing the political ladder. As early as 1836, he made a bid for Congress, but lost. Before he became a judge, he did a short stint as Illinois secretary of state (1840).

In 1842 he was elected to Congress and then to the Senate (1846). His first assignment was chairman of the important Senate Committee of Territories.

Douglas moved to Chicago in 1847. He became involved in the passage of the Illinois Central Railroad Bill and the enactment of the Compromise of 1850. The Democrats created a "Young America" wing and selected Douglas as their candidate for the presidency. He lost, but was re-elected to the Senate.

In 1847 Stephen Douglas married Martha Denny Martin. She died six years later. In 1856 he married Adele Cutts (great-niece of Dolley Madison).

In 1858 he challenged and debated Lincoln for the Senate seat and won. In 1860 the two debated again for the presidency. The Democrats split North and South. A separate candidate for the South was selected. Thus divided, Lincoln won. Douglas firmly supported Lincoln to preserve the Union.

On a speaking tour, he contracted typhoid fever and died in Chicago at age 48. A 4¢ stamp issued in 1958 shows Douglas debating Lincoln.

Frederick Douglass

Scott 1290
Born: February 1817, Tuckahoe, Maryland
Died: February 20, 1895, Anacosta Heights, D.C.

His name was Frederick Augustus Washington Bailey. He was a slave. His master sent him to a household in Baltimore when he was nine years old to be a servant boy. There he learned to read and write. When he reached the age of 16 he was returned to his master to labor in the fields. He attempted to escape when he was 19, and shortly thereafter was apprenticed out to a ship caulker in Baltimore. Two years later he disguised himself as a sailor and went to New York City. In 1838 he moved to New Bedford, Massachusetts, where he changed his name to Douglass.

At a meeting of the Massachusetts Anti-Slavery Society in Nantucket in 1841, he gave a speech that won him a job as a speaker for the society. He traveled throughout the north and east. He spoke so well that people began to doubt that he was ever a slave. He wrote and published in 1845 his *Narrative of the Life of Frederick Douglass, an American Slave*, in which he identified his former master.

He used his lecture fees to aid fugitive slaves. Fearing capture, he fled to England and continued his anti-slavery program. Two years later he was back in the United States. Public subscription was sufficient to buy his freedom.

With Martin R. Delany, he founded the abolitionist newspaper *North Star*. After 1851, it was called *Frederick Douglass's Paper*. It lasted 16 years.

He was accused of financially aiding John Brown's raid on Harper's Ferry, Virginia, and fled to Canada in 1859. When black troops for the Union Army were organized in the Civil War, he helped. He was an active supporter of the Republican party.

After the war, he was on the Santo Domingo commission. He served as marshal of the District of Columbia (1877-1881), recorder of deeds (1881-1886) and minister to Haiti (1889-1891). Douglas is shown on a 25¢ stamp issued in 1967 as part of the Prominent Americans.

Charles Richard Drew

Scott 1865
Born: June 3, 1904, Washington, D.C.
Died: April 1, 1950, near Burlington, North Carolina

Charles Richard Drew was the son of Richard Thomas and Nora R. (Burrell) Drew. Charles Drew began his education at Amherst College, graduating in 1926. He received degrees of master of surgery and doctor of medicine from McGill University, Montreal, Canada, in 1933. He completed an externship in 1932-33 at the Royal Victoria Hospital in Montreal, and an internship (1933-34), followed by a residency in medicine (1934-35) at Montreal General Hospital. He returned to Washington, D.C., and was an instructor in pathology from 1935 to 1936 at Howard University.

From 1938 to 1940, he had the Rockefeller Fellowship in Surgery at the College of Physicians and Surgeons, Columbia University, and was resident in surgery at the Presbyterian Hospital, New York City. In 1941 he headed the Department of Surgery at Howard University.

From 1940 to 1941, he was the first director of the Blood Transfusion Association, supplying blood to the British. In 1941 he was the first director of the American Red Cross blood bank, supplying plasma to the U.S. Armed Forces. The first large-scale blood bank was established at Cook County Hospital in 1937. Blood plasma was used instead of whole blood because it could be stored in powder form for as long as five years and could be made ready for use at any time by adding sterile water.

From 1946 to 1947, Drew was chief of surgery and chairman of the staff at Freedman's Hospital, Washington, D.C. In 1949 he became a surgical consultant for the European Theater.

Drew was a diplomat of the American Board of Surgery. He was an examiner in 1942. He was a recipient of the Springarn award in 1944. He also directed the District of Columbia National Funds for Poliomyelitis in 1946 and was a District of Columbia director for the Crippled Children Memorial Fund and a member of the American-Soviet Science Committee.

In 1950 Charles Drew died in an automobile accident near Burlington, North Carolina. A 35¢ stamp was issued in 1981 to honor Drew. The stamp is part of the Great Americans series.

John Foster Dulles

Scott 1172
Born: February 25, 1888, Washington, D.C.
Died: May 24, 1959, Washington, D.C.

John Foster Dulles devoted more than 50 years to international law and diplomacy. He was the son of the Reverend Allen Macy and Edith Foster Dulles. He was born in Washington D.C. His family was closely associated with governmental affairs, so it was a natural path for Dulles to take, although it was his original intention to follow the ministry. He was the grandson of John Watson Foster, who served as secretary of state under Benjamin Harrison. He was the nephew of Robert Lansing, a secretary of state under Woodrow Wilson. His brother, Allen Welsh Dulles, was a distinguished lawyer, diplomat and public official. Allen served with the Office of Strategic Services (OSS) during World War II and was director of the Central Intelligence Agency (CIA) from 1953 to 1961.

In 1907 John Foster's grandfather took him to the Hague Conference. His grandfather served there as secretary to the Chinese delegation. This experience set John Foster on the road of international law and diplomacy. He graduated the following year from Princeton University. He studied at the Sorbonne in Paris. He received his law degree from George Washington University, was admitted to the New York bar in 1911 and joined the law firm of Sullivan and Cromwell. He served with the War Trade Board and was counsel to the Reparations Commission at Versailles in 1919.

He was a U.S. delegate to the San Francisco conference of the United Nations in 1945 and to the U.N. General Assembly for four separate sessions. He served as adviser to the secretary of state at the Councils of Foreign Ministers (London, Moscow and Paris). He served in the Senate to fill a vacancy in 1949. President Truman appointed him ambassador to negotiate the peace treaty with Japan in 1952. Under Eisenhower, he was secretary of state (1953-1959).

A 4¢ John Foster Dulles Memorial issue was released in 1960.

Paul Laurence Dunbar

Scott 1554
Born: June 27, 1872, Dayton, Ohio
Died: February 9, 1906, Dayton, Ohio

Paul Laurence Dunbar was a persistent poet. His perseverance and achievements were recognized by many black Americans in the naming of their schools and societies for him. In the Dayton (Ohio) public schools, he was a popular member of the literary society and editor of the school publication. He also composed the school song when he graduated in 1891. Dunbar would have liked to have been a lawyer or a minister but he never had the chance. Until 1895, he earned his living as an elevator operator, spending his leisure moments writing poetry.

His poetry was published in newspapers, and in 1895 his collection of poems, *Oak and Ivy*, was privately published at Christmastime. At the World's Columbian Exposition in Chicago in 1893, he worked for Frederick Douglass at the Haitian exhibition. In 1895 he published a second collection of poems titled *Majors and Minors*. It was given a fine review by William Dean Howells in *Harper's Magazine*, which increased the poem's demand.

Dunbar became a fashionable poet with his *Lyrics of Lowly Life*. An introduction by Howells increased and broadened his acceptance as a poet. He was often invited to do readings. In 1897 he was invited to England. When he returned, he served as an assistant at the Library of Congress for over a year.

His verse was written in Negro dialect transmitting the feelings of the slaves in the old plantation days and their feelings about emancipation. Dunbar was the son of former slaves. Later he wrote in standard verse to escape the racial stigma brought on by the dialectical technique he used in his verses and short stories. He wrote several novels, but to his regret, they were not as popular as his poems and short stories. He also wrote the Tuskegee Institute school song.

The 10¢ American Arts issue released in 1975 depicts Dunbar.

Edward Patrick Francis Eagan

Scott 2499
Born: April 26, 1897, Denver, Colorado
Died: June 14, 1967, Rye, New York

Eddie Eagan's father was a railroad engineer who died in a railway accident when Eddie was one year old. Eddie's mother raised him and his four brothers. Eddie was fascinated with boxing and learned the techniques of the sport from Abe Tobin. He fought as an amateur in the mining towns of Colorado. He entered the University of Denver. He completed one year of college before enlisting in the army, answering the call for World War I soldiers. He was commissioned a lieutenant in the artillery.

Following World War I, he entered Yale University. He continued as an amateur boxer, fighting in the 1919 Amateur Athletic Union (AAU) championships as a heavyweight. He represented the United States in the Inter-Allied Games in Paris, winning the middleweight competition. In 1920 Eagan won the Olympic light heavyweight title at Antwerp, Belgium.

He graduated from Yale University in 1921, then entered Harvard University Law School. In 1924 he competed in the Olympic Games at Paris as a boxer in the heavyweight class but was eliminated in the first round. He spent the next three years at Oxford University on a Rhodes scholarship.

He continued boxing by participating in exhibition bouts with heavyweight champion Jack Dempsey. He went on a world tour for two years. He trained the new heavyweight champion, J.J. "Gene" Tunney, for a rematch with Dempsey in 1928. Tunney won. It was during this time that Eagan married Margaret Colgate. They had two children, Sidney and Caroline.

He achieved an Olympic first when he joined the U.S. Olympic bobsled team for the Lake Placid Games in 1932. He won a gold medal, thus becoming the first Olympian to win a gold in both the summer and the winter games.

Later in 1932 Eagan was admitted to the New York State Bar. He served a five-year term as assistant district attorney for southern New York. He was attached to the Air Transport Command during World War II. He retired as a lieutenant colonel in 1945. In 1956 President Eisenhower selected Eagan to be the first to head the People to People Sports Committee.

Eagan is portrayed on a 25¢ Olympians stamp issued in 1990.

Amelia Earhart

Scott C68
Born: July 24, 1898, Atchison, Kansas
Died: July 3, 1937, near Howland Island, South Pacific

Amelia Earhart married publisher George P. Putnam in 1931, but she retained her maiden name. She learned to fly in the early 1920s. She crossed the Atlantic by air in 1928 as a passenger and flew it alone in 1932, thus being dubbed "Lady Lindy." She wrote about aviation. She set many aviation records and was an inspiration to aviators.

Earhart and her flying partner, Fred Noonan, were making an equatorial flight around the world in 1937. Positioned at Lae, New Guinea, they were ready to fly to Howland Island. Bad weather delayed their departure for two days. On July 2, 1937, they took off. During the night, the administrator of Nauru Island heard Earhart's radio transmission reporting overcast weather. The Coast Guard cutter *Itasca* was afloat near Howland and picked up some of her messages. Richard B. Black, the representative from the Department of the Interior, left the *Itasca* to be at the Howland landing field to welcome Earhart and Noonan. Fires were set on Howland to help guide them.

The ship's crew crowded the deck and searched the early morning skies for a first glimpse of the twin-engined Lockheed Electra. At 8:44 a.m., her last message was received, "We are on the line of position 157-337, flying north and south." To the north of the *Itasca*, Commander Thompson saw a dark and ominous weather front. He surmised that Earhart and Noonan were in that direction. At 9:30 a.m., he ordered the *Itasca* to steam northward and begin a wide search. The search soon involved several ships. The search covered 250,000 square miles. Nothing was ever found.

However, in 1989 on the atoll Nikumaroro in the Pacific Ocean, 650 miles north of Pago Pago, a navigator's aluminum bookcase was found. The Federal Bureau of Investigation ran laboratory tests on the bookcase. It is possible that it belonged to Noonan and was on Earhart's plane.

Earhart is shown on an 8¢ airmail stamp released in 1963.

George Eastman

Scott 1062
Born: July 12, 1854, Waterville, New York
Died: March 14, 1932, Rochester, New York

George Eastman began making money early in life. At age 14, he worked in an insurance office, then later as a bookkeeper in a Rochester, New York, bank. Photography fascinated him and became his avocation. To make it easier, in 1879, he invented and patented the machine that applied the gelatin emulsion to glass, making dry photographic plates. When this proved successful, he began manufacturing the machines for other photographers. At that time, there were very few photographers. Hoping to increase the number of photographers, he devised an inexpensive box camera, called the Kodak, and loaded it with flexible film. His slogan was "You push the button; we do the rest." To get film developed, the customer sent the camera to Eastman's company, The Eastman Dry Plate and Film Company. The photos were returned, along with the reloaded box camera.

In 1889 he introduced the flexible transparent film. In 1892 he organized the Eastman Kodak Company, relocated his company to Eastman Park and put to work 3,000 profit-sharing employees. The Eastman laboratories continued to improve on cameras and film. By 1901 they had so great a hold on the market that the Eastman Kodak Company of New Jersey, a holding company, ran into difficulties with the government for antitrust violations.

Eastman was an international cartel by 1908. By 1927 his company held a virtual monopoly in the industry. In 1928 he gave all 10-year-olds born in the year of the armistice a free Brownie box camera, as a promotional effort to sell more film.

Eastman's philanthropic gifts totaled more than $100 million. Major benefactors included Institute of Technology, the Hampton and Tuskegee institutes, and the University of Rochester. In 1919 he established the Eastman School of Music and the Eastman School of Medicine and Dentistry at the University of Rochester.

George Eastman is depicted on a 1954 3¢ commemorative stamp.

Thomas Alva Edison

Scott 945
Born: February 11, 1847, Milan, Ohio
Died: October 18, 1931, West Orange, New Jersey

Young Thomas Edison's teacher described him as "addle brained." After three months, he quit school. His mother, a former teacher, educated him at home. When he was nine years old, his mother gave him a primer on physics, which included many interesting experiments he could do at home. He performed these experiments over and over. He set up his own chemical laboratory in the cellar of the Edison home.

When he was 12, he got a job on the Grand Trunk Railway selling newspapers and candy. He set up his laboratory in the baggage car. On layovers between trains in Detroit, he read everything he could find on physics and chemistry at the city library. When he was 15, he bought a printing press and set it up in the baggage car and printed his own newspaper, *The Weekly Herald*. At 16, he learned telegraphy and worked as a telegrapher. He dreamed of being an inventor. He read Michael Faraday's *Experimental Researches in Electricity*, and his ambitions were set afire.

His first success came when he repaired a broken stock price transmitter for its inventor, S. Laws. Laws hired him for $300 a month. Edison then made improvements on this stock ticker and ended up making $40,000. He opened a shop in Newark, New Jersey, to manufacture tickers and the duplex and quadraplex telegraph.

He moved to Menlo Park, New Jersey, and established the first invention factor to invent useful products, such as the carbon telephone transmitter and phonograph (1877). In 1878 he improved upon the incandescent lamp and envisioned a widespread lighting system. He completed his dreams by discovering the right filament. It was the final adaptation of the alternating current (AC) by Nikola Tesla that made it universal.

Edison moved to West Orange, New Jersey, where many modern inventions came about. In 1892 his companies merged to become the General Electric Company.

Edison is portrayed on a 3¢ stamp issued in 1947 to mark the centenary of his birth.

Albert Einstein

Scott 1774
Born: March 14, 1879, Ulm, Germany
Died: April 18, 1955, Princeton, New Jersey

If Albert Einstein had a code name it would be E=MC², for he is best known for his special and general theories of relativity. He also made important contributions to the kinetic theory of matter and the theory of specific heats. He was one of the pioneers of the quantum theory.

Einstein was born in Ulm, Germany. His family moved to Munich when he was only one year old. His uncle ran a small electrochemical factory in Ulm. Einstein was an average student in school. At home, his uncle showed him the mechanics of algebra.

He passed the entrance examination into the Federal Polytechnic in Zurich, Switzerland, in 1896 on the second attempt. He worked mostly on his own, studying the classics of theoretical physics by Helmholtz, Boltzlamm and Mach, and especially Maxwell's electromagnetic theory.

Einstein gained Swiss citizenship and worked in the patent office in Bern in 1902. He published four papers in the 1905 *Annalen der physic*. In 1909 he was given an academic post at the University of Zurich. He spent a year in Prague in 1911, then returned to Zurich and to the Federal Polytechnic. In 1913 he went to Berlin for research in the Kaiser Wilhelm Society.

He published his theory of relativity. A total eclipse of the sun in 1919 proved his predictions of light of a distant star bending as it passes close to the sun. His work on the photoelectric effect won him the Nobel Prize in 1921.

Fortunately, Einstein was in California when Hitler came to power in Germany in 1933, for he was a prominent Zionist Jew and a prime Nazi target. He took a permanent post at the Institute of Advanced Study in Princeton and was given U.S. citizenship in 1941. He warned Franklin Roosevelt of Germany's development of the atomic bomb.

Einstein was honored on a 15¢ stamp in 1979.

Dwight David Eisenhower

Scott 1393
Born: October 14, 1890, Denison, Texas
Died: March 28, 1969, Washington, D.C.

Dwight David Eisenhower was the 34th president of the United States. He held the permanent rank of five-star general of the U.S. Army. He attended West Point (U.S. Military Academy) from 1911 to 1926. In World War I, he commanded a tank training center. He finished first in the Army Command and General Staff School in 1926 and graduated from the Army War College in 1928. He was stationed in Washington D.C., in the office of the chief of staff, General Douglas MacArthur, from 1933 to 1935 and was with MacArthur in the Philippines from 1935 until the start of World War II.

Eisenhower became chief of staff of the War Plans Division of the Army General Staff after the attack on Pearl Harbor. In June 1943 he was commanding general of the European Theater (ETO), and in November he assumed command of the Allied Forces in North Africa. He was made supreme commander of the Allied Expeditionary Forces for the invasion of western Europe and directed the Normandy landing on June 6, 1944. In December 1944 he was promoted to five-star general, and on May 7, 1945, he received the unconditional surrender from Germany.

He resigned from active duty in February 1948 and assumed the presidency of Columbia University until December 1950, when he was appointed commander of the supreme headquarters of NATO. He resigned in mid-1952 to accept the Republican nomination for the presidency against Democrat Adlai E. Stevenson, whom he defeated. He was inaugurated January 20, 1953.

His first term was marred by a severe heart attack. He was re-elected for a second term, again defeating Stevenson. During his administration, the Korean War was terminated (July 1953). The International Atomic Energy Agency and the South East Asia Treaty Organization (SEATO) were formed. After two terms in office, Eisenhower retired to his farm to write.

Eisenhower was honored on a 6¢ stamp in 1969.

Charles William Eliot

Scott 871
Born: March 20, 1834, Boston, Massachusetts
Died: August 22, 1926, Northeast Harbor, Maine

Intelligent, gifted and the son of a socially prominent family in Boston, Charles William Eliot made good on all the advantages he was born into. He graduated second in his class from Harvard and was awarded a teaching assignment. Eliot studied in Europe from 1863 to 1865 and returned to the United States to accept a professorship at the Massachusetts Institute of Technology. He published his observations and views of European and American education, which led to his appointment as president of Harvard College in 1869 at age 35.

During his tenure, the college's faculty increased tenfold, and the student body quadrupled, greatly increasing the faculty/student ratio. Three more schools were added, and the schools of law, medicine and the sciences were brought up to top-notch standard. These changes made Harvard one of the world's most outstanding schools of learning.

By 1892, Eliot had reduced required subjects to only English and modern languages, with all else being electives. He served as the president of Harvard for 40 years. He was the chairman of the National Education Association's Committee of Ten, and he believed that all subjects should be pursued by students with the utmost verve. Eliot also believed that even secondary school subjects should be open to elementary-grade students who qualified and showed desire and talent.

He foresaw the need to find the right field for which a person is most fitted — be he "future peasant, mechanic, tradesman, merchant, or one of the professions of arts and science." It might be said that Eliot believed all persons had a genius, if only that genius could be discovered and cultivated.

In 1903 he was elected president of the National Civil Service Reform League and helped edit the 50-volume *Harvard Classics*.

He is honored as an educator on a 1940 3¢ stamp in the Famous Americans issue.

97

Thomas Stearns Eliot

Scott 2239
Born: September 26, 1888, St. Louis, Missouri
Died: January 4, 1965, London, England

Thomas Stearns Eliot was a playwright, poet and critic who was better known as "T.S." than Thomas Stearns. He was the youngest of seven children of Henry Ware Eliot and Charlotte Champe Stearns. He was the grandson of William Greenleaf Eliot, a Unitarian minister who settled in St. Louis, Missouri, where he founded Washington University. "T.S." did not attend Washington University. He went to Smith Academy in St. Louis and Milton Academy in Milton, Massachusetts. He entered Harvard College in 1906 and received his bachelor's degree in 1909 and his master's degree a year later, studying under such greats as Irving Babbitt and George Santayana. In 1910 and 1911 he studied at the Sorbonne in Paris, where he heard lectures by Henri Bergson, the celebrated French philosopher. He returned to the United States as a graduate student in philosophy at Harvard from 1911 to 1914, then continued his studies at the University of Marburg, Germany.

When World War I broke out, he headed for Merton College in Oxford, England. He taught at a boys school near London from 1915 to 1917, during which time he submitted his doctoral dissertation to Harvard (on the English philosopher F.H. Bradley). He did not return to accept his doctorate.

He failed the physical examination for navy service.

An expatriate, he made England his home. In 1927 he became a British subject and a member of the Church of England. He was editor of *The Egoist* (1917-1919), a British literary magazine, and in 1922 he founded *The Criterion*, a quarterly review. It suspended publication in 1939. He was director of the publishing house Farber and Farber.

Among the honors awarded Eliot were the American Medal of Freedom in 1946, the Noble Prize for literature in 1948 and the British Order of Merit in 1948. He was honored on a 22¢ Literary Arts stamp in 1986.

98

Edward Kennedy 'Duke' Ellington

Scott 2211
Born: April 29, 1899, Washington, D.C.
Died: May 24, 1974, New York, New York

During his lifetime, Duke Ellington wrote more than 6,000 compositions, including a ballet, a pageant of black history and background music for
films. For many years, his musical signature was *The A Train*, written by Billy
Strayhorn. Ellington started playing the piano when he was seven years old.
He also was talented in art and was offered a scholarship at the Pratt Institute
in Brooklyn to study graphic art, but he chose music instead. At age 19, he
started a small band in Washington, D.C., with some success, but when he
tried to form a band in New York, it didn't materialize. Nevertheless, he was
exposed to music by Harlem jazz pianists, such as Thomas "Fats" Waller,
who encouraged Ellington and influenced his musical rhythm and style.

In 1923 his band, the Washingtonians, played at Baron's in Harlem, then
at the Holiday Club on Broadway. At the club, his band made its first
recordings and radio broadcasts. Then came his nightly radio broadcasts from
the famous Cotton Club of Harlem, where Ellington's band became nationally recognized. Many of Ellington's instrumentalists stayed with him for
years. This enabled him and his co-arranger Billy Strayhorn to write music
that fit their musicians' individual talents.

Ellington's short compositions, *Black and Tan Fantasy*, *Creole Love
Call*, and *Mood Indigo*, are jazz classics. Songs such as *Sophisticated Lady*,
Satin Doll and *I Got it Bad* continue to be popular.

Ellington fused jazz tempo with Latin rhythm, creating a new and
unusual beat. He extended his compositions into longer forms beyond the
usual 12 or 32 bars in the chorus. Duke Ellington brought jazz into the church
and dignity to the art of jazz.

He is depicted in front of a piano keyboard on a 1986 22¢ stamp.

Lincoln Ellsworth

Scott 2389
Born: May 12, 1880, Chicago, Illinois
Died: May 26, 1951, New York, New York

Lincoln Ellsworth was the son of James William and Eva (Butler) Ellsworth. He attended school in Pottstown, Pennsylvania, and graduated from Hill School. After two years at Columbia University, he received his master of science degree. At the Sheffield scientific school at Yale University in New Haven, Connecticut, he received his doctorate in law. His first job was wielding an ax on the first survey of the Grand Pacific railroad across Canada in the early 1900s. Next, he was the resident engineer for the Prince Pupert Terminal. He worked in Montreal as a construction engineer. He also worked for the Canada Pacific Railway and prospected for gold.

For Johns Hopkins University, he organized the Ellsworth Expedition, making geological studies of the Andes mountains. In 1925 he teamed up with Roald Amundsen to fly from Spitsbergen to Alaska over the North Pole, but bad weather grounded them. The next year, in the dirigible *Norge*, he and Amundsen, with Colonel Umberto Nobile, coasted across the North Pole.

With Sir George Hubert Wilkins, he helped chart a submarine expedition to the arctic. When the dirigible *Graf Zeppelin* made its arctic flight, Ellsworth was aboard. A blizzard stopped a flight he attempted in 1935, and he had to be rescued. In 1935 he made a flight of 2,500 miles across the Antarctic, claiming 30,000 square miles of new land for the United States. He flew into the Antarctic in 1939 from a base in the Indian Ocean and claimed more than 81,000 square miles of territory for the United States.

In 1941, as a lieutenant commander, he led an exploration for the U.S. navy into the heart of the Inca lands of Peru in search of the emperors' tombs.

He wrote about *The Last Buffalo Hunt* in 1915, *Our Polar Flight* in 1925, and of the *First Crossing of the Polar Sea* in 1927. In 1932 he wrote *Search* and *Beyond Horizons* in 1938.

He was awarded a gold medal from the Norwegian Parliament for saving two companions from drowning in 1925 and received several medals from Italy, Norway and the United States, including a medal from President Hoover from Congress in 1931.

He is featured on one of four 1988 25¢ Antarctic Explorers stamps.

Ralph Waldo Emerson

Scott 861
Born: May 25, 1803, Boston, Massachusetts
Died: April 27, 1882, Concord, Massachusetts

Until Ralph Waldo Emerson was eight years old, he was influenced by his father, a somewhat liberal minister of the First Unitarian Church of Boston and editor of the *Monthly Anthology*. Many dignitaries visited the Emerson home. In 1811 the Reverend William Emerson died. Ralph's mother, Ruth, had to sell her husband's library, and the children went to live with relatives.

Ralph moved in with his intellectually inclined aunt, Mary Moody Emerson, in Boston, where he attended the Latin School, kept his own journal, wrote poetry, formed a small museum, strolled along the harbor and frequented the library. At age 14, he entered Harvard College and, after graduating, taught at his brother William's School for Young Ladies in Boston. In February 1825, he entered middle class at the Harvard Divinity School. His studies were halted because of family problems.

Emerson returned to teaching at Chelmsford, and until 1826, he struggled with eye problems. He gave his first sermon at the Middlesex Association and was licensed to preach. He went to Florida but returned in 1827 to preach at Concord, New Hampshire, where he met and married Ellen Tucker. A year and a half later she died of tuberculosis.

Emerson later became the permanent minister of the Second Church in Boston, but resigned in 1832 to spend a year in Europe. An inheritance from his wife's estate improved his finances.

He met Lydia Jackson while preaching in Plymouth. They were married in 1835, moved to Concord, Massachusetts, and had four children. Emerson entered into an active community life, and edited the *Dial*, traveled and lectured. He wrote poems and essays, and protested the wrongs in politics and society. After an active and happy life, his mind gave way to senile dementia. He died of pneumonia one month before his 79th birthday.

Emerson was honored as an author on a 3¢ stamp issued in 1940 as part of the famous Americans series.

John Ericsson

Scott 628
Born: July 31, 1803, Langbanshyttan, Varmland Province, Sweden
Died: March 8, 1889, New York, New York

At the young age of 13, John Ericsson served as a draftsman for the engineers building the Gota Canal. He entered the Swedish army at age 17 and became a land surveyor. He developed an engine that used superheated air instead of steam to power the motor. Thus, he was anticipating the future gas turbine motor. His motors were called caloric engines.

Ericsson went to London in 1826 to find someone to sponsor his dream. While in England, he developed the screw propeller and used it in two small ships built in 1837 and 1839.

In 1839 he moved to New York City. With Ericsson's help, the *Princeton* was launched by the United States in 1843. It was the first metal-hulled, screw-propelled warship that had its engines below the waterline for ballast, convenience and protection. He devised the revolving gun turret protected by armor, which was installed on the *Monitor*, the famous naval vessel that battled the *Virginia* (*Merrimack*) in Hampton Roads, Virginia, in 1862, during the Civil War. All subsequent warships were built on these principles and brought Ericsson his place in history.

Ericsson's inventions did not stop with these innovations. He also devised a method of extracting salt from brine and invented fans that forced air where ventilation was needed, an on-board depthometer, the first useful steam fire engine, surface condensers for marine steam engines and small pumper caloric engines. He pioneered such advanced physical phenomena as capturing useful energy from the sun. Ericsson was a compulsive inventor and innovator. Many of his inventions transcended the technology of his time.

He died in New York City in 1889. In 1890 his body was carried to Sweden on the *USS Baltimore*. The Ericsson stamp was issued in connection with the unveiling of his statue in Washington, D.C., May 29, 1926.

Leif Erikson

Scott 1359
Born: circa 980, Iceland
Died: circa 1020, Brattahlid, Greenland

Leif Erikson was the son of Eric the Red, who established the first settlement in Greenland. Around the year 1000, when Leif was returning by ship from Norway, he was blown off course by a wild wind south of Greenland. He came to Vinland, the location of which is still disputed. After staying there for a year, he returned to Greenland with a cargo of valuable timber and clumps of wild grapes. On his way home, he rescued a crew of Norsemen sailors who, according to one Icelandic saga, had been shipwrecked off Greenland. According to another story, he may have made a planned and deliberate voyage to a land that had been sighted southwest of Greenland by earlier sailors. He went to investigate it.

Erikson led what was probably the first European expedition to the mainland of North America. Some historians believe he and his men explored northern Newfoundland, where Norwegian archaeologists found the remains of an old Norse settlement in the 1960s. Other historians believe Erikson sailed farther south, around Cape Cod. The logs and grapes Erikson brought to Greenland from Vinland made him a wealthy and highly respected man.

Eric the Red died soon after his son's return from Vinland. Leif inherited Brattahlid on Ericsfiord, Eric the Red's estate in Greenland. According to legend, Leif brought Christianity to Greenland after he had been converted from the pagan religion of Nordic theology at the court of Olaf Tryggvason. This assumption is supported by the fact that the first Christian church stood at Brattahlid. In 1961 Leif Erikson's grave also was supposedly identified as being an unmarked grave in the cemetery adjoining Brattahlid.

Erikson had two sons, Thorgils and Thorkel. Thorkel, the legitimate son, inherited Brattahlid, supposedly in the year 1020, when Leif died.

Leif Erikson is portrayed on a 6¢ 1968 commemorative stamp.

Ray C. Ewry

Scott 2497
Born: October 14, 1873, Lafayette, Indiana
Died: September 29, 1937, New York, New York

When Ray Ewry was a child, he was stricken with infantile paralysis (now called poliomyelitis) and nearly died. After his recovery, his legs were considerably weakened. To combat his disability, he exercised with unrelenting determination and regularity. After graduating from high school in 1890, Ewry entered Purdue University in West Lafayette, Indiana, He was a star performer on the track team and lettered one year in football. He continued his studies as a mechanical engineer, earning a graduate degree in 1897. He moved to New York City, where he worked as a hydraulic engineer.

Not neglecting his physical fitness exercises, he became a member of the New York Athletic Club. When the second modern Olympics was staged in Paris in 1900, Ewry had earned a place on the U.S. team. He won all three of the events he entered — the standing high jump, the standing broad jump, and the standing hop, step and jump. He set Olympic records in all three events.

In 1904 he qualified for the third U.S. Olympics held in St. Louis, where he won all three of his special events and set a new Olympic record in the standing broad jump at 11 feet, four and one-half inches. In 1906, in Athens, Greece, he won two of his events. His third athletic forte — the hop, step and jump — had been discontinued. At age 35, he again qualified for the fourth Olympics, in London, England, and won two more gold medals. His official Olympic wins amounted to eight gold medals. With the two Athens medals, his total was 10. Ewry's record of eight Olympic gold medals stood for 64 years until Mark Spitz won nine medals in swimming at the Munich Games in 1972. Counting the Athens medals, however, Ewry, is unsurpassed with 10.

After the 1912 Olympics, the standing high jump and standing broad jump were dropped from the Olympic contests. Until he was honored on a 25¢ Olympians stamp on July 6, 1990, Ewry's name was no more than a statistic buried in the almanacs and sports' records books. Nevertheless, Ray C. Ewry is another example of a person depicted on a stamp who gained success by overcoming a crippling handicap.

Douglas Fairbanks

Scott 2088
Born: May 23, 1883, Denver, Colorado
Died: December 12, 1939, Santa Monica, California

Douglas Fairbanks was the son of his mother's second husband, whose surname was Ulman. His real name was Douglas Elton Thomas Ulman. His mother divorced Ulman in 1900 and took the name of her first husband, Fairbanks. Douglas Ulman became Douglas Elton Fairbanks and throughout his career was known simply as Douglas Fairbanks.

Fairbanks grew up in Denver and attended the Colorado School of Mines. He gained dramatic training locally and met Frederick Warde, who encouraged him to pursue the theater. In 1900 he and his mother moved east and joined one of Warde's repertory theater groups. His first major role was the juvenile lead in *A Gentleman from Mississippi*, in New York (1909-1911).

He was lured to Hollywood by the movies. He was photogenic, athletic, graceful and met all the requirements of the silent movies. He worked well with the cameras and stunted admirably. He portrayed heroic young American characters in *The Americano* (1916), *Knickerbocker Buckaroo* (1919) and others. He wrote several books that showed that his real life characteristics were as gallant as his film characterizations. Like other stars of his time, such as Charlie Chaplin and Mary Pickford (whom he later married, and divorced), he was much idolized by the film-going public. He joined Charlie Chaplin and D.W. Griffith and founded the United Artists company, which produced swashbuckling spectaculars in which he played the major role.

After 1935, he spent much time in Europe. He married Lady Sylvia Ashley. In 1939 he formed a film-producing company, whose first production, *The Californian*, starred his son (by his first wife, Anna Beth Sully) Douglas Fairbanks, Jr., who became an outstanding actor in his own rights.

Douglas Fairbanks, Sr. was commemorated in the Performing Arts series with a 20¢ stamp issued in 1984.

Philo Taylor Farnsworth

Scott 2058
Born: August 19, 1906, Beaver, Utah
Died: March 11, 1971, Salt Lake City, Utah

Philo Farnsworth grew up on a sheep ranch near Rigby, Idaho. Until he was 14 years old, he had no knowledge of electricity. However, by studying all the information available to him, he soon grasped the physical principles involved. Farnsworth read about Boris Rosing in Russia, who was transmitting moving pictures by electricity. While still in high school, Farnsworth worked out the basic principles involved and drew up a schematic diagram.

He attended Brigham Young University from 1923 to 1925, until he found financial backing for his proposed practical development of a television system. As early as 1928, he was able to demonstrate his image-dissector camera, which turned a scene into electric currents by electronic rather than mechanical means. The image-scanning was done much faster than had been accomplished by Rosing and others.

The Philco Corporation assumed the development of his system. In a few years, Farnsworth was able to demonstrate clear moving images at the Franklin Institute. Philco withdrew its support, and Farnsworth moved to Fort Wayne, Indiana, to continue his work. World War II halted his progress. He turned to radar and related work for the war effort.

After the war, one of Rosing's students perfected the iconoscope and won the backing of Radio Corporation of America (RCA), which pushed production. The Farnsworth Television & Radio Corporation then became the research arm of the International Telephone and Telegraph Company (ITT). Farnsworth worked as the research consultant.

After 1949, Farnsworth moved into research work for electric power by atomic fission and fusion. He had accumulated more than 300 patents and was honored worldwide for his pioneering accomplishments in electrical engineering and television.

A 1983 20¢ stamp in the American Inventors set depicts Farnsworth and a television camera.

David Glasgow Farragut

Scott 311
Born: July 5, 1801, Stony Point, near Knoxville, Tennessee
Died: August 14, 1870, Portsmouth, New Hampshire

At age six, James Farragut moved with his family to New Orleans. At age nine, he was adopted by Captain David Porter and appointed midshipman in the Navy. He served under Captain Porter on the *Essex* from 1811 through the War of 1812. At age 12, he was briefly in charge of a captured ship. When he was 13, he changed his first name to David in honor of his foster father (or his foster brother, David Dixon Porter, born in 1813).

Farragut served on several different ships, mostly in the Mediterranean, and studied under the U.S. consul at Tunis. He studied diligently and became proficient in several languages, but seamanship was his specialty. He spent much of his time around New Orleans. He again joined Captain David Porter (1823-24) to repel the pirates in the Caribbean. In 1825 he was promoted to lieutenant. He was made commander in 1841 and became captain in 1855. He saw duty both at sea and ashore, including the Mexican War.

At the outbreak of the Civil War (1861) and at the recommendation of his foster brother, Commander David Dixon Porter, he was put in command to capture New Orleans and control the Mississippi. In April 1862, with cunning and fearless seamanship, he won the forts and captured the city. He was promoted to rear admiral. For two years he blockaded the Gulf Coast and controlled the river traffic. In 1864 he was ordered to capture Mobile Bay. His iron-clad *Tecumseh* was sunk by a torpedo. Fort Morgan's guns were directed at his fleet, as were guns from the Confederate's *Tennessee*. "Damn the torpedoes — Full speed ahead!" he ordered. The *Tennessee* was engaged and defeated. Fort Morgan capitulated. The South was demoralized.

Farragut was promoted to vice admiral, and in 1866 the rank of admiral was created especially for him.

He is shown with David D. Porter on the 3¢ 1937 U.S. Navy issue.

William Faulkner

Scott 2350
Born: September 25, 1897, New Albany, Mississippi
Died: July 6, 1962, Oxford, Mississippi

William Faulkner wrote novels and short stories about people in the South. His great-grandfather, William Cuthbert Falkner (1825-1879), wrote a novel. His great-grandfather was known as the "Old Colonel" because he led a volunteer cavalry regiment in the Civil War. Before that he fought in the Mexican War, and was twice acquitted for murder. After the war, he became a lawyer, built railroads, and was finally shot dead in a gun duel. William Faulkner's grandfather was known as the "Young Colonel."

In 1902 Faulkner's parents, Murry C. and Maud Butler Falkner (the novelist himself later added the "u" to the family name), moved to nearby Oxford, Mississippi. The novelist spent most of his life in that area. His formal education was not impressive. He never finished high school. He attended the University of Mississippi in his hometown of Oxford but didn't finish the freshman year. He worked on student publications and wrote poetry and short stories. He spent some time in New York City, New Orleans and Europe.

In New Orleans he was inspired by Sherwood Anderson to write a novel, *Soldier's Pay* (1926). Anderson advised him to write about the rural South, the subject he knew best. From this came *Sartoris* and *The Sound and the Fury* (1929). From these stories and others, the reader became acquainted with Yoknapatawpha County, an imaginative place inhabited by people from all evils of life and through whose history the trials and tribulations of the South were described.

Faulkner did not become well-known until he was awarded the Nobel Prize for literature in 1949. In 1955 he was awarded the first two Pulitzer Prizes. In 1946 Malcolm Cowley edited *The Portable Faulkner*, which made Faulkner popular. *The Reivers*, written in 1962, was Faulkner's last book.

He was honored with a 22¢ Literary Arts stamp issued in 1987.

W.C. Fields

Scott 1803
Born: April 9, 1879, Philadelphia, Pennsylvania
Died: December 25, 1946, Pasadena, California

W.C. Fields' real name was Claude William Dunkerfield. He ran away from home when he was 11, became a petty thief and spent some time in jail. He drifted into vaudeville. Fascinated by the jugglers, he taught himself the art. He started out in Atlantic City, New Jersey, and ballyhooed himself as "W.C. Fields, the Tramp Juggler" or "the greatest comedian in the world." As a comic juggler, he made his reputation. In 1901 he played a command performance for King Edward VII of England. In 1915 he joined the Ziegfield Follies and for six years shared top billings with Will Rogers, Fanny Brice and many other stars. On Broadway he was Eustace McGargle, the preposterously fraudulent comic in *Poppy*.

Then came the inevitable transition to the films. His charming personality was that of a cantankerous and crusty wit, characterized as an intruding old boozer noted for bombast, whimsy, awkward salaciousness, chicanery and utter disregard for sentimental conventions, particularly those concerning socially prominent persons, pompous officials, little old ladies, children and dogs. His raspy voice and sarcastic drawl, bulbous nose and befuddled mannerisms were a delight. His character did not vary. Fields was Fields from Eustace McGargle (1924) to Mr. Micawber (1935). His best films may be listed as *Million Dollar Legs* (1932), *David Copperfield* (1935), *Poppy* (1936), *You Can't Cheat an Honest Man* (1939), *My Little Chickadee* (1940), *The Bank Dick* (1940) and *Never Give a Sucker an Even Break* (1941). His first film was *Sally of the Sawdust* (1925), directed by D.W. Griffith.

On radio he carried on a running battle of wits with Edgar Bergen's Charlie McCarthy — offering Charlie a "dose of termites," or a "piggyback ride on a buzz saw." W.C. Fields was the lovably obnoxious character the audience delighted in despising.

A 15¢ Performing Arts stamp released in 1980 portrayed the actor.

Millard Fillmore

Scott 818
Born: January 7, 1800, Cayuga County, New York
Died: March 8, 1874, Buffalo, New York

Except for about six months of formal education at the New Hope Academy in 1819, Millard Fillmore was self-educated. He was the oldest of five sons of poor parents, Nathaniel and Phoebe Millard Fillmore. He was a clerk in the law office of Judge Walter Wood in Montville, New York. Later he studied law in a Buffalo law firm while teaching school. He was admitted to the bar in 1823. He married Abigail Powers in 1826. Fillmore opened a law office in East Aurora, in association with Nathan Kelsey Hall.

In 1828 he entered politics on the Anti-Masonic ticket, guided by Thurlow Weed. He served three terms in the state assembly. On the Anti-Jackson ticket, he was elected in 1833 to the House of Representatives. He was re-elected to the House in 1836 and remained a congressman until 1843. Along with his friend Weed, he changed to the Whig coalition and supported Henry Clay. In 1844 he lost the vice-presidential nomination as well as a term for governor of New York. In 1848 he was nominated and elected vice president with Zachary Taylor.

Taylor died July 9, 1850, and Fillmore became the thirteenth president of the United States. His administration passed the legislation that led to the War Between the States. With Douglas (in Clay's absence), Fillmore supported the passing of Omnibus bill (Clay's Compromise of 1850), which Taylor opposed. He authorized the Commodore Matthew C. Perry expedition (1852 and 1854), opening trade with Japan. He lost the presidential nomination in 1952 to General Winfield Scott, who lost the election to Franklin Pierce.

Fillmore stumped the South and West for re-election again but lost to James Buchanan in 1856. His wife died in 1853. He remarried a wealthy Albany widow, Caroline Carmichael McIntosh, in 1858 and moved to Niagara Square in Buffalo. She became a chronic invalid (1860). He became a paralytic (1874) from a stroke and soon died.

Fillmore is portrayed on the 13¢ stamp in the 1938-43 Presidential series.

Edward Joseph Flanagan

Scott 2171
Born: July 13, 1886, Roscommon, Ireland
Died: May 15, 1948, Berlin, Germany

Edward Joseph Flanagan was 18 years old when he emigrated to the United States. Between the day he landed in 1904 and the day he became a U.S. citizen in 1919, he accomplished a great deal. Flanagan spent two years at Mount St. Mary's College in Emmitsburg, Maryland. He then spent one year at St. Joseph's Seminary in Dunwoodie, New York, another year at the Gregorian University in Rome, Italy, and three years at the Jesuit University in Innsbruck, Austria. He was ordained a priest in the Roman Catholic Church in 1912. His first assignment was in O'Neill, Nebraska, for one year. In 1913, he became the assistant priest of St. Patrick's church in Omaha.

Flanagan established a Workingmen's Hostel in Omaha to help poor derelicts. He soon realized that unemployable thieving winos were for the most part beyond redemption and that their troubles went back to unfortunate childhoods. "There are no bad boys," he reasoned. Flanagan decided that the time and place to attack such social problems was in childhood.

In 1917, he rented a house and began his Home for Homeless Boys with five boys. Flanagan bought a small tract of land outside Omaha in 1918 and built Father Flanagan's Boys Home. By 1922, his home had grown to such proportions that it was incorporated as a municipality called Boys Town. It even had a town government of boys elected by the boys. By 1939, Boys Town included 500 boys. Each of the young men at Flanagan's home had responsibilities, educational opportunities and a goal in life.

The place was dramatized in the film *Boys Town* in 1938. The movie starred Spencer Tracy, who won an Academy Award for his role. The film popularized the home, which grew and prospered with annual Christmas seals and generous donations.

Flanagan became the adviser to the U.S. government on youth programs in occupied countries. He died in Berlin in 1948.

A 1986 4¢ Great Americans stamp features the gentle and generous Father Flanagan.

111

Henry Ford

Scott 1286A
Born: July 30, 1863, Springwells Township, Wayne County, Michigan
Died: April 7, 1947, Fair Lane, Dearborn, Michigan

Henry Ford grew up on a farm and went to a rural school. Early in life, he became fascinated with machinery and engines. When he was 16, he apprenticed himself to a mechanic in Detroit and improved his mechanical knowledge and skills. When he finished his apprenticeship, he took a job in southern Michigan repairing Westinghouse steam engines. After about a year, he returned to the family farm and built a sawmill and a machine shop.

On April 11, 1888, he married Clara J. Bryant of Greenfield, Michigan. Three years later, the couple moved to Detroit, where Henry took a job with the Detroit Edison Illuminating Company. He was chief engineer of the Illuminating Company until 1899, when he resigned to form the Detroit Automobile Company and to serve as its chief engineer. The Ford's only child, Edsel Bryant Ford, was born November 6, 1893.

By June 1896, Henry Ford had built a car, a light horseless carriage powered by a two-cylinder engine. The car was the basis for the Detroit Automobile Company. The Detroit Automobile Company went bankrupt in two years but reorganized as the Henry Ford Company.

In 1901 Barney Oldfield drove a Ford racer to victory in a Grosse Pointe, Michigan, race. In March 1902, Ford left the Henry Ford Company, which abandoned his name. With the backing of Alexander Y. Malcolmson, he organized the Ford Motor Company in 1903. In midwinter 1904, Ford drove his "999" speedster to a world's record of one mile in 40 seconds over the ice on Lake St. Clair, approximately 66 miles per hour.

Ford Motor Company began manufacturing in 1903. By 1906, Ford was the president of the company. Two years later, Ford replaced his Model N with the sturdy black four-cylinder, 20-horsepower Model T. Between 1908 and 1927, Ford sold 15 million Model T's and significantly changed lifestyles in the United States. The Model T was manufactured on the assembly-line concept and sold at a price that the common man could afford.

Ford is pictured on the 12¢ definitive in the Prominent Americans series.

Stephen Foster

Scott 879
Born: July 4, 1826, Lawrenceville, Pennsylvania
Died: January 13, 1864, New York, New York

It hardly seems possible that Stephen Foster would write charming and tender music when his background was one of hardship and stern discipline. His father was a colonel, and his family roots could be traced to the early pioneers. He was the youngest child. His formal education ended after a month of college in 1841. Foster went to work as a bookkeeper for his brother in Cincinnati, but he showed little aptitude for handling his own money. His publishers exploited him unscrupulously.

He had no music education. He lacked self-confidence, but music was in his blood. He wrote his first waltz at age 13. In 1844 his first song, *Open thy lattice, Love*, was published.

While in Cincinnati, he joined a singer's club. For them he wrote two songs, *Old Uncle Ned* and *Lou'siana Belle*. They were published, but Foster signed away the royalties. The songs produced $10,000 in sales, but Foster received nothing. His songs *Way Down South* and *Oh, Susanna!* were popular. He was the first American composer to win popularity in Europe.

With this success, he moved to Allegheny City, New York, to devote his life to composing music. Despite the success of his songs, his yearly income was only about $1,000. He returned to his Pennsylvania home in 1849 and concluded a satisfactory agreement with E.P. Christy of the Christy Minstrels. He wrote some of his best works, including *Massa's in de Cold, Cold Ground, Camptown Races, Nelly Bly, Jeanie With the Light Brown Hair, Old Black Joe* and *Beautiful Dreamer*.

His unhappy family life brought about a divorce in 1860. He succumbed to alcoholism, and his songs lacked the charm they once had. Stephen Foster died in debt in New York's Bellevue Hospital with 35¢ in his pocket.

He is one of the composers honored in the Famous Americans issue of 1940. He is portrayed on the 1¢ stamp.

Francis of Assisi

Scott 2023
Born: 1181 or 1182, Assisi, Perugia Province, Umbria, Italy
Died: October 3, 1226, Portiuncula Chapel, near Assisi, Italy

Francis was the oldest son of Peitro di Bernardone, a prosperous textile merchant in the ancient city of Asisium, a commune in Perugia province, Umbria, located in central Italy on the south slope of Monte Subasio, 12 miles southeast of Perugia. His mother was a member of the distinguished Pica family. The Pica family had French roots, and for this reason John de Bernardone (his real name) was nicknamed Francisco, "the Frenchman."

When Francisco was in his early twenties, he wanted to become a military hero. He joined the army of Walter of Briene in Apulia. Walter was fighting for the causes of Innocent III of Anagni. While in Spoletium (near his own home), Francisco became ill. He heard a voice in an apparition say to him, "Why do you desert the Lord for his vassal?" And again in 1207, while he was praying in an old crumbled down church in San Daminano near his home, the voice said to him, "Francisco, repair my house." Francisco stole several bolts of his father's cloth and sold them for money to repair the old church. This angered his father so much that Francisco was brought before the bishop's court. The young man returned all the money and the shirt off his back. His father disinherited him.

Francis followed his calling to repair churches. He served the leper colonies. He spent hours with animals. In the chapel of St. Mary of the Angels, called the Portinuncula, he recalled the words of St. Matthew (x.7-10): "And as you go, preach the message, The Kingdom of Heaven is at hand! Cure the sick, raise the dead, cleanse the lepers, cast out devils. Freely you have received, freely give. Do not keep gold, or silver, or money in your girdles, no wallet for your journey, nor two tunics, nor sandals, nor staff; for the laborer deserves his living." Penniless, he went to Assisi to preach to the poor.

He is shown with birds on a 20¢ stamp issued in 1982.

Peter Francisco

Peter Francisco 🌸 *Fighter Extraordinary*

Scott 1562
Born: unknown
Died: unknown

Peter Francisco was a Portuguese-French immigrant. When he was 15 years old, he joined the Continental Army. A large man, he displayed strength in and around the army camps and during battles. He could shoulder a canon piece as heavy as 1,000 pounds, and he swung a sword that was six feet long.

Francisco played an important role in several battles of the Revolutionary War. The object of the campaign of 1777 was the capture of Philadelphia by the British. The British general put his troops on board ships and sailed to Chesapeake Bay. George Washington marched his army into Pennsylvania, and the two forces met at Brandywine Creek. The Americans were defeated on September 11, and the British took Philadelphia. All the operations in Pennsylvania turned out badly for the Americans. At the end of 1777, the ragged American troops established their winter quarters in Valley Forge.

In 1781 the Americans began to have success in the South. The first success was at Cowpens, South Carolina, where an American detachment under Morgan defeated a British force led by Tarleton. The next action was at Guilford Court House, North Carolina. The losses in this fight were equal.

The last battle of the war was fought at Yorktown, Virginia. In the summer of 1781, Cornwallis was at Yorktown with 8,000 troops. Washington was near New York City. He suddenly changed his plan and marched quickly to Yorktown, reaching there at the end of September. He was joined by French troops that had arrived at the Chesapeake Bay in a fleet commanded by Count Grasse. The allied French and American armies laid siege to Yorktown. Cornwallis surrendered on October 19, 1781.

In all these battles Francisco fought with great valor. He is featured on an 18¢ American Bicentennial stamp.

Benjamin Franklin

Scott 1030
Born: January 6, 1706 (old style), Boston, Massachusetts
Died: April 17, 1790, Philadelphia, Pennsylvania

Benjamin was the youngest of 10 children of Josiah and Abiah Folger Franklin. Ben's father was a candlemaker and a skilled mechanic. His forebears were Calvinistic protestants who emigrated to the American colonies from England about 1682. As a young boy, Ben found a job as a printer. Later he went to England to learn more about the printing trade. He returned in 1726 and set up his own press. He printed and published the *Pennsylvania Gazette*. He started spreading homespun American morality in his *Poor Richard's Almanack* about 1732.

Franklin did most of the printing for the province, establishing partnerships with printers from Nova Scotia to Antigua. He clerked for the Pennsylvania Assembly, operated a bookstore in Philadelphia and was the Philadelphia postmaster. At age 42, he was nearly retired, living off the income from his printing business. Free from financial worries and the ties of labor, he made himself available for a variety of public services, such as the first postmaster general of the United States.

He was determined to improve Philadelphia. He organized the Junto discussion club, a circulating library, a fire company, an insurance company and a hospital. In 1743 he organized the American Philosophical Society, which in 1749 became the University of Pennsylvania. His 40 years of public life began in earnest when he was elected to the Pennsylvania Assembly in 1751. He dabbled in scientific experimentation. He showed that lightning was a form of electricity, and developed many practical innovations.

Franklin was the leading American spokesman in England before the Revolution. He helped draft the Declaration of Independence and promptly signed it. As a commissioner to France in 1776, he served in a variety of diplomatic capacities. He urged ratification of the Constitution and proposed George Washington for president.

Franklin is shown here on a 1/2¢ stamp from the 1954-68 Liberty series.

116

John Charles Fremont

Scott 288
Born: January 21, 1813, Savannah, Georgia
Died: July 13, 1890, New York, New York

John Fremont's mother was Anne Whiting Pryor of Richmond, Virginia. His father was Jean Charles Fremont, a French emigre. The couple ran off to Savannah, Georgia, but never married. John was born in Savannah. The family moved around in the South. When John was five, his father died. He and his mother moved to Charleston, South Carolina, where he went to school and entered Charleston College, only to be expelled for "incorrigible negligence." Thus was John Charles Fremont's beginning in life.

When he was 20, he taught mathematics on the sloop-of-war *Natchez*, cruising South America. In 1836 he surveyed the Carolina and Tennessee mountains for the railroad, and in 1838 went on a scientific expedition to Minnesota and the Dakotas for U.S. Topographical Corps. On October 19, 1841, he eloped with Senator Thomas Hart Benton's daughter, Jesse. She aided him considerably with his popular exploration reports and his *Memories of My Life* (1887).

In 1842, with Senator Benton's support, he explored the Oregon trail with Kit Carson. The following year he made a more extensive mapping of the western areas and returned to St. Louis in 1844. On a third journey (1845), with orders from President Polk, he made it to California. He raised the American flag on Hawk's Peak at Sutter's Fort.

In January 1847 he captured Los Angeles and secured California. He was governor for two months. General Stephen Kearny arrested him for disobedience. He was court-martialed in 1848, but Polk suspended his sentence. In California he made a fortune in gold. He was nominated for president in 1856 but was defeated by Buchanan.

During the Civil War, he directed the Department of the West. In Virginia he fought against "Stonewall" Jackson. He lost a fortune in western railroad and land speculations. He was the Arizona Territory governor (1878-1883) and retired on pension. He died while on a visit to New York.

Fremont is shown holding a flag on the Rocky Mountains on the 5¢ denomination of the 1898 Trans-Mississippi Exposition issue.

Daniel Chester French

Scott 887
Born: April 20, 1850, Exeter, New Hampshire
Died: October 7, 1931, Stockbridge, Massachusetts

The timeless statuary created by Daniel Chester French shows that he was a meticulous and diligent worker. His fame as a sculptor could be established by any number of his works, but the two most widely publicized are the *Minute Man* and *Lincoln*. The *Minute Man* was unveiled by Ralph Waldo Emerson in 1875 and placed on the Old North Bridge in Concord, Massachusetts. The statue's image was chosen to decorate defense bonds, stamps and posters during World War II, and is used as the symbol of an insurance company. The seated marble *Lincoln* (1922) in the Lincoln Memorial, Washington, D.C., is viewed by many thousands of visitors every year.

French created the *Minute Man* when he was only 23 years old. It established his reputation and brought him numerous, important commissions. Among these commissions were the busts of Ralph Waldo Emerson and Bronson Alcott, and a statue of John Harvard at Harvard University, Cambridge, Massachusetts. French is also known for *Dr. Gallaudet and His First Deaf-Mute Pupil*, which was done for the Columbia Institute for the Deaf and Dumb in Washington, D.C.; the 75-foot *Statue of the Republic* for the World's Columbian Exposition in Chicago in 1893; *Death Staying the Hand of the Sculptor*, in memory of Martin Milmore in Forest Hills Cemetery, Boston; and, in collaboration with Edward Potter, the equestrian statues of General Grand in Fairmount Park, Philadelphia, and George Washington in Paris, France. He also created the Boston Public Library's low-relief bronze doors, the standing *Lincoln* at the capitol in Lincoln, Nebraska.

French had little formal art education. William Morris Hunt showed him color value. He spent one year at the Massachusetts Institute of Technology studying drawing with William Rimmer and two years with Thomas Ball in Italy. French studied intently and learned rapidly.

His sculptures may be seen on the April 4, 1925, 5¢ Lexington-Concord issue (Scott 619) and the May 30, 1959, 4¢ Lincoln Sesquicentennial issue (Scott 1116). French is commemorated on a 5¢ 1940 Great Americans issue.

118

Robert Lee Frost

Scott 1526
Born: March 26, 1874, San Francisco, California
Died: January 29, 1963, Boston, Massachusetts

When Robert Frost was 11, his father, William Prescott Frost, died. His mother, Belle Moodie Frost, with Robert and his sister, Jeanie, moved from California to New England. Belle taught school in Salem, New Hampshire. Educated by his mother, he was admitted to high school. Upon graduation, he tied for valedictorian with Elinor White, who later became his wife.

Frost entered Dartmouth College in 1892 but dropped out before the semester was completed. He lived with his mother and did odd jobs, while writing poetry. In 1894 his first poem, *My Butterfly: An Elegy*, was published. After marrying Elinor White, he taught in his mother's private school at Lawrence, Massachusetts, for about two years. While a student at Harvard (1897-1899), Belle became ill with cancer, Elinor became pregnant with their second child, and Frost contracted a fever. He left Harvard. His grandfather purchased the West Derry farm, their home for the next 12 years. In mid-summer of 1900 their first child died, and in the fall, Belle died. Farming was productive and so was the family. Five more children were born to the Frosts, but the last died in infancy in 1907. Frost farmed, but his first love was poetry.

In 1912 he and Elinor went to England. With encouragement from Ezra Pound, his poems were well-received. He returned to Boston in 1914 as an established poet. He moved to a farm in Franconia, New Hampshire. In 1916 he accepted a position at Amherst College, where he remained until 1937. His works poured forth. In the 1940s he moved to a farm in Ripton, Vermont.

He won four Pulitzer prizes, the gold medal of the Poetry Society of America, poet laureate of Vermont, the Congressional Gold Medal and honorary degrees in 17 colleges in England and America. He read a poem at J.F. Kennedy's presidential inauguration in 1961. He is portrayed on a 10¢ stamp issued in 1974.

Robert Fulton

Scott 1270
Born: November 14, 1765, near Lancaster, Pennsylvania
Died: February 24, 1815, New York, New York

It might be said of Robert Fulton that he was far ahead of his time. Had France and England heeded his inventive ideas, they would have had a considerable military edge over the rest of the world.

Fulton began as an artist. In Philadelphia, at 17, he supported himself by selling his paintings and mechanical drawings. When he was 21, he went to England to study under Benjamin West, and in 1791, he exhibited two portraits in the Royal Academy.

Canal navigation was an early interest of his, and in 1796 he published a *Treatise on the Improvement of Canal Navigation*. In 1797 he envisioned the submarine and submitted his illustrations to the French government, showing how they could destroy British warships. In 1800 he launched a 24 1/2-foot long vessel, the *Nautilus*, at Rouen. The vessel carried him and three mechanics to a depth of 25 feet for four and one-half hours. At Brest, he showed how the *Nautilus* could fire a torpedo underwater and blow up a sloop. But France and England showed no interest. Even Thomas Jefferson did not follow through on Fulton's recommendations.

Fulton then went to work on steam engines for riverboats. He met U.S. Ambassador Robert Livingston in Paris. Together they formed a business partnership to ply the waters by steam. They demonstrated it on the Seine with an eight-horsepower steam engine turning a 12-foot paddle.

In August 1807, they launched the *Clermont*, which ran from New York City to Albany and back on steam. In the following eight years, 13 more steamboats (including a warship) were launched, and used on the Hudson, Potomac and Mississippi rivers, cutting freight costs 25 percent.

Fulton established engine works in New Jersey, and in 1812 designed the *Demologus*, which could have fired a 100-pound projectile to protect New York Harbor. The War of 1812 ended before it could be used, but steamboating was established.

Fulton is portrayed, along with the *Clermont*, on a 5¢ stamp issued in 1965 to commemorate the 200th anniversary of the inventor's birth.

Clark Gable

Scott 2446
Born: February 1, 1901, Cadiz, Ohio
Died: November 16, 1960, Hollywood, California

Clark Gable was called "the King" and the "all-time number one film star." His work for several years in the Oklahoma oil fields helped develop a strong physique and an authoritative way of speaking, which he carried with him into the films. Before Hollywood, he worked with a small group of touring actors in the west and northwest. He then joined a company of actors in Portland, Oregon. In 1928 he appeared on Broadway in *Machinal*. This led to a part in the sound film *The Painted Desert*, which led to the leading role in *Dance, Fools, Dance* and the starring role in *A Free Soul*. All of these were released in 1931. Forty-one of his films grossed a total of $63 million.

As a young boy, Gable aspired to be a doctor but gave it up when he was 15 years old to become a callboy in an Akron, Ohio, theater.

He served in the Army Air Force during World War II, flying photographic missions in the European Theater of Operations. His first two marriages, to Josephine Dillon in 1924 and to Rhea Franklin in 1930, ended in divorces. In 1939 he married Carole Lombard, who was killed in an airplane crash in 1942. From 1949 to 1952, he was married to Lady Sylvia Ashley. In 1955 Kay Spreckels became his fifth wife.

Gable received the Academy Award in 1934 for his starring role in *It Happened One Night*. Other films of note were: *Red Dust, No Man of Her Own, Call of the Wild, Mutiny on the Bounty, San Francisco, Boom Town, Test Pilot, Command Decision, Mogambo* and *The Hucksters*. The role he is most associated with is Rhett Butler in Margaret Mitchell's *Gone With the Wind* (1939). He had just completed his role in *The Misfits* on November 6, 1960, when he suffered a major heart attack. Ten days later he died.

Clark Gable is shown with Vivien Leigh in a scene from *Gone With the Wind* on a 25¢ Classic Films stamp issued in 1990.

Albert Gallatin

Scott 1279
Born: January 29, 1761, Geneva, Switzerland
Died: August 12, 1849, Astoria, Long Island, New York

Albert Gallatin was born in Geneva, Switzerland, to a socially prominent and well-to-do French family. He was influenced in his early years by the writings of the political theorist and idealist Jean Jacques Rousseau. At the young age of 19, Gallatin fled to Massachusetts. He taught French at Harvard and polished up on his English at the same time. He also sold goods to settlers on the Maine frontier, with little success.

When the Revolutionary War was over, he acquired land in the frontier area of Fayette County, Pennsylvania. He then opened a store, farmed and speculated in land. Intelligent, educated and Republican, he was elected to the Pennsylvania legislature. Gallatin won the position as a result of his involvement with the anti-federalist convention in 1788 at Harrisburg. He served three terms.

In 1793 Gallatin was elected to the Senate, but his office was rescinded. He was elected to the House of Representatives in 1795 and served for six years. He was responsible for organizing the committee of finance. In 1801 Thomas Jefferson appointed Gallatin as the secretary of the treasury. He handled the national finances extremely well, from the Louisiana Purchase to the Barbary pirate war.

However, he then ran into the costly War of 1812 with England. Gallatin went to Russia as a mediator, but it was not until the Treaty of Ghent that he finally settled the peace.

He moved to France in 1815 to serve seven years as the United States minister. In 1823 he accepted the U.S. vice presidency nomination, but later withdrew. In 1826 John Quincy Adams appointed Gallatin the minister to England. After a year there, he settled in New York City and became the president of the National Bank. In 1836 he published a treatise on the American Indian tribes. He founded the American Ethnological Society in 1842 and was its first president.

Gallatin lived to the ripe old age of 88. He is shown on a 1967 1 1/4¢ value in the Prominent Americans issue.

Thomas Hopkins Gallaudet

Scott 1861
Born: December 10, 1787, Philadelphia, Pennsylvania
Died: September 10, 1851, Hartford, Connecticut

In Washington, D.C., at the Gallaudet Institute for the Deaf and Dumb, is one of Daniel Chester French's famous sculptures, *Dr. Gallaudet and His First Deaf-Mute Pupil*. It is a tribute to Thomas Hopkins Gallaudet, who devoted his life to helping the deaf learn to read, write and speak audibly. When Thomas Gallaudet became acquainted with a young girl, who was deaf, it sparked his interest in the education of deaf youngsters.

The Gallaudet family had moved to Hartford, Connecticut, when Thomas was a boy. He graduated from Yale in 1805. He studied law, tutored at Yale and even engaged in business. He then became interested in the ministry. He entered Andover Theological Seminary in 1812 and graduated two years later, but he was not physically fit for the rigors of the ministry.

In 1816 a young girl's father and friends financed Gallaudet's trip to Paris to study methods of educating the deaf at the Institut Royal des Sourds-Muets. He returned in 1816 and brought with him Laurent Clerc. Together they opened a free school for the deaf in Hartford in 1817. The school later became the state-supported American Asylum. Gallaudet was its principal until his retirement in 1830.

Gallaudet saw the school grow and become a training center for other teachers. He gave support to establishing other schools for the deaf throughout the country. He was a staunch supporter of manual training and for establishing normal schools to qualify women and black persons as teachers.

It was Gallaudet's younger son, Edward Miner Gallaudet, along with Amos Kendall (former postmaster general under Andrew Jackson), who in 1864 established the Columbia Institute for the Deaf and Dumb, Washington, D.C., now called Gallaudet College, in honor of his father. It is a liberal-arts college exclusively for the deaf.

Thomas Gallaudet is portrayed on a 20¢ stamp issued in 1983 as part of the Great Americans series.

Bernardo de Galvez

Scott 1826
Born: July 23, 1746, Macharavialla, Spain
Died: November 30, 1786, Mexico City, Mexico

At age 16, Bernardo de Galvez was already a veteran of the war with Portugal. At that time, in 1762, Spain entered the Seven Years' War as an ally of France. British expeditions had captured Havana and Manila. Galvez went to Mexico with his uncle, Jose de Galvez. By the Treaty of Paris (1763), Spain ceded Florida to Great Britain and received Havana, and France ceded Louisiana to Spain. As a result of the Seven Years' War, France was temporarily eliminated, and Britain and Spain became the great colonial powers. Charles III introduced reforms, raising Spain to a position of power.

During this period, Galvez led several military strikes against the Apache northwest of Chihuahua, Mexico. He then returned to Spain and was wounded in the Algerian campaign in 1775. He returned to Louisiana as its regimental commander. In January 1777 he was appointed governor.

The American Revolution afforded Spain an opportunity to check British expansions. Galvez supplied arms to the patriots and seized British frigates. War was declared between Spain and Great Britain in 1779, and Galvez was ordered to drive the British out of Louisiana and the Gulf area. He enlisted French colonial, black and Indian volunteers, and forced the British to surrender Baton Rouge and Fort Panmure at Natchez. He captured Fort Charlotte at Mobile in 1780 and the next year took Fort George at Pensacola.

Charles III made Galvez a count and lieutenant general. Galveston, Texas, and Galveston Bay were named in honor of Galvez. In 1784 Charles III appointed him captain general of Louisiana, Florida and Cuba. In 1785 Conde de Galvez was promoted to viceroy of New Spain (Mexico). He offered peace to the Indians, and provided them with guns and goods. He also worked to relieve the famine and the scarlet fever epidemic. He contracted the disease in Mexico City and died at the age of 40.

General Galvez is depicted on a 1980 15¢ issue.

124

Mohandas Karamchand Gandhi

Scott 1174
Born: October 2, 1869, Porbandar, India
Died: January 30, 1948, Delhi, India

Born to a well-to-do family, Gandhi had advantages over the average youngster in India. In 1887, when he was 18, his father sent him to London to study law. Four years later, he was admitted to the bar. An Indian firm in South Africa engaged him for legal services in 1893, and he became aware of the suppression under which Asiatic people in South Africa were suffering.

Gandhi devoted his life to public service by following a path of self-discipline called *satyograha*. He read from the *Bhagavad Gita* and the New Testament, and studied the writings of John Ruskin, Leo Tolstoy and the poet Raychanddbhai. He believed that life is best lived near the soil. His altercations with the South African government landed him and his wife and companions in jail. Nevertheless, when the empire was under stress, he supported Great Britain in the Boer War of 1899-1902 and the Zulu Rebellion in 1906 by organizing ambulance corps.

In 1913 he led a group of Indian demonstrators from Transvaal to repeal some acts against them and won. In 1915 he returned to India, convinced that India was ready for self-rule. Until 1934, Gandhi actively supported the National Congress Party. The Rowlatt Acts of 1919 gave the government extraordinary power that was used with violence against a political demonstration at Amritsar in April 1919. After the Mopla rebellion in 1922, Gandhi was imprisoned for two years. He then undertook a hunger strike to bring Hindus and Moslems to mutual toleration.

In 1927 the British government appointed a parliamentary commission to consider India's self-government. By urging boycotts, going on self-imposed fasts, and accepting imprisonments, Gandhi became known by his people as Mahatma, the Great-Souled.

Gandhi strove for his country's independence until January 30, 1948, when he was assassinated by a high-ranking Brahman, who feared Gandhi's program of tolerance for all creeds and religions.

Mohandas Gandhi appears on a 1961 4¢ Champion of Liberty stamp.

James Abram Garfield

Scott 2218b
Born: November 19, 1831, near Cleveland, Ohio
Died: September 19, 1881, Elberon, New Jersey

Born in a log cabin, James Garfield was the youngest of five children. When he was two years old, his father, Abram, died. His mother, Eliza Ballou Garfield, raised her children in poverty. James worked for a short time on a canal boat, but he returned home because he became ill. He graduated from Williams College in 1856, after he had attended a seminary, taught in district schools and studied and taught at the Western Reserve Eclectic Institute (now Hiram College), Hiram, Ohio. He returned to Hiram and became principal of the Eclectic Institute in 1858. He was a popular lay preacher and lecturer. He married his former classmate, Lucretia Rudolph, in 1858. In 1859 he was elected to the Ohio State Senate as a Republican opposed to slavery. At this time, he studied law and was admitted to the bar.

During the Civil War, he rose from lieutenant colonel to major general. He led a brigade in eastern Kentucky and another at Shiloh and Corinth. In 1863 he became chief of staff to General William S. Rosencrans, commander of the Cumberland army, and served at Tullahoma and Chickamouga. He resigned his commission to serve in the House of Representatives, having been elected in 1862. He served until 1880. He supported black suffrage, congressional reconstruction and the impeachment of President Andrew Johnson. He led the establishment of the U.S. Department of Education and was a regent of the Smithsonian Institution. He backed Rutherford B. Hayes for president, and was House minority leader under Hayes.

After a dispute to nominate a candidate in May 1880, Garfield was nominated for the presidency. Chester Arthur was his running mate. On July 2, 1881, he was shot down by a mentally deranged and disappointed office seeker, claiming he was a stalwart who supported Arthur.

James A. Garfield's portrait is shown on a 22¢ stamp of the Presidential sheetlets issued in 1986 for the Ameripex international stamp show.

Giuseppe Garibaldi

Scott 1168
Born: July 4, 1807, Nice, France
Died: June 2, 1882, Caprera, Italy

Giuseppe Garibaldi, like his forefathers, went to sea at age 15 and was a ship's master at age 25. He joined Giuseppe Mazzini in an unsuccessful insurrection at Genoa, Italy, in 1834. For this, he was condemned to death by the Piedmont government of Sardinia. Garibaldi fled to South America, where he gave his services to the state of Rio Grande do Sul against Brazil. He also fought for an Italian legion against Argentina for Uruguay.

He returned to Italy and, after helping Milan against the Austrian government of Lombardy, he again went to serve Mazzini's Roman Republic. Once defeated, Garibaldi led a daring escape and fled to the United States. He worked as a candlemaker and a ship's captain, and intended to become an American citizen.

He was called back to Italy in 1854 to command the first Italian screw-propelled steamer. In 1856 he settled in Caprera, a barren and secluded island off the northern tip of Sardinia. His home is now a national shrine.

In 1859 Garibaldi organized the Cacciatori delle Alpi, a volunteer group of 1,000 men known as the Redshirts. Using South American guerrilla warfare tactics, Garibaldi's troops crossed to the mainland and expelled Francis II from Naples, thus defeating the Kingdom of the Two Sicilies. Italy, united with Sardinia, proclaimed Victor Emmanuel king in 1861.

Garibaldi made two similar attempts to expel Pope Pius IX from Rome in 1862 and 1867. Both were unsuccessful. During the Franco-Prussian War (1870-71), he held a command with France. He returned to Italy, was elected to Parliament in 1874 and then retired to his Caprera island estate in 1876.

This Italian patriot and freedom fighter was honored with a 1960 4¢ commemorative in the Champion of Liberty issue.

Judy Garland (Frances Gumm)

Scott 2445
Born: June 10, 1922, Grand Rapids, Minnesota
Died: June 22, 1969, London, England

Frances Gumm was born "backstage," or so she professed. She appeared on stage with her parents review act before she was three years old and made her official stage debut when she was five. Later she sang in a trio with her elder sisters. In 1936 a film test was successful, and Gumm, as Judy Garland, was soon launched on an impressive list of hits that followed.

Among her earlier hits was the *Andy Hardy* series (with Mickey Rooney). A number of screen musicals, notably *Meet Me in St. Louis*, *The Pirate* (with Gene Kelly) and *Easter Parade* (with Fred Astaire), followed, after which she returned to the stage in vaudeville and singing shows. She developed a scintillating manner on stage and screen, and an effective singing technique.

The songs she made memorable are numerous, especially *You Made Me Love You, I Cried For You, For Me and My Gal, I Got Rhythm, Embraceable You, Look for the Silver Lining* and *Meet Me Tonight in Dreamland*.

During the filming of *Annie Get Your Gun* in 1950, Garland suffered a nervous breakdown. Two years later she appeared at the London Palladium at the start of a British tour that was a fantastic success. At her farewell-to-England performance in Birmingham, the audience rose, joined hands and sang *Auld Lang Syne* for her.

She appeared in her own show at the Palace Theater, New York City, and later took the show on tour.

In addition to problems with nervous exhaustion, drug dependency (barbituates) and the battle with obesity, she was plagued with unhappy marriages to composer-conductor David Rose, director Vincente Minnelli and producer Sidney Luft. She had three children.

Judy Garland immortalized the song, her lifelong theme song, *Over the Rainbow* in *The Wizard of Oz*.

She died of an overdose of sleeping pills (barbituates) in London 12 days after her 47th birthday. She is shown on one of four 25¢ stamps in the Classic Films set issued in 1990.

128

Horatio Gates

Surrender at Saratoga 1777 by Trumbull
US Bicentennial 13 cents

Scott 1728
Born: 1727, Maldon, Essex, England
Died: April 10, 1806, Manhattan Island, New York, New York

In 1817, artist John Trumbull was commissioned by Congress to paint *The Surrender of Burgoyne*, depicting General Horatio Gates receiving the surrender of General John Burgoyne at Saratoga in October 1777. The painting was for the rotunda wall in the U.S. Capitol.

Horatio Gates first served for the British Army in Nova Scotia from 1749 to 1750. He served in the French and Indian War and was wounded while attacking Fort Duquesne in 1755. In 1761 he was involved in the capture of Martinique. In 1765 he retired at half pay as a major. At the recommendation of George Washington, he moved with his family to Virginia. He was appointed a lieutenant colonel in the Virginia militia, and when the Revolution began, he remained with the United States. He was made adjutant general of the army in 1775.

Boston was evacuated in 1776. Gates was made major general and assigned to command the northern American army, which had retreated from Canada. General Philip Schuyler was in command of the Northern Department. A conflict arose. Congress settled in favor of Schuyler. Gates returned to Philadelphia. In 1777 Schuyler's army was defeated, and Gates took over command below Ticonderoga as Burgoyne advanced. Two battles, Bemis Heights and Freeman's Farm, resulted in Burgoyne's defeat and surrender, which was accepted by Gates at Saratoga.

Late in 1777 Gates was appointed president of the Board of War. In 1778 he was appointed to command the army in Boston. In 1780 he commanded the southern army. His troops dispersed and ran in disorganized confusion.

Gates was replaced by Nathanael Greene. He did not return to active duty. His only son died during the war and his wife soon after.

In 1786 Gates married a wealthy widow. In 1790 he sold his Virginia plantation, freed his slaves and moved to a Manhattan island farm.

Trumball's painting of Burgoyne's surrender to Gates is reproduced on a 13¢ stamp issued in 1977 as part of the American Bicentennial series.

129

Henry Lou Gehrig

Scott 2417
Born: June 19, 1903, New York, New York
Died: June 2, 1941, New York, New York

Lou Gehrig is one of America's professional baseball immortals. He was a New Yorker all his life. He attended Columbia University in New York City for two years before joining the New York Yankees. He was a steady dependable first baseman, a powerful left-handed hitter, and an all around spark to the team. He played for the Yankees for 14 years (1925 to 1939) and established an enviable career batting average of .340. He set a record of consecutive major league games played — 2,130. This record has yet to be broken. Gehrig missed his first game on May 2, 1939. For his long career he was dubbed "Iron Horse." His Columbia University days also won him the locker-room nickname of "Columbia Lou."

Gehrig's best year was 1934, when he won the league batting title with an average of .363. That year he had 49 homeruns and 165 runs batted in (RBIs). In 1931 he had 184 RBIs. He was selected the most valuable player of the American League in 1927, 1931, 1934 and 1936. He played in the World Series in 1926, 1927, 1928, 1932, 1936, 1937 and 1938.

Gehrig retired from baseball in 1939 at age 36 and became New York City's parole commissioner. He was dying of a rare form of spinal paralysis, amyotrophic lateral sclerosis, in which portions of the spinal cord harden causing degeneration of the muscles of the body. Today, the disease is often referred to as Lou Gehrig's disease. Despite the fact that swallowing and talking were difficult for Gehrig, a drama came into the homes of Americans when they heard him say, over radio, before 60,000 tearful fans at Yankee Stadium, "I consider myself the luckiest man on the face of the earth."

Gehrig died just 17 days before his 38th birthday in 1941. In 1939 he was inducted into the Baseball Hall of Fame, Cooperstown, New York.

Gehrig is honored on a 25¢ stamp issued in 1989.

Walter F. George

Scott 1170
Born: January 29, 1878, Preston, Georgia
Died: August 4, 1957, Vienna, Georgia

Walter George was an associate justice of the Supreme Court of the state of Georgia when he resigned in 1922 to fill the vacancy in the United States Senate. Prior to his state supreme court judgeship he had been the solicitor general of the Cordele, Georgia, judicial circuit.

He had served as a state superior court judge and state court of appeals judge. From 1922 to 1956, George had served continuously as a U.S. senator. He declined re-election in 1956, because of poor health. But his years spanned a longer term in the Senate than any of his colleagues. He served in the administrations of Coolidge, Hoover, Roosevelt, Truman and Eisenhower.

George's path in the Senate was usually smooth, except perhaps in the Roosevelt administration. He sometimes supported Roosevelt's New Deal legislation, but more often opposed it. He especially opposed Roosevelt's attempt to pack the Supreme Court. Liberal Democrats persuaded Roosevelt to purge a number of legislators in the 1938 Democratic primaries, in particular senators George, Smith and Tydings, but all three won handily. George was a leader in America's bipartisan foreign policies at the time of World War II and its aftermath.

After George's long span in the Senate, Eisenhower appointed him ambassador to the North Atlantic Treaty Organization (NATO). The United States was one of the 15 member countries comprising almost eight million square miles and representing 500 million people who were "determined to safeguard the freedom, common heritage, and civilization of their peoples, founded on the principles of democracy, individual liberty and the rule of law."

The 4¢ Senator George Memorial issue was released in 1960.

George Gershwin

Scott 1484
Born: September 25, 1898, Brooklyn, New York
Died: July 11, 1937, Hollywood, California

Jacob Gershvin's parents were poor Russian Jewish immigrants. George, as he was called, left high school when he was 15 to pursue a career in music. He had been playing the piano since he was 12 and got a job "piano-pounding" in Jerome Remick's music publishers office. His first song composition was published when he was 16. He moved to Harms Publishing Company in 1918. He changed the spelling of his name to Gershwin. In 1919 he wrote *Swanee*, popularized by Al Jolson. He contributed numbers to several shows, and in 1919 composed his first full score, for the operetta *La, La, Lucille*. From 1920 to 1925, he composed the musical scores for the *George White's Scandals*.

Paul Whiteman, the "King of Jazz," invited him to write a symphonic jazz work for a concert Whiteman was organizing in New York at Aeolian Hall. Gershwin wrote the composition in 10 days. Ferde Grofe, Whiteman's arranger, orchestrated the composition, and it was presented as *Rhapsody in Blue* in 1924. Gershwin was launched as a jazz symphony writer. In 1925 he followed with *Concerto in F*, commissioned by Walter Damrosch. In 1928 he composed *An American in Paris*. *Second Rhapsody* came in 1932.

He was influenced by DeBose Heyward's novel *Porgy*. He spent a summer in the black quarters of Charleston studying their way of life and their songs. The libretto was by Heyward and the lyrics by Heyward and George's older brother, Ira Gershwin. Two years later the opera *Porgy and Bess* was completed. It was performed in New York in 1935.

Gershwin composed numerous musical scores with lyrics by Ira for motion pictures featuring such stars as Fred Astaire, Ginger Rogers and Ethel Merman. *Of Thee I Sing* won the Pulitzer Prize in 1931 and *An American in Paris* won an Academy Award in 1951.

Gershwin died in 1937 of a brain tumor at age 38, but in his short lifetime, he firmly established symphonic jazz.

He is honored in the 1973 American Artists issue on an 8¢ stamp.

132

Amadeo Peter Giannini

Scott 1400
Born: May 6, 1870, San Jose, California
Died: June 3, 1949, San Mateo, California

Amadeo Peter Giannini was the son of Italian immigrants. His stepfather, Lorenzo Scalena, put him to work as a clerk in his produce commission house in San Francisco, when he was 12 years old. When he was 19 years old, he was a partner in the business. In 10 years he expanded the wholesale produce business until it was the largest of its kind in the area. Then he sold it.

Giannini was a director of a bank, but after five years, not happy with the bank's practices, he founded the Bank of Italy (capitalized at $150,000). He could then put into practice the unconventional and liberal practices he wanted to pursue. He made small loans to farmers and businessmen, and even advertised his bank's services.

Then, in 1909, came the disastrous earthquake and fire in San Francisco. Giannini rescued the gold and securities in the bank's vault. When the rebuilding came about, he was able to make many small loans to those in need. The next year saw a financial panic, which Giannini's bank again was able to survive by relying on gold reserves. He eventually acquired small banks in the area and made them branch banks.

In 1919, Giannini established the Bancitaly Corporation, which was transformed into the Transamerica Corporation as a holding company for the stock of his banks in less than 10 years.

In 1930 the Bank of Italy became the Bank of America National Trust and Savings Association, making loans and doing business with large and small enterprises alike.

Giannini was the financial backing of much of the expanding motion-picture industry. He retired in 1930, but within a year was back on the board of the Transamerica Corporation as chairman. He again retired in 1945, but kept in close touch with the bank. By 1948 the Bank of America had more than 500 branches with more than $6 billion in deposits. It was the largest bank in the United States and the largest private bank in the world.

Giannini is depicted on the 1973 21¢ regular issue.

133

Lillian Evelyn Moller Gilbreth

Scott 1868
Born: May 24, 1878, Oakland, California
Died: January 2, 1972, Phoenix, Arizona

Lillian Gilbreth applied her knowledge and experience to the efficiency of the home as well as to the factory. Her expertise was that of an industrial engineer, one of the few women in the field. Fewer than one in 200 engineers were women during her time. She was the mother of 12 children and still found time to work in close coordination with her husband Frank Bunker Gilbreth (1868-1924), a contracting engineer and efficiency expert. The two oldest of the 12 Gilbreth children took what they had learned from their parents on efficiency in industry and applied it to the home in a book they wrote, *Cheaper By the Dozen*, followed by a movie (and television serial) of the same name.

When Lillian Gilbreth's husband died in 1924, she continued his work. Frank Bunker Gilbreth had worked in Boston from 1904 to 1911 and from 1911 until 1924 in New York City. He worked on what was termed the Taylor System of Scientific Management and published, in 1911, *The Principles of Scientific Management*. In 1912 Lillian Gilbreth published *Psychology of Management*, in 1927 *The Homemaker and Her Job*, and the next year *Living With Our Children*. She collaborated with her husband on two major references, *Fatigue Study* (1919) and *Time Study* (1920), which were widely read and relied upon by managers and executives of factories, large and small.

Gilbreth's home was across the Hudson River from New York City in Montclair, New Jersey. She devoted her expertise and knowledge to the students of engineering and management all over the world. She not only extended her husband's work but she expanded it as well. Her husband had laid the foundation of the industrial engineering field as it is known today, and she built upon that foundation.

Lillian Gilbreth is portrayed on a 40¢ stamp issued in 1984 as part of the Great Americans series.

Robert Hutchings Goddard

Scott C69
Born: October 5, 1882, Worcester, Massachusetts
Died: August 10, 1945, Baltimore, Maryland

While still in high school, Robert Goddard was interested in rocketry and space. He was inspired by H.G. Wells' *War of the Worlds*.

In 1908 Goddard graduated from Worcester Polytechnic Institute, and in 1911 he received his doctorate from Clark University, also in his hometown of Worcester. He had already anticipated solid- and liquid-propellant rocket motors and the two-stage rocket idea, the use of hydrogen and oxygen, electric propulsion, and solar energy for propulsion. Astronauts would be protected from acceleration, weightlessness and vacuum.

Goddard received financial support from the Smithsonian Institution after publishing *A Method of Reading Extreme Altitudes*. In 1926, at Auburn, Massachusetts, he launched the world's first liquid-propellant rocket. The Guggenheims supported his experimentation, which led to the publication of *Liquid-Propellant Rocket Development*. In Roswell, New Mexico, he launched a liquid-propellant rocket with instruments.

During World War II, he was the director of the Bureau of Aeronautics (U.S. Navy). His work was ignored by the United States during the war, but Germany used his patents for their V-2 rockets. His work served as the basis for the U.S. space exploration. The Goddard Space Flight Center in Greenbelt, Maryland, is named in his honor.

An 8¢ airmail stamp released in 1964 honors Goddard.

George Washington Goethals

Scott 856
Born: June 29, 1858, Brooklyn, New York
Died: January 21, 1928, New York, New York

Goethals had originally planned to study medicine after he had finished public school. He entered the College of the City of New York, then switched to civil engineering and transferred to West Point Military Academy. He graduated in 1880. He was assigned to the Army Corps of Engineers and served as an engineer on the Ohio and Cumberland river projects. Goethals also worked on the Muscle Shoals Canal on the Tennessee River. He spent two stints teaching at West Point from 1885 to 1889 and from 1898 to 1900.

The Hay-Bunau-Varilla Treaty between the United States and Panama was signed on November 18, 1903. The treaty stated that the United States was to build a canal across the Isthmus of Panama. The land that extended for five miles on either side of the canal was known as the Canal Zone. The project would employ 30,000 workers who needed food, housing, medical care, recreational facilities and government, including policing.

The project itself was enormous, but the most trying of all the problems was the human element. President Theodore Roosevelt chose George Washington Goethals as chief engineer, following the resignations of two predecessors. The project began in 1904, and Goethals took over in 1907. He was given near dictatorial powers. He held the workers together with spirited partisanship, and the job was completed six months ahead of schedule. The canal was pronounced finished when the first ship passed through on August 15, 1914. The canal shortened ocean voyages between the Atlantic and the Pacific by thousands of miles.

By appointment of President Woodrow Wilson, Major General Goethals stayed on as the first governor of the Canal Zone until 1917. He was then a member of the War Industry board for two years.

The Panama Canal issue was released in 1939. The 3¢ commemorative honors the 25th anniversary of the canal's opening and depicts Theodore Roosevelt and Goethals.

136

Samuel Gompers

Scott 988
Born: January 27, 1850, London, England
Died: December 13, 1924, San Antonio, Texas

Samuel Gompers' father was a cigarmaker in London. The family lived in the tenement district. Samuel left school when he was 10 years old to become a cigarmaker like his father. In 1863, when he was 13, the family emigrated to New York City, where they lived on the Lower East Side. In 1864 Gompers joined the Cigarmakers' Union, and the next year became an American citizen. He was influenced by the writings of Karl Marx and the socialistic trends of the poor immigrants in the city. He worked for unionization of the laboring class.

In 1877 he reorganized the Cigarmakers' Union. By using the strike and the boycott and avoiding political action or affiliation, he fought for higher wages, benefits and security measures. He had high dues, and strike and pension funds, and established his union on a national scale.

In 1881, to counter the control of the Knights of Labor, he founded the Federation of Organized Trades and labor Unions of the United States of America and Canada. In 1886 the name was simplified to the American Federation of Labor (AFL), with Gompers as its president. With the exception of one year (1895), he remained president until his death in 1924. In the 1890s the Knights of labor began to decline and officially ended in 1917.

The AFL insisted on trade and craft unionism and did not include unskilled workers. This brought on the radical IWW (Industrial Workers of the World) in 1905, the Wobblies, which lasted until their treasonable strikes against the war industries in 1917, resulting in the arrest of their leadership and the proscription of their union.

To offset the socialist anti-war influence by the Wobblies, Gompers vigorously marshaled labor support for the domestic war effort and advocated pure and simple unionism, from which evolved the principles followed today by America's organized workers.

A 3¢ stamp was released in 1950 to commemorate the centennial of Gompers' birth.

Ulysses Simpson Grant

Scott 255
Born: April 27, 1822, Point Pleasant, Ohio
Died: July 23, 1885, Mount McGregor, New York

Baptized Hiram Ulysses, Ulysses was the eldest son of Jesse Root and Hannah Simpson Grant. A year later they moved to Georgetown, Ohio, where "Lyss" grew up. He went to Maysville Seminary and the Ripley Presbyterian Academy. In 1839 he was nominated to West Point as Ulysses Simpson Grant (the name he retained). He graduated second lieutenant in 1843 and was sent to Jefferson Barracks, Missouri (where he met his future wife, Julia Dent), then to the southwest frontier (1844).

He served under General Zachary Taylor (1846) and General Winfield Scott (1847) in the Mexican War, and was advanced to first lieutenant. He and Julia were married August 22, 1848. In 1852 he was assigned to Fort Vancouver to dull and discipline-oriented duty, so he resigned two years later.

He tried farming (1854-1858) and the real-estate business (1858-1861), then returned to Galena, Illinois, to clerk in his father's leather goods store.

The South seceded, and the Civil War began. President Lincoln made Grant a brigadier general in 1861. He saw action in Missouri in 1861. At Forts Donelson and Henry (February 1862) he won victories. As a major general, he secured Shiloh (April 1862) and Corinth (September 1862). He was charged with taking Vicksburg and succeeded in July 1863. He was made major general in the regular Army and was victorious around Chattanooga. As lieutenant general, he commanded all the Northern Armies. He threw all the force of the Union at the Confederates. Overwhelmed, General Lee surrendered at Appomattox Court House on April 9, 1865. Grant was made full general in 1866.

He was elected president of the United States in 1868. He served two terms, but fraud, scandal, and blunders in fiscal matters and policy marred his administration. He ran for a third term, but he lost to Hayes. He again ran, but lost to Garfield. He turned to business, ended up bankrupt, and retired to write.

U.S. Grant's portrait first appeared on a 5¢ stamp in June 1890, five years after his death. He is shown here on the 5¢ regular stamp of 1894.

138

Francois Joseph Paul Grasse

Scott 703
Born: September 13, 1722, Chateau du Bar, Toulon, France
Died: January 11, 1788, Paris, France

By virtue of his inheritance, Francois Joseph Paul Grasse was Marquis de Grasse-tilly and Compte de Grasse. At age 12, he serviced on the galleys of the Order of Malta, and at age 18, he entered the French service. He served throughout the War of the Austrian Succession, which lasted from 1740 until 1748. During that war, he was wounded and captured. He also served in the Seven Years' War, between 1756 and 1763. Sixteen years later, when France and the United States joined forces in the Revolutionary War, Grasse was sent to America by Louis XVI to help the colonies fight the British.

Between 1779 and 1780, he fought the English off the West Indies. In 1781 he was promoted to the rank of admiral and commander in chief of the Atlantic fleet, having defeated Admiral Samuel Hood in taking Tobago.

Washington and Rochambeau were to march to Virginia to join forces with Lafayette against Cornwallis. Washington requested the assistance of Grasse's French fleet. Grasse sailed in the flagship *Ville de Paris*, carrying 104 guns and 4,000 men of the Haiti garrison under General Marquis de Saint-Simon. He sailed from the West Indies to the Chesapeake Bay and was joined by a fleet under Compte de Barras. They were engaged by Admiral Thomas Graves, but the French fleet easily overpowered the British, forcing Graves to withdraw. The French fleet held supremacy in the waters off Yorktown, prevented the British from giving aid to Cornwallis and brought in men and supplies. Helpless, Cornwallis surrendered and his troops stacked arms.

On April 12, 1782, the tides turned. Grasse's fleet met with a superior fleet under Admiral George Rodney in the West Indies. The *Ville de Paris* was seized and Admiral Grasse was taken prisoner. His career had ended. On his return to Paris, he made charges against his captains and published his *Memoire justificatif*. He was acquitted in 1784.

Francois Joseph Paul Grasse is depicted with George Washington and Count de Rochambeau on a 1931 2¢ commemorative stamp.

Horace Greeley

Scott 1177
Born: February 3, 1811, Amherst, New Hampshire
Died: November 29, 1872, Pleasantville, New York

When Horace Greeley was nine years old, his father lost the family farm to creditors. The family moved to Westhaven, Vermont. When Horace was 15, his family moved again to a small clearing in Erie County, Pennsylvania. Horace had quit his intermittent schooling to take a job at East Poultney, Vermont, on the *Northern Spectator*. Four years later he rejoined his parents and found a job with an Erie, Pennsylvania, newspaper. In 1831 he left for the city to establish his future.

He arrived in New York City a gaunt, tattered, tow-headed, 20-year-old teetotaler, mostly self-educated from the printing press but confident of his own over-average intelligence. He worked hard as a journeyman printer and in 1834 published the *New Yorker* magazine, which consistently hung on the brink of bankruptcy.

On July 5, 1836, he married Mary Youngs Cheney, a neurotic peevish teacher. He patiently endured their tedious and discordant misalliance.

Greeley wrote clear-cut simple prose. Politically, he was an impartial Whig. This attracted Thurlow Weed, who engaged him as editor of the weekly *Jefferson*, supporting William Henry Seward. In 1840 he published the *Log Cabin*, another weekly. In 1841 he founded the New York *Tribune*, a penny daily and a dream come true.

He became more active in the political scene. The *Tribune* editor helped shape the Republican platform. Greeley hated war and spoke for a quicker peace, embarrassing Lincoln. "Universal Amnesty and Impartial Suffrage" summed up his Southern policy.

In 1867 he signed a bail bond for Jefferson Davis. He was a bitter critic of Andrew Johnson. He accepted the ill-advised presidential nomination of the Liberal Republicans and Democrats in 1872, but the popular Ulysses S. Grant defeated him decisively.

Greeley's wife died on October 30, 1872. He died a month later.

He is portrayed on a 4¢ stamp issued in 1961.

Adolphus Washington Greely

Scott 2221
Born: March 27, 1844, Newburyport, Massachusetts
Died: October 20, 1935, Washington, D.C.

Adolphus Greely enlisted in the army at the beginning of the Civil War (1861). He fought in several historic battles, was wounded seriously three times, and advanced from a private to a brevet major in rank. He remained in the regular army after the war, holding the rank of second lieutenant. An arctic expedition was planned by the International Polar Year (1882-1883). Greely volunteered for the project in 1881.

As a first lieutenant, he was put in charge of 25 men, who sailed on the *Proteus* and landed on the eastern shore of Ellesmere Island in August 1881. They set up camp, Fort Conger, where the scientific observations were to be carried out. They discovered Lake Hazen and Greely Fjord.

In May 1882 they arrived at 83 degrees 24 minutes north latitude, their most northern point. Supply ships failed to reach Fort Conger. Greely retracted south to Cape Sabine. They could go no further and faced the winter. When relief arrived in June 1884, Greely and five of his men had survived.

Greely was promoted to captain in 1886. The following year he was appointed chief of the Signal Service and was made brigadier general by President Grover Cleveland. For the next 20 years, he strung thousands of land miles of telegraph wires and laid many nautical miles of underwater cables in Puerto Rico, Cuba, the Philippines, Alaska and elsewhere. He also headed the U.S. Weather Service.

In 1891 he was transferred to the Department of Agriculture. He was promoted to major general in 1906, commanding the Northern Military Division to oversee relief operations following the San Francisco earthquake. He retired in 1908 and wrote several books relating his adventures, including *Reminiscences of Adventure and Service* (1927).

He was widely honored for his contributions to science. He is portrayed on a 22¢ stamp in the Arctic Explorers block of four released in 1986.

141

Nathanael Greene

Scott 785
Born: August 7, 1742, Potowomut, Warwick, Rhode Island
Died: June 19, 1786, Mulberry Grove, Georgia

Nathanael Greene's father was an ironmaster and successful farmer. They were Quakers. Nathanael read extensively and was personally tutored by clergyman Ezra Stiles, who later was president of Yale College. In 1770 Nathanael managed his father's foundry in Coventry, Rhode Island, and served in the Rhode Island Assembly. Because he supported the military, he was expelled from the Society of Friends. He raised a militia, but because the Rhode Island governor was a Royalist, he was not allowed to give support to the Massachusetts conflict (April 1775).

The legislature appointed Greene brigadier in command of three regiments that served in the Boston siege and its occupation in 1776, then aided in the defense of New York. To avoid being trapped on Manhattan Island, Greene recommended that the American troops withdraw. Their escape was a narrow one. As major general he lost Fort Washington, but then aided General George Washington in action at Trenton, Brandywine, Germantown in 1777 and Monmouth in 1778.

He served as quartermaster general (in addition to field duty) from March 1778 until August 1780, when he assumed command of the entire army. In the fall of 1778 he presided over the trial of Major John Andre, the British spy who was hanged when Benedict Arnold's treason was discovered. In the fall he was sent to replace General Horatio Gates in the South and to reorganize Gates' demoralized troops. Facing the British in several battles in early 1781, he finally drove Cornwallis to retire towards Yorktown, Virginia. After the surrender of Cornwallis in October 1781, Greene continued to harass the enemy for nearly a year before the British withdrew completely.

He had invested heavily in the revolutionary efforts and in supporting his troops. His money had been mismanaged, and he was unable to recover many government contracts. He retired to Georgia.

He is shown with General George Washington and Mount Vernon on the 1¢ stamp of the 1936-37 Army issue.

David Wark Griffith

Scott 1555
Born: January 22, 1875, Crestwood, Kentucky
Died: July 23, 1948, Hollywood, California

D.W. Griffith seemed destined for a stage and screen career. Although his family was part of the aristocratic South, and his father a Confederate army officer, the Civil War left the family impoverished. He went to Louisville, Kentucky, when he was 16 to work in a newspaper office. He won a small part in a production by the Mefert stock company, and for several years, he went on tour. He wrote his first play in 1907, but it quickly sank into oblivion. He obtained a job as a movie actor when he wrote a scenario of *Tosca*. He worked briefly at the Edison studio in West Orange, New Jersey, then moved to the Biograph Company.

Griffith directed his first film in 1908, the first of nearly 500 in the next 23 years. He discovered and developed numerous filming tricks and stage effects that were to be used for many years in movie making. He focused his films on history, philosophy and social statements. His *Birth of a Nation* (1915) introduced the controversial element of racism. It was also a wonder in techniques of the cinematic arts. In 1916 he produced the epic *Intolerance*. His other films included *Broken Blossoms* (1919), *Way Down East* (1920), *Orphans of the Storm* (1922), *America* (1924) and *Abraham Lincoln* (1931).

He introduced many actors and actresses to the movie-going world. Among them were Mary Pickford, Douglas Fairbanks and Charlie Chaplin, with whom he formed the United Artist Company. He directed films with Dorothy and Lillian Gish, Lionel Barrymore, Joseph Schildkraut, Harry Carey, Mack Sennet and Donald Crisp. He noted W.C. Field's success with *Poppy* and in 1925 made it into a movie.

He had more than a speaking acquaintance with Amedeo Peter Giannini, the banker who financed much of the young motion-picture industry, to the rich advantage of both. Griffith retired in 1930 and sold his United Artists interest in 1933.

D.W. Griffith's portrait appears on a 10¢ stamp issued in 1975 as part of the American Arts series.

Nathan Hale

Scott 551
Born: June 6, 1755, Coventry, Connecticut
Died: September 22, 1776, Manhattan Island, New York

"Howe hung Hale, the man from Yale." So went the little ditty learned by many history students to help them remember the story of America's most celebrated Revolutionary War hero and martyr — Nathan Hale. Hale graduated from Yale College in 1773 and taught school at East Haddam and New London, Connecticut. After the Battle of Lexington, he gave a speech that rung of patriotism and brought much attention to him. On July 1, 1775, the Connecticut General Assembly commissioned him a lieutenant.

His unit saw action in the siege of Boston. He was promoted to captain on January 1, 1776. It was anticipated that General Howe would attack New York. The Boston troops moved to New York to bolster the defenses. The Americans were defeated at Brooklyn Heights and retreated to Manhattan.

Hale was captain of Lieutenant Colonel Knowlton's Rangers. General George Washington asked Knowlton for a volunteer from his company to infiltrate the British camps in Long Island and learn their strategy. Hale was the only volunteer. Disguised as a schoolmaster and carrying his Yale diploma, he made his way from Connecticut to Long Island. When he infiltrated the British positions, the Continental army had their backs to the north end of Manhattan. Hale followed the enemy.

On September 21, he was spotted and captured. The information he carried with him, for what little good it was, was enough to incriminate him. Hale did not deny his mission. General Howe ordered that the spy be hung at sunrise the next day.

As he stood on the gallows, before the rope was put around his neck, he made a speech in which he spoke the famous words, "I only regret that I have but one life to lose for my country." The story of Hale's execution on September 22, 1776, became a standard of American Revolutionary patriotism. Hale is portrayed on the 1/2¢ stamp of the 1922-25 regular series.

Alexander Hamilton

Scott 1086
Born: January 11, 1757, Nevis, Leeward Islands, West Indies
Died: July 12, 1804, New York, New York

Alexander Hamilton and his older brother, James Jr., were abandoned by their unwed parents, Rachel Faucitt Lavien and John Hamilton, the son of the Lord Cambuskeith (Scotland). Presbyterian clergyman Hugh Knox raised funds to send Alexander to New York to school (1773), where he studied at King's College (Columbia University).

He supported the colonial cause. George Washington appointed him his aide-de-camp. Hamilton denounced the Conway Cabal, which suggested replacing Washington with General Gates after Saratoga. He became a friend of the Marquis de Lafayette and was given a command at Yorktown.

On December 14, 1780, he married Elizabeth Schuyler, daughter of General Philip Schuyler. They had eight children. He noted defects in the Articles of Confederation. He studied law and was admitted to the bar in July 1782, and practiced law in New York City. He was a member of the Continental Congress (1782, 1783, 1787, 1788), and represented New York in the Annapolis Convention in 1783. With Madison and Jay, he supported the new constitution in *The Federalist* (1787-1788).

Hamilton was the first secretary of the treasury of the United States. (1789-1795) and established the first fiscal system. He strengthened the central government, stimulated trade and enterprise, developed the national resources, and placed the government's credit on a sound basis. He was appointed inspector general of the armies with the rank of major general.

Thomas Jefferson was elected president of the United States in 1801 by the House of Representatives as a result of Hamilton's decision to throw the Federalist votes to him rather than to Aaron Burr, who had tied Jefferson in electoral votes. Burr later sought the governorship of New York. Hamilton openly doubted Burr's integrity. A duel at Weehawken, New Jersey, was demanded on July 11, 1804, and Hamilton was mortally wounded. He died the following day.

Alexander Hamilton is shown on a 3¢ stamp issued in 1957 to commemorate the 200th anniversary of his birth.

145

Dag Hjalmar Agne Hammarskjold

Scott 1203
Born: July 29, 1905, Jonkoping, Sweden
Died: September 18, 1961, near Ndola, Northern Rhodesia

Dag Hammarskjold's father, Hjalmar (1862-1953), was prime minister of Sweden during World War I (1914-1917) and was a member of the Swedish Academy. Upon his father's death, Dag took over the academy seat. In 1958 he, along with the other 17 academicians, awarded the Soviet poet Boris Pasternak the Nobel Prize for literature. In 1961 Dag Hammarskjold won the Nobel Peace Prize, posthumously.

Dag Hammarskjold began his career as a political economist and diplomat when he was a lecturer of political economy at Stockholm University. Between 1936 and 1952, he held various offices. In 1952 he became chairman of Sweden's United Nations delegation. The following year he became second secretary general of the United Nations for a five-year term.

Using his quiet diplomacy, he was responsible for the release of 11 United States airmen held captive in China in 1955. He had been requested by the general assembly to go to Peking for negotiations. The prisoners were released later in the year.

He was elected for a second five-year term in 1957. His tenure of duty saw many problems in the Middle East and the Congo. Except for the landing of British and French troops in the Suez Canal in 1956, the French in Bizerte in 1961, and United States troops in Lebanon in 1958, he was effective in preventing direct intervention of the great powers.

The Soviets wanted to replace the secretary general with a "troika" made up of communists, western and uncommitted. Premier Krushchev demanded Hammarskjold's resignation in 1960.

Hammarskjold had organized 19,000 troops from 21 lesser nations for a U.N. peace force in the Congo and was on his way to negotiate a cease-fire between the U.N. troops and forces of the Katanga province, Congo, when his plane mysteriously crashed.

Hammarskjold is shown on a 4¢ commemorative issued in 1962. When this stamp was discovered with an inverted color (yellow), the U.S. Post Office ordered the printing of an additional 40 million inverts.

William Christopher Handy

Scott 1372
Born: November 16, 1873, Florence, Alabama
Died: March 28, 1958, New York, New York

William Handy's father was a strict Methodist minister in Florence, located in the northwest corner of Alabama. William sang in the church choir and learned to play the church organ. He was not permitted to play any instrument other than the church organ. However, he secretly bought himself a cornet and played with the hometown brass band. With his cornet, he walked barefoot 125 miles to Birmingham to study music. He obtained a job teaching school and also worked at a steel mill.

In 1893 he organized a quartet to play at the Chicago World's Columbian Exposition. He later drifted around the country with Mahara's Minstrels, playing solo cornetist and doing odd jobs. He finally settled in Memphis, Tennessee, to pursue music seriously.

Shifting to the music he had grown up with — spirituals, work songs, rambling folk ballads and jazz — he combined them with "blue-notes," flatted thirds and sevenths, to what he called the "blues." He wrote a song, *Mr. Crump*, in 1909 to be used in a political campaign for mayor. In 1911 he polished it and called it the *Memphis Blues*. It was a new mode and was followed by a flood of similar songs. The immortal *St. Louis Blues* in 1914, and *Beale Street Blues*, *Yellow Dog Blues*, and some 60 others all were published in several anthologies.

In 1941 his autobiography was published under the well-deserved title of *Father of the Blues*. In his later years his health was poor. He was nearly blind, but he continued to direct his own music publishing company in New York City until his death.

Handy comes to mind as the creator of the highly specific type of music known as the blues. He is shown on a 6¢ commemorative issued in 1969.

147

John Hanson

John Hanson
President Continental Congress
USA 20c

Scott 1941
Born: April 13, 1721, Mulberry Grove, Maryland
Died: November 22, 1783, Oxon Hill, Maryland

John Hanson was elected to the Maryland assembly in 1757 and remained there for the next 22 years. He played a major role in pre-independence debates resisting efforts on the part of the Loyalists to undermine defense preparations. He anticipated the Revolutionary War and was an early advocate of colonial independence. He was elected to the Continental Congress in 1779. Hanson took the seat in Congress the following year and worked to resolve the disputes over the western lands between Virginia, Maryland and other states. This action prepared the way for the ratification of the Articles of Confederation in 1781.

On November 5, 1781, after the Articles of Confederation had been ratified, Hanson was appointed president of the United States in Congress Assembled. He was, therefore, the presiding officer of Congress under the Articles of Confederation. However, he had little executive authority at the time. As recorded in George Washington's papers at the Library of Congress, on November 30, 1781, General Washington congratulated John Hanson and noted that he had been elevated to "the most important seat in the United States." Such a statement has sparked some historians to regard Hanson as the first president of the United States. Since the office of the president of the United States was not officially created until the United States Constitution was adopted, it is likewise argued that Hanson was only president of the Congress and not a chief executive.

Hanson completed a term of one year and retired. Two hundred years has established that George Washington, not John Hanson, was the first president of the United States and the father of our country. Yet some historians doggedly cling to the claim that it was John Hanson who was our first president.

The 1981 John Hanson issue was released as a 20¢ value.

Warren Gameliel Harding

Scott 684
Born: November 2, 1865, Blooming Grove, Ohio
Died: August 2, 1923, San Francisco, California

The Harding administration following World War I in many ways paralleled that of Grant's following the Civil War, except that Harding did not live to finish his term. Both were fraught with mismanagement. Grant's cabinet was packed with corrupt associates and Harding's with the "Ohio gang" cronies who brought his government down to a low ebb. Nevertheless, Harding's cabinet included several distinguished figures: Charles Evans Hughes, Herbert Hoover, Andrew Mellon, Henry Wallace and ex-president William H. Taft. Harry M. Daugherty, Charles R. Forbes and Albert B. Fall fell into widespread corruption with the Teapot Dome oil-lease transfers.

In June 1923 Harding took off on a transcontinental tour, a "Voyage of Understanding," and on to Alaska where he received a message from Washington informing him that much corruption was to come to light. He headed south to California, but was struck with food poisoning and other ills on the way. He died in San Francisco on August 2, 1923.

Forbes and Fall were convicted of bribery and went to prison. Daugherty was dismissed by President Coolidge. Scandal after scandal came to light.

Nan Britton, a former Marion, Ohio, girl 31 years Harding's junior and mother of his daughter Elizabeth Ann, blackened him in a book she published. His longtime affair with the wife of a Marion merchant smeared his reputation. His wife, "the Duchess," as he called her, was a domineering divorcee.

Marion, Ohio, was his lifelong home. He owned the *Marion Star* newspaper and gradually evolved into politics from a local level to the United States Senate. His career was undistinguished. He fell into the presidency by the quirks of politics. He defeated James M. Cox primarily because of the nation's war weariness and his oratory for a "return to normalcy." Coolidge inherited his problems.

Harding is shown on the 1 1/2¢ stamp of the 1930 regular issue.

Joel Chandler Harris

Scott 980
Born: December 9, 1848, Eatonton, Georgia
Died: July 3, 1908, Atlanta, Georgia

Joel Chandler Harris quit school when he was 13 years old. He continued his education as he apprenticed with the *Countryman*, a weekly newspaper. The publication was printed and published on a local plantation during the Civil War. Harris became a master of the Negro dialect and plantation stories. He worked on newspapers in Macon, New Orleans and Savannah, and eventually established himself as a humorist. He finally settled at the *Atlanta Constitution* in 1876, where he remained a staff member for 24 years.

In 1879 he published *The Tar-Baby Story*, the first of his Uncle Remus series. This series culminated in the establishment of *Uncle Remus' Magazine* in 1907. With the help of his son Julian, Harris edited the magazine in the last year of his life.

Harris' writings came at a time when slavery had been recently abolished and plantation life was reorganizing — the Reconstruction and post-Reconstruction period. His Uncle Remus stories preserved the good side of the South's antebellum plantation life. Uncle Remus relates tales to his master's little son about animals who behave like Negroes and white folks. Brer Rabbit was usually the hero of the story. "Brer Rabbit," Harris said, "is victorious in contests with the bear, the wolf, and the fox. It is not virtue that triumphs, but helplessness; it is not malice, but mischievousness."

The humor in Harris' stories helped mollify the bad feelings left by the Grant administration, the panic of the early 1870s and the Ku Klux Klan menace. His stories were effective through World War I, the Great Depression of the 1930s, World War II and even shortly after.

Eventually, stories like *Little Black Sambo*, *Uncle Tom*, *Ole Black Joe*, and *Uncle Remus* were suppressed. Still, Harris must be regarded as a master of humor and dialectic reporting. His fresh stories are truly enlightening and are genuine fables of American literature.

The 3¢ Joel Chandler Harris issue was released in 1948 to commemorate the Georgia writer.

150

Benjamin Harrison

Scott 2218e
Born: August 20, 1833, North Bend, Ohio
Died: March 13, 1901, Indianapolis, Indiana

Benjamin Harrison, the second of nine children, grew up in North Bend, Ohio, in the limelight of several political figures in the family, including his grandfather, William Henry Harrison, the ninth president of the United States. His father, John Scott Harrison, was a U.S. congressman. His mother was Elizabeth Irwin, from Pennsylvania.

Benjamin went to Cincinnati to attend Cary's Academy (later Farmer's College) at age 14. At age 17, he registered as a junior in Miami University in Oxford, Ohio. He graduated with first honors in June 1852. He read law with Storer and Gwynn, a Cincinnati firm, was admitted to the bar in 1854 and moved to Indianapolis. He had married Caroline Scott the previous year.

In 1855 William Wallace joined his law firm. Harrison campaigned for Republican presidential candidate John C. Fremont in 1856. In 1857 he was elected Indianapolis city attorney. He served as the state's secretary of the central committee and was elected state supreme court reporter in 1860.

For helping elect President Rutherford B. Hayes, he was appointed to the Mississippi River Commission (1879-1881). He supported James Garfield in 1880 and was elected to the U.S. Senate, where he served from 1881 to 1887.

James G. Blaine declined the Republican presidential nomination, and Harrison was nominated. He became the 23rd president of the United States by an electoral vote majority. Four important laws in 1890 marked his term: the Sherman Antitrust Act, the Sherman Silver Purchase Act, the McKinley Tariff Act and the Dependent Pension Act. His foreign policies included the two-ocean navy, the first Pan American conference (1889), and arbitration settlements with Great Britain and Germany. He lost to Grover Cleveland for re-election. He returned to Indianapolis to manage his lucrative law practice.

Benjamin Harrison's portrait appears on a 22¢ stamp in the Presidential sheetlets issued in 1986 for the Ameripex international stamp show.

William Henry Harrison

Scott 2216i
Born: February 9, 1773, Charles City County, Virginia
Died: April 4, 1841, Washington, D.C.

William Henry Harrison's father, Benjamin Harrison, was a signer of the Declaration of Independence, governor of Virginia and a delegate to the first two Continental Congresses. William Henry was elected the ninth president of the United States. He contracted pneumonia a month after entering office and died. Vice President John Tyler followed as president on April 4, 1841.

Harrison and Tyler campaigned on the Whig platform with the slogan, "Tippecanoe and Tyler, too," based on Harrison's victory in 1813 over the Indians at Tippecanoe and the more decisive victory over Indian Chief Tecumseh at the Battle of the Thames. The victory secured the Northwest Territory border. The Indians were fighting on the side of the British to save their sacred hunting grounds.

Harrison joined the army in 1791 after he had studied medicine for two years at Richmond and Philadelphia. He served in various places in the northwest and became aide-de-camp to General Anthony Wayne, with whom he fought in the Battle of Fallen Timbers in 1794. He witnessed the Treaty of Greenville and became commandant of Fort Washington, Cincinnati.

He quit the army in 1798 and moved to North Bend, Ohio, where he built his estate. He was then appointed secretary of the Northwest Territory and delegated to Congress. In 1800 he was appointed governor of the Indiana Territory. He moved to Vincennes, the territorial capital.

In 1814 he resigned his commission and began his political career. He was a U.S. senator (1819-1821) and for a short term was minister to Colombia, but was incompatible with Simon Bolivar. In 1836 he took the road to the presidency. He lost the first election in 1839 but owing to economic hard times, won the next election over Democrat Van Buren.

Harrison's portrait appears on one of the 22¢ stamps of the Presidential sheetlets issued in 1986 for the Ameripex international stamp show.

Bret Harte

Scott 2196
Born: August 25, 1836, Albany, New York
Died: May 5, 1902, Camberley, England

Bret Harte was born Francis Brett Hart. His father changed the name to Harte shortly before his death in 1845. His mother remarried and moved to California. Young Bret joined his mother in California in 1854. He wandered about the countryside, spending time in gold-mining camps, and doing various odd jobs. He finally settled in San Francisco, where he worked as a secretary and clerk in government offices and also as a printer. He read extensively, wrote and had some of his writings published. In 1862 he married Anna Griswold.

His short story *M'liss* (previously known as *The Work on Red Mountain*), published in 1860, was well-accepted. Harte gradually developed into a writer of fiction about the American West. In 1867 he published two books and a collection of his poetry. From 1868 to 1871 he was editor of the *Overland Monthly*. His writings soon centered on California. For 30 years he wrote about people and places in contemporary California.

While in San Francisco, Harte became the literary guide to such greats as Mark Twain and Ambrose Bierce. His story *The Luck of Roaring Camp* (1868) and his verse "The Heathen Chinee," a satiric parody known first as "Plain Language from Truthful James" (1870), brought him international recognition. He and Mark Twain produced it into a play called *Ah Sin* (1877). It was a flop.

Harte obtained a U.S. government job in Germany in 1878. He lectured in England, where he was popular. From 1880 to 1885, he was the U.S. consul at Glasgow. He left his wife and children and moved to London, where he produced many of his later works. He is now little known except for a few stories, but his works fill 20 volumes. They influenced Hollywood's Western films and writers of Western culture. As a parodist, he is considered the best.

Harte is portrayed on a $5 stamp issued in 1987 as part of the Great Americans series.

David Hartley

Treaty of Paris 1783
US Bicentennial 20 cents

Scott 2052
Born: 1731
Died: 1813

David Hartley's father was a famous physician, philosopher and psychologist who founded the Associationist School of Learning. Since they both had the same name, the son was known as "the younger." The younger Hartley was a fellow of Merton College in Oxford and a member of Parliament for Kingston-upon-Hull. He served from 1774 to 1779 and again from 1782 to 1784. When the final Treaty of Paris came about, Hartley had been appointed by the Fox-North ministry as a plenipotentiary to negotiate with the Americans and to place his signature on that historic treaty.

America's peace commissioners had been selected even before the surrender of Cornwallis at Yorktown, October 11, 1781. They were John Adams, Benjamin Franklin, Thomas Jefferson, John Jay and Henry Laurens. Jefferson declined the appointment.

Laurens was being held captive in the Tower of London and was released too late to be at the proceedings. The negotiations began in Paris in the spring of 1782, with Benjamin Franklin the only American delegate at hand. Jay and Adams arrived later.

Comte Charles Gravier de Vergennes was the minister of foreign affairs under Louis XVI, representing France in the negotiations of the treaty. Spain was an ally of France. The 13 United States were no ally of Spain, but were an ally of France.

Vergennes feared that the United States would be too powerful if the Mississippi were to become its western boundary. The British and the United States agreed on a preliminary treaty on November 30, 1782. The final treaty, signed September 3, 1783, which accepted the terms of the preliminary treaty, annoyed the French. First Jay, then Adams and finally Franklin decided to ignore instructions from Congress and to go it alone, and sign the treaty their way. Hartley quietly signed for Britain.

Hartley is shown with John Adams, Benjamin Franklin and John Jay on the 1983 20¢ Signing of Treaty of Paris issue.

154

John Harvard

Scott 2191
Born: 1607, Southwark, London, England
Died: September 14, 1638, Charlestown, Massachusetts Bay Colony

The seated bronze visage of John Harvard, sculpted by Daniel Chester French in 1884, looks out from University Hall, in Cambridge, Massachusetts. The likeness was rendered nearly 250 years after Harvard's death. For more than 100 years, it has been the presiding spirit in the leafy, weathered-brick Harvard Yard. It stares out over a vast, flourishing arena that today ranks as one of the world's most distinguished centers of learning. Three hundred fifty years ago it was a farmhouse surrounding a one-acre cow pasture.

The plague in London in 1625 left more than 40,000 people dead. Among the victims was John Harvard's father, Robert Harvard, a butcher and tavern owner. Robert Harvard had married twice. His second wife was Katherine Rogers, daughter of an alderman and cattle dealer in Stratford-upon-Avon. Soon after Robert's death, she remarried a man of means.

John Harvard entered Emanuel College in Cambridge, England, in 1627 and graduated in 1632 with a bachelor of arts degree. Three years later he was awarded his master's degree. The next year he married Ann Sadler. He had inherited considerable wealth in 1635 and considered entering the clergy. He and his bride sailed for America, (probably on the *Hector*) in 1637 and settled in Charlestown, Massachusetts Bay Colony.

Harvard became a teaching elder in the church and a leading member of the community. He died in 1638, at age 31, "of consumption." In his will he left half of his estate (£400) and his 400-volume library to the proposed school or college which in 1636 the Great and General Court of Massachusetts Bay Colony had authorized. The £400 had been set aside by the court for the college. Classes began in the summer of 1638. On March 13, 1639, the school was officially named Harvard College.

Harvard is portrayed on the 56¢ stamp issued in 1986 as part of the Great Americans series.

Nathaniel Hawthorne

Scott 2047
Born: July 4, 1804, Salem, Massachusetts
Died: May 19, 1864, Plymouth, New Hampshire

The Hathorne's were an old family in Salem. Nathaniel changed the spelling of his name to Hawthorne when he was in Bowdoin College. His father was of the fifth generation in Salem. He was a sea captain who died when Nathaniel was only four years old. An early Hathorne forefather, William, had been a soldier and judge, and had ordered a Quaker woman to be flogged. Judge William Hathorne's son John was one of the three judges at the Salem witchcraft trial in 1692, when one of the condemned women put the hex on the Hathornes. His mother's family also could be traced to the early history of Salem. When Nathaniel's father died, his mother became a recluse.

Nathaniel returned from college in 1825 to devote himself to writing. He had become a close friend of his classmates Franklin Pierce and Henry Wadsworth Longfellow while in college.

In 1837 he produced the first volume of *Twice Told Tales*. His boyhood friend, educator Elizabeth Palmer Peabody, introduced him to her sister Sophia, whom he later married. Elizabeth's other sister, Mary, was married to Horace Mann. Sophia and Nathaniel moved to Concord, where he was a quiet visitor of the transcendentalist group headed up by Emerson, Thoreau and Bronson Alcott. In 1846 he returned to Salem where, in 1850, he published *The Scarlet Letter*. He moved to Lenox, in western Massachusetts. He became a close friend of Herman Melville. He wrote *The House of Seven Gables* and two delightful children's books.

In 1852 he returned to Concord and wrote a campaign bibliography for Franklin Pierce. He was appointed U.S. consulate in Liverpool for four years, then two years in Italy, and another year in England, finally returning to Concord. His last work was in 1863, *Our Old Home*. He died in Plymouth, New Hampshire, while on a trip with Franklin Pierce.

Hawthorne was honored with a 20¢ stamp issued in 1983.

156

Rutherford Birchard Hayes

Scott 563
Born: October 4, 1822, Delaware, Ohio
Died: January 17, 1893, Fremont, Ohio

Hayes attended a Methodist seminary at Norwalk, Ohio, and then the Isaac Webb private school at Middletown, Connecticut (later part of Wesleyan University). He graduated from Kenyon College in Gambier, Ohio, in 1842. After studying law privately, he went to Harvard Law School. He earned his law degree in 1845, mainly to satisfy the wishes of his domineering sister, Fanny. He began practicing law in Lower Sandusky (later Fremont), Ohio. He moved to Cincinnati. He married Lucy Ware Webb, from Chillicothe, Ohio, in 1852. They had seven sons and a daughter. He helped found the Ohio Republican party in 1856 and was elected city solicitor in 1858.

When the Civil War broke out, he served with the 23rd Ohio Volunteers. He was wounded five times and rose to the rank of major general. He was nominated and elected to the House of Representatives in 1864 and again in 1866, but resigned the following year to run for governor of Ohio. He was re-elected in 1869, but refused the third term to retire to Fremont.

The Democrats with their greenback and Reconstruction issues pushed Hayes to campaign for a third term as governor. The campaign attracted national attention.

In 1877 he was nominated over James G. Blaine, a Republican, for president of the United States. Democrat Samuel J. Tilden appeared to have won, but the Republicans challenged the returns of four states. A commission was formed and settled on Hayes as the 19th president of the United States by one electoral vote (185-184).

Hayes was inaugurated on March 5, 1877. He kept his promise to withdraw troops from the South. He followed a sound fiscal policy, took a firm stand on the railroad strike of 1877, and adhered to a pledge not to run for a second term in 1880. He returned to Ohio and busied himself in various humanitarian causes.

Hayes is shown on the 11¢ stamp of the 1922-25 regular issue.

157

Ernest Miller Hemingway

Scott 2418
Born: July 21, 1899, Oak Park, Illinois
Died: July 2, 1961, Ketchum, Idaho

In high school, Ernest Hemingway did well in English and sports. He went into journalism after graduation. Poor vision kept him out of military service in World War I, but he joined the Red Cross as an ambulance driver in Italy. In 1920 he worked for the *Toronto Star* as a European correspondent in Paris. He published his first book, *Three Stories and Ten Poems*, in 1923, the same year he went to Spain and became fascinated with bullfighting. In the next few years, he wrote some of his best works: *In Our Time* (1925), *The Sun Also Rises* (1926) and *Men Without Women* (1927). He lived in Key West, Florida, after returning from Europe. He returned to Paris in 1929. *A Farewell to Arms* was published, and in 1932 it was made into a film.

In 1937 he returned to Spain. He allied with the Loyalists in their fight against Franco, from which experiences he wrote *For Whom The Bell Tolls*. He reaped commercial success from this book. He covered the Sino-Japanese War in 1941. In 1944, in England, he reported on the war in Europe. He participated in the activities in France after the Allied invasion.

Following World War II, Hemingway lived in Cuba. He revived his reputation with *The Old Man and The Sea* (1952), which won him the Pulitzer Prize. In 1954 he won the Nobel Prize and that same year took off for an African safari. He wrote several novels, including *Death in the Afternoon* (1932), *Green Hills of Africa* (1935), *To Have and Have Not* (1937), *The Fifth Column* (1938) and *Across the River and into the Trees* (1950).

In 1959 the Cuban revolution forced him to move to Ketchum, Idaho. In poor health and mentally disturbed, he shot himself in the head with a shotgun. Ernest Hemingway was married four times and had three sons. His book on his Paris reminiscences of 1920 was published posthumously in 1965 as *A Moveable Feast*.

A 25¢ Literary Arts stamp issued in 1989 portrayed the author.

Patrick Henry

Scott 1052
Born: May 29, 1736, Studley Plantation, Hanover County, Virginia
Died: June 6, 1799, Red Hill, Charlotte County, Virginia

Patrick Henry's father was a well-educated, well-to-do Scotsman who served in Virginia as a county surveyor, colonel and county court judge. His mother, of Welsh descent, was knowledgeable in music. Patrick did fair in school, but as a farmer and storekeeper, he failed miserably. His forte was history and law. At age 24, he was admitted to the bar (1760). In 1765 he entered the House of Burgesses.

With the announcement of the Stamp Act that same year, he introduced a number of radical resolutions against the act and showed his extraordinary oratorical ability. He was the recognized leader of the radical faction in his home state and gained recognition throughout the colonies for his leadership and his remarkable speeches.

As a member of Virginia's first Committee of Correspondence and a delegate to the first two Continental Congresses, he carried the convention with his speech in which he said, "I know not what course others may take, but as for me, give me liberty or give me death."

He became commander of the Virginia militia but resigned. In 1776 he helped draft the Virginia constitution and was the state's governor (1776-1779) through the war years. In 1778 he sent George Rogers Clark to conquer the old Northwest.

He served in the legislature again from 1780 to 1784. He advocated equitable treatment for former Loyalists after the Treaty of Paris in 1783. He followed Benjamin Harrison for another term of governor from 1784 to 1786 and served again in the legislature from 1787 to 1790.

Because of several oppositions, he refused to be a delegate to the Constitution Convention in 1787, but he was responsible for the 10 amendments comprising the Bill of Rights. In 1788 he retired.

Patrick Henry is portrayed on the $1 stamp of the 1954-68 Liberty series.

Matthew Alexander Henson

Scott 2223
Born: 1866, Charles County, Maryland
Died: March 9, 1955, New York, New York

Matthew Henson grew up in Washington, D.C., where he lived with an uncle, having been orphaned when he was quite young. He worked in a restaurant and went to the N Street School for a half-dozen years. Captain Childs, commander of the *Katie Hinds* out of Baltimore, hired Henson in 1879. He was just 13 years old when he began working as a cabin boy. Henson learned seamanship as he sailed through the Straits of Magellan, crossed the Pacific Ocean to the China Sea, crossed the Atlantic Ocean and even sailed into the Baltic Sea. After six years with Captain Childs, he went to work in Boston as a stevedore, then worked as a bellhop in Providence and as a coachman in New York City. When Henson was 19 years old he returned to Washington, D.C., a much traveled and experienced young man.

In 1887 he chanced to meet Robert Peary in a store. The owner of the store recommended Henson as a valet to accompany Peary on his trip to survey a canal route through Nicaragua. With his experience, abilities to chart courses through the jungles and expert seamanship, Henson soon became more of a colleague than a valet. Except for Peary's first trip to the arctic, Henson was at Peary's side on all the arctic excursions that he undertook. The most notable of these was the last one (1908-1909), when Henson, Peary and four Eskimos made it to the North Pole on April 6, 1909.

Commander MacMillan said in his book, *How Peary Reached the North Pole*, "Henson, the colored man, went with Peary because he was a better man than any of the white assistants." Peary said, "He is a better dog driver and can handle a sledge better than any man living except some of the best Eskimo hunters. I couldn't get along without him."

Afterward, Henson worked as a clerk in the New York Customs House from 1913 to 1936. In his later years he received numerous honors and medals for his exploits with Peary. On April 6, 1988, the 79th anniversary of the day Peary and Henson placed the American flag on the North Pole, Henson's body and the body of his wife, Lucy Ross Henson, were reinterred with full military honors from an obscure New York grave site to Arlington National Cemetery in Arlington, Virginia.

Henson and Peary are depicted on the 1986 22¢ Polar Explorers issue.

Victor Herbert

Scott 881
Born: February 1, 1859, Dublin, Ireland
Died: May 26, 1924, New York, New York

In 1886, Walter Damrosch invited Victor Herbert to come to the United States to accept the position of first-chair cellist at the Metropolitan Opera House in New York City. Herbert previously had been a cellist for the orchestra conducted by the younger Johann Strauss in Vienna. Early in life, Herbert showed exceptional musical ability, At age 7, he was sent to Germany to study. Before joining Strauss, he toured Europe as a solo cellist. He studied under several masters, learning the flute and piano. He composed for the cello, played for several European orchestras and conducted.

In the United States, he played for Theodore Thomas' orchestra and the New York Philharmonic, in which he gave the premiere performances of his composition *Concerto and Suite for Cello* (1887) and his *Second Concerto* (1894). He also conducted the New York 22nd Regiment Band for five years, during which time he began composing delightful operettas for the New York City stage. *The Wizard of the Nile* was his first successful operetta (1895). It was followed by such classics as *The Serenade* (1897), the *Fortune Teller* (1898), *Babes in Toyland* (1903), *Mlle. Modiste* (1905), *The Red Mill* (1906), *Little Nemo* (1908), *Naughty Marietta* (1910) and *Her Regiment* (1917).

He conducted the Pittsburgh Symphony Orchestra from 1898 to 1904. In 1904 he returned to New York City and organized his own orchestra. He wrote two grand operas, *Notama* (1911) and *Madeleine* (1914), as well as numerous short pieces. His song *Ah! Sweet Mystery of Life* has become a classic.

In 1914 Herbert founded ASCAP, the American Society of Composers, Authors and Publishers. He composed the first film music score ever, for the classic *The Fall of a Nation*, and in 1919, 1921 and 1924, wrote the music for the *Ziegfield Follies*.

He is one of five composers honored in the 1940 Famous Americans series. He is depicted on the 3¢ stamp.

161

Nicholas Herkimer

Herkimer at Oriskany 1777 by Yohn
US Bicentennial 13 cents

Scott 1722
Born: 1728, near German Flats (nowHerkimer), New York
Died: August 16, 1777, near Oriskany, New York

Nicholas Herkimer fought in the French and Indian War and was a militia officer when the Revolution began. As a brigadier general, he mobilized 800 militiamen on July 14, 1777, to help relieve Fort Stanwix, near Rome, New York. Colonel Barry St. Leger, with his force of 800 British regulars and American Tories, bolstered by more than a thousand Indians, besieged the fort. Colonel St. Leger was on a march to Albany to join other British troops from Canada. He challenged Herkimer near Oriskany, New York, on August 6, 1777. The American militiamen lost more than half their command in casualties. Herkimer was mortally wounded and died 10 days later.

Prior to this attack, St. Leger's force was one of two divisions made up by General Burgoyne. His army was encumbered by officers' wives, children and an enormous quantity of baggage. It took nearly a month to reach Fort Edward, which had been abandoned. Just to carry one month's supplies required 180 Canadian bateaux, hauled by relays of oxen and horses over the portages between the two lakes.

St. Leger's troops moved up the St. Lawrence to Oswego, then across country toward Fort Stanwix, where Sir John Johnson had promised a large turnout of Loyalist militia and Mohawk braves.

Herkimer led his Patriots but was ambushed by St. Leger's Mohawks near Oriskany. St. Leger reached Fort Stanwix the next day, August 7. A small force under Benedict Arnold went to the Mohawk River to relieve Fort Stanwix. Arnold spread a false rumor about large numbers of advancing reinforcements, which panicked the Mohawks, causing St. Leger to give up Fort Stanwix and retreat through the woods to Canada on August 22, 1777. The retreat occurred one week after Herkimer died of battle wounds.

Herkimer lost the battle but won the war. He is depicted at the Battle of Oriskany on a 1977 13¢ U.S. Bicentennial stamp.

162

James Hoban

Scott 1936
Born: 1762, Callan, County Kilkenny, Ireland
Died: December 8, 1831, Washington, D.C.

James Hoban studied architectural drawing and design at the school of the Dublin Society. He assisted in the drawings and design of several Dublin buildings before he emigrated to the United States in 1785. He settled in Philadelphia, and later in South Carolina, where he designed the state capitol. In 1792 he moved to the District of Columbia to take advantage of the new city being built and to enter in the design competition for the new capitol and the president's house.

Although the facade of the president's mansion in Hoban's design resembled somewhat the Leinster House in Dublin, his inspiration came from an illustration in James Gibbs' *Book of Architecture* (1728). One plan submitted, anonymously, was by Thomas Jefferson, but Hoban's design won. However, his design for the U.S. Capitol was not selected. That went to William Thornton.

From 1793 to 1800, he supervised the construction of the mansion. He used Virginia freestone on its front. The rest was painted white, so the mansion was soon called the White House. Lincoln preferred "executive mansion," but in 1902 Theodore Roosevelt adopted White House as its official name when he had the West Wing added. In 1942 Franklin D. Roosevelt had the East Wing added.

Hoban also designed two hotels in Washington, D.C. He was able to acquire considerable real-estate in the area, and from 1802 until the year he died, he was a member of the city council of Washington, D.C. When the War of 1812 destroyed the White House, he supervised the rebuilding project. Restoration was completed in 1817. He also designed and built the offices of the State Department and the War Department.

The South Portico was added to the White House in 1824 and the North Portico in 1829. The building was completely renovated in 1952.

The 1981 18¢ Hoban stamp was issued on the same day as a 20¢ stamp with the same design in anticipation of an increase in postal rates.

163

Chief Hollow Horn Bear

Scott 565
Born: near the Niobrara River, Sheridan County, Nebraska
Died: March 15, 1913, buried in Washington, D.C.

Like the highly respected American Eagle with arrows in one claw and an olive leaf in the other, Hollow Horn Bear, or Mati-he-hlogeco as he was called in Indian language, was a highly respected American Prairie Indian chief clutching a tomahawk in one fist and a piece pipe in the other. At age 16, Hollow Horn Bear went with his father, Chief Iron Shell, to fight the Pawnee tribe. He proved himself to be a true Indian brave. He took part in many raids on the encroaching white men along the Bozeman and Oregon trails in Montana, Wyoming, Nebraska and the Dakota country.

When Captain W.J. Fetterman left Fort Phil Kearny to guard a wood train and (disobeying orders) instead attacked Red Cloud on December 21, 1866, Hollow Horn Bear was alongside Red Cloud, leaving Fetterman and his men as food for the vultures. Hollow Horn Bear also raided Union Pacific Railroad crews and labor camps.

After the Treaty of Fort Laramie was signed in 1869, Hollow Horn Bear continued his raids. But in 1873, he too joined Spotted Tail on the reservation. At the Crow Agency on the Rosebud Reservation, Hollow Horn Bear was appointed captain of the Indian police. When Spotted Tail was assassinated by the disgruntled Crow Dog in 1881, Hollow Horn Bear hunted down the murderer and arrested him.

In 1889 Hollow Horn Bear, as spokesman-representative of the Brule Sioux, negotiated with General George Crook in the United States government's attempted breakup of the large Indian reservations. Crook was taking advantage of the internal rift among the Brule Indians. Even though Hollow Horn Bear vigorously protested General Crook's tactics, Crook brushed aside the chief's efforts to protect the Indian's basic rights. He went from tribe to tribe to obtain their agreements. Crow Dog signed this agreement.

Hollow Horn Bear rode in Theodore Roosevelt's inaugural parade in Washington, D.C., in 1905, proudly representing all the Indians of the West. In 1923, the U.S. Post Office honored Hollow Horn Bear by picturing him on a 14¢ definitive stamp.

164

Oliver Wendell Holmes

Scott 1288
Born: March 8, 1841, Boston, Massachusetts
Died: March 6, 1935, Washington, D.C.

Oliver Wendell Holmes' father, Oliver Wendell Holmes Sr. (1809-1894), was a physician, educator and author and Boston's unofficial laureate. Two of his best poems, *The Chambered Nautilus* and *One Hoss Shay*, are classics. The senior Holmes was a professor of anatomy at Harvard. He suggested the name for the *Atlantic Monthly* and, by request, was a contributing editor along with James Russell Lowell. Thus, Oliver Wendell Holmes Jr. had a very illustrious parenthood, which undoubtedly steered his thinking. His father had enrolled in Harvard Law School, but found law too dull and switched to medicine, even though the literary field was his first love.

Oliver Wendell Jr., on the other hand, made law his entire life's endeavor. He entered Harvard in 1857, and proved to be a rather unconventional student, influenced by his father and Ralph Waldo Emerson. He graduated in 1861 as the class poet.

He entered the Civil War with the 20th Massachusetts Volunteers as a lieutenant. He saw action at Ball's Bluff, Antietam and Fredericksburg, and was seriously wounded each time. After three years of facing stark reality and deeply influenced by war, he mustered out, a lieutenant colonel, in 1864.

He entered Harvard Law School, earned his law degree in 1866, went on the customary trip to Europe, and then opened a law practice in Boston. He was married to Fanny Bowdith Dixwell of Cambridge from 1872 to 1929, when she died. He became editor of the *American Law Review* and lectured on constitutional law and jurisprudence at Harvard. He wrote the book, *The Common Law* (1881).

In 1882 he was appointed justice of the Massachusetts Supreme Judicial Court; he became chief justice in 1899. At age 60, he was appointed associate justice of the Supreme Court by President Theodore Roosevelt. He served until 1932. His credo was "self-assurance, not just learning, makes the man."

Oliver Wendell Holmes is portrayed on a 15¢ definitive stamp in the 1965-78 Prominent Americans series.

Herbert Clark Hoover

Scott 1269
Born: August 10, 1874, West Branch, Iowa
Died: October 20, 1964, New York, New York

When Herbert Hoover was a boy, his parents died. He was sent to Oregon to live with an uncle. His parents had been Quakers. After high school, at age 17, he entered Stanford University in California, and worked to pay for his education. He graduated in 1895 with an engineering degree. He went to work for Bewick, Moreeing and Company, London, and was sent to Australia in 1897. In 1899 he was assigned to the Chinese government in its Bureau of Mines during the Boxer Rebellion. He married Lou Henry (1874-1944) that year and took her to China with him. She became a partner of his company.

Seven years later, he returned to New York and established his own offices in New York, San Francisco and London. In London he assisted the return of stranded Americans at the onset of World War I.

In late 1914 he was made chairman of the Commission for Relief in Belgium. In 1917 he became U.S. food administrator. In 1921 he was appointed U.S. secretary for commerce under President Harding. He was nominated for the presidency and defeated Alfred E. Smith in 1928. In 1929 he was confronted with the stock market collapse and the Great Depression, which led to his defeat for a second term to Franklin D. Roosevelt.

He retired to private life until 1946, when he served as coordinator of food supply for world famine. He was chairman of the first Hoover Commission in 1947 and the second in 1953, officially known as the Organization of the Executive Branch of the Government. He addressed seven Republican national conventions, the last in Chicago in 1960.

He wrote at least 30 books including *The Ordeal of Woodrow Wilson* and his *Memoirs*, as well as *An American Epic*. He held honorary degrees from 85 U.S. and foreign institutions, was an honorary citizen of 24 European cities, and was awarded 67 gold medals from U.S. and foreign organizations.

Hoover was honored with a 5¢ stamp in 1965, one year after his death.

Johns Hopkins

Scott 2194A
Born: May 19, 1795, "Whitehall," Anne Arundel County, Maryland
Died: December 24, 1873, Baltimore, Maryland

Johns Hopkins was named after his great-great grandfather Richard Johns. The first-known Hopkins ancestor, William Hopkins, was living in Anne Arundel County in 1657. Johns' mother, Hannah, was a member of the Tucker-Janney family of Loudoun County, Virginia. His father, Samuel Hopkins, operated a tobacco plantation. In 1807 Samuel freed his slaves and put his sons to work on the plantation. Johns was 12 and had been going to South River school. Five years later his uncle Gerard, a wholesale grocer and commission merchant in Baltimore, took Johns in with him to learn the business. Two years later Gerard put Johns in charge for several months while he was away in Ohio.

Even while the British fleet threatened the city, Johns carried on with the business extremely well. This gave Johns confidence in himself as a business-man. When Johns was 24, he and his uncle had a dispute when Johns wanted to marry his cousin Elizabeth. His uncle forbade it. Neither Johns nor Elizabeth ever married, but they remained close friends.

In the depressed year of 1819, the country customers could only pay for their goods with whiskey. Gerard objected, and Johns then set up his own business. He succeeded, and he and his brothers, Philip, Gerard and Mahlon, established the Hopkins Brothers. They accepted whiskey for payment and sold it as Hopkins Best.

His business spread to several surrounding states. He expanded his enter-prises into banking, warehousing and railroads. Next to the city and the state, he was the third largest shareholder of the rapidly expanding Baltimore and Ohio Railroad. He invested in steamship lines, insurance companies and banks. His financing saved Baltimore during the Civil War and the 1873 panic. Epidemics of cholera and yellow fever in Baltimore influenced him in 1870 to leave $7 million to build a hospital, nursing school, medical school and a university founded upon European ideas under the influence of philanthropist George Peabody. Both institutions bear Johns Hopkins' name.

Hopkins is portrayed on a $1 Great Americans stamp issued in 1989.

Mark Hopkins

Scott 870
Born: February 4, 1802, near Stockbridge, Massachusetts
Died: June 17, 1887, Williamstown, Massachusetts

In 1824 Mark Hopkins graduated from Williams College, a privately endowed school of liberal arts. The college was a men's school (now co-educational) in Williamstown, Massachusetts. Hopkins attended Berkshire Medical College at Pittsfield, Massachusetts, and graduated with a degree in medicine in 1829. He practiced medicine in New York City but, after a few months, returned to Williams College to accept the chair as professor of moral philosophy and rhetoric and mentor in charge of the senior-class instruction. He remained in this position until his death. He was president of Williams College from 1836 to 1872.

Despite having no formal schooling in theology, he was nevertheless ordained in the Congregational church in 1836. He was the great-nephew of Samuel Hopkins (1721-1803), who was the first Congregationalist to speak out against slavery, and who worked to establish missions in Africa. Samuel Hopkins had been associated with and studied under Jonathan Edwards at the church in Great Barrington (about 10 miles south of Stockbridge). After Edwards left to become president of the College of New Jersey (now Princeton), Samuel liberalized and modified Congregational theology, to what became known as Hopkinsianism.

Therefore, Mark Hopkins' roots had been well-established in the nearby area by Samuel. This no doubt influenced Hopkins' philosophy considerably.

He developed what was called the gospel of wealth. He stressed individualism, the pursuit of wealth and progress and that possession is a form of stewardship. According to Hopkins, wealth should be a trust, administered for the good of society as a whole.

He is portrayed as an educator on a 2¢ stamp in the 1940 Famous Americans series.

Samuel Houston

Scott 1242
Born: March 2, 1793, Rockbridge County, Virginia
Died: July 26, 1863, Huntsville, Texas

Sam Houston grew up near Lexington, Virginia, and the frontier region of Tennessee. When he was 15, rather than take a job in a local store, he lived with the Cherokee Indians for three years. He joined the army and served under Andrew Jackson in the War of 1812. He fought in the Battle of Horseshoe Bend against the Creek. He became an Indian agent and helped move the Cherokee to Arkansas. After five years, he began studying law. In 1823 he was elected to the House of Representatives, and held that position for two terms. He returned to Tennessee and was elected governor for two terms. He married Eliza Allen in January 1829. She deserted him.

He resigned as governor and returned to the Cherokee Indians. He was adopted by them. He traveled to Washington, several times, pleading for equitable treatment of the Indians. President Andrew Jackson sent him to Texas to negotiate with Indian tribes. Texas was agitating for independence, and Houston took up the cause. He attended the San Filipe convention in 1833. He petitioned the Mexican government for statehood, and wrote a state constitution. He settled permanently in Texas in 1835, where he commanded a small army. In April 1836, he defeated and captured General Santa Anna.

In September 1836 he was elected president of the Republic of Texas and served until 1838. From 1838 to 1840, he was in the Texas legislature, and from 1841 to 1844, he was again president. Texas was admitted to the Union in 1845, and Houston was sent to the Senate, where he remained for 14 years as a Union Democrat. He opposed the Kansas-Nebraska Bill.

He was again elected governor in 1859. At first, he opposed secession, then refused to swear allegiance to the Confederacy, for which he was deposed as governor in March 1861. He retired to Huntsville, Texas.

A 5¢ stamp issued in 1964 marks the centenary of Houston's death.

Elias Howe

Scott 892
Born: July 9, 1819, Spencer, Massachusetts
Died: October 3, 1867, Brooklyn, New York

Elias Howe invented the lockstitching sewing machine. Isaac M. Singer became interested in the machine after watching a friend attempt to repair several machines. Singer made a few important changes in the invention, using a straight needle instead of Howe's curved needle. In 1854, after Howe had won a suit against Singer for his royalties, four manufacturers, including Singer and Howe, pooled their patents and expertise, protecting themselves in a sewing machine combination that expired in 1870. From this combination came the mass production of clothing.

Howe grew up on a farm and had little formal education. He was interested in machines and tools and worked in his father's gristmill and sawmill. He later worked as an apprentice in several machine-tool shops and then went to Boston to work for a watchmaker. While apprenticed to a scientific-instrument maker in Cambridge, Howe heard men talking about the idea of a sewing machine. This so inspired him that he went to work on this device. By 1845, he had created the eyed needle to carry the upper thread and a shuttlelike holder to carry the lower thread, working together to fasten stitches. The following year, Howe's machine could sew 250 stitches a minute. He obtained a patent, but his machine did not sell. He took it to England, where a corset manufacturer, William Thomas, bought his machine and the British royalty. Destitute, Howe returned to Boston in 1849. He vindicated his patent rights, formed a company at Bridgeport, Connecticut, and proceeded to put sewing-machine manufacturing on a sound basis. This lasted until the 1870s.

Today, the name of Singer is uppermost in sewing machine manufacturing, but it initially was Howe's invention. Elias Howe appears on a 1940 5¢ stamp from the Famous American Inventors series.

Julia Ward Howe

Scott 2177
Born: May 27, 1819, New York, New York
Died; October 17, 1910, Newport, Rhode Island

Although Julia Howe spent most of her life as a reformer and abolitionist, her claim to fame was that she wrote the words to *The Battle Hymn of the Republic* (1861), which later was sung to the tune of *John Brown's Body*. She wrote the words while she was visiting Union troops under the command of General George B. McClellan near Washington, D.C. in 1861. It was published in the *Atlantic Monthly* magazine in 1861 and became popular with the partisans of the Union cause. Because of the song's success, Howe was the first woman to be elected to the American Academy of Arts and Letters.

She also wrote *Is Polite Society Polite?* (1895), a social criticism. She wrote a biography (*Margaret Fuller*), travel sketches (*A Trip to Cuba*), and three books of verse. Her writings tell of the social and political scene in the latter half of the 19th century.

In 1843 she married Dr. Samuel Gridley Howe (1801-1876), who was 18 years her senior. He was a teacher of the blind in Europe. He taught in Boston in 1832 at the New England Asylum for the Blind, later called the Perkins School for the Blind. He worked with books for the blind, using raised type (Boston line type) and became known for teaching the deaf-blind child, Laura Bridgman. This encouraged other states to establish schools for the deaf and blind, to which he gave his expertise. He supported Horace Mann in his fight for better public schools. He aided Dorothea Dix in her crusade.

Julia and Samuel were active abolitionists and supporters of John Brown. They edited the major abolitionist periodical called the *Commonwealth*. Julia Howe was president of the New England Woman Suffrage Association. She died at age 91.

A 14¢ stamp issued in 1987 in the Great Americans series honors Howe.

171

Charles Evans Hughes

Scott 1195
Born: April 11, 1862, Glens Falls, New York
Died: April 27, 1948, Osterville, Massachusetts

Charles Evans Hughes' parents were the Reverend David Charles Hughes and Mary Catherine Connelly Hughes. Charles was their only son. He graduated from Brown University in 1881. Hughes studied law and taught for a few years, then entered Columbia Law School, where he graduated with honors in 1884. From 1891 to 1893, he taught at Cornell Law School.

In 1905 he was nominated for mayor of New York, but declined the nomination. The next year he accepted the nomination for governor, defeating William Randolph Hearst. During Hughes' two terms (1906-10), he instigated reform of the state's government. In 1910 he was appointed to the Supreme Court by President Taft. In 1916 he resigned from the court to run for president. He was narrowly defeated by incumbent Woodrow Wilson. Hughes' loss was primarily due to the fear that the Republicans might take the United States into World War I. After his defeat, he retired to a private law practice. President Wilson promptly took the United States into war.

Under President Harding, Hughes was appointed secretary of state. He was involved in negotiating a separate peace treaty with Germany, organized the Washington Disarmament Conference in 1921 and the Open Door policy in China, and negotiated a 15-nation treaty at the Pan American Conference. He was a member of the Hague Tribunal and served as a judge at the World Court in the Hague.

In 1930 President Herbert Hoover appointed Hughes chief justice of the Supreme Court. Hughes took a middle-of-the-road stance when the court began to question the constitutionality of President Roosevelt's New Deal legislation. However, his decision against the National Industrial Recovery Act showed his conservatism. Hughes denounced President Roosevelt's proposed court-packing plan in 1937, resulting in its defeat. He retired in 1941.

The 4¢ Charles Evans Hughes issue was released in 1962.

Cordell Hull

Scott 1235
Born: October 2, 1871, Byrdstown, Tennessee
Died: July 23, 1955, Bethesda, Maryland

Cordell Hull went to Montvale College in Celina, Tennessee, then on to the National Normal University in Lebanon, Connecticut, in 1889. An avowed Democrat, he transferred to Cumberland University Law School in 1890, graduated and was admitted to the bar in 1891. In 1893 he was on his way in politics to the state legislature. He recruited a company of volunteers and served with the 4th Tennessee regiment in Cuba in the Spanish-American War. In 1903 Hull was elected a Tennessee circuit court judge. From 1907 to 1931, except for one term, he served in the House of Representatives. He prepared the first federal income-tax bill in 1913 and its revision later. In 1916 he wrote the federal inheritance-tax law.

Hull supported Woodrow Wilson in the League of Nations and his non-trade barriers for the promotion of world peace. In 1931 he was elected to the Senate. Two years later he was appointed secretary of state under President Franklin D. Roosevelt. He attended four Pan American conferences formulating the good-neighbor policy: Montevideo (1933), Buenos Aires (1936), Lima (1938), and Havana (1940). He was instrumental in getting the passage of the Trade Agreements Act passed in 1934 to stimulate trade with the Latin American countries and give power to the president to adjust tariffs.

The outbreak of World War II thwarted hopes of neutrality, and Hull backed President Roosevelt's programs of supporting the Allies. In 1943 he headed the delegation to the conference of foreign ministers in Moscow.

He attended the Dumbarton Oaks Conference in Washington, where the basis for the founding of the United Nations at San Francisco was organized. President Roosevelt called him the Father of the United Nations.

In that same year he won the Nobel Peace Prize for his peace efforts. Hull is depicted on a 1963 5¢ issue.

Washington Irving

Scott 859
Born: April 3, 1783, New York, New York
Died: November 28, 1859, "Sunnyside," Tarrytown, New York

Washington Irving's father owned an importing firm. The family was well-to-do and provided Washington with a home life of learning and culture. He did not see the need for going to school or college. He studied and apprenticed himself to a lawyer. He spent the better part of six years traveling. He spent time in Europe from to 1804 to 1806 for his health.

During this period, he wrote for his brother's *Morning Chronicle*, and produced satirical "Letters of Jonathan Oldstyle, Gent." About 1806 he returned to New York and was admitted to the bar. In the next two years, he published *Salmagundi: Or, the Whim-Whams and Opinions of Launcelot Langstaff, Esq. and Others*. In 1809 he published a comic history of Dutch New York, A History of New York by "Diedrich Knickerbocker." He also published poetry by Thomas Campbell and edited the *Analectic Magazine*, while lobbying for the family firm.

He took a position on the governor's military staff during the War of 1812. He then sailed to England on behalf of the family importing business. He associated with Sir Walter Scott and other literacy figures.

The family firm went bankrupt, and he returned to writing. In 1819 and 1820 he published in England and the United States *The Sketch Book of Goeffrey Crayon, Gent* , which contained *Rip Van Winkle, The Legend of Sleepy Hollow*, and *The Spectre Bridegroom*, which are considered the first modern short stories.

Later he was secretary to the U.S. legation in London (1829-1832), and U.S. minister to Spain (1842-1846), between which time he established his home, "Sunnyside," on the Hudson River, near Tarrytown. In the mid-1830s he traveled west and wrote adventure stories. As a historian, he wrote about Columbus and produced five volumes on George Washington.

Washington Irving's portrait appears on the 1¢ Authors stamp of the 1940 Famous Americans series.

Queen Isabella I

Scott 244
Born: April 22, 1451, Madrigal, Old Castile, Spain
Died: November 26, 1504, Medina del Campo, Spain

Isabella was the queen of Castile. She was the legitimate daughter of John II of Castile and Isabella of Portugal. Her half-brother, Henry IV, died, and she was heir to the throne. However she had to contest her claim with Juana la Beltraneja, whom her half-brother Henry had claimed as his daughter, though this turned out to be doubtful. Isabella's victory was due in part to the generalship of her husband Ferdinand of Aragon, whom she had married in 1469. Thus the two ruled over Castile, and Leon and Aragon.

Her chief mission as queen was to expand the power of the royalty.

Isabella had blue eyes, a clear, fresh complexion that graced her handsome regular features framed by auburn hair, so admired by the Spanish because of its rarity. Her manners were gracious, dignified and affable. She showed tact and intelligence in dealing with people, which made her a great ruler. Her tastes were simple. She was temperate in her diet, and did not overdo frivolous entertainment. Nevertheless, she showed tendencies to intolerance and bigotry.

Christopher Columbus convinced the sovereigns that his Enterprise of the Indies was possible. However, their finances were strained by war with the Moorish kingdom of Grenada. They could not back him. Columbus had given up hope of the sovereigns financing his plans of discovery, even though the queen had pledged her jewels. Dejected and downhearted, he packed his mule, took what little money he had earned and was joined by his friend Fray Juan. The two departed Sante Fe and set out for France.

The queen was persuaded by Luis de Santangel, the family treasurer, to back the voyage. Grenada, the last remaining Moorish stronghold in Spain was captured. Isabella sent a messenger to find Columbus. He returned to the court in Santa Fe, and the long-awaited for voyage became a reality.

Isabella is shown with Columbus on the $4 value of the 1893 Columbian Exposition issue.

Andrew Jackson

Scott 2216g
Born: March 15, 1767, Waxhaw Settlement, South Carolina
Died: June 8, 1845, Hermitage Plantation, Nashville, Tennessee

Andrew Jackson was the third son of immigrant parents, Andrew Jackson and Elizabeth Hutchinson, from northern Ireland. Andrew was born in a frontier settlement along Crawford's Creek, a branch of Waxhaw Creek, in north-central South Carolina. Andrew's father died a few days before he was born. Young Andrew served in the American Revolution as a messenger when he was 12 years old and, for a time, was a British prisoner. During the war, his mother and his two brothers died of illness. Jackson moved west to the Tennessee territory. He studied law in Salisbury, North Carolina, and was admitted to the bar at age 20. In 1788 he used his legal training to collect debts. He married Rachel Robards, whose divorce had been in question.

In the 1790s he served in the Tennessee Constitutional Convention, the U.S. House of Representatives and the Senate. He built the Hermitage plantation in Nashville.

In 1812 he was made commander of the Tennessee troops against the Creeks. He defeated the Indians at Horseshoe Bend in 1814. He won the Battle of New Orleans as a major general. He then invaded Florida, captured Pensacola, and was involved in the scandal for hanging two Englishmen.

He returned to the Senate in 1823. In 1824 he lost his first bid for the presidency to John Quincy Adams. However, in 1828 he won handily over Adams. As president, he greatly expanded the power and prestige of the office of chief executive, developed domestic reform and moved toward a hard-money currency policy. He was easily re-elected in 1832 over Henry Clay. He had differences with his vice-president, John C. Calhoun, and instead selected Martin Van Buren, who succeeded him as the eighth president. "Old Hickory" Jackson retired to his Hermitage as a gentleman farmer.

Jackson is shown on one of the 22¢ stamps from the Presidential sheetlets issued in 1986 for the Ameripex international stamp show.

176

Thomas Jonathan Jackson

Scott 788
Born: January 21, 1824, Clarksburg, West Virginia
Died: May 10, 1863, Guinea Station, Chancellorsville, Virginia

Thomas "Stonewall" Jackson was one of Confederate General Robert E. Lee's ablest lieutenants. He received a sketchy education and was unprepared for the Military Academy. However, when one candidate resigned, Jackson filled his place. He graduated in 1846 and chose the artillery. He went to Mexico as a second lieutenant with K Company under General Zachary Taylor, then transferred to General Winfield Scott's army and participated in the Vera Cruz and Cerro Gordo battles. He earned the rank of major at the end of the Mexican war because of his outstanding soldiering and remained in Mexico in the occupation force.

After a tour of duty in various eastern forts, he was sent to the Seminole Indian Department. Following an altercation with the post commander, he resigned from the army. He taught for 10 years at the Virginia Military Institute at Lexington, Virginia. He married Eleanor Junkin in 1854. She died in childbirth. He married Mary Ann Morrison in 1857.

When John Brown was hung in October 1859, Jackson took some of his Virginia Military Institute cadets to witness the incident. He remained a Union man until Virginia seceded in April 1861. He received a commission as colonel in the Virginia state forces and defended Harpers Ferry for the Confederates. He turned the post over and assumed command of Shenandoah. He won the Battle of Falling Waters and was made brigadier general. He went to aid General Beauregard at Manassas and fought like a "stone wall" at the Battle of Bull Run.

In 1861 he was commissioned a major general. His campaign against Romney, Virginia, was unsuccessful, but his later Shenandoah Valley campaign ended up victorious, making him a Confederate hero. He won the second Battle of Bull Run. He won numerous battles. He was defeated at Fredericksburg, his last battle, in December 1862. On reconnaissance in May 1863, he was mistaken for a Federal and shot in the left arm. The arm was amputated, but he contracted pneumonia and died.

"Stonewall" Jackson is portrayed with Robert E. Lee on the 4¢ stamp of the 1936-37 Army issue.

177

John Jay

Scott 1046
Born: December 12, 1745, New York, New York
Died: May 17, 1829, Bedford, New York

John Jay was well-qualified for diplomatic service. Coming from a family of wealth, John Jay was able to receive an excellent education. In 1764 he attended King's College (now Columbia University), and earned a master-of-arts degree in 1767, studying law. He was admitted to the bar in 1768 and practiced law for six years. He married Sarah van Brugh Livingston, daughter of New Jersey's Governor William Livingston. To them were born two sons, Peter and William.

His first political assignment was in 1773 as secretary to the Royal Mixed Commission. He opposed independence as a member of the Continental Congress, but when the vote went in favor of independence, he supported it with unwavering patriotism. On July 6, 1776, he drafted the resolutions confirming independence for the New York Provincial Congress. On December 10, 1778, he was elected president of the Continental Congress.

In September 1779, congress sent Jay to Madrid to seek aid and Spain's recognition of United States independence. Both were flatly denied despite concessions. In 1782 Jay joined John Adams and Benjamin Franklin for the peace commission, which culminated in the Treaty of Paris in 1783. Jay returned to New York to find that he had been selected secretary for foreign affairs, a position with which he struggled for the next six years.

He was a strong supporter of the Constitution and contributed five essays to the Federalist papers (1787-1788). When the new government became activated in 1789, he was the first chief justice of the Supreme Court. Thomas Jefferson assumed Jay's foreign affairs duties as secretary of state.

Jay organized the Supreme Court and established the court's procedures. He returned and resigned from the Supreme Court to serve two terms as governor of New York before retiring in 1801.

John Jay is shown on the 15¢ Liberty series stamp issued in 1958.

178

John Robinson Jeffers

Scott 1485
Born: January 10, 1887, Pittsburgh, Pennsylvania
Died: January 20, 1962, Carmel, California

In 1914 John Robinson Jeffers' uncle died and left him an estate. This relieved him of the necessity of working for a living. Before this time, he had pursued a career in medicine. He graduated from Occidental College in Los Angeles in 1905. He studied medicine at the University of Southern California and at the University of Zurich. He later studied forestry at the University of Washington in Seattle. He quit school and settled in Carmel, California. He built his own home on a cliff overlooking the Pacific Ocean.

He wrote poetry that was pessimistic and bitter. He expressed his feelings with sharp expressions and in clearly defined terms.

His work is best described as a modern adaptation of ancient Greek tragedies, such as Euripede's *Medea*. His version of this tragedy was produced on Broadway. His first two volumes of poems, *Flagons and Apples* and *Californians*, were traditional in both subject and form.

His post-graduate studies in science and medicine influenced his work. He implied anti-humanistic and anti-religious tones, especially in *Tamar and Other Poems* (1924). *Dear Judas and Other Poems* (1929) recalls the Passion but with Judas as the hero and Jesus as the traitor because Christ advocated love, which, according to Jeffers, is the trap that keeps man from welcoming annihilation.

Oswald Spengler (1880-1936) diagnosed Western civilization as being in a state of decline. He predicted worldwide struggle, paving the way for the rise of Hitler. In *The Double Axe and Other Poems* (1948), Jeffers offended his readers with his Spenglerian comments about World War II.

Jeffers is shown on an 8¢ stamp in the 1973 American Arts issue.

179

Thomas Jefferson

Scott 1278
Born: April 13, 1743, Shadwell, Albermarle County, Virginia
Died: July 4, 1826, Monticello, near Charlottesville, Virginia

Thomas Jefferson studied at the College of William and Mary in Williamsburg, Virginia, from 1760 to 1762. He was the son of Peter Jefferson, a well-to-do planter and surveyor, and Jane Randolph, a member of a well-known Virginia family. He attended private schools that emphasized the classics. It was with Governor Francis Fauquier that he read law (1762-1769).

He married the wealthy Martha Wayles Skelton in 1772, thus doubling his land inheritance. He began building his beautiful Monticello.

As a delegate to the Continental Congress, he drafted the Declaration of Independence. In 1776 he entered the Virginia House of Delegates. He served as the second governor of Virginia, but quit that post when the British invaded Virginia in 1781. He was sent to Congress in 1783. In 1785 he was appointed minister to France. In 1789 Washington appointed him secretary of state. Because of his opposition to Hamilton, he resigned on the last day of 1793.

In 1796 he was elected vice president of the United States. He continued to be the spiritual leader opposing Federalism.

He was elected the third U.S. president in 1801 by the House of Representatives as a result of Hamilton's decision to throw the Federalist votes to him rather than to Aaron Burr, who had tied him in electoral votes. He was the first president to be inaugurated in Washington.

The purchase of Louisiana from France in 1803 was the most notable act of his administration. Re-elected in 1804, he kept the United States out of the Napoleonic Wars by employing the unpopular embargo policy.

He retired to Monticello in 1809. He helped found the University of Virginia in 1819, thus pursuing his never-flagging interests in education. He died on the 50th anniversary of the proclamation of the Declaration of Independence, a few hours in advance of John Adams. He is shown on a 1986 22¢ Presidents stamp.

Andrew Johnson

Scott 822
Born: December 29, 1808, Raleigh, North Carolina
Died: July 31, 1875, Carter Station, Tennessee

Andrew Johnson was born in a one-story log cabin. His father died when Andrew was three years old, leaving the family impoverished. His mother remarried, and when Andrew was 10, he was apprenticed to a tailor. He had no formal education, learning much on his own. When his parents moved to Greeneville, Tennessee, he opened his own tailor shop. He married Eliza McCardle in 1827. They had five children. He soon became involved in politics and served in the House of Representatives (1843-1854), as governor of Tennessee (1853-1857) and as senator (1857-1862). He was primarily a Jacksonian Democrat, fighting for a more equitable land policy.

As a senator, he stood by the Union during the Civil War, the only Southern senator to do so. In 1863 he became war governor of Tennessee and carried out his office with great courage under difficult circumstances. In 1864 he became Lincoln's running mate to make a balanced ticket.

When Lincoln was assassinated, Johnson succeeded him as president and tried to continue Lincoln's policies. But he did not have the same skill. He came into hopeless conflict with the Radical Republicans, who were able to dominate the Congress, passing measures over his vetoes. They attempted to limit the executive powers of appointments and removals of office with the Tenure of Office Act, a conscious effort by Congress to usurp presidential power. Johnson tested its constitutionality by removing E.M. Stanton as secretary of war and appointing U.S. Grant.

On February 25, 1867, Johnson was formally impeached. The trial followed, but the vote was one short of the two-thirds majority needed for conviction. Johnson left office embittered.

The purchase of Alaska and the removal of French forces from Mexico in 1867 occurred during his presidency. He returned to the Senate in 1875 but died a few months after taking office.

His portrait appears on the 17¢ value of the 1938-43 Presidential series.

181

James Weldon Johnson

Scott 2371
Born: June 17, 1871, Jacksonville, Florida
Died: June 26, 1938, near Wiscasset, Maine

James W. Johnson is best remembered for his novel *The Autobiography of an Ex-Colored Man* (1912) and his work with the National Association for the Advancement of Colored People (NAACP). He was secretary of the NAACP from 1916 to 1930. His novel, which many people believed was his own life story, was more an essay than a work of fiction. It listed many of the grievances the black society had against the racial policies of the white society. Johnson is also known for his poetry, especially his *God's Trombones: Negro Sermons in Verse*, based on negro folk preaching. He wrote a history of the black theater in New York, *Black Manhattan*. He edited *The Book of American Negro Poetry* and *Negro Spirituals*.

Johnson graduated from high school in Atlanta, then the Atlanta University in 1894. He returned to Jacksonville to establish a secondary school for blacks and was principal of their school. He studied law at this time and was admitted to the Florida bar in 1897, the first black to do so.

With his brother, John Rosamond Johnson, he wrote songs. Especially notable are *Congo Love Song, Since You Went Away* and *Lift Every Voice and Sing*, which later became the black national anthem. In 1901 he went to New York City to continue his studies. He earned his master-of-arts degree from Atlanta University. He also studied at Columbia University. He aided Theodore Roosevelt in his campaign for president and in 1906 was appointed consul in Porto Cabrello, Venezuela. He was the consul in Corinto, Nicaragua, from 1909 to 1912. He was awarded the NAACP's Springarn Medal in 1925. He was professor of creative literature at Fisk University and visiting professor at New York University from 1934. He received an honorary doctorate from Talladega College, Alabama, and Howard University.

At age 62, Johnson was killed in an automobile crash. A 22¢ stamp in the Black Heritage series was released in 1988 honoring Johnson.

182

Lyndon Baines Johnson

Scott 1503
Born: August 27, 1908, Stonewall, Texas
Died: January 22, 1973, LBJ Ranch, San Antonio, Texas

Lyndon B. Johnson came from a family of preachers and teachers. His father and grandfather served in the Texas House of Representatives. Lyndon Johnson graduated from Southwest Texas State Teachers College and taught school for two years, then accepted a position as secretary to Representative Richard M. Kleberg in 1932. Johnson and Claudia Alta Taylor were married that same year. Mrs. Johnson was popularly known as "Lady Bird." Two daughters were born to them.

Johnson was an ardent supporter of Franklin Roosevelt and an avid Democrat. He became administrator in Texas for the National Youth Administration in 1935, and in 1937 he was elected to Congress. During World War II, he served in the Navy in the Pacific.

In 1948 he was elected to the Senate, and by 1953 he was the Senate Democratic leader. He sought the nomination for the presidency in 1960 but lost to John F. Kennedy. Surprisingly, he accepted the vice presidency.

On November 22, 1963, in a motorcade in Dallas, Texas, Kennedy was shot and killed. Johnson immediately took the oath of office in the presidential jet at the airport. As president, he enacted the civil-rights bill, the voting-rights bill, a Medicare program, an educational improvement bill, and declared war on poverty. In 1964 he was elected president over Republican Barry Goldwater. His Great Society program turned to expanding the Vietnam conflict and dispatching troops to the Dominican Republic to fight communism. Opposition to his administration's policy grew, and his popularity ebbed. On March 31, 1968, he announced that he would not seek or accept re-election. The assassinations of Martin Luther King Jr. and Robert F. Kennedy sent the Democratic National Convention into shambles.

Johnson retired in January 1969 to his LBJ ranch. He suffered a fatal heart attack in 1973. An 8¢ stamp was released that year to honor Johnson.

Louis Joliet

Scott 1356
Born: Baptized September 21, 1645, near Quebec, New France (now Canada)
Died: circa May 1700, on an island in the St. Lawrence River, Quebec

Louis Joliet left Canada for France in 1667 and took up the study of hydrography. He had originally studied for the priesthood, taking minor clerical orders in 1663 when he was 18 years old. But he saw a greater future in mapping the waterways of North America.

In 1668, he returned to New France (Canada) and took up fur trading in the Great Lakes country, establishing a fur-trading post at Sault Sainte Marie, near Lake Superior. He met Father Jacques Marquette, the Jesuit missionary, at Sault Sainte Marie. An Iroquois Indian guide returned Joliet to Quebec by way of Lake Huron and the Detroit River into Lake Erie, establishing a new route for the French from Quebec to their western trading posts.

By 1671, Simon Francois Daumont, the Sieur de St. Lusson, was accompanied by Joliet back to Sault Sainte Marie where Daumont formally annexed the Upper Great Lakes to New France. Joliet had become well-acquainted with the Indian tribes around the Great Lakes and knew well the waterways and the terrain. The Ojibway Indians of the Wisconsin forests spoke of a stream that flowed south. The Indians called it "Missi Sipi." Joliet knew this meant "Great River."

Comte de Frontenac et de Palluau, the governor of New France, hoped that the river would lead to the Pacific Ocean, and thus be a passageway to the Orient. Frontenac commissioned Joliet to explore the Great River. Joliet took two canoes. In his party, he included Father Marquette and five voyageurs. In May 1673, the explorers left from St. Ignace, now in Upper Michigan near Mackinac Island. They went to Green Bay, ascended the Fox River, portaged to the Wisconsin River and descended to the Mississippi. After a month, they were floating down the Mississippi, finally reaching the Arkansas River in July. They knew that it emptied into the Gulf of Mexico and not the Pacific, so they returned to Green Bay, but by a different route. They portaged over the area that is now Illinois, including what became Chicago, covering a total of 3,000 miles and opening the area for settlement and colonization.

Joliet was a hydrographer and skilled cartographer. On the 1968 Father Marquette stamp, he is seated in the canoe and is holding a map.

John (Casey) Jones

Scott 993
Born: March 14, 1864, Cayce, Kentucky
Died: April 30, 1900, Vaughan, Mississippi

John Luther Jones grew up near Cayce, Kentucky, and became a railroad worker at age 16. In 1890, he became an engineer on the Illinois Central Railroad. Since he came from the town of Cayce, he was nicknamed Casey by his fellow workers.

Jones was the throttle-puller on the Illinois Central *Cannonball*. On April 30, 1900, he was making a run on Number 382 for a friend who was ill. Near Vaughan, Mississippi, he was shoveling for more steam ahead, when the main track was suddenly blocked by two freight trains. Jones stayed with the train and jammed on the brakes. He died in the crash, but saved the lives of his passengers and crew.

His death in the collision was immortalized in a ballad originally composed by Wallace Saunders, a black railroad worker. The ballad has since been revised in many versions. In 1938 a bronze tablet in Jones' honor was dedicated at Cayce, Kentucky. The Casey Jones State Museum was erected at Vaughan, Mississippi.

The T. Lawrence Siebert version of the song's first verse and chorus sets the flavor of the ballad:
"Come all you rounders that want to hear
"The story of a brave engineer.
"Casey Jones was the rounder's name,
"On a big eight wheeler, boys, he won his fame.
"Casey Jones mounted on his cabin
"Casey Jones with his orders in his hand.
"Casey Jones mounted in his cabin,
"And he took his farewell trip to the promised land."

When they found his body in the wreckage, one hand was on the throttle, and one hand was on the brake. Jones became a railroader's hero, especially because of the labor movement in the early 1900s.

The Railroad Engineers issue of 1950 features two trains and a picture of Casey Jones.

John Paul Jones

I have not yet begun to fight

John Paul Jones
US Bicentennial 15c

Scott 1789
Born: July 6, 1747, Arbigland, Scotland
Died: July 18, 1792, Paris, France; entombed U.S. Naval Academy chapel

When John Paul Jr. was 12 years old, his father apprenticed him to a merchant shipper as a cabin boy. He sailed to Fredericksburg, Virginia. By 1769 he had his own ship, the *John*. Paul was accused of murder, for whipping the ship's carpenter, but was cleared. In 1773 he commanded a ship in the West Indies and again killed a man, causing him to flee to Fredericksburg and change his name to Jones. For the American Revolution, John Paul Jones was commissioned senior lieutenant of the Continental navy.

In 1776, on the *Alfred*, he sailed to the Bahamas, under the Grand Union flag, under command of Esek Hopkins. The small fleet captured war goods at New Providence. He commanded the sloop *Providence* and in August captured several prizes. In October he took command of the *Alfred*, returned to the Bahamas and in December won more prizes.

He sailed the frigate *Ranger* in 1778 to France to buy the *Indien*, but it was sold to France instead. He sailed the *Ranger* around the British Isles and captured a sloop. In August 1779 he sailed on the *Bonhomme Richard* around the British Isles and again captured prizes. In September he confronted the *Serapis* escorting a Baltic trading fleet and engaged it in a fierce battle. Advised to surrender he replied, "I have not yet begun to fight!" The *Serapis* surrendered, but the *Bonhomme Richard* sank. He cruised the *Alliance*, returning to Paris, where he was honored by Louis XVI.

In 1781 Congress appointed him to command the huge 74-gun *America*, but the ship was given to France. He went to France to negotiate war payments and to Denmark on a similar mission.

In 1788 Empress Catherine commissioned him rear admiral in the Russian navy. He served against Turkey, was dismissed in 1789 and retired to Paris. John Paul Jones is honored on a 1979 15¢ stamp.

Robert Tyre Jones Jr.

Scott 1933
Born: March 17, 1902, Atlanta, Georgia
Died: December 18, 1971, Atlanta, Georgia

Bobby Jones, the pride of Atlanta, was the world's greatest amateur golfer. With his smooth swing and his putter, nicknamed "Calamity Jane," he established a record that has never been equaled, the "Grand Slam of Golf." The Grand Slam involves winning the four major tournaments in a single year. In 1930, Jones won the United States Open, the U.S. Amateur, the British Amateur and the British Open. He won 13 of the 27 major tournaments in which he competed. He was a member of the U.S. Walker Cup team five times between 1922 and 1930. In 1930 Jones made a series of golfing films.

He began playing golf when he was a boy. He won a junior tournament when he was nine years old. In 1916, at age 14, he was Georgia state champion. That year he advanced as far as the third round of the U.S. National Amateur tournament. Jones graduated from the Georgia School (now Institute) of Technology in 1922 and received a degree in English literature from Harvard in 1924. He studied law at Emery University, Atlanta, 1926-27. He was admitted to the Georgia bar in 1928 and opened a law practice in Atlanta.

He helped establish the Augusta National Golf Club, and in 1934 he founded the prestigious annual Masters tournament at Augusta. Because of his golfing ability, Jones was nicknamed "Emperor Jones," but he quit tournament play at age 28. In 1948 he was confined to a wheelchair after suffering a crippling back injury. In 1958 he became the first American since Benjamin Franklin to be honored with the freedom of the burgh of St. Andrews, Scotland, site of the world's most famous golf course. In 1960 he published the book *Golf is My Game.*

He is pictured on a 1981 18¢ stamp wearing plus fours. He made the sports knickers, four inches longer than ordinary knickers, the popular golf attire of his era.

187

Scott Joplin

Scott 2044
Born: November 24, 1868, Texarkana, Arkansas
Died: April 11, 1917, New York, New York

Scott Joplin earned his living traveling up and down the Mississippi valley doing odd jobs and playing the piano. He spent time in St. Louis, playing in honky-tonks. He worked at the World's Columbian Exposition in Chicago in 1893 as a band leader. He moved to Sedalia, Missouri, in 1896, where he attended George Smith College for Negroes. He studied harmony and composition seriously. He and his fellow musicians were the attraction at such bistros as the Maple Leaf Club in the sporting district of Sedalia. As the "professor" (the piano player) at the club, he met music publisher John Stark. Stark published Joplin's first ragtime piece to appear in sheet music, his *Original Rag*, and the most famous of American jazz compositions, his *Maple Leaf Rag Time* (1899).

Stark and Joplin moved to St. Louis. Joplin established the basis for the evolving school of jazz that was developing. The inspiration came from tunes in the cake walks of the Negroes, and the polkas, quadrilles, minuets and waltzes, which were currently popular in New Orleans, Memphis and St. Louis, adding typical Negro rhythmic complications in conflict with the 2/2 or 4/4 time. The peculiarities of ragtime boil down to its lively syncopated rhythm and the fact that it is almost exclusively connected with the piano.

Joplin also wrote *Sugar Cane Rag*, *Wall Street Rag* and *Gladiolus Rag*. He wrote two ambitious ragtime operas, *A Guest of Honor*, produced in St. Louis in 1903, and *Tremonisha*, which he produced in New York City's Harlem for a single performance in 1911. Joplin's ragtime has been hailed as "the precise American equivalent, in terms of a native style of dance music, of minuets by Mozart, mazurkas by Chopin, or waltzes by Brahms." A 20¢ Black Heritage stamp was issued in 1983 to honor Joplin.

Chief Joseph

Scott 1364
Born: 1840, Joseph Creek, Wallowa Valley, Oregon
Died: September 21, 1904, Nespelem, Washington

Young Chief Joseph's grave is located just north of the town of Nespelem, in the Colville Indian Reservation, near the Nespelem River in Washington. On his monument is inscribed: "HIN-MAH-TOO-YAH-LAT-KEKT/ Thunder Rolling in the Mountain ***Erected June 20, 1905, by the Washington University State Historical Society*** He led his people in the Nez Perce War of 1877/Died Sept. 21, 1904/Aged about 60 years."

His father, Twaeet Tu-Eda-Kas, became the head of the Wallowa Nez Perce. Old Joseph was a Cayuse, and his squaw was a Nez Perce. Blind and enfeebled near the end of his life, Old Joseph told his sons, Ollokat and young Joseph, "Never sell your country." Old Joseph had been baptized by the Presbyterian missionary H.H. Spalding at the Lapwai Mission in November 1839. Old Joseph took his children to Spalding to be baptized, but in their later lives they turned away from Christianity, for to them their land was sacred and their beliefs were not harmonious with that of the white man's. The white man was taking away their sacred land.

It was the discovery of gold in the Salmon River in western Idaho that precipitated an invasion of the country of the peaceful Nez Perce. Chief Joseph struck back, but to no avail. In 1877 he began a retreat eastward over 1,500 miles of mountain and plain that remains the most memorable feat in the annals of Indian warfare. Near the Canadian border the feeble remnants of the Nez Perce were captured and exiled to Oklahoma.

Chief Joseph spoke for all his race, "I am tired of fighting. Our chiefs are killed. The little children are freezing to death. I want to have time to look for my children and see how many of them I can find. Maybe I can find them among the dead. Hear me, my chiefs. My heart is sick and sad. I am tired."

The 1968 6¢ American Indian issue depicts the noble Chief Joseph.

Kamehameha I

Scott 799
Born: 1737 (?), Kohala, Hawaii
Died: May 8, 1819, Kailua, Hawaii

In 1782 Kamehameha I conquered all but two of the Sandwich Islands, and in 1795 he made himself ruler. The other two islands, Kauai and Niihau, joined him in 1810. He allowed trade with foreign ships and established a workable government on his islands. He put an end to feudal anarchy and petty wars. Kamehameha prepared the way for a more civilized way of living and for the admission of Christian missionaries, although he himself clung to the religion of his ancestors.

Just where Kamehameha's grave is located is an unsolved mystery. When he was dying, he told his high chief, Ulumaheihei Hoapili, "You must hide my remains. The people who hid my father's body betrayed him when they revealed the hiding place."

Kamehameha's head queen was Keopuolani. When Kamehameha I died, the throne went to their son, Liholiho, who then called himself Kamehameha II. He encouraged Christianity and trade with foreign countries, especially the United States. He destroyed pagan temples and idols, and abolished the ancient taboo system. He was supported strongly by Queen Kaahamanu, the favorite wife of Kamehameha I, who proclaimed herself regent of the islands.

In 1842 the United States recognized the independence of the islands and received Pearl Harbor as a coaling and naval station in 1887. In 1891 Lydia Lilluokalani became queen, and in 1893 she attempted a coup d'etat. American marines landed to protect the islanders and soon set up a provisional government. On July 4, 1894, the Republic of Hawaii was established. In 1898 the islands were transferred to the United States as a territory, and finally, in 1940, the electorate of Hawaii voted 2-to-1 in favor of statehood.

A statue of Kamehameha I represents Hawaii in Statuary Hall in Washington, D.C. The 1937 Hawaii Territorial issue shows a statue of him.

Elisha Kent Kane

Scott 2220
Born: February 3, 1820, Philadelphia, Pennsylvania
Died: February 16, 1857, Havana, Cuba

Elisha Kent Kane began his education in 1838 at the University of Virginia with hopes of becoming an engineer. About this time, he became ill with rheumatic fever, which permanently damaged his heart valves.

He transferred to medical school at the University of Pennsylvania. In 1843, Kane received his medical degree and joined the Navy as a surgeon to get medical experience and to see the world. He spent time in India, China, Ceylon and the Philippines. In the Philippine Islands, he explored the crater of a volcano.

Kane served in Africa and contracted a lingering fever that further damaged his health. He returned to the United States and served in the Mexican War with distinction.

In 1850, he was assigned to the U.S. Coast Survey.

Kane's first assignment was with naval Lieutenant E.J. DeHaven in the first Grinnell expedition to seek out information on the lost British arctic explorer, Sir John Franklin. Franklin was searching for the elusive Northwest Passage and disappeared in the Lancaster Sound region just west from Baffin Bay. They found no trace of Franklin, but Kane wrote about his experience in *The U.S. Grinnell Expedition in Search of Sir John Franklin.* This book was reissued in 1915 as *Adrift in the Arctic Ice Pack.*

In May 1853, Kane sailed again, commanding the *Advance* with the same mission. He passed through Smith Sound to new waters not before described. These waters are now called Kane Basin. The *Advance* became frozen in ice. The brig traveled 1,200 miles through icy waters and arrived half way down the west coast of Greenland in August 1855. Kane wrote *The Second Grinnell Expedition for Sir John Franklin, 1853, '54, '55* in 1856.

He traveled to England and then to Havana, Cuba, where he died in 1857.

In 1857, Captain MacLintock's expedition discovered Franklin's records. Sir Franklin died June 11, 1845, and was buried at sea.

Kane is depicted on one of the block of four 22¢ Arctic Explorers stamps released May 28, 1986.

Stephen Watts Kearny

Scott 944
Born: August 30, 1794, Newark, New Jersey
Died: October 31, 1848, St. Louis, Missouri

Seven miles east of the town of Kearney in south central Nebraska was once Fort Kearny. Kearney was originally named Kearny Junction in 1871. When the town was incorporated in 1873, an "e" found its way into the spelling and remained. The fort was established in 1848 for the protection of settlers traversing the region along the Oregon Trail in wagon trains. When the railroad was established in 1871, the fort was no longer needed.

Fort Kearny and the subsequent town were named for Stephen Watts Kearny. Kearny attended Columbia College in 1811, but left the next year to serve in the War of 1812. He served for many years with General Henry Atkinson on the western frontier. Kearny fought in many Indian battles and established outposts.

In May 1846, Kearny was named commander of the Army of the West, and shortly after that he was promoted to the rank of brigadier general. As commander of the Army of the West, he marched 1,700 men into Santa Fe, New Mexico, on August 18, 1846, and for a month served as the military governor. He then headed west to California and joined up with Commander Robert F. Stockton. By January 1847, Kearny had taken San Diego, San Gabriel and Los Angeles. The defeated Californians surrendered to Fremont, not Stockton or Kearny. Kearny won final authority, promptly removed Fremont and court-martialed him. Fremont resigned from the Army.

Kearny was military governor of California until August 1847. In September 1848, he was sent from Fort Leavenworth, Kansas, to Mexico, where he served as governor general of Veracruz and, later, Mexico City. In September, he was promoted to major general, despite the opposition strenuously offered by Senator Thomas Hart Benton (Lieutenant Colonel John C. Fremont's father-in-law). Kearny contracted a tropical disease and died six weeks later in St. Louis.

The 1946 Kearny Expedition issue commemorates the 100th anniversary of General Kearny's capture of Santa Fe.

Helen Adams Keller

Scott 1824
Born: June 27, 1880, Tuscumbia, Alabama
Died: June 1, 1968, Westport, Connecticut

At age 19 months, Helen Keller was left blind, deaf and dumb by a severe fever. When she was six, Alexander Graham Bell examined her and put her in the hands of Anne Mansfield Sullivan from the Perkins Institute in Boston, which Bell's son-in-law directed. Sullivan (later Mrs. John A. Macy) remained with Keller until 1936, the year of Sullivan's death. After the death of Sullivan, Keller depended upon her secretary, Polly Thomson.

Sullivan communicated with Keller by a touch system. She taught her to read Braille and to write on a special typewriter. In 1890, soon after she was 10 years old, Keller learned to speak through special instructions from Sarah Fuller of the Horace Mann School for the Deaf in Boston. She attended the Wright-Humason School for the Deaf in New York City from ages 14 to 16 (1894-1896) and the Cambridge School for Young Ladies from ages 16 to 20. She entered Radcliffe College and in four years graduated with honors.

Keller devoted her life to stimulating public interest in and support for the physically handicapped. She lectured, wrote several books and made one motion picture based on her life. She appeared on the Orpheum circuit for two years to help support herself and to expose her handicap to the public to show how the handicapped can be helped. She served on the Massachusetts Commission for the Blind.

Following World War II, she visited American Veterans' Hospitals and made tours abroad to encourage and lend hope to all handicapped people.

Among her several books were *The Story of My Life* (1903) and *Midstream—My Later Life* (1930). Her last was *The Open Door* (1957).

Helen Keller and Anne Sullivan are portrayed on a 15¢ stamp issued in 1980 to mark the centenary of Keller's birth.

John Fitzgerald Kennedy

Scott 2219h
Born: May 29, 1917, Brookline (Boston), Massachusetts
Died: November 22, 1963, Dallas, Texas

John F. Kennedy's credo, "Ask not what your country can do for you —
ask what you can do for your county," appealed to the youthful, vigorous,
confident and politically pragmatic intellectual. John was the second son of
Joseph P. and Rose Kennedy. He was educated in private schools, entered
Princeton at age 18, transferred to Harvard, and graduated in 1940. He served
as secretary to his father, who was then U.S. ambassador in London. During
that time, he wrote and published *Why England Slept.*

John Kennedy worked at Stanford University before enlisting in the navy
in 1941. He commanded a PT boat. He was discharged from the navy in 1945
and entered politics. He was elected to the House of Representatives and re-
elected in 1948 and 1950. In 1952 he defeated Henry Cabot Lodge for the U.S.
Senate. In 1952 he married Jacqueline Lee Bouvier of Newport and Washington. In 1956 he published *Profiles in Courage.*

Kennedy was re-elected to the Senate in 1958. In November 1960 he was
elected president, defeating Richard M. Nixon. He was the youngest man
inaugurated and the first Catholic ever to serve as president. He instigated the
New Frontier program, and was immensely popular.

The negatives that occurred during his administration were the ill-con-
ceived Bay of Pigs Cuban invasion, the building of the Berlin Wall, and the
Cuban missile crisis in October 1962, as well as intensifying conflicts in Laos
and Vietnam. The Alliance for Progress, aimed to aid Latin America, and the
Peace Corps program were positive actions.

Kennedy favored civil-rights and integration movements headed by
Martin Luther King Jr. With the Soviet Union in September 1963 he signed
the treaty banning all but underground tests of nuclear devices. The next
month he was shot and killed by Lee Harvey Oswald in Dallas.

He is portrayed on a 22¢ Presidents stamp issued in 1986.

Robert Francis Kennedy

Scott 1770
Born: November 20, 1925, Brookline (Boston), Massachusetts
Died: June 6, 1968, Los Angeles, California

Robert was the younger brother of John Fitzgerald Kennedy, sons of Joseph P. and Rose Kennedy. He was a graduate of Harvard (1948) and the University of Virginia Law School (1951). His goal was public service. He began as an attorney for the criminal division of the Department of Justice. He resigned that post to manage John F. Kennedy's campaign for the U.S. Senate seat from Massachusetts in 1952.

Robert Kennedy served on several Senate committee staffs. From 1958 to 1960, he was the chief counsel of the Select Committee on Improper Activities in the Labor or Management Field leading up to the jailing of James R. Hoffa, president of the International Brotherhood of Teamsters. In 1960 he managed his brother's campaign for the Democratic presidential nomination and then for the presidential race.

When John became president, Robert was appointed attorney general. After John was assassinated, Robert remained attorney general under President Lyndon B. Johnson but resigned in 1964 to run for U.S. Senate from New York. He won the election in November.

In March he announced his candidacy for the Democratic presidential nomination. When President Johnson announced he would not accept the nomination for re-election, it enhanced Robert's chances for the nomination. However, the state primaries were mixed. In June he appeared to have won the nomination from Senator Eugene J. McCarthy in the important state of California and was celebrating his victory at the Ambassador Hotel in Los Angeles when he was shot by an Arab immigrant, Sirhan Bishara Sirhan. He died 25 hours later in Good Samaritan Hospital in Los Angeles. He was survived by his wife, Ethel Skakel Kennedy, and 10 children. The eleventh child was born after Robert's death.

Robert Kennedy was honored with a 15¢ stamp issued in 1979.

Jerome David Kern

Scott 2110
Born: January 27, 1885, New York, New York
Died: November 11, 1945, New York, New York

Jerome Kern's musical compositions were being published at the rate of two or more a year from 1910 until 1942. Although he was born in New York City and died there, he actually spent only the first 10 years of his life in New York City and then moved to Newark, New Jersey. Kern started writing songs while he was still in high school in Newark. He went back to New York in 1902 to study piano and harmony at the New York College of Music. He continued his studies in England and Germany, supporting himself by writing music for various London musical shows. In 1910 he wrote his first complete musical, *Mr. Wix of Wickham.*

A steady worker, Kern produced almost a show a year, with hits like *The Red Petticoat* (1912) and *The Girl from Utah* (1914), which introduced the song *They Didn't Believe Me.*

Have a Heart was adapted for the 1916 *Ziegfield Follies.* On many of his shows, he collaborated with other playwrights and songwriters. His greatest production was in collaboration with Oscar Hammerstein II in 1929 to produce the classic *Show Boat* adapted from Edna Ferber's novel by the same name. *Show Boat* was a story about a theatrical family on the Mississippi River. It introduced such songs as *Can't Help Loving That Man, Why Do I Love You, Only Make Believe, Bill, You Are Love,* and especially *Ol' Man River,* sung by Jules Bledsoe and later in the movie by Paul Robson. This song dared to present, for the first time in a musical play, a dignified tragic black man. Other Kern favorites are *I've Told Every Little Star* from *Music in the Air, The Way You Look Tonight* from *Swing* (1939), *All the Things You Are* from *Very Warm for May, Smoke Gets in Your Eyes* from *Roberta* (1933) and many more.

Jerome Kern is featured on a 1985 22¢ Performing Arts issue.

196

Francis Scott Key

Scott 962
Born: August 1, 1779, Frederick (now Carroll) County, Maryland
Died: January 11, 1843, Baltimore, Maryland

Francis Scott Key began practicing law in Fredericktown, Maryland, in 1801 after he graduated from St. John's College. After one year in Fredericktown, he moved to Georgetown, near Washington, D.C., and became a successful attorney. A Maryland physician, Dr. William Beanes, was being held prisoner on a British ship retiring from the burning of Washington in the War of 1812. Key was sent to the ship to negotiate the release of the doctor. His mission was successful, but while he was returning to Washington, he was detained when the British fired on Baltimore during the night of September 13-14, 1814. The ship he was on lay off the besieged Fort McHenry.

At dawn, Key looked to see if the American flag on Fort McHenry was still flying. It was. He dashed off a verse, "Defence of Fort M'Henry." A flyer with his poem on it was circulated around Baltimore the next day and was published in the newspaper. It was set to the oft-sung English drinking song, *To Anacreon in Heaven* and became a patriotic song throughout the colonies.

Key's other poems and writings were of little note. However his credo, "And this is our Motto, in God is our Trust," became a standby.

He practiced law in Georgetown and Washington the rest of his life and held the office of U.S. attorney for the District of Columbia from 1833 to 1841. His song, *Defence of Fort M'Henry*, continued to be popular. In 1889 it was adopted by the U.S. Navy, and by the Army in 1903. It continued to be the number one patriotic song and the unofficial national anthem under the title *The Star Spangled Banner*.

In 1931 it was adopted as the official national anthem by Congress. Some objections have been raised because the song is difficult to sing and because it is oriented to war.

Key is honored on a 3¢ stamp issued in 1948.

Martin Luther King Jr.

Scott 1771
Born: January 15, 1929, Atlanta, Georgia
Died: April 4, 1968, Memphis, Tennessee

Born Michael Luther Jr., his father changed their names to Martin Luther King. Young Martin entered Morehouse College at 15, was ordained a minister in 1947 and graduated from Morehouse in 1947. At Crozer Theological Seminary, he received a bachelor of divinity degree in 1951 and was deeply influenced by the Gandhian philosophy of passive resistance. He was awarded a doctorate of philosophy from Boston University in 1955.

In December 1955, in Montgomery, Alabama, Rosa Parks was arrested because she refused to give up her seat on a bus to a white man. This led to a boycott of Montgomery's segregated buses by the black community. Martin Luther King Jr., the young minister of the Dexter Avenue Baptist Church in Montgomery, was placed in charge of the boycott, which marked the beginning of the civil-rights movement.

After a year of agitation, the Supreme Court ruled against racial discrimination in interstate and intrastate transportation. This success led to the formation of the Southern Christian Leadership Conference early in 1957 in an effort to broaden civil-rights activities over the entire South.

In 1959 King moved to Atlanta as co-pastor in his father's Ebenezer Baptist Church. He was conspicuous in his leadership in anti-discrimination demonstrations and voter registration drives at Selma and Birmingham, Alabama, and Albany, Georgia. In his famed March on Washington in 1963, he immortalized himself with his forceful sermon-speech, "I Have A Dream."

In December 1964 King was awarded the Nobel Peace Prize. He carried his campaign to the North. He met with bigoted opponents, was jailed, stoned and beaten. His home was bombed, and he received many threats on his life. On April 4, in Memphis, Tennessee, he was shot to death by a sniper, James Earl Ray.

King is portrayed on a 15¢ Black Heritage stamp issued in 1979.

198

Henry Knox

Scott 1851
Born: July 25, 1750, Boston, Massachusetts
Died: October 25, 1806, Thomaston, Maine

Henry Knox was the seventh of 10 sons born to Scottish-Irish immigrants. He quit school when he was 12 to work in a bookstore to support himself and his mother. When he was of age, he opened his own bookshop and was successful. He gave up business in 1772 to become a soldier in the Boston Grenadier Corps. He specialized in artillery. He married the daughter of the royal secretary of the province in 1774. Despite lucrative offers to remain loyal to the crown, he left Boston with his wife and was commissioned a colonel in charge of the Continental army artillery in 1775.

Ethan Allan had captured 55 British artillery pieces at Ticonderoga. Knox hauled them back to use against the British. He captured Boston in March 1776 and forced the British to leave, including his in-laws.

Knox was adviser to General George Washington. He was closely involved in almost every important engagement of the war, including Yorktown. He was at New York, and was with Washington at the crossing of the Delaware. After the Battle of Trenton, he was promoted to brigadier general. He was with Washington at Valley Forge.

Knox helped found military academies and sat on court-martials. In 1781 he was promoted to major general. In December 1783, when Washington bade farewell to his officers, Knox was the first to shake Washington's hand. From 1782 to 1784, he commanded the fort at West Point. He organized the Society of the Cincinnati in 1783 and was its secretary for years. Congress elected him secretary of war. When Washington became the first U.S. president, Knox was retained on the cabinet.

Knox's quarrels with Alexander Hamilton muddied his tenure of office. In December 1794 he resigned and retired to his estate at Montpelier, Thomaston, Maine. On October 25, 1806, he choked to death on a chicken bone.

Knox is shown on an 8¢ stamp issued in 1985 as part of the Great Americans series.

199

Thaddeus Kosciusko

Scott 734
Born: February 12, 1746, Bolorussia, Grand Duchy of Lithuania
Died: October 15, 1817, Solothurn, Switzerland

Thaddeus Kosciusko (also spelled Tadeusz Kosciuszko) learned to read and write from an aged uncle who took an interest in his learning. The young Kosciusko read Plutarch's *Lives*, which tells of 50 distinguished Greeks and Romans. The book inspired him for military glory. Kosciusko was commissioned a captain in the Polish army shortly after he graduated from the Royal School at Warsaw in 1769.

Bored with no active duty, he went to Paris to study military engineering and painting. In Paris, Kosciusko heard about the American Revolution, which stirred him to apply to Benjamin Franklin for service in the Continental Army. He was accepted and arrived in Philadelphia in August 1776. He was commissioned a colonel of engineers on October 18, 1776. He served with valor at Ticonderoga and contributed substantially to the victory over General John Burgoyne at Saratoga. In 1778 Kosciusko was in charge of building West Point. In addition, he served with Gates and Greene in the Carolina campaigns. In 1784 he left New York for Paris, looking for more action. Instead he returned to rural life in Poland.

Kosciusko was back in action in 1789 as a major general, leading a weak contingent of Poles against the Russians. Poland became divided again in 1793. Kosciusko retired to France, but returned to Poland in 1794 to lead an uprising. He was defeated by the overpowering Russians and taken prisoner. Czar Paul I, however, decided to set him free if he promised he would never again take up arms against Russia.

The United States paid Kosciusko what he had earned during the American Revolution, plus 500 acres of Ohio land. He retired to Fontainebleau. He kept his promise to the czar and refused to aid Napoleon against Russia in 1806.

Kosciusko moved to Switzerland in 1816. The next year, he was thrown from a horse and died. His remains were removed to Krakow and interred in the cathedral. Money from his U.S. estate went to establishing the Colored School at Newark, New Jersey, and to freeing slaves.

A 1933 5¢ stamp honored the Polish soldier.

Lajos Kossuth

Scott 1117
Born: September 19, 1802, Monok, Hungary
Died: March 20, 1894, Turin, Italy

Hungarian independence from Austria was Lajos Kossuth's goal, although his family came from noble rank and provided for him a fine education in law. He practiced law and entered the Parliament in Pest as the deputy of absent magnates. However, at the same time, he edited a newspaper that had to be printed in manuscript because of the stringent press laws. In this manner he published the parliamentary debates, and for that he was condemned to four years imprisonment in 1837. He was released in 1840.

From 1840 to 1844, he edited the *Pest Journal*, a paper with advanced views of reform. In 1844 he organized the National League in opposition to the Viennese government. The National Party elected him to the Hungarian Diet in 1847, and the following year he became minister of finance in the Hungarian government. He headed the insurrection in 1848 and was made dictator. But Kossuth resigned on August 11, 1849, when Russia intervened against the Magyars. Arthur von Gorgey replaced him.

Kossuth accused von Gorgey of treachery and took refuge in Turkey. There he was imprisoned until 1851, when Great Britain and the United States intervened for him. He thereafter visited both countries and received a hero's welcome. Without success, he attempted to enlist the aid of both Victor Emmanuel II of Italy and Napoleon III of France to act against Austria on Hungary's behalf. Hungary offered Kossuth amnesty to return home, but he refused. He could not reconcile to the union of Austria and Hungary. He remained in Italy.

His son, Ferenc Kossuth (1841-1914), was an engineer prior to 1894. Born in Budapest, Ferenc returned to Hungary following the restoration of the constitution. He became a leader of the party of independence in the Hungarian parliament, and in 1906 he was the minister of commerce in the Sandor Wekerle cabinet.

Lajos Kossuth was often called the Hungarian George Washington by Americans. He is depicted on the 1958 4¢ Champion of Liberty issue.

Marquis de Lafayette

Scott 1716
Born: September 6, 1757, Chateau Chavaniac, Auvergne, France
Died: May 20, 1834, Paris, France

In 1770, at age 13, Lafayette inherited the family wealth. Marie Joseph Paul Yves Roch Gilbert du Motier, the Marquis de Lafayette, attended the College du Plessis from 1768 to 1771. He enlisted in the company of musketeers and later transferred to a regiment of dragoons. He arranged, through Silas Deane in Paris, for a commission in the Continental Army. In July 1777 he was commissioned a major general. The young general proved himself in the Battle of Brandywine on September 11, 1777, and was wounded. He was given his own command and spent the winter with George Washington at Valley Forge. He was appointed to lead the expedition into Canada, which failed.

As liaison with France, he was instrumental in establishing a growing alliance. In 1779 the Marquis returned to France a hero and worked to obtain aid from that country, obtaining a force under Count de Rochambeau.

Lafayette was restored to his command of Virginia's light troops. In April 1781 he held a command in the campaign in Virginia against General Cornwallis, which led to the final capitulation at Yorktown and the virtual end of the war. In 1782 he returned to France. He came to the United States in 1784, then returned to France to play an important role in the French Revolution, after which he was in command of the Paris militia.

By 1790, he and the king were the two most powerful figures in France. He again went to war in 1791 against Austria but was captured. He remained for five years (1792-1797). He returned to France in 1799. Not until 1815 was he active again. He sat in the Chamber of Deputies in 1815 and again from 1818 to 1824. When Lafayette visited America in 1824, President Monroe gave him land and money. Lafayette laid the corner stone for the Bunker Hill monument. He again served in the Chamber of Deputies in 1830, supporting liberal causes and attacking Louis Philippe for unkept promises.

Lafayette is portrayed on a 13¢ stamp issued in 1977 as part of the American Bicentennial issue.

Fiorello Henry La Guardia

Scott 1397
Born: December 11, 1882, New York, New York
Died: September 20, 1947, New York, New York

Because Fiorello Henry La Guardia advanced welfare for so many people in need and fought against crime and graft, he was called the chronic dissenter by those he opposed. Those who held him in high esteem for his commitments to his needed programs, however, called him by his Italian first name, Little Flower.

Fiorello Henry La Guardia attended high school in Prescott, Arizona, then went to St. Louis as a reporter on the *St. Louis Dispatch*. At age 16, he worked in Budapest at the United States Consulate and then went to the Trieste and Fiume Consulates, ending up at Ellis Island as an interpreter. While in New York, he attended the New York University law school. La Guardia graduated in 1910 and was admitted to the bar.

In the 14th Congressional District he had established a free-of-fee legal-aid bureau to represent poor people in court. He was easily elected to the House of Representatives on the Republican ticket in 1916. La Guardia commanded an American bombing squadron on the Italian-Austrian front in World War I and returned to finish his term in 1918. He was president of the New York City board of aldermen in 1920-21 and was re-elected to the House of Representatives in 1922.

He championed child labor laws and women suffrage, opposed Prohibition and pork-barrel legislation, and exposed some federal judges for graft. In 1933 he unseated Tammany Hall in New York City's election for mayor. He was re-elected twice. La Guardia went to work on everything from slums and gangsters to official corruption. He improved the fire and police departments, and built bridges, roads, health clinics, low-cost housing, playgrounds and an airport that bears his name.

In 1941 he was named director of the U.S. Office of Civilian Defense, and in March 1946 he became director general of the United Nations Relief and Rehabilitation Agency. He resigned from that post in December 1946.

La Guardia is shown in front of the New York City skyline on the 1972 14¢ regular issue.

Samuel Pierpont Langley

Scott C118
Born: August 22, 1834, Roxbury, Massachusetts
Died: February 27, 1906, Aiken, South Carolina

Samuel P. Langley is often mentioned in the early historical writings concerning aviation. He was on the verge of flying man in a heavier-than-air machine, but as bad luck would have it, his flying machine plummeted into the Potomac. It seems the charts he used to calculate the air pressure on curved surfaces, the basis of aerodynamics, were inaccurate.

Langley was a man who learned by studying and experimenting. His formal education went no further than high school, where his main interest was astronomy. He graduated in 1851. In 1857 he went to Chicago and then St. Louis, where he worked in engineering and architecture. Near the end of the Civil War, he sailed to Europe with his brother, John Williams Langley, for travel and study. After a year, he returned and was given an assistantship at the Harvard Observatory. The next year he taught mathematics at the U.S. Naval Academy. For 20 years he was professor of physics and astronomy at the Western University of Pennsylvania (now the University of Pittsburgh) and the director of the Allegheny Observatory.

In 1878 he invented the bolometer, an instrument that detects and measures minute amounts of radiant energy. He led an expedition in 1881 to Mount Whitney in California to test his bolometer. He measured the solar constant (heat falling on the earth from the sun). This is used to measure light from stars, infrared radiation and the power output of microwave equipment.

In 1887 he moved to Washington, D.C., as secretary of the Smithsonian Institution. In Washington he established the Astrophysical Observatory and the National Zoological Park.

Langley experimented with flying machines. He was 62 when he first demonstrated any notable success. On May 6, 1896, near Washington, D.C., his steam engine *Aerodrome No. 5* flew over the Potomac River. The War Department had allocated $50,000 toward his experiments.

Langley never succeeded in getting man off the ground in a flying machine, but he was still alive to learn about the successes of the Wright brothers at Kitty Hawk on December 17, 1903. In late 1905 Langley suffered a paralytic stroke and died the next year.

Langley is portrayed on a 45¢ airmail stamp issued in 1988.

Sidney Lanier

Scott 1446
Born: February 3, 1842, Macon, Georgia
Died: September 7, 1881, Lynn, North Carolina

In his short lifetime, Sidney Lanier contributed some lasting works to American literature. He was a musician and a teacher, as well as a poet and a writer. Early in life, Lanier developed a deep interest in music and literature. He graduated from Oglethorpe University in 1860. He joined the fight for the Confederacy in 1861 and served three years. In 1864, he was captured and imprisoned in Maryland. While he was in prison, Lanier contracted tuberculosis, which gradually led to his early death.

After the Civil War, he went to work in his father's law office. During this time, he wrote his first book, *Tiger-Lilies*. This first accomplishment prompted him to devote his time to the arts.

Lanier left his father's law office and moved to Baltimore, where he became the first flutist with the Peabody Orchestra. In 1875, he finished two of his finest poetic works, *Corn* and *The Symphony*. Both were well-received. For the 1876 exposition in Philadelphia, he contributed the *Centennial Meditations*. In 1879 Lanier was appointed a lecturer in English literature at Johns Hopkins University. He extended his study of poetry and produced *The Science of English Verse* in 1880 and *The English Novel* in 1883. In the spring of 1881, he went to the mountains in North Carolina in quest of regaining his health. However, he died in September.

A book, *Poems*, was published three years after his death. It included many favorite works, such as *The Marshes of Glynn*.

Had it not been for the devastating Civil War and his imprisonment where he contracted consumption, Lanier may have lived to become one of America's major poets.

He is honored with the 8¢ Sidney Lanier issue released in 1972.

Frank Charles Laubach

Scott 1864
Born: September 2, 1884, Benton, Pennsylvania
Died: June 11, 1970, Benton, Pennsylvania

Frank Charles Laubach was the son of John Brittain and Harriet L. Laubach. The younger Laubach studied at Bloomsbury, Pennsylvania, then progressed to the State Normal School in 1901. He was a student at the Perkiomen Seminary from 1904 to 1905 and received his bachelor of arts degree at Princeton University in 1909. Laubach studied at the Student Union Theological Seminary from 1911 to 1914. He married Effa Seely on May 15, 1912, and he received his master of arts and doctor of philosophy degrees from Columbia University in 1915. To add to his diplomata, he was later awarded a doctor of philanthropy degree in 1952 and a doctor of Hebrew literature from Wooster College in 1950.

Laubach was an American missionary, preacher and educator who won international recognition for teaching illiterate people to read. His system used symbols to represent phonetic sound. He first used the system while serving as a missionary in the Philippines from 1915 to 1936. Governments of many countries later sponsored his program. Laubach co-authored more than 200 primers in more than 165 languages for illiterate adults. His creative phonetic methods of combining letters and pictures to educate people who had no previous schooling in reading and writing was very effective. They could be applied to many different languages in many different countries and were even helpful in regular schools for persons with reading difficulties.

He also developed alphabets and written languages in remote areas where previously none existed. Among his many books, *Forty Years with the Silent Billion* was not only an explanation of his methods, but also was somewhat of an autobiographical treatise. His work has been extended and expanded, and is in continuous use.

Frank Laubach is honored on a 1984 30¢ commemorative in the Great Americans issue.

206

Jason Lee

Scott 964
Born: June 28, 1803, Stanstead, Ontario, Canada
Died: March 28, 1845, Stanstead, Ontario, Canada

At age 23, Jason Lee was converted to Methodism and promptly attended Wesleyan Academy in Massachusetts. He returned to his hometown of Stanstead, Vermont (now Stanstead, Quebec, Canada), and served as a minister for two years. The New England conference of the Methodist Episcopal Church wanted to establish a mission for the Flathead Indians in the Oregon country. Lee was selected to head the mission.

Lee and his party reached Fort Vancouver in September 1834. They were joined by Nathaniel J. Wyeth's expedition. Together, they were able to establish a base in the Willamette Valley, near present-day Salem, Oregon. Other settlements were soon established in the valley.

In 1838 Lee traveled east and petitioned Congress for territorial status for Oregon. In 1840 he returned to Oregon by sea with a reinforcement of 50 persons. He was more bent on the settlement of Oregon by white people, than on missionizing the Indians. He established the Oregon Institute in 1842 (later Willamette University), the first institution of higher learning in the far west.

By 1843, following an initial meeting in 1841 at Champoeg, a territorial government was established with Lee at the leadership. Because of the fear that Lee was taking too many liberties in overexpansion, the missionary society replaced him. He learned of this while he was on his way back east in 1844. Other misunderstandings were also involved in his removal as a missionary.

Lee defended himself admirably and was exonerated from the charges, but he was not reappointed to his missionary posts.

He returned to his hometown in ill health and disappointed that his accomplishments were not understood by the New England conference of the Methodist Episcopal Church. The situation in the West was too far away from the church heads in the East for them to comprehend.

A statue of Lee represents the state of Oregon in Statuary Hall. The 1948 Oregon Territory issue features Lee, John McLoughlin and a wagon on the Oregon Trail.

Robert Edward Lee

Scott 788
Born: January 19, 1807, Stratford, Westmoreland County, Virginia
Died: October 12, 1870, Lexington, Virginia

Robert E. Lee was the son of Henry ("Light-Horse Harry") Lee. Robert attended school in Alexandria. In 1825 he was appointed to West Point, graduating in 1829. He was assigned to work on Mississippi River projects and Atlantic coastal defenses. In 1846 he joined General Winfield Scott in Mexico and, by distinguished service, rose to the rank of colonel. In 1852 he was appointed superintendent at West Point until 1855, when he was sent to command a frontier cavalry regiment in Texas.

While on leave in October 1859, he was ordered to Harpers Ferry to dislodge John Brown from the federal arsenal. Secession began. Lee declined an offer of the command of all Federal forces and, instead, accepted an appointment as commander of the Virginia forces with the rank of general. As military adviser to Confederate President Jefferson Davis, he was sent to fortify the southern Atlantic coastal region.

In March 1862 Lee sent General "Stonewall" Jackson on his spectacular Valley Campaign. Lee commanded the Army of Northern Virginia in 1862. In the Seven Days' Battles (June 26-July 2, 1862), he forced General McClellan to retreat and defeated General John Pope at the second Battle of Bull Run (Manassas). In December 1862 he repulsed General Burnside's attack at Fredericksburg and won a major victory at Chancellorsville, where "Stonewall" Jackson died.

From July 1 to 3, 1863, Lee met his disastrous defeat at Gettysburg. In May 1856 General Grant headed for Richmond with a force twice that of Lee's. Lee fought defensively, finally entrenched hopelessly at Petersburg.

In February 1865, he was named general-in-chief of all the armies of the failing Confederacy. Richmond fell, and Lee surrendered at Appomattox Courthouse on April 9, 1865. Afterward, he was the president of Washington College in Lexington, Virginia. The college was renamed Washington and Lee University in 1870.

Lee is portrayed on the 4¢ stamp in the 1936-37 Army issue.

Vivien Leigh

Scott 2446
Born: November 5, 1913, Darjeeling, India
Died: July 7, 1967, London, England

Of the several actresses considered for the role of Scarlet O'Hara in the 1939 movie *Gone With the Wind*, the selection of Vivien Leigh was a stroke of excellent casting. She perfectly complimented Clark Gable, who played the male lead Rhett Butler. For her portrayal of this role, she received an Academy Award. In 1940 she married actor Sir Laurence Olivier. She won her second Oscar in the role of Blanche du Bois in Tennessee Williams' *A Streetcar Named Desire* in 1952.

Leigh gained her first notable role in London on the stage in *The Mask of Virtue* in 1935. After her marriage, she appeared in *Romeo and Juliet* in New York in 1940, *The Skin of Our Teeth* in London in 1945. She led London's Old Vic Company to Australia and New Zealand in 1948.

In 1949 she was back in London starring in *Antigone* by the French dramatist Jean Anouilh, written in 1942 during the war and the German occupation of France with the Vichy regime.

With her husband, Sir Laurence Olivier, Vivien Leigh provided theater-goers with a dramatistic delight. Like her leading man, Clark Gable, Sir Laurence had many of the desirable qualities of a great actor. He had striking good looks. He had inherent aristocratic intelligence and likewise developed most all of the other features of a great actor. These qualities complemented his actress-wife and partner of 20 years.

In the United States, Vivien Leigh is most often associated with her role in *Gone With the Wind*. She also won many awards for other acting contributions to the stage and screen. In 1957 she won the Knight's Cross of the Legion of Honor and in 1965 a French award for her portrayal of an American divorcee in her last Hollywood film, *Ship of Fools*.

She died while rehearsing Edward Albee's play, *A Delicate Balance*. She was suffering from tuberculosis.

Leigh is shown with Clark Gable in a scene from *Gone With the Wind* on a 25¢ stamp issued in 1990. The stamp is part of the Classic Films set.

Harry Sinclair Lewis

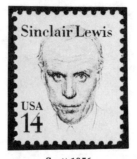

Scott 1856
Born: February 7, 1885, Sauk Centre, Minnesota
Died: January 10, 1951, Rome, Italy

Harry Lewis was a small-town renegade. He had two older brothers. One became a successful surgeon and the other a hometown galoot. Harry Sinclair was somewhere in between. He was awkward, odd-looking and a loudmouth. To prepare for college, he went to Oberlin Academy in Ohio. He was a Yale graduate, although he left Yale in his senior year to spend time with Upton Sinclair's Helicon Hall, a socialist community in New Jersey. He was a janitor. He knew he wanted to be a writer and dropped the Harry from his name. In his lifetime, he produced 22 novels and three plays, as well as numerous short stories for the *Saturday Evening Post* and other popular magazines. In 1930 Sinclair Lewis was the first American to win the Nobel Prize for literature. He won the Pulitzer Prize in 1926 but refused it.

In 1914 he married Grace Hegger, who was on the staff of *Vogue* magazine. Their marriage lasted until early 1928. They had a son, Wells Lewis, a brilliant young man, who was killed in World War II. In May 1928, Sinclair Lewis married American journalist Dorothy Thompson. Their marriage soon fell apart, but was not legally dissolved until 1942. They, too, had one son, Michael, who became an actor.

In the 1940s Sinclair Lewis tried the theater, but was unsuccessful as a dramatist and as a summer-stock actor. He was well-to-do financially, but traveled around a lonely lost person in decline. Alcohol was one of his problems. He died in Rome, Italy, and his ashes were returned to Sauk Centre, Minnesota. Lewis' first major work was *Main Street* (1920), then *Babbit* (1922). *Arrowsmith* appeared in 1925 and *Elmer Gantry* in 1927. In 1929 *Dodsworth* was published and *It Can't Happen Here* in 1935. *Kingsblood Royal* (1947) was his last work. Lewis appears on a 14¢ stamp issued in 1985 as part of the Great Americans series.

Meriwether Lewis

Scott 1063
Born: August 18, 1774, near Charlottesville, Albermarle County, Virginia
Died: October 11, 1809, on Natches Trace, near Nashville, Tennessee

Meriwether Lewis had been a longtime friend of Thomas Jefferson. He spent his early years in Virginia. His family then moved to Georgia. He returned to Virginia for his education, then entered the local militia. In 1794 he took part in the Whiskey Rebellion, then enlisted in the regular army and served until he became Jefferson's aide in 1801. For a period he served under William Clark.

In 1801 Jefferson began laying plans for Lewis' expedition. On November 30, 1803, the Louisiana Territory was handed over by the Spanish governor to the French prefect. Three weeks later it was transferred to the United States. Jefferson did not wait long to send his friend, Lewis, and William Clark on a quest to find a waterway to the Pacific. The logical route was up the Missouri River from St. Louis. They followed to what is now Bismark, North Dakota. They stayed at Fort Mandan for the winter. They proceeded up the Missouri, having acquired guides Toussaint Charbonneau and his Shoshone wife, Sacagawea. They followed the Missouri, crossed the Rockies at Lemhi Pass, then canoed down the Clearwater, Snake and Columbia rivers to the Pacific Ocean and established Fort Clatsop (Astoria, Oregon). After several months, they set out on their return trip, floating downstream on the Missouri to St. Louis. Jefferson was delighted with their report when they returned in 1806, even though no waterway was found to the Pacific Ocean.

Lewis was made governor of the new Louisiana Territory in 1807. On a return trip to Washington, in October 1809, he was mysteriously killed along the Natchez Trace south of Nashville.

Meriwether Lewis is show with William Clark and Sacagawea on a 3¢ stamp issued in 1954 to mark the 150th anniversary of the expedition.

211

Abraham Lincoln

Scott 1036
Born: February 12, 1809, near Hodgenville, Kentucky
Died: April 15, 1865, Washington, D.C.

Abraham Lincoln was born in a log cabin in Hardin County, Kentucky. From the time he was a young boy, he learned the meaning of hard work. He learned early in life to study. He was raised in Indiana and Illinois, where he split rails for fences. He also worked on Mississippi flatboats, and helped run a country store. He served in the Black Hawk War. He was postmaster at New Salem, Illinois, and was an assistant county surveyor. This gave him the means to study law and politics.

He served two terms in the Illinois legislature and went to Congress for a term in the House of Representatives. He also practiced law in Springfield, Illinois. When he received the nomination for the presidency in 1860, he left his law practice. On March 14, 1861, be became the 16th president of the United States.

Immediately after the election in November 1860, South Carolina seceded from the nation, followed by six other southern states. A month before Lincoln took office, these states formed the Confederate States of America with Jefferson Davis as their president. Lincoln said to the South, "You can have no conflict without being yourselves the aggressors . . ."

On April 12 the Confederates fired on Fort Sumter in Charleston Harbor. The fort surrendered in two days. The Civil War began. In the 1864 election, Lincoln won by a large margin over Democrat George B. McClellan. On April 9, 1865, Confederate General Robert E. Lee surrendered his entire army after evacuating the town of Richmond, Virginia, and the next day Lincoln and General Sherman entered Richmond. Lincoln returned to Washington and gave his last public speech.

On April 14, 1865, Lincoln attended Ford's Theater, where Laura Keen was performing in *Our American Cousin*. John Wilkes Booth entered Lincoln's box and shot him in the head. He died the next morning.

Lincoln's portrait appears on the 4¢ stamp of the 1954-73 Liberty series.

Thomas 'Tad' Lincoln

A Nation of
Readers
USA 20c

Scott 2106
Born: April 4, 1853, Springfield, Illinois
Died: July 15, 1871, Springfield, Illinois

Thomas Lincoln, called "Tad," was the youngest of the four sons of Mary Todd Lincoln and Abraham Lincoln. The oldest son, Robert Todd (1843-1926), became a well-educated attorney, businessman and public official.

Robert was a graduate of Phillips Exeter Academy and Harvard University (1864). The Lincolns' second son, Edward Baker (1846-1850), died at the early age of four. The third son, William Wallace (1850-1862), died at age 12. Tad outlived his father but still died at the young age of 18.

An early photograph taken in 1861 shows the Lincoln family of mother, father and sons Thomas, William and Robert. In the picture, Abraham Lincoln is reading to Tad, then age eight. A 1984 20¢ stamp, honoring a Nation of Readers, was based on an 1865 photograph taken by Matthew Brady, not the 1861 photograph.

Abraham Lincoln, who had only the barest formal education, undoubtedly wanted his sons to have the education he was denied. When Abe was only nine, his mother died of milk sickness.

In 1819 Abraham Lincoln's widower father married Sara Bush Johnston, a kindly, hard-working widow with three children. In the next two years, she saw to it that Abe received enough additional schooling to be able "to read, write and cipher to the rule of three," as Abe often reported. He was eager to learn more. He borrowed books wherever he went. His favorites were *Robinson Crusoe*, *Pilgrim's Progress*, Aesop's *Fables*, William Grimshaw's *History of the United States*, and Parson Weems' *Life and Memorable Actions of George Washington*.

The only book that young Abe Lincoln's family owned was the Bible. He read it so many times he could quote any portion of the scriptures that fitted his needs. Abe's father, Thomas, whom Tad was named for, could barely scrawl his name.

213

Walter Lippmann

Scott 1849
Born: September 23, 1889, New York, New York
Died: December 14, 1974, New York, New York

Walter Lippmann wrote 26 books and more than 4,000 newspaper columns, syndicated internationally. He also contributed articles to more than 50 magazines, earning him the unofficial title of Dean of American Political Journalism. He graduated with honors from Harvard University in 1910, after receiving private undergraduate tutoring. At Harvard, he was influenced by British political thinker Graham Wallas, a member of the Fabian Society who wrote *Human Nature in Politics.*

William James was a professor of philosophy at Harvard University from 1885 to 1907, and he also influenced Lippmann's early thinking. George Santayana, who joined the Harvard philosophy staff in 1889 and wrote *The Life of Reason*, also had an impact on Lippmann's life.

Woodrow Wilson selected Lippmann to assist in formulating the Fourteen Points and in developing the concept of the League of Nations. In World War I, Lippmann was a captain in U.S. military intelligence. He attended the Versailles Peace Conference. Before the war, he founded the *New Republic*, a liberal weekly magazine. In 1921, he joined the staff of the *New York World*. He left in 1931 to join the *New York Herald Tribune*, where his syndicated column, Today and Tomorrow, appeared in some 200 newspapers.

Walter Lippmann won the Pulitzer Prize in 1958 and 1962, and other honors that established him as America's foremost analyst of social, political and ethical problems.

He is featured on a 1985 6¢ Great Americans stamp.

214

Robert R. Livingston

Scott 323
Born: November 27, 1746, New York, New York
Died: February 26, 1813, Clermont, New York

Robert R. Livingston's great-grandfather, also named Robert Livingston, migrated indirectly from Scotland, via Holland, to Massachusetts in 1673. He settled in Albany, New York, and in 1679 married Alida Schuyler. The marriage added more land and wealth to his own. In 1686, he manipulated his claim to 160,000 acres of land on the east side of the Hudson River, thus establishing the huge Livingston estate. His land and wealth gave him and his descendants the prestige and wherewithal to serve the state of New York and the nation in various political and administrative positions.

Thus, the younger Robert Livingston's inherited wealth allowed him to obtain an education at King's College, now Columbia University. He was admitted to the bar in 1770 at age 24.

He served as a delegate to the Continental Congress in 1775-76 and helped draft the Declaration of Independence. In 1777, he was chosen as chancellor of New York state, an office he held until 1801. In August 1781, Livingston was elected by Congress as the first secretary for foreign affairs, a position he held until 1783.

For the state of New York, he assisted John Jay and Gouverneur Morris in drafting the state's constitution. As a Federalist, he figured prominently in securing New York's ratification in 1788 of the U.S. Constitution. He opposed Alexander Hamilton and supported Thomas Jefferson. He ran unsuccessfully against John Jay for governor of New York in 1798.

In 1801 President Jefferson named Livingston minister to France. Livingston negotiated the Louisiana Purchase with eloquent finesse. It was his most notable accomplishment. He resigned his post in 1804. He met Robert Fulton in Paris and worked with him on building the steamship. In 1807, their partnership sent a steamboat, the *Clermont*, successfully up the Hudson River to Albany.

Livingston spent the happiest times of his life as a scientific farmer at his home in Clermont, New York. In 1875, a statue of Livingston was placed in the U.S. Capitol in Washington, D.C.

He is the subject of the 1904 1¢ Louisiana Purchase Exposition stamp.

215

Belva Ann Bennett Lockwood

Scott 2179
Born: October 24, 1830, Royalton, New York
Died: May 19, 1917, Washington, D.C.

Belva Bennett married a young farmer, Uriah McNall, at age 18 and was widowed six years later. She left her young daughter with her parents while she went to Genesee College. She graduated in 1857. She had been a teacher, and after college, she continued to teach in upper New York state until 1868. She then went to Washington, D.C., to study law, and that same year married Ezekiel Lockwood.

Belva Lockwood matriculated into National University Law School, but as a female, she was not allowed to attend classes. She was tutored privately. She graduated, but the other students, all male, objected to her graduating with them, so she was denied her diploma. She finally received her diploma, and in 1873 was admitted to the bar to practice in the lower courts. She wrote a resolute letter stating her rights to Ulysses S. Grant who, as president of the United States, was the titular head of the university. When she was a teacher, she received only half the pay that her male counterparts received. These and the many other indignities to the female sex persuaded her to devote her life's work to obtaining equal rights for women.

In Washington, Lockwood drafted a bill for equal-pay-for-equal-work-by-women in the civil service. The bill was enacted into law. She also drafted a bill for a law allowing women to practice law before the Supreme Court. She was the first to argue a case before the nation's highest judicial tribunal. Although women could not vote, they could be voted for, she said. In 1884 and 1888, the Equal Rights Association nominated her for president.

Lockwood was active in a wide range of reform movements, from charitable organizations to women's suffrage to peace movements. She worked for equal rights of guardianship for children and property rights for women. Most of her goals have since been accomplished. She also successfully defended land rights of the North Carolina Cherokee Indians.

Belva Lockwood is depicted on a 1986 17¢ Great Americans stamp.

John Griffith 'Jack' London

Scott 2183
Born: January 12, 1876, San Francisco, California
Died: November 22, 1916, Glen Ellen, California

Jack London grew up in poverty. His natural father was W.H. Chaney, an itinerant astrologer from Maine. His mother, Flora Wellman, was a Welsh farm girl-spiritualist from Ohio. Chaney left Flora. When Flora's illegitimate baby was a few months old, she married a local grocer, John London. The child was named John Griffith London and was called Jack.

Jack London managed to finish the eighth grade at Oakland, California. From then on, his life was undisciplined. He loafed around the waterfront and became involved with opium-smugglers, harpooners and sealers. At age 15, he bought a sloop and became an oyster pirate, even though he was employed by the San Francisco Bay fish patrol. He sailed on the *Sophie Sutherland*, hunting seals off the Siberian coast and making unruly excursions into Japanese ports. After a year, he tried to settle down in Oakland but could not find work of any satisfaction.

In 1894 he drifted to New York. As a vagrant, he was incarcerated in the Erie County Penitentiary for a month. That incarceration may have had its effect, for he returned to California to make something of himself. He completed high school in a year, and entered the University of California in 1896. He was an avid reader. He was much influenced by socialists Herbert Spencer and Karl Marx.

In 16 years, he published 43 volumes. After his death seven more were published. Most of his books were autobiographical, relating to his early experiences. He was twice married — to Elizabeth Maddern, 1900 (divorced 1905) and Charmain Kittredge, 1905. He had two daughters by his first wife. He built a home near Glenn Ellen, California, which burned down in 1913.

In 1916, ill with alcoholism and depression, he took a drug overdose and died at age 40.

Jack London is portrayed on a 25¢ stamp issued in 1986 as part of the Great Americans series.

Dr. Crawford Long

Scott 875
Born: November 1, 1815, Danielsville, Georgia
Died: June 16, 1878, Athens, Georgia

Dr. Crawford Long was probably the first doctor to use ether for freedom from pain during surgical procedures. After receiving his medical degree from the University of Pennsylvania, he worked in New York City hospitals and later practiced in Jackson County, Georgia. In 1841 he was asked to use laughing gas (nitrous oxide) at a student party. He substituted ether instead. Long observed that those made insensible by the gas bruised themselves but were oblivious of the pain. From this experience he recommended the use of ether on a patient, James Venable, who had been unwilling to undergo removal of two neck tumors. On March 30, 1842, Long successfully operated on the tumors while Venable was under the influence of ether.

So successful was his use of ether that Long used it in operations several more times during the next four years, but he did not publish his results until 1849. This was three years after others, notably William T.G. Morton in Boston, had announced the use of ether in surgical operations. The early history of the introduction of ether anesthesia in America was the subject of much controversy, but the principal facts may be briefly stated as follows:

It was sometimes customary for early 19th-century surgeons to intoxicate the patient with alcohol or opium in cases requiring complete muscular relaxation, such as reductions of fractures or operations for hernia. Hypnosis and suggestion were also employed.

In March 1842, Dr. Long performed his surgical procedure using ether. This was vouched for by resident physicians of his locality. The original documents in support of Dr. Long's claim were effectively brought together by Dr. H.H. Young in *Bulletin Johns Hopkins Hospital, Baltimore*.

Dr. Long is depicted on a 1940 2¢ Famous Americans issue.

Henry Wadsworth Longfellow

Scott 864
Born: February 27, 1807, Portland, Massachusetts (now Maine)
Died: March 24, 1882, Cambridge, Massachusetts

Henry Wadsworth Longfellow was a tender, gentle, romantic but somewhat melancholic person. This was reflected in his poetry. His life was a combination of peace and beauty and tragedy. He grew up in the Wadsworth-Longfellow mansion in Portland, where he received private tutoring. His father was a Harvard graduate, lawyer and congressman. His mother was the daughter of General Peleg Wadsworth.

At age 14, Longfellow entered the Bowdoin College in Brunswick, Maine, 25 miles north of Portland, where he met Nathaniel Hawthorne. Henry's father wanted him to study law, but he had already made up his mind to make teaching, translating and writing his life's work.

Longfellow graduated in 1825, and after a tour in Europe, he returned to teach modern language at his alma mater. His tenure of teaching at Bowdoin lasted from 1829 to 1835, at which time he was offered the Smith professorship of modern languages at Harvard. In 1831 he married Mary Storer Potter of Portland. Five years later, while studying again in Europe, Mary died in Rotterdam of puerperal fever. In 1837 Longfellow took up lodging at historic Craigie House in Cambridge and began lecturing at Harvard. In 1843 he married Fanny Appleton of Boston and received the Craigie home as a gift from his wealthy father-in-law.

His life was the picture of tranquility — six children and a brilliant career. In 1861 tragedy struck again when his wife died of burns after her dress caught afire. To relieve his grief, Longfellow directed his energies to the prolonged translation of Dante's *Divine Comedy*, published in three volumes between 1865 and 1867.

His tender and somewhat trite poetry showed the power of mythmaking. He made Paul Revere a hero. His poems about the fictional village blacksmith, Miles Standish and Evangeline are famous. A bust of Longfellow is in Westminster Abbey. Oxford and Cambridge conferred honorary degrees upon him in 1868.

Longfellow is shown on a 1¢ Famous Americans stamp released in 1940.

Louis XVI

French Alliance
1778

US Bicentennial 13c

Scott 1753
Born: August 23, 1754, Versailles, France
Died: January 21, 1793, Paris, France

Though he and his queen, Marie Antoinette, were beheaded on the guillotine in Paris' Place de la Revolution, condemned by the Commune for treason, Louis XVI was not entirely responsible for the French Revolution. It was more the fault of his predecessors, Louis XIV and Louis XV.

Louis XVI was the last of the Bourbon kings to govern France as an absolute ruler. He was the third son of the Dauphin Louis and the grandson of Louis XV. In 1770 he married Marie Antoinette, the frivolous and extravagant daughter of Marie Theresa and Francis I of the Holy Roman Empire. Louis became king of France on May 10, 1774.

The king did not help the cause when Turgot, his economist comptroller-general, attempted to balance the budget while Louis and his queen drained the treasury with extravagant expenditures. Turgot was succeeded by Necker and Calone, but they also failed. During the American Revolution, France incurred large military expenditures by supplying men, arms and ships.

General Burgoyne surrendered at Saratoga October 17, 1777, causing a change in France's policy. Comte de Vergennes, King Louis' able foreign minister, knew that France supported the American Revolution and that the French industrialists craved more direct access to the American markets. He feared that Lord North would be eager to recognize American independence (which he was), but England's King George III refused. North appointed a peace commission with broad conciliations if America would acknowledge the sovereignty of the king.

But 11 days before the North bill passed Parliament, Benjamin Franklin signed treaties of commerce and alliance with Vergennes. Great Britain declared war on France. Spain entered as an ally of France. Thus, by 1780 the war had spread around the world. Louis XVI was in the thick of it.

The king is shown with Franklin on a 13¢ stamp issued in 1978 to honor the French Alliance. The stamp is part of the American Bicentennial series.

Juliette Magill Kinzie Gordon Low

Scott 974
Born: October 31, 1860, Savannah, Georgia
Died: January 17, 1927, Savannah, Georgia

Julliette Gordon was the daughter of a prominent Georgia family. She was educated at private schools in Virginia and New York City. In 1886 she married William W. Low, and the two divided their time between the United States and England. It was while she was in England that she met the Boer War hero Sir Robert Baden-Powell, who in 1907 founded the Boy Scouts in England. Baden-Powell's sister had founded a similar organization, Girl Guides. Juliette Low became interested in this organization and organized several Girl Guide companies in Scotland.

On March 12, 1912, in Savannah, Georgia, she held the first meeting of a group of girls on a tennis court at her home and called them the Girl Guides of America, then Girl Scouts of the USA. Low contributed her time and money to the new organization and was its national president until 1920. She was given the title of founder.

Membership grew rapidly and within three years the organization counted 5,000 members. Its headquarters was first established in Washington, D.C. In 1916 New York City became the permanent headquarters.

By 1927 the membership of Girl Scouts grew to more than 140,000. Since then, more than 52 million girls and adults have participated in this world's largest voluntary organization. The organization was incorporated as the Girl Scouts of the USA in 1915. In 1950 the U.S. Congress granted a charter to the Girl Scouts of the USA, which protects the scouts uniform, insignia and program, and defines the responsibilities of the group. The Girl Scouts are divided into four age group levels: Brownie, Junior, Cadette and Senior.

Today, nearly 90 nations participate in scouting through membership in the World Association of Girl Guides and Girl Scouts.

Juliette Low is pictured on a 3¢ stamp issued in 1948.

James Russell Lowell

Scott 866
Born: February 22, 1819, Cambridge, Massachusetts
Died: August 12, 1891, Cambridge, Massachusetts

In the late 19th century, James Russell Lowell was acknowledged as America's leading man of letters.

At age 19, he graduated from Harvard University. Two years later he received a law degree. Writing, teaching and diplomatic service was to become his life's work. In 1841 he published *A Year's Life*, his first volume of poetry. Two years later he began the publication *Pioneer*, featuring works by Edgar Allan Poe, Nathaniel Hawthorne and John Greenleaf Whittier.

His wife, Marie White Lowell, influenced him to write articles on abolition, a cause she championed. In 1846, Lowell published a series of articles as letters featuring Hosea Biglow. He combined these articles on slavery in *Biglow Papers* in 1848. He continued to write and travel until 1855, when he succeeded Henry Wadsworth Longfellow as the professor of modern languages at Harvard. Lowell held this post for 20 years.

For four years, he edited the *Atlantic Monthly*, which he helped found. During the Civil War, he published the second series of his *Biglow Papers*. From 1864 to 1872, he edited and published the *North American Review* with Charles Eliot Norton. Lowell also produced numerous books and essays between 1864 and 1888.

In 1878 he contributed his services to the presidential campaign of Rutherford B. Hayes. For Lowell's contribution to a successful election, Hayes appointed him U.S. minister to Spain for three years. He then spent five years as minister to Great Britain, a post for which he was well-suited.

Between 1847 and 1853, his wife and three children died, leaving him with one daughter, Maria. Four years later, he married his daughter's governess, Frances Dunlap, and settled in Elmwood, his childhood home in Cambridge, Massachusetts.

In his final years of retirement, Lowell made several trips to England and produced more poetry, criticism and political essays.

He is depicted in the Famous Americans series on a 1940 3¢ stamp.

Sybil Ludington

Scott 1559
Born: 1761, Colony, New York
Died: February 26, 1839, Putnam County, New York

Sybil Ludington was the oldest child in a family of 12. Her father, Henry Ludington, was a commander of a regiment of minutemen scattered around for several miles. Colonel Ludington's small farm was 10 miles east of the Hudson River and 15 miles northwest of Danbury, Connecticut. During the Revolution, the Army stored large quantities of flour, meat and military supplies at Danbury.

On April 26, 1777, approximately 2,000 Redcoats led by Colonel William Tyron, sailed from New York to Norwalk across Long Island Sound. They then marched to Danbury and set fire on the unprotected town. A weary messenger raced to Ludington's farm and shouted to the colonel, "Look to the southeast, Sir! Danbury's burning!" The regiment had to be mustered at once, but the messenger and his horse were too tired to go on. Colonel Ludington called for 16-year-old Sybil and ordered her to take a horse named Star and wake up the minutemen. She donned her mother's heavy red cloak, mounted Star and rode off to tell the minutemen to gather at Ludington's Mill.

She galloped to Shaw's Pond by way of Horse Pond. "Look to the East, Danbury's burning," she shouted. The men knew what to do. On to Mahopac Pond she rode the tiring horse through the mud and brush. It was midnight when she reached Red Mill. Stormville was yet ahead. On the way she met a company of Redcoats. She hid in the trees. Once danger had passed, she raced to Stormville, where troops were already gathering. Her alarm was spread.

She returned home, where 400 minutemen were ready to march. They overtook the Redcoats at Ridgefield, eight miles south of Danbury, forcing them back to their ships at Fairfield.

Sybil married Edmond Ogden, and they had six children. She lived to be 78 years old. General George Washington visited the Ludington home to thank Sybil personally. Historical markers trace her route, and a statue of Sybil on Star stands in Carmel, New York.

The 1975 8¢ American Bicentennial issue honoring contributors to the cause depicts Sybil on horseback. The words "Youthful Heroine" are featured beside her name.

Martin Luther

Scott 2065
Born: November 10, 1483, Eisleben, Halle District, Germany
Died: February 18, 1546, Eisleben, Halle District, Germany

Martin Luther studied law at the University of Erfurt. He received his bachelor of arts degree in 1502 and his master of arts degree in 1505. In his *Tischreden* (Table Talk), it is related that on July 2, 1505, he was caught in a thunderstorm. He prayed to St. Anne and promised that if he were saved he would become a monk. He renounced the world. A few weeks later, against his father's wishes, he entered the Augustinian monastery at Erfurt. He celebrated his first Mass on May 2, 1507.

He lectured on the Scriptures at the University of Wittenberg in electoral Saxony. He was also the parish priest at Wittenberg. His parishioners were buying indulgences. On October 31, 1517, Luther blasted the indulgences with his "95" Thesis, denouncing papal venality, and jurisdiction over purgatory, and also the accumulation of merits of the saints. The "95" Thesis brought condemnation from Rome. In October 1518, Luther was examined in Augsburg by Cardinal Cajetan. He debated with Johann Eck at Leipzig in July 1519. Luther proclaimed that he would accept only the Scripture as his authority. He emerged from the debate a national hero, winning support from the German nationalists who hated Roman exploitation.

In 1520 he issued three major tracts protesting the hierarchical-papal structure of the church and rejected the canon law that served as its legal justification. On December 10, 1520, he burned the Papal Bull and a copy of the canon law. Emperor Charles issued the Edict of Worms that condemned Luther. Frederick the Wise hid Luther in the remote Wartburg castle, where he translated the entire New Testament from Greek into German.

Luther returned to Wittenberg in 1522. He married Katherina von Bora. They had five children. The effect of Luther's attack on canon law occasioned the calling of the Council of Trent (Trento, Italy, 1545-1563), which regulated the life, structure and law of the Catholic Church for 400 years.

In 1983 a 20¢ stamp was issued portraying Martin Luther.

Mary Lyon

Scott 2169
Born: February 28, 1797, Buckland, Massachusetts
Died: March 5, 1849, South Hadley, Massachusetts

Mary Lyon was the founder of Mount Holyoke Female Seminary in South Hadley, Massachusetts. She studied at both Ashland and Amherst academies. She also attended Byfield Academy. It was there that she was influenced by the headmaster to promote education for women. Lyon taught at Ashford Academy for three years. In 1828, after teaching at the Adams Female Academy in Londonderry (later Derry) for 10 years, she teamed up with Zilpah Grant to establish a seminary in Ipswich, Massachusetts. Grant was the principal of Adams Female Academy. Lyon was the dominant factor in the academy, and she stayed on until 1834 when she resigned.

She spent the next three years raising funds to establish a school for women that would provide high educational standards at an affordable cost. To fund such a school from donations was an almost impossible task. However, through her persuasiveness and persistence, she was able to collect enough contributions to establish the school in 1837.

She opened her seminary with 80 students. It was named Mount Holyoke Female Seminary for the 878-foot mountain north of South Hadley. In 1888, the name was changed to Mount Holyoke Seminary and College. In 1893, it became Mount Holyoke College. The college now offers two years of general education in the liberal arts and two years of concentrated study in one of 24 academic departments. The college campus spreads over 770 acres and includes the Williston Memorial Library and an observatory. The residence halls provide French- and Russian-language dormitories. Today, the enrollment is more than 1,900 students.

Mary Lyon is depicted on the 2¢ Great Americans issue released February 28, 1987.

Clara Maass

Scott 1699
Born: June 28, 1876, East Orange, New Jersey
Died: August 24, 1901, Havana, Cuba

Clara Maass grew up in East Orange, New Jersey, just five miles northeast of the center of Newark. East Orange was settled by citizens of Newark in 1678 and was part of the city of Orange until 1863. It was settled by the Dutch, probably ancestors of Clara Maass.

Clara was the oldest of the nine Maass children. She trained to be a nurse at Newark German Hospital (now Maass Memorial Hospital), where she graduated and received the hospital's distinctive nurse's cap in 1895. In 1898 she became a United States Army nurse when the Spanish-American War broke out. She soon was working in Cuba.

The war was fought in the bay of Santiago with a decided victory by Schley and Sampson. On the ground, 15,000 American forces had little opposition from the 1,700 Cuban raw recruits who fell at San Juan Hill.

But for every one of the 286 men killed or wounded, 14 times as many died of disease. Poor sanitation was one reason; yellow fever another.

Dr. Walter Reed was sent to Cuba, which was then occupied by the American Army. Reed was to head a group to study yellow fever. The mosquito was considered the transmitter of the disease. It had been shown that a two-week lapse was necessary before the disease became dangerous to others. Volunteers were purposely bitten by infected mosquitoes. The tests determined that the cause of the disease was a virus and that it was not caused by person-to-person contact. Twenty-two cases were produced experimentally: 14 by infected bites, six by injection of blood and two by injection of filtered blood serum, which proved the viral theory. Claire Maass was among the volunteers.

On August 25, 1901, Maass' mother received a cable from Havana. It read: MISS MAASS DIED TWENTY-FOUR at SIX-THIRTY GORGAS. The sender was Major William C. Gorgas, Army sanitation officer.

Clara Maass was honored for her heroics on a 1976 13¢ stamp. The stamp reads, "Clara Maass/She gave her life."

Douglas MacArthur

Scott 1424
Born: January 26, 1880, Fort Dodge, Little Rock, Arkansas
Died: April 5, 1964, Washington, D.C.

Douglas MacArthur grew up on military posts. He was the son of Lieutenant General Arthur MacArthur, a hero of the Civil War and Spanish-American War. From West Point, Douglas MacArthur graduated first in his class in 1903. During World War I, he organized and commanded the 42nd Rainbow Division with the rank of brigadier general. He won honors in the war and, afterward, commanded the U.S. occupation zone. He was superintendent of West Point from 1919 to 1922. From 1928 to 1930, MacArthur commanded the Philippines Department, and was army chief of staff from 1930 to 1935. In 1932 he routed the Bonus Army of unemployed veterans' marching on Washington, D.C. In 1935 he was appointed field marshal of the Philippines. He resigned in 1937 to avoid reassignment.

When U.S. forces in the Philippines merged with the Philippine forces in 1941, MacArthur was recalled to command the Far East Forces as lieutenant general. On December 7, 1941, the same day as the attack on Pearl Harbor, Japan invaded the Philippines. MacArthur retreated to Bataan peninsula, and then to Corregidor, which finally surrendered. He became supreme commander of the Allied Forces in the Southwest Pacific area and began his island-hopping strategy. In October 1944, MacArthur landed in the Philippines, fulfilling his promise, "I shall return." He was promoted to general of the army. In September 1945, following the atomic bombing of Japan, he accepted the surrender of Japan aboard the battleship *Missouri*.

For the next six years, he served as supreme commander of the occupation forces in Japan. He was named U.N. commander in Korea, where he recaptured Seoul. From the Yalu River advancement, his forces were driven back to the 38th parallel. To avoid a war with China, President Truman recalled MacArthur in April 1951. MacArthur returned as a national hero.

He appears on a 1971 6¢ stamp.

John McCormack

Scott 2090
Born: June 14, 1884, Athlone, Ireland
Died: September 16, 1945, Dublin, Ireland

At the tender age of nine, John McCormack faced his first audience when he sang at the Marists Brothers School. His first appearance as a professional singer was at *Feis Ceoil*, the Irish National Festival in Dublin, Ireland, in May 1903. In 1904 McCormack made a phonograph recording for the Edison Company. He went to Italy to study in 1905 and performed in several operas.

In London, he was at first less successful and earned his living by singing in cabarets and restaurants. But after a concert at the Queen's Hall, engagements began to follow. In October 1907, McCormack obtained his first Covent Garden part, as Turiddu in *Cavalleria Ruticana*.

McCormack's debut at the Manhattan Opera House, engaged by Oscar Hammerstein, was in *Traviata* on November 10, 1909. He later gave concerts all over Europe and also appeared several times at the Metropolitan Opera in New York City. Gradually, he abandoned opera and devoted himself entirely to concert work. He was made a papal count in 1928.

McCormack's income from phonograph records was second only to Caruso's. He appeared in several films, including *Song of My Heart*. A critic wrote, in an attempt to analyze McCormack's popularity, "His voice is exquisite ... His enunciation ... particularly in English ... is like music itself. His diction has life and pulse, it is a thing of beauty and eloquence to sway a multitude. His song, be its burden grave or gay, bears the impulse of a simple, wholesome personality."

In addition to singing in the Metropolitan Opera and the Manhattan Opera company, he appeared at the Chicago Opera Company and the Monte Carlo Opera. McCormack became a United States citizen in 1919. His retirement was marked by a farewell tour in 1938. In 1984, the U.S. Postal Service honored McCormack with a 20¢ Performing Arts issue.

228

Cyrus Hall McCormick

Scott 891
Born: February 15, 1809, Rockbridge County, Virginia
Died: May 13, 1884, Chicago, Illinois

Cyrus Hall McCormick followed what was for his family a three-generation involvement in farm machinery. McCormick's father, Robert, was a Virginia landowner. He had invented several farming implements, some of which he had patented, but a workable reaper seemed to be his enigma. In July 1831, the younger McCormick constructed a workable reaper that had all the essential components used in later commercial machines. McCormick patented his invention in 1834, a year after Obed Hussey had announced a reaper of his own. McCormick began manufacturing his machine on the family farm in 1837 and, in 1843, licensed manufacturers in other parts of the country.

In 1847, McCormick established a factory in Chicago. A year later, his patent ran out, and Hussey and others instigated legal action for certain rights. While lawyers Abraham Lincoln, Edwin M. Stanton and William H. Seward argued about the case in court for several years, McCormick forged ahead using business and sales techniques to overwhelm his rivals.

McCormick's brother, Leander James, assisted him as superintendent of manufacturing operations in Chicago beginning in 1849. From 1859 to 1881, the brothers were partners.

McCormick's son, also named Cyrus Hall McCormick, succeeded his father as president of the McCormick Harvesting Machine Company in 1884, the year his father died. In 1902 Cyrus McCormick Jr. reorganized the company in combination with his and rival companies as the International Harvester Company. He remained the president of the new company until 1919. The International Harvester Company became one of the greatest industrial establishments in America. Cyrus Hall McCormick Sr. is pictured on a 1940 3¢ Famous American Inventors stamp.

Thomas Macdonough

Scott 791
Born: December 31, 1783, The Trap (now Macdonough), Delaware
Died: November 10, 1825, at sea

Thomas Macdonough's father was a Continental Army officer who encouraged his son to enter the U.S. Navy in 1800 at age 17. The younger Macdonough served as a midshipman on the *Constellation* and the *Philadelphia* during the Tripolitan War. He was made second officer on a prize vessel taken from the Moors. Macdonough later served under Stephen Decatur, with whom he made a daring raid to scuttle the captured *Philadelphia*.

Macdonough served as a lieutenant from 1807 to 1810, then resigned and went into the private trading business.

The War of 1812 brought him back to active duty. He commanded a small fleet on Lake Champlain to guard against the British.

In September 1814, Macdonough skillfully outwitted the British Navy. He captured the English fleet and saved Vermont and New York State from certain occupation by British Redcoats. Thus, the British invasion of the Hudson Valley was thwarted. Macdonough did it by deploying his forces at Plattsburgh Bay and maneuvering his flagship *Saratoga* to its best advantage. The *Saratoga* already had been hit by the British flagship *Confiance* and had lost its starboard battery and a fifth of its crew. While at anchor, he pointed his port guns at the *Confiance* and three other vessels. The British commodore lost his life, and the commander, Sir George Provost, retreated to Canada. This most decisive victory won Macdonough his captaincy.

He served as commandant of the Portsmouth Navy Yard (1815-18), then as captain of the *Guerriere* (1818-20) and the *Ohio* (1820-24). Finally, he became the commander of the Mediterranean squadron (1824). He became ill and died at sea on the *Edwin*.

Macdonough is shown with Stephen Decatur on the 1937 2¢ Navy issue.

Edward Alexander MacDowell

Scott 882
Born: December 18, 1861, New York, New York
Died: January 23, 1908, New York, New York

Edward Alexander MacDowell began studying music when he was a child. His father recognized his talents, furthered his studies and encouraged him by placing him under the tutorship of Juan Buitrago in New York City.

At age 17, MacDowell was sent to France to study at the Conservatoire. After two years, he went to Germany to study at the Frankfurt Conservatory, where he was more suited. He was made head piano instructor at the Darmstadt Conservatory in 1881. A year later he played his A-minor concerto, *First Modern Suite*, for Franz Liszt, who arranged to have MacDowell perform before the Allgemeiner Deutscher Musik-Verein held in Zurich.

MacDowell continued to compose for the next several years, using German landscapes and literature for his inspiration.

In 1884 he returned to the United States and married Marian Nevins, who was one of his pupils in Germany. They returned to Wiesbaden to live until 1888. They then returned to Boston. His compositions that followed his return were strictly American in theme, despite his French and German exposure. These compositions included *Indian Suite* (1892), *Woodland Sketches* (1896), *Sea Pieces* (1898), and New *England Idyls* (1902).

He became the director of the Columbia University music department in 1896, integrating an orchestra and chorus with other academic curricula.

He wanted to pattern American music instruction after the European methods, but met with stubborn opponents who insisted that talented American musicians must study in European conservatories. Unable to bring his farsighted methods to the fore, MacDowell resigned his post at Columbia in 1904 and retired to his farm in Petersborough, New Hampshire.

After his death, his wife organized the MacDowell Colony at their farm as a summer residence for composers, writers and artists.

MacDowell was elected to the Hall of Fame for Great Americans in 1960. He is honored in the Famous Americans issue on a 5¢ 1940 stamp.

Ephraim McDowell

Scott 1138
Born: November 11, 1771, Rockbridge County, Virginia
Died: June 25, 1830, Danville, Kentucky

Ephraim McDowell, at age 13, moved with his family to Danville, Kentucky, in 1784. His father, Samuel McDowell, was a prominent member of Danville society and aided in the creation of the Kentucky constitution. The young McDowell's medical education was somewhat informal. He studied with Dr. Alexander Humphreys in Staunton, Virginia, and attended the University of Edinburgh's medical school in Scotland for one year. He also studied privately under Dr. John Bell in Scotland.

McDowell returned to Danville in 1795, became renowned as a surgeon and began attracting students to his office.

He became especially proficient in ovariotomies, bladder surgery and hernia repairs. He performed both a bladder operation and a hernia repair on James K. Polk, who later became president of the United States.

McDowell's most famous case was 47-year-old Jane Todd Crawford, from whom he removed a 20-pound ovarian tumor. She lived 30 more years to tell about it. McDowell reported Crawford's case and two others in April 1817 and reported two more cases in 1819. Of the 13 operations he performed on ovarian tumors and cysts, he had a record eight recoveries. He sent his results to Dr. Bell, who was living his last days in Italy and did not see the letter. But Bell's successor, John Lizars of Edinburgh, published McDowell's results in his *Observations on Extraction of Diseased Ovaria*. In the meantime, Dr. Nathan Smith had performed an ovariotomy at Norwich, Virginia, in July 1821, not knowing about McDowell's work.

Later, especially with the introduction of ether anaesthesia, such surgeons as John L. Atlee of Pennsylvania performed the operation 78 times with 64 recoveries. The operation became firmly established in England and France in the next several years, and within 50 years, it was commonplace.

The Ephraim McDowell issue was released in 1959 on the 150th anniversary of his first successful ovarian operation in the United States.

232

William McKinley

Scott 559
Born: January 29, 1843, Niles, Ohio
Died: September 14, 1901, Buffalo, New York

William McKinley studied at Union Seminary in Poland, Ohio, and Allegheny College in Meadville, Pennsylvania. He taught school, served as a postal clerk in Poland, and when the Civil War broke out, enlisted as a private on June 11, 1861. McKinley fought his first battle in September of that year. From 1862 to 1864, he participated in several battles, and rose from a private to a major. When he was mustered out, he was acting adjutant general on the staff of General S.C. Carroll.

McKinley studied law in Youngstown, Ohio, and was admitted to the bar in Warren, Ohio, in March 1865. He practiced at Canton. In 1877 he was elected to Congress as a Republican. He served until 1891.

McKinley served as chairman of the Ways and Means Committee in 1890. That year he also secured passage of the McKinley Tariff Act. The following year, he became governor of Ohio. He was re-elected in 1893.

The Republicans chose McKinley to oppose William Jennings Bryan in the 1896 presidential campaign. McKinley was elected by a substantial margin. His administration began quietly until 1898, when the Spanish American War broke out. The U.S. battleship *Maine* was sunk in Havana Harbor in February, and in April war was declared. The Spanish fleet in Manila Bay was destroyed and soon thereafter the Philippine Islands were captured. Peace was signed in December.

By February 1899, the United States had obtained Puerto Rico, Guam and the Philippines. With the annexation of Hawaii, Wake and American Samoa, the United States was a Pacific power.

The Open Door policy toward China involved U.S. troops in China's Boxer Rebellion in 1900.

In 1901 McKinley won the presidency over William J. Bryan. In September, while attending a reception in the Music Hall at the Pan American Exposition, he was shot twice by Leon Czolgosz, an anarchist. McKinley died nine days later. His portrait appeared on a 7¢ definitive issued May 1, 1923.

233

John McLoughlin

Scott 964
Born: October 19, 1784, La Riviere du Loup, Quebec, Canada
Died: September 3, 1857, Oregon City, Oregon

After studying medicine in Scotland and Quebec, John McLoughlin returned to Canada and entered the service of the North West Company. He became a partner in 1814. The company merged with the Hudson Bay Company in 1821, and McLoughlin was placed in charge of the fur trade in the Columbia River area, which included all of what are now the states of Washington and Oregon. The area had previously been operated by John Jacob Aster's American Fur Company, but that company left at the time of the War of 1812.

McLoughlin first erected Fort Vancouver in 1825 (now Vancouver, Washington), which was the only white settlement in the area until 1834. He controlled the Indian trade, thwarting the efforts of the United States traders to break the British monopoly. But he gave assistance to new settlers who came to the area after 1840. McLoughlin was especially helpful to Jason Lee, who came with the first group of missionaries to Oregon in 1834. He helped those who came via the Oregon Trail, but discouraged settlement north of the Columbia River.

In 1846 the 49th parallel became the United States-Canadian boundary. McLoughlin retired from the company in 1846. He claimed land for himself at the falls of the Willamette River and developed a town, Oregon City (20 miles south of Vancouver). Oregon became a territory in 1848. Under the Donation Land Act of 1850, however, McLoughlin was denied his claim. He went along with the government's claim to his land until his death in 1857. Rights to the land were restored to McLoughlin's heirs for the payment of a nominal fee in 1862. Oregon had been admitted to the Union as a state in February 1859, but McLoughlin did not live to see this happen.

He is known as the father of Oregon. The McLoughlin Institute in Oregon City was established in 1907 in his honor, and Oregon placed his statue in the U.S. Capitol in 1953. McLoughlin is depicted along with Jason Lee and a wagon on the Oregon Trail on the 1948 3¢ Oregon Territory issue.

Brien McMahon

Scott 1200
Born: October 6, 1903, Norwalk, Connecticut
Died: July 28, 1952, Washington, D.C.

James O'Brien McMahon, who later changed his name to Brien, graduated from Fordham University in 1924, and from Yale University in 1927. He opened a law practice in Norwalk, Connecticut, and by 1933 was the city judge. He followed Attorney General Homer S. Cummings to Washington in 1935 as his special assistant. The next year, he was assistant attorney general in charge of the Criminal Division. In 1939 he returned to private law practice in Norwalk, and in 1940 he married Rosemary Turner.

A Democrat and a Catholic, he enjoyed considerable political support from his area. In 1944 he was easily elected to the United States Senate. McMahon strongly supported Franklin D. Roosevelt's programs, and was a liberal and internationalist. When Truman took office, he supported Truman's programs, such as civil rights, American membership in the United Nations, the Marshall Plan, NATO, Point Four and the Japanese Peace Treaty. He opposed the Taft-Hartley Act.

Senator McMahon played a leading role in the shaping and passage of the Atomic Energy Act of 1946, which gave control of the atom to the Atomic Energy Commission, headed by civilians. McMahon supplemented his battle for atomic buildup with disarmament and peace proposals. Early in 1950 he called for arms reduction and a fund for worldwide economic development to be contributed largely by the United States but administered by the United Nations. Secretary of State Dean Acheson deemed the proposal unrealistic. McMahon was re-elected to the Senate in 1950, even though Senator Joseph McCarthy campaigned vigorously against him.

In 1952 he was considered for the vice presidency, but withdrew because he was seriously ill. McMahon died of cancer four days later.

The 1962 Senator Brien McMahon stamp was issued to honor his role in opening the way to peaceful uses of atomic energy.

Dolley Madison

Scott 1822
Born: May 20, 1768, Guilford County, North Carolina
Died: July 12, 1849, Washington, D.C.

Historians have substantiated that Dolley Madison spelled her name with an "e" and not without the "e," as it is usually spelled. Dolley's parents, John and Mary Payne, were Quakers who took good care in raising her. Because she was female, she received very little education. When she was 15, her parents moved to Philadelphia. When she was 22, she married John Todd Jr. The couple had two children, John Payne Todd and an infant son, who died in the 1793 yellow fever epidemic. Her husband also died of yellow fever at the same time, leaving her widowed at age 25.

She was introduced to Representative James Madison by Senator Aaron Burr. Madison, who was 17 years older than Dolley, married her on September 15, 1794. They had no children together. Dolley was expelled from the Society of Friends because she had married a non-Quaker.

When Jefferson appointed Madison secretary of state in 1801, the couple moved to Washington, D.C. Dolley was noted for her hospitality as a hostess, and when Thomas Jefferson was widowed, she occasionally served as hostess of the president's house. After James Madison's two terms as president, the couple retired to Montpelier, his plantation in Orange County, Virginia. James Madison served from there in the Virginia Constitution Convention of 1829. Upon the death of Thomas Jefferson, July 4, 1826, he served as acting rector of the University of Virginia until his own death on June 28, 1836. Dolley returned to Washington to continue her role in Washington society, until her death at age 81.

Dolley Madison is pictured on a 1980 15¢ definitive stamp.

236

Helene Madison

Scott 2500
Born: June 19, 1913, Madison, Wisconsin
Died: November 25, 1970, Seattle, Washington

Helene Madison lived a life of success and failure, of glory and loneliness, of fanfare and frustration. She moved from Madison, Wisconsin, to Seattle with her parents. She learned to swim in West Green Lake in Seattle. The swimming instructor at the Washington Athletic Club, Ray Daughters, recognized Helene as a potential champion. Daughters taught her the six-beat crawl stroke, which she mastered.

By 1928, Helene was the champion her coach envisioned. In a few years, she earned 87 trophies, including three 1932 Los Angeles Olympic Games gold medals and 20 national championships. She set world records for 20 distances from 100 yards through one mile and the metric equivalents, except the 800 meters. In 1929 she forced the 1928 100-meter freestyle Olympic gold medalist Albina Osipowich to tie the world's record to barely win the junior outdoor Amateur Athletic Union championship match. This encouraged her to "go for the gold," which she did in Los Angeles in 1932. She swam it in 1 minute 6.8 seconds, an Olympic and U.S. record. She captured the 400-meter freestyle, with a time of 5 minutes, 28.5 seconds, another Olympic record and world record. She won her third gold medal as anchor swimmer in the 100-meter freestyle relay contributing to a world record of 4 minutes 38 seconds.

In 1931 she was selected by the Associated Press as the Female Athlete of the Year. In 1930 and 1931 she was a top contender for the prestigious James E. Sullivan Memorial Trophy, given annually to America's best amateur athlete. In 1966 she was elected to the International Swimming Hall of Fame in Fort Lauderdale, Florida, just two years after its inception.

She retired from competition at age 19. She won a minor role in a movie, *The Warrior's Husband*. She tried several careers.

In 1937 she married Luther C. McIver. One child resulted of that union. The McIvers divorced in 1958. She married William Kapphahu in 1959 and divorced again in 1961. In 1970 she died of cancer and diabetes at age 56.

She is portrayed on a 25¢ stamp in the Olympians issue of 1990.

James Madison

Scott 808
Born: March 5, 1750 (old style), Port Conway, Virginia
Died: June 28, 1836, Montpellier, Virginia

James Madison came from a family of well-to-do Virginia planters. He studied at the Donald Robertson School in King and Queen County, Virginia. A sickly child, Madison received two years of private tutoring from an Anglican rector. In 1769 he entered the College of New Jersey, now Princeton University. He graduated in 1771 and remained for postgraduate study for six months. At home, he studied theology and law. On December 22, 1774, Madison was elected to the Orange County, Virginia, Committee of Safety. Two years later, he served on a committee that drafted a new Virginia constitution and the Virginia Declaration of Rights. Through the 1770s and 1780s, he championed the reform programs of Thomas Jefferson and favored a strong central government. Madison collaborated with Alexander Hamilton and John Jay on the Federalist papers, which advocated the adoption of the Constitution.

In 1794 he married Dolley Payne Todd. They had no children together, but raised Dolley's son by her first husband.

In the new Congress, Madison opposed Hamilton's financial program and pro-British foreign policies. He retired from Congress in 1797 to Montpellier, where he drafted the Virginia Resolution, which protested the Alien and Sedition Acts. In 1801 Jefferson appointed him secretary of state. In 1809 Madison succeeded Jefferson as the fourth president of the United States, defeating Charles C. Pinckney.

Increased tension with Britain culminated in the War of 1812, the year Madison was re-elected over Federalist DeWitt Clinton. In 1814 the British captured Washington, forcing Madison to flee to Virginia. Upon returning to Washington, he capitulated to the Hamiltonian policies, signing bills for a U.S. bank and higher tariff. He retired to his Montpellier farm in 1817.

James Madison appears on a 1938-54 4¢ Presidential stamp.

Ramon Magsaysay

Scott 1096
Born: August 31, 1907, Iba, Luzon Island, the Philippines
Died: March 17, 1957, Cebu Island, the Philippines

Ramon Magsaysay joined the United States Army under General MacArthur at the outbreak of World War II in 1941. He was well-educated, having graduated from the University of the Philippines in 1931. Magsaysay also studied at Jose Rizal College in Manila from 1932 to 1933. He was commissioned a captain in April 1942.

He organized guerrilla forces in western Luzon during the Japanese occupation. The guerrillas were consolidated under an American commander responsible only to General MacArthur, and they soon began their devastating work of sabotage and intelligence. By October 20, 1944, the guerrillas were powerfully equipped and strategically dispersed throughout the Philippines. On every island, these daring men and women contributed mightily to the overthrow of the Japanese and to minimizing American battle losses.

In February 1945, General MacArthur appointed Magsaysay the military governor of his home province, Zambalese, just north of the Bataan peninsula. A year later in 1946, when the Philippine Islands were granted independence, Magsaysay was elected to the new congress. He was re-elected in 1949. He began a determined effort to eradicate the Communist-led Hukbalahap guerrillas, known as the Huks.

Magsaysay also attacked the conditions that had produced the Huks. From 1951 to 1953, he was secretary of national defense. In this position, he reorganized the military and completely eradicated the Hukbalahap terrorism. He was awarded the United States Legion of Merit in 1952.

Magsaysay was elected president of the Philippine Islands in 1953. Until his untimely death in March 1957 in a plane crash on Cebu, he worked endlessly to reconstruct his country and make it a more advanced nation. He instigated public works programs, social welfare and land reforms. He supported the West and was a co-sponsor of the Southeast Asia Treaty Organization (SEATO) established in 1954 at Manila.

Magsaysay is featured on a 1957 8¢ Champion of Liberty issue.

239

Horace Mann

Scott 869
Born: May 4, 1796, Franklin, Massachusetts
Died: August 2, 1859, Yellow Springs, Ohio

Horace Mann graduated from Brown University in 1819, taught school for two years and then studied for his law degree, being admitted to the Massachusetts bar in 1823.

He had a flourishing law practice in both Dedham and Boston, Massachusetts. He was a representative in the Massachusetts state legislature from 1827 to 1833, and from 1833 to 1837, he was a Massachusetts state senator. He was appointed to the Massachusetts Board of Education as secretary, with the task of revising and reorganizing the state's public school system.

Mann became so involved with his new endeavor that he gave up his law practice and turned away from politics to devote his entire time and energies to the field of public education. He saw inadequate and run-down school buildings staffed with poorly paid, ill-prepared teachers attempting to teach a trite and narrow curriculum. Unless a youngster was fortunate enough to have private instruction and attend one of the few colleges, his education barely reached past basic reading, writing and arithmetic.

In his new position, Mann prepared a series of 12 annual reports (1837-48) and presented them so forcefully that the need for improvement became widely known. He showed the need for educating teachers, and normal schools were established as a result. He convinced others that taxes should be used for public education. The modernized public school system stemmed from his endeavors, first in Massachusetts then throughout the country.

Mann was elected to Congress as a Whig (1848-53), but ran for governor unsuccessfully in 1852. After his congressional tour, he accepted the presidency of Antioch College in Yellow Springs, Ohio, and taught there until his death in 1859.

Mann, who has been called the father of the common schools, was elected to New York University's Hall of Fame when it was established in 1900 to honor great Americans. He is honored on the 1940 1¢ Famous American Educators issue.

240

Carl Gustaf Emil Mannerheim

Scott 1165
Born: June 4, 1867, Askainen, Russia (now Finland)
Died: January 27, 1951, Lausanne, Switzerland

Carl Gustav Emil Von Mannerheim came from a family of nobility. He was educated for a military and diplomatic career at Nikolayev Cavalry School in St. Petersburg, Russia. At age 22, Mannerheim was commissioned a second lieutenant in the Imperial Russian Army. He served in the Russo-Japanese War from 1904 to 1905 and also in World War I. For his service in the retreat from Manchuria, Mannerheim was decorated three times. He was a lieutenant general in the Russian army at the time of the Bolshevik Revolution in October 1917. When Finland declared independence, Mannerheim resigned his commission and returned to his home in Finland.

The brief war between Finland and Russia in 1918 was fought between the White Guard, organized by Mannerheim, and the Bolshevist-supported Red Guard. With assistance from Germany, the White Guard won. In December 1918, Mannerheim became the temporary ruler of Finland, but was defeated in the July 1919 election. He directed the Mannerheim Child Welfare League from 1919 to 1931 and, in 1920, founded and presided over the Finnish Red Cross. In 1931 he was appointed head of the nation's defense council. He established the Mannerheim Line across the Karelin Isthmus, the 65-mile southeastern frontier.

Mannerheim led the Finnish armies unsuccessfully against the Russian aggression between 1939 and 1940. From 1941 to 1944, he joined the Germans against the Russians, hoping to regain lost Finnish territory. In 1944, when the Germans were retreating from the Russian front, Mannerheim was chosen president of Finland to negotiate a separate treaty with Russia. In September 1944, Finland withdrew from the war. Mannerheim opened the new Finnish legislature in April 1945, after the end of World War II, but became ill in September. He was forced to resign as president in March 1946.

He spent his retirement in Switzerland and Sweden until his death.

Carl Gustav Emil Von Mannerheim is portrayed on a 1960 4¢ Champion of Liberty stamp.

Jacques Marquette

Scott 1356
Born: June 1, 1637, Laon, France
Died: May 18, 1675, near present-day Ludington, Michigan

Jacques Marquette was the son of Nicolas Marquette (Sieur de la Tombelle), counselor-elect of Laon, and Rose de la Salle, who was the grand aunt of St. Jean Baptiste de la Salle, founder of the Christian Brothers. His sister was the founder of the Marquette sisters community school. Marquette taught school in Reims, Charlecille, and Langres after completing his novitiate at Nancy and studying at Pont-a-Mousson. At age 17, he became associated with the Society of Jesus. In 1666 he was called to go to Quebec, New France, to work as a missionary among the Indians.

Marquette spent the first five years in the New World studying the language and customs of the local Indians. He worked initially with the Three Rivers trading station, then in 1668 with the Ottawa tribe at Sault Sainte Marie, in what is now Ontario. His third station was at La Pointe de St. Esprit at Chequamegon Bay on the southwest shore of Lake Superior. In 1671 he retreated with the Hurons and Ottawas to the St. Ignace mission on Mackinac Island because of a fierce battle between the Sioux and the Huron tribes. In December 1672, Louis Joliet arrived at St. Ignace. Father Marquette joined Joliet and five French traders to explore the great river hoping to find a waterway to the South Sea, now known as the Pacific Ocean. They reached the great river on June 17, 608 miles from Sault Sainte Marie. They floated down the Mississippi River to the mouth of the Arkansas. Here, they learned that the great river flowed into the Gulf of Mexico, not the South Sea. They returned to St. Francis Xavier.

Marquette made copies of Joliet's report, and after Joliet lost his journal in a canoe accident, Marquette published his copy and received the credit. Marquette's health was poor after the journey from what is now Green Bay, Wisconsin, to the area of Ottawa, Illinois, where he intended to establish a mission among the Kaskaskia Indians. Marquette reached his destination, but his health continued to fail. He died on the east coast of Lake Michigan.

Jacques Marquette appears with Louis Joliet on a 1968 6¢ stamp.

George Catlett Marshall

Scott 1289
Born: December 31, 1880, Uniontown, Pennsylvania
Died: October 16, 1959, Washington, D.C.

In 1901 George C. Marshall graduated from the Virginia Military Institute in Lexington, Virginia. He served in the Philippines in 1902 as a second lieutenant, then returned the next year to attend the Army School of the Line and the Army Staff College at Fort Leavenworth, Kansas, graduating in 1907. The next year he completed studies at the Command and General Staff School. He served again in the Philippines from 1913 to 1916 as aide-de-camp to General Hunter Liggett.

Although he wanted a combat command in World War I, Marshall's abilities in planning and administrative assignments with the American Expeditionary Force in Europe were needed more. After the war, he served as an aide to General John J. Pershing. After a three-year tour of duty in China, he returned to teach at the Army's infantry school at Fort Benning, Georgia.

From 1933 to 1939, Marshall was senior instructor for the Illinois National Guard. He emerged as the army's chief of staff, a position he held until the end of World War II. He also served as chief adviser to President Franklin D. Roosevelt on military strategy. He attended, with the president, all major Allied planning conferences, from Casablanca to Potsdam.

In 1944 he was made a four-star general. After World War II, President Harry S Truman commissioned Marshall to mediate the civil war in China. His mission was unsuccessful. In 1947 he was appointed secretary of state under President Truman. In June 1947, he proposed a European Recovery Program that became known universally as the Marshall Plan.

In 1949 Marshall resigned from the cabinet because of poor health, but returned the next year to lead the Department of Defense when the Korean War broke out. He retired permanently from public service in 1951, after serving as president of the American Red Cross in the 1949-50 term. In 1953 he received the Nobel Peace Prize, primarily for his Marshall Plan.

George Catlett Marshall is shown on a 1967 20¢ stamp.

John Marshall

Scott 2415
Born: September 24, 1755, Germantown, Fauquier County, Virginia
Died: July 6, 1835, Philadelphia, Pennsylvania

John Marshall was appointed chief justice of the Supreme Court on January 20, 1801, by President John Adams. He held this position for 34 years. Neither a Republican nor a Federalist, Marshall condemned the Alien and Sedition Laws vigorously. He was a Virginian and a third cousin of Thomas Jefferson. His parents were well-to-do and well-educated, although he received little formal schooling.

In 1775 Marshall joined the Virginia minutemen and saw action in the battles of Brandywine, Germantown, Monmouth, and Valley Forge. He returned to Virginia in 1779 to spend a brief time at home studying law and one month at the College of William and Mary. He began his law practice in 1880, then turned toward local politics, serving in the state legislature.

He declined President George Washington's offer to become U.S. attorney for Virginia to lead the Federalist's party at Richmond.

In 1797 he went to France to answer questions concerning French interference with American trade. This was known as the XYZ Affair. X, Y, and Z were the foreign ministers representing Talleyrand of France in an effort by President Adams to establish commerce and friendship. The French demanded large sums of money before they would negotiate. America refused. Marshall sailed home.

The storm of war was mercifully averted. Napoleon Bonaparte made a treaty of peace with the United States in 1800.

Marshall brought order to the Supreme Court. He oversaw the transition of the country from a confederation to a nation.

In 1807, on circuit court in Richmond, Marshall presided over the treason trial of Aaron Burr.

Marshall died in Philadelphia and was buried in Richmond, Virginia. His portrait appears on a 1990 25¢ Supreme Court Bicentennial stamp.

244

Tomas Garrigue Masaryk

Scott 1147
Born: March 7, 1850, Hodonin, Moravia
Died: September 14, 1937, Prague, Czechoslovakia

Tomas Masaryk's father was a coachman on an Austrian imperial estate. Thus, Masaryk was able to learn both the Czech and German languages. Masaryk gave private tutoring lessons to support his studies in Vienna and Leipzig. During this time, he married Charlotte Garrigue, an American. He apprenticed to be a blacksmith, but teaching was his ambition.

Masaryk wrote *Suicide and Modern Civilization* in 1881. It was his first notable sociological work. A year later, he joined the newly organized Czech University of Prague as a professor of philosophy. He founded the *Athenaeum*, a critical monthly review, and the *Times*, a weekly that reported on political affairs. From 1891 to 1893, he served at the Austrian Reichsrat (Federal Council). He then resigned this post and founded *Our Epoch*, another monthly review. In 1898, Masaryk wrote *The Philosophical and Sociological Foundations of Marxism* and helped organize the Realist Party. He was gearing his activities to forming an independent Czechoslovakia.

His party elected him to Parliament in 1907. Masaryk aired his ideas and intentions at the Agram (Zagreb) high treason trials. He attempted to prevent the declaration of war against Serbia in 1914. He went on a trip to Italy to avoid being arrested. He headquartered in London during World War I. With Benes, Durich and Stefanik, he organized the national council of an independent Czech government in Paris.

In Russia, Masaryk organized Czech prisoners to join the French army in 1917. In this way, they stayed out of the Russian civil war. He traveled to the United States and got formal recognition by the Allied powers.

When Czechoslovakia became an independent nation in 1918, he was its first president. Masaryk was re-elected in 1920, 1927 and 1934.

He successfully put into effect all the reforms he had planned. Masaryk was assisted by his son, Jan Garrigue Masaryk (1886-1948).

The 1960 4¢ Champion of Liberty issue honored Masaryk on the 110th anniversary of his birth.

George Mason

Scott 1858
Born: 1725, Stafford (now Fairfax) County, Virginia
Died: October 7, 1792, Gunston Mansion, Lorton, Virginia

George Mason grew up on a typical Virginia plantation on the high ground west of the Potomac River and south of Mount Vernon near Alexandria City (founded 1749). He had no formal education, but his guardian uncle taught him well and encouraged him to read law. Being interested in the settlement of the West, Mason became treasurer of the Ohio Company from 1752 to 1773.

Although he had disdain for politics and politicians, as a large landowner (5,000 acres high above the Potomac River, south of Gunston Cove), he could not avoid public affairs and service to his local and national government. By 1759, Mason was a member of the Virginia House of Burgesses. In the 1760s and 1770s, during the conflicts between the colonies and the crown, he wrote numerous tracts defending the colonists. He was involved in the Townshend duties and the Fairfax Resolves disputes. Mason was a member of the July 1775 Virginia Convention and the state's Committee of Safety. In 1776, he drafted the Virginia Constitution and the Declaration of Rights, which was drawn upon by Thomas Jefferson for the Declaration of Independence.

From 1776 to 1788, he was a member of the Virginia House of Delegates and was instrumental in assisting the George Rogers Clark expedition to the northwest country.

In 1778 Mason was an active delegate to the Federal Constitutional Convention in Philadelphia. He opposed the Constitution as it was written and left the convention early. He retired to his home to oppose the Constitution's ratification. The adoption of the Bill of Rights was due to his influence.

Mason declined any further public service, even though he was chosen to become one of Virginia's first senators. He spent his remaining days at his home, Gunston Hall, and managed his plantation until his death. He is depicted on the 1981 18¢ Great Americans issue. The Gunston Hall issue, released in 1958 (Scott 1108), shows his home.

Edgar Lee Masters

Scott 1405
Born: August 23, 1869, Garnett, Kansas
Died: March 5, 1950, Melrose Park, Pennsylvania

When Edgar Lee Masters was a boy, his parents moved to Lewistown, Illinois, 50 miles northwest of Springfield, near the Spoon River, a small feeder of the Illinois River. He attended Knox College in Galesburg, Illinois, for one year, and was admitted to the bar in 1891. He practiced law in Chicago. For a time, he was in law partnership with Clarence Seward Darrow, a nationally known labor lawyer whose rationalism and ingrained skepticism were expressed in a number of Masters' books.

Masters' legal practice developed slowly, which gave him ample time to ply his pen to poetry. He socialized with the young writers of Chicago and, in 1914, published a series of poems in a St. Louis literary paper under the pen name of Webster Ford.

Masters began writing seriously after he received a copy of *The Greek Anthology* by Marion Reedy, editor of *Reedy's Mirror* in St. Louis. Masters' work consisted of five-verse monologues of corpses who spoke from their burial plots in the cemetery of the fictitious town of Spoon River. In 1915 it was published under the title of *Spoon River Anthology*. It portrayed a direct and somber view of human nature in its simple verse form. By 1940, it had been published in 70 editions and had been translated into several languages.

Masters abandoned his legal practice after the success of his poetry. He moved to New York City to devote his entire energies to writing poetry, biographies and novels. His novels of boyhood, in the *Mitch Miller* series, were his best. His biographies of Vachel Lindsay, Walt Whitman and Mark Twain were notable, but his biography of Abraham Lincoln, *Lincoln, the Man*, aroused a storm of controversy, since it took a debunking approach to the so-called Lincoln myth. Masters published his autobiography, *Across Spoon River*, in 1936.

He is depicted on a 1970 6¢ stamp.

Charles Horace Mayo

Scott 1251
Born: July 19, 1865, Rochester, Minnesota
Died: May 26, 1939, Chicago, Illinois

Charles Horace Mayo was the son of William Worrall Mayo and the younger brother of William James Mayo. The father of the two sons emigrated from England in 1845. He studied medicine in Indiana. He settled in Minnesota in 1855 and soon became the most prominent doctor in the area.

Charles Mayo was born the year the Civil War ended, and grew up in Rochester. He received his formal medical training from the Chicago Medical College, now the medical school of Northwestern University, where he graduated in 1888. Mayo then became a member of the St. Mary's Hospital staff. The hospital was built by the Sisters of St. Francis after a ruinous tornado damaged the town in 1883. With his father and older brother, Mayo helped build a new hospital.

Rochester had the most adequate surgical and medical facilities for much of Minnesota, Iowa and the Dakotas. The hospital received many referrals from other doctors in those outlying areas. The Mayo brothers kept up with the most modern surgical techniques and advances by traveling and studying, as well as practicing. Charles Mayo specialized in surgery of the thyroid and the nervous system and in ophthalmology. He was known for reducing the death rate in goiter surgery. He worked closely with Edward Calvin Kendall, who isolated thyroxine in 1916 while at the Mayo Clinic, and became the head of the biochemistry section.

Mayo was a professor of surgery at the Mayo Graduate School of Medicine from 1915 to 1936. He also served as president of the American Medical Association in 1917, and as health officer of Rochester from 1912 to 1937. He served in the armed forces during World War I and became a brigadier general in the Medical reserve in 1921.

Charles Horace Mayo appears with is brother William James Mayo on a 1964 5¢ stamp.

248

William James Mayo

Scott 1251
Born: June 29, 1861, Le Sueur, Minnesota
Died: July 28, 1939, Rochester, Minnesota

William James Mayo was the son of William Worrall Mayo and older brother of Charles Horace Mayo. Mayo's father emigrated from England in 1845, and studied medicine in Indiana and at the University of Missouri before opening practice in and around Le Sueur, Minnesota.

William was born at the beginning of the Civil War. He grew up in Rochester and, along with his brother, aided his father in the practice of medicine. He studied formally at the University of Michigan, and received his medical degree in 1883. Along with his father and brother, he completed the staff of the new St. Mary's Hospital built by the Poor Sisters of St. Francis. They developed a huge practice that attracted other physicians and surgeons.

After their father died in 1911, the Mayo brothers began to create a group clinic as other surgeons joined them. In 1915 they established the Mayo Education and Research Foundation, which was affiliated with the University of Minnesota.

William specialized in gallstone, cancer and stomach surgeries. During World War II, he and his brother were special consultants to the Surgeon General's Office and were awarded the Distinguished Service Medal. In 1906 Mayo was president of the American Medical Association. He served in the Army Medical Corps during World War I and became a brigadier general in the medical reserves in 1921.

William Mayo appears with his brother Charles on a 1964 5¢ stamp.

Philip Mazzei

Scott C98
Born: December 25, 1730, Poggio a Caiano, Italy
Died: March 9, 1816, Pisa, Italy

Philip Mazzei was a physician in Turkey, a wine merchant in England, an experimental farmer in the United States, a royal adviser in Poland and a pensioner in Russia. He studied medicine in Florence, Italy, and practiced in Turkey, before moving in 1755 to London and becoming a wine merchant.

In 1773 Mazzei set sail for the American colonies, intending to launch the development of olive and grape growing in Virginia.

He established an experimental farm next to Thomas Jefferson's home of Monticello. As a good neighbor of Jefferson, he soon became enveloped in the independence movement, and he strongly favored Virginia's strides toward that goal. Mazzei accepted a commission from Virginia's governor, Patrick Henry, to seek a loan from the Duke of Tuscany. He was captured by the British while on this mission and spent three months in prison. When he finally arrived in Europe to continue his mission, Mazzei found he was being blocked by Benjamin Franklin, who contended that the national government alone could contract foreign debts, not individuals.

Mazzei stayed in Europe until 1783. He collected valuable political and military information for Jefferson. He returned briefly to the United States in quest of a foreign-service post of some kind, but none was available. He went back to Europe and published his lengthy four-volume treatise, *Recherches historiques et politiques sur les Etats-Unis de l'Amerique septentrionale*, which included his historical notes and political opinions of New England.

In 1792 he became an adviser to Stanislow II, the last king of independent Poland, and in 1802 he began to receive a pension from Russia.

Mazzei continued to correspond with Jefferson, even to criticize the Federalists and George Washington. The newspapers printed one such letter, and it caused an uproar. In 1813 he published, in Italian, an account of his life.

A 40¢ Philip Mazzei airmail stamp was issued in 1980.

Andrew William Mellon

Scott 1072
Born: March 24, 1855, Pittsburgh, Pennsylvania
Died: August 26, 1937, Southampton, New York

    Andrew Mellon was the son of Thomas Mellon of Pittsburgh, who was a successful banker, as well as a lawyer and judge. Andrew attended the public schools of Pittsburgh and then went to Western University of Pennsylvania, now the University of Pittsburgh. He would have graduated in the class of 1872 had he not left school in his final year, at age 17, to operate his lumber business. Ten years later, Mellon's father transferred the ownership of the Thomas Mellon and Sons family bank to him.

    Mellon had the ability to recognize the potential growth of certain businesses. By aiding them financially, he watched them develop into large companies. Some companies he helped develop include Aluminum Company of America, the Carborundum Company, the Gulf Oil Corporation, and the Union Steel Company, which merged with United States Steel.

    Mellon became secretary of the treasury under President Harding in 1921. He reduced the government's World War I debt by $9 million, and Congress substantially cut income-tax rates. Mellon also served as secretary of the treasury under Calvin Coolidge and Herbert Hoover. He negotiated agreements with countries in debt from World War I. All defaulted except Finland. In 1932 he was made ambassador to Great Britain, a position he held until 1933. In 1937 he gave his $25 million art collection to the U.S. government. He also donated $15 million for a museum to house it.

    Andrew William Mellon appears on a 1955 3¢ stamp.

Herman Melville

Scott 2094
Born: August 1, 1819, New York, New York
Died: September 28, 1891, New York, New York

Herman Melville came from a distinguished and prosperous family. His father, Allan, was a well-to-do importer in New York, but his business began to ebb when Herman was nine years old. Two years later, he was bankrupt. At age 11, Melville found himself in Albany, New York, where his father had taken the family, hoping to regain his fortune. The elder Melville worked himself to physical exhaustion and mental ruin. Within two year, he died, leaving his four sons and four daughters and wife, Maria, in poverty.

The tragic death of Melville's father had a deep effect on him. Two years later he quit school to take odd jobs to help support his family. He worked in a bank, did farm work, clerked in a store, tried teaching and then, at age 19, signed on as a cabin boy aboard a New York-Liverpool trader boat. This four-month round trip led him to write *Redburn*, an autobiographical sketch.

In 1841, at age 22, Melville signed on with the whaler *Acushnet*, bound for the South Seas out of Fairhaven, Massachusetts. After 18 months, he jumped ship and hid out in the jungles of Nuku Hiva, one of the Marquesas Islands, where the Taipi cannibals treated him kindly and tried to keep him on the island. Melville recounted this in his first book, *Typee*. His experiences on Tahiti and the nearby island of Moorea were related in *Omoo*. On the navy frigate *United States*, Melville was inspired to write *White-Jacket*.

Whaling was the theme of his next book, *Moby-Dick*, also titled *The Whale*. He wrote the book in 1850 at his Pittsfield, Massachusetts, farm, where he was encouraged by his neighbor Nathaniel Hawthorne.

To make a living, Melville worked as deputy inspector of customs in the Port of New York from 1866 to 1885. In addition to novels, Melville also wrote poetry and short stories.

Herman Melville is commemorated on a 1984 20¢ stamp.

Moina Belle Michael

Scott 977
Born: August 15, 1869, Good Hope, Georgia
Died: May 10, 1944, Athens, Georgia

Moina Belle Michael was the daughter of John Marion and Alice Sherwood (Wise) Michael. Michael attended school at the Teachers College in Athens, Georgia, and Columbia University. She taught in the public schools in Georgia for many years. In 1913 she became the social director of the Winnie Davis Hall and the general secretary for the Young Women's Christian Association (YWCA) at the Georgia State Teachers College. Michael was the president of the Georgia Council of Deans of Women and Social Directors of Schools and Colleges of Georgia in 1933.

She served with the American Committee of World War, Rome, Italy, in 1914, and with the Young Men's Christian Association (YMCA), at overseas headquarters, Columbia University, in 1918. She was also a member of the Daughters of the American Revolution, Daughters of the Confederacy, and an honorary member of the Spanish-American War Veterans Auxiliary. She was a registered Democrat and a Southern Baptist.

In November 1918, Michael originated the Flanders Field Memorial Poppy Commemoration to honor the men and women who have served in the United States armed services. The day, known as Poppy Day, is usually celebrated on the Saturday before Memorial (Veteran's) Day. Volunteers, sponsored by several veterans' groups, sell poppies to the public for the benefit of disabled and needy veterans. The money collected is used for medical and educational services.

The poppy, which bloomed on the battlefields of France, became the symbol of the tragedy of war after the World War I. Artificial poppies are sold in the United States.

Michael was awarded the Distinguished Service Medal by the American Legion Auxiliary in Boston in 1930, and was cited as a distinguished citizen by the Georgia legislature in 1931.

The 1948 3¢ Moina Michael issue depicts Michael and a bunch of poppies in honor of the founding of Flanders Field Poppy Day.

253

Edna St. Vincent Millay

Scott 1926
Born: February 22, 1892, Rockland, Maine
Died: October 19, 1950, Austerlitz, New York

Edna St. Vincent Millay and her two younger sisters were raised in Rockland, Maine, by their mother, a widow. Millay's mother recognized and encouraged her daughter's poetic talent. In 1911 Edna submitted a poem titled *Renascense* in an anthology contest. Although she did not win any awards for it, she gained a sponsor who sent her to Vassar College in Poughkeepsie, New York. Millay was 21 years old when she enrolled. Upon graduation in 1917, she participated in the Vassar Daisy Chain, the traditional part of the commencement festivities. She published *Renascense and Other Poems* the year she graduated.

To cultivate her talents and to associate with other artists and writers, she moved to Greenwich Village in New York City. She wrote poems and short stories for magazines and skits for the Provincetown Players, with whom she occasionally acted. She sometimes used the pseudonym Nancy Boyd.

In 1923 Millay married Eugen Jan Boissevain. The couple moved into a remotely located house situated in the foothills of the Berkshires near Austerlitz, New York. In 1923 Millay won the Pulitzer Prize for *The Harp Weaver and Other Poems*. She contributed poetry, books and plays to the publishers, mostly in the 1920s and 1930s. The Metropolitan Opera Company commissioned her to write an opera with Deems Taylor, which culminated in *The King's Henchman*. It was first produced in 1927 with much success. It was published in book form and sold extensively.

With George Dillan, Millay translated Baudelaire's *Flowers of Evil* in 1936. Her later poetry concentrated on modern history.

Millay was a member of the American Academy of Arts and Letters. In 1943 the Poetry Society of America awarded her a medal for her contribution to the humanities.

Edna St. Vincent Millay is pictured on a 1981 18¢ stamp.

Robert Andrews Millikan

Scott 1866
Born: March 22, 1868, Morrison, Illinois
Died: December 19, 1953, San Marino, California

Robert Millikan was born in Morrison, Illinois, located in the northwest part of the state. He then moved to Maquoketa, Iowa. He attended Oberlin College in Oberlin, Ohio, and graduated in 1891. Millikan received his doctorate from Columbia University in New York City in 1895. He spent two more years of post-graduate study at the universities of Berlin and Goettingen, Germany. Millikan returned to the United States and was appointed instructor at the University of Chicago in 1896. He became a full professor of physics in 1910.

His early investigations concerned the electrical charges of electrons. He determined that the charge was a discrete constant and not a statistical average. In recognition of this, Millikan won the Comstock prize of the National Academy of Sciences. He confirmed Einstein's photoelectric equation and made an accurate evaluation of the Max Planck constant.

During World War I, he served as chief of the science and research division of the Army Signal Corps. In 1921 he left the University of Chicago to direct the Norman Bridge Laboratory of Physics of the California Institute of Technology (Caltech) in Pasadena. In 1923 he was awarded the Nobel Prize for isolating the electron and measuring its electric charge, and also for his work on photoelectricity.

Millikan determined that a certain mysterious discharging of a charged electroscope was due to a stream of atomic nuclei of an extremely penetrating character. This stream entered Earth's atmosphere from outer space, bombarding the atmospheric atoms to produce mesons and secondary particles. He called these cosmic rays, and thought them to be the birth cries of new atoms.

During World War II, he worked on jet and propulsion systems, and won the Presidential Medal of Merit.

The 37¢ value released in 1982 as part of the Great Americans issue commemorates Millikan and his discoveries.

255

Margaret Mitchell

Scott 2168
Born: November 8, 1900, Atlanta, Georgia
Died: August 16, 1949, Atlanta, Georgia

Margaret Mitchell spent most of her life in Atlanta, except one year that she spent studying medicine in Smith College, Northampton, Massachusetts. She returned home in 1919 when her mother died. Margaret's father, Eugene Mitchell, was a fifth generation Atlantan, president of the Atlanta Bar Association and the Atlanta Historical Society. Her mother, Maybelle Stephen Mitchell, was an Irish-Catholic who helped found the women's suffrage movement in Georgia. From her parents and elder family members, as well as the family servants, Margaret heard many stories told repeatedly about the Civil War and its aftermath.

She was a reporter for the *Atlanta Journal* and continued on its *Sunday Magazine* even after she married John R. Marsh in 1926. Her first husband, Berrein "Red" Upshaw, an alcoholic, committed suicide in Galveston, Texas, in January 1949.

While recovering from an injured ankle, Mitchell began to write a book. She worked on it for 10 years. Her heroine, Scarlet O'Hara, was much like herself. Biographers say Mitchell was an outrageous flirt. She was little, at four-feet 11 inches. She was also amusing and good-looking, with blue eyes and brown hair. The book, *Gone With the Wind*, was a 1937 Pulitzer Prize winner. A movie based on the book won nine Academy Awards in 1939. The story's hero and heroine, Scarlet O'Hara and Rhett Butler, are two of the best-known figures in American fiction. Mitchell never understood why the book was such a phenomenal success. She never wrote another.

Her life also was cut short. On August 11, 1949, while walking to the theater with her husband, she was struck by an automobile driven by an off-duty taxi driver who had a record of 24 arrests. She died five days later from severe brain damage. The driver was convicted of involuntary manslaughter and sentenced to one year in jail.

Margaret Mitchell is portrayed on a 1¢ Great Americans stamp.

256

James Monroe

Scott 2216e
Born: April 28, 1758, Westmoreland County, Virginia
Died: July 4, 1831, New York, New York

James Monroe left his studies at the College of William and Mary to serve in the Revolutionary War. He was wounded at Trenton. He became a major, but left the army in 1780 to study law under Virginia's governor, Thomas Jefferson. In 1782 Monroe was elected to the Virginia legislature, and from 1783 to 1786, he served in Congress. He was a delegate to the Annapolis Convention. In 1790 he was elected to the Senate as a Jeffersonian Democrat. In 1794 George Washington appointed him minister to France. Monroe attempted to justify the pro-British Jay's Treaty unsuccessfully. Washington called him back to the United States in 1797.

From 1799 to 1802, Monroe was governor of Virginia. In 1803 President Jefferson sent him to aid Robert Livingston in the Louisiana Purchase. As minister to Great Britain between 1804 and 1805, Monroe attempted unsuccessfully to buy Florida from Spain. In 1807 in London, he joined William Pinkney to rectify Jay's Treaty without success. In 1808 James Madison defeated Monroe for the presidency. In 1810 Monroe again was a Virginia legislator. In 1811 Madison appointed him secretary of state. In 1814 he acted as secretary of war for six months.

He was nominated for the presidency in 1817 and won easily. He was re-elected in 1820. His eight years were known as "the era of good feeling." In 1817 the Seminole Indians, encouraged by the Spanish authorities in Florida, instigated an uprising against the people of Georgia. General Andrew Jackson was sent into Florida and promptly took Fort St. Marks and Pensacola. This led to negotiations with Spain, and eventually the acquisition of Florida. For $5 million, Spain ceded Florida to the United States.

In 1820 the Missouri Compromise was settled, and in 1822 the Monroe Doctrine was proclaimed. Monroe refused re-election.

His portrait appears on a 22¢ Presidential stamp issued in 1986.

257

John Bassett Moore

Scott 1295
Born: December 3, 1860, Smyrna, Delaware
Died: November 12, 1947, New York, New York

John Bassett Moore held many important positions in his lifetime, any one of which would have assured him his place in American history. A graduate of the University of Virginia, he studied law in an office in Wilmington, Delaware. He was admitted to the Delaware bar in 1883. In 1885 he was a clerk in the Department of State. Moore was selected as the secretary to the conference on Samoan affairs and as the U.S. secretary at the conference on North Atlantic fisheries in 1887 to 1888. In 1891, he was made professor of diplomacy and international law at Columbia University in New York City. He often took leave from this position to serve his government.

At the beginning of the Spanish-American War, he served as assistant secretary of state. At the Peace Conference in Paris, he was secretary and counsel. Moore was the U.S. agent before the United States and Dominican arbitration tribunal in 1904, the U.S. delegate to the fourth International American Conference at Buenos Aires in 1910 and the special U.S. plenipotentiary to the Chilean centennial in 1910. He also served as the U.S. delegate to the International Commission of Jurists in Rio de Janeiro in 1912, the counselor to the Department of State from 1912 to 1914, and U.S. delegate to the Pan-American Financial Congress in 1915.

In 1921 Moore was appointed to the Permanent Court of International Justice. However, he resigned in April 1928 to edit a historical collection of treaties. He also resigned from his position at Columbia University in 1924 to edit a comprehensive digest of international adjudications throughout history with legal commentaries. From 1922 to 1923, he was the U.S. delegate and chairman of the International Conference on Rules for Aircraft and Radio in Time of War held at The Hague. In addition, Moore wrote volumes on international law, diplomacy and legal history.

He is depicted on the $5 Prominent Americans issue released in 1966.

258

Marianne Craig Moore

Scott 2449
Born: November 15, 1887, Kirkwood (St. Louis), Missouri
Died: February 5, 1972, New York, New York

Marianne Craig Moore's poetry, marked by wit and irony, stands out in the literary world not for a great quantity of verses but rather for its unique quality. *Complete Poems*, published in 1967, contained only 242 pages and included a mere 120 poems. The list of awards Moore won best illustrates the reception her poetry received. The enviable list includes The Dial Award in 1924 for *Observations* and the Ernest Harstock Memorial Prize in 1935 for *Selected Poems*. Other awards Moore received included the Harriet Monroe Poetry Award in 1944; the coveted Bolingen Prize, the National Book Award for Poetry and the Pulitzer Prize in 1951; the M. Carey Thomas Memorial Award and the Gold Medal of the National Institute of Arts and Letters in 1953, and the MacDowell Medal in 1967.

In addition to poetry, Moore translated *The Fables of La Fontaine* in 1954. She won France's Croix de Chevalier des Arts et Lettres for her efforts. She published *Predilections*, a collection of prose essays, in 1955. She received her degree at Bryn Mawr College in Pennsylvania in 1909. She then studied at the Carlisle Commercial College and taught vocational education at the Carlisle Indian School in Carlisle, Pennsylvania.

During World War I, she moved to New York City. Moore spent the rest of her adult life in New York. From 1925 to 1929, she served as acting editor of *The Dial* magazine. In 1929 she settled in Brooklyn.

In 1921 friends first published her *Poems* in London. *Observations* appeared in the United States in 1923, which inaugurated her as a poet of note. Moore also wrote critical essays about her favorite authors, including herself. Her essays "Feeling and Precision" and "Humility, Concentration, Gusto" are examples. She wrote several books in her later years. These included *The Arctic Ox* in 1964, and *Tell Me, Tell Me* in 1966.

Marianne Craig Moore appears on a 1990 25¢ stamp.

Robert Morris

Scott 1004
Born: January 31, 1734, Liverpool, England
Died: May 8, 1806, Philadelphia, Pennsylvania

Robert Morris' father was a tobacco merchant in the village of Oxford, Maryland. At age 13, Robert left Liverpool, England, to join his father. He went to school in Philadelphia but, after a short time, joined the Willing family's mercantile house. At age 20, he became a member of the firm.

Morris was sympathetic toward the cause for independence, siding with the conservative Pennsylvania Whigs rather than the radicals of Thomas Paine. He accepted the post of vice president of the Pennsylvania Committee of Safety, serving between 1775 and 1776. He was a delegate to the Continental Congress from 1776 to 1778. While a member of Congress, he headed two committees, one that obtained war materials and the other that instructed the country's diplomats in Europe.

At first, Morris was reluctant to sign the Declaration of Independence, but did so after its adoption. He was elected to the Pennsylvania Assembly and served until 1779. He brought attention and investigation upon himself when he openly directed business to his mercantile firm for profit.

He again was in the assembly between 1780 and 1781. He served as superintendent of finance at the insistence of Congress, who needed his talents. He immediately established the Bank of North America in Philadelphia and prevented national bankruptcy.

Morris personally helped finance the transfer of George Washington's army from New York to Yorktown to assure the surrender of Cornwallis in 1781. He retained his post until 1784 when he resigned. He was again in the assembly from 1785 to 1787. In 1786 he attended the Annapolis Convention and the Constitutional Convention the following year. He was one of Pennsylvania's first Federalist senators, serving from 1789 to 1795.

Morris supported Alexander Hamilton's fiscal policies. He sold his mercantile business, invested in Western land ventures, and failed. From 1798 to 1801, he languished in debtor's prison. His health declined rapidly.

Robert Morris appears with Betsy Ross, George Washington and George Ross on a 1952 3¢ stamp.

260

Samuel Finley Breese Morse

Scott 890
Born: April 27, 1791, Charlestown, Massachusetts
Died: April 2, 1872, New York, New York

Samuel Morse, developer of the first successful electric telegraph in the United States, became interested in this idea on a trip from Europe aboard the ship *Sully* in 1832. After learning that electricity could be sent instantly over any known length of wire, Morse spent the rest of the trip making notes and sketches. Five years earlier, he had attended lectures on electricity by James Freeman Dana, where the electromagnet was demonstrated.

After reaching New York City, Morse, with the help of Leonard Dunnell Gale, made a crude model, which he demonstrated to friends. Morse corresponded with physicist Joseph Henry, who had published a detailed proposal for a telegraph six years earlier. By 1838, Morse had a working model and also a workable code, which bears his name. The International Morse Code translates letters and numbers into dots and dashes.

Alfred Vail, the son of a New Jersey ironmaster, was interested in Morse's project. With his help, Morse convinced Congress to appropriate $30,000 to build a telegraph line from Washington, D.C., to Baltimore, a distance of 40 miles. The line was built by Ezra Cornell. On May 24, 1844, Morse tapped out, "What hath God wrought!" Lawsuits for rights ensued, but Morse's claims finally were validated in 1854.

Morse was associated with Cyrus Field in laying a transatlantic telegraph cable in 1858. Rulers from other countries decorated Morse for his achievements. He founded Vassar College and was professor of painting and sculpture at the University of the City of New York, now known as New York University. He founded the National Academy of Design in 1826, and for many years served as its president.

Samuel Morse appears on a 1940 2¢ Famous Americans stamp.

261

Horace Moses

Horace Moses
Founder, Junior Achievement
USA 20c

Scott 2095
Born: April 21, 1862, Ticonderoga, New York
Died: April 22, 1947, Springfield, Massachusetts

In 1918, Horace Moses, a paper manufacturer and active participant in local civic affairs, had the idea of creating an organization that would stimulate young people in the principles of business. He had worked his way up from a poor farm boy to become one of the leading U.S. industrialists. He graduated from Troy Academy of Poultney, Vermont, in 1881. He was the founder of Junior Achievement in 1919. The purpose of the organization is to stimulate interest in developing business skills with hands-on experience.

Junior Achievement is directed to American high school students. In the fall of the year before the school term, a student who wishes to participate chooses a product to sell or a service to provide. The student joins the Junior Achievement company and can form a miniature corporation to market the product or service. The youngster sells shares for $1 each. At the end of the year, the corporation is dissolved, and the capital and profits are divided among the shareholders.

The youngsters receive advice and guidance from adult volunteer business and professional personnel. The business endeavors are varied and imaginative. The students' corporations may involve articles bought and sold or manufactured and sold. The services, for instance, may vary from secretarial or repair work to labor. Some endeavors may be creative, such as writing for newspapers and magazines, painting or photography.

Junior Achievement now involves approximately a half million students in four regions and 245 groups, with 8,000 companies guided by 254 autonomous corporations. More than 10 million students have participated in the Junior Achievement program since its inception.

Horace Moses was the honorary chairman of the national organization at the time of his death in 1947.

The 20¢ Horace Moses stamp was issued in 1984.

Lucretia Coffin Mott

Scott 959
Born: January 3, 1793, Nantucket, Massachusetts
Died: November 11, 1880, Philadelphia, Pennsylvania

For two years, Lucretia Coffin attended the public schools in Boston, at her father's insistence, to learn the ways of democracy and to escape the whalers of Nantucket. She later enrolled at a Quaker boarding school in the town of Nine Partners, New York, in the vicinity of Poughkeepsie. There she studied and taught, and met James Mott, a fellow teacher.

Her father moved to Philadelphia, and she joined him at his new home. When she was 18, she and James Mott were married in Philadelphia. She was a good speaker, and within a few years she was recognized as a minister of the Society of Friends. When the Society of Friends split in 1820, she followed the liberal branch and became active traveling around the country and lecturing on religion and social reform. She spoke frequently about temperance, the abolition of slavery and peace.

Mott helped found the American Anti-Slavery Society after she had organized the Philadelphia Female Anti-Slavery Society and was named its president. She met with considerable opposition and rebuff, but she made her crusade known. At a women's rights convention in Seneca Falls, New York, in 1848, she worked with Elizabeth Cady Stanton to organize the women's rights movement.

After the Fugitive Slave Law was adopted in 1850, she and her husband opened their home to runaway slaves as a station in the Underground Railroad. Her husband helped her establish Swarthmore College just four years before his death in 1868. He lived to see their efforts become a reality when President Lincoln signed the Emancipation Proclamation on New Year's Day in 1863. This led to the 13th Amendment to the Constitution, which abolished slavery and involuntary servitude on December 18, 1865.

Lucretia Mott witnessed the inductions of the 14th Amendment, making blacks citizens, and the 15th Amendment, giving blacks the right to vote, in 1868 and 1870, respectively.

Mott is depicted on the 1948 3¢ Progress of Women issue with Carrie Chapman Catt and Elizabeth Stanton.

John Muir

Scott 1245
Born: April 21, 1838, Dunbar, Scotland
Died: December 24, 1914, Los Angeles, California

John Muir was a great walker and a lover of nature. He came from Scotland with his parents when he was 11 years old and grew up near the Fox River at Portage, Wisconsin. He attended the University of Wisconsin from 1859 to 1863, but did not receive a degree. He studied only what interested him and took extensive trips on foot into the Midwest and into Canada.

An eye injury in 1867 changed his course of study from mechanical inventing to viewing nature and keeping volumes of records on what he observed. In 1868, Muir went to California to study nature. He made Yosemite Valley his main central camp for six years. He roamed into Utah, Nevada and the Northwest, where he studied the forests and glaciers of the Sierra Nevada mountain range. In 1879 he went to Alaska, where he first recorded his views of Glacier Bay and a great glacier, which is now named Muir Glacier. He also tramped along the upper reaches of the Yukon and Mackenzie rivers.

In 1880, Muir went with George De Long on a search expedition to the arctic. He also traveled in the Caucasus, Siberia, Manchuria, Japan, India, Egypt, Australia and New Zealand.

Muir wrote many articles for magazines and newspapers, urging creation of national parks. Both Sequoia and Yosemite National Parks were the results of his efforts. He was also responsible for bringing about the passage of federal conservation laws protecting forests. Muir Woods National Monument, 10 miles north of the Golden Gate Bridge, is a 491-acre monument. It preserves the only groves of redwood trees within a national park.

The 1964 John Muir issue was released to honor the conservationist. It shows Muir and a redwood forest.

Luis Munoz Marin

Scott 2173
Born: February 18, 1898, San Juan, Puerto Rico
Died: April 30, 1980, San Juan, Puerto Rico

Luis Munoz Marin was the son of publisher and patriot Luis Munoz Rivera, who led the autonomist forces in achieving Puerto Rico's independence from Spain before the U.S. takeover. Munoz Marin grew up in Puerto Rico and in Washington, D.C., where his father was the island's resident commissioner until he died in 1916. Munoz Marin attended Georgetown University in Washington, D.C., where he studied law. He later turned to writing and moved to New York City in 1919, where he submitted articles to such publications as the *Nation, Smart Set,* and the *American Mercury.*

He advocated Puerto Rican independence from the United States and espoused socialism. In 1926 he returned to Puerto Rico to edit his father's newspaper, *La Democracia,* later called *Diario de Puerto Rico.* He left the paper in 1928, but returned when he was elected to the Puerto Rican senate in 1932 on the Liberal Party ticket.

Through Franklin D. Roosevelt, Munoz Marin was able to obtain U.S. government spending directed to Puerto Rico. He lost his senate seat in 1936, returned to the United States, and broke with his Liberal party. In 1937 Munoz Marin returned to his father's hometown, Barranquitas, and founded the Popular Democratic Party, which won its first senate victory in 1940.

Munoz Marin served as president of the senate from 1940 to 1948, when his party lost the election, and he forfeited his leadership. When Rexford G. Tugwell took office as the U.S.-appointed governor, Munoz Marin worked with Tugwell to improve the island's conditions.

Puerto Rico was given the right to elect its own governor. Munoz Marin was elected the first governor and was re-elected three more times, in 1952, 1956 and 1960. He was effective in changing the island's status.

On July 25, 1952, the new Commonwealth Constitution went into effect. In 1964 Munoz Marin refused re-election but returned to the senate.

Luis Munoz Marin appears on a 5¢ stamp issued in 1990 as part of the Great Americans series.

Ethelbert Woodbridge Nevin

Scott 883
Born: November 25, 1862, Edgeworth, Pennsylvania
Died: February 17, 1901, New Haven, Connecticut

Ethelbert Woodbridge Nevin was an American pianist, composer, teacher and recitalist. He had a sound tutelage, having studied with Franz Boehme in Dresden, Germany (1877-78); B.J. Lang and Stephen A. Emery in Boston (1881-83); and Karl Klindworth and Carl Bial in Berlin, Germany (1884-86). On December 10, 1886, upon his return to the United States, he made his debut at a recital in Pittsburgh. He then settled in Boston in 1887.

Nevin taught music and was a popular performer at recitals. He often played his own compositions of songs and piano pieces, which were widely accepted and performed. In 1891 he moved to Europe with his wife and children and remained there until 1897, when he returned to New York City. In his New York studio, Nevin taught and composed. He was in poor health at the time, and he and his family soon moved to New Haven, Connecticut. In 1901 Nevin died at age 38.

His compositions were lyrical and graceful and probably became popular because of their wonderful sentimentality, which was quite fashionable at that time. The best examples of his piano pieces are in *Water Scenes*, which includes the popular *Narcissus* (1891). *In Arcady* was published in 1892. *May in Tuscany* (1896) and *A Day in Venice* (1898) were also widely performed. Nevin's best-known songs were *Oh, That We Two Were Maying* (1888) and *One Spring Morning* (1888). The two songs that are even today included in many vocal recitals are *The Rosary* (1898) and *Mighty Lac' a Rose* (1901).

His unfinished cantata, *The Quest of the Heart's Desire* was completed by Horatio Parker and published the year after Nevin's death. Also published after Nevin's death was *Tempo di Valse*, a sketchbook of songs and piano pieces. His song *The Rosary* was performed in a concert at Madison Square Garden in New York City on February 15, 1898. Its immediate popularity assured his fame.

Nevin was commemorated for his talents with a 1940 10¢ stamp for famous American composers in the Famous Americans issue.

Jean Nicolet

In 1618, at age 20, Jean Nicolet went to Quebec, New France (Canada). He accompanied Samuel de Champlain, who was his patron and mentor. Nicolet was assigned to live with the Indians on Allumette Island to learn their language and mores. In 1624 he was sent by Champlain to live with the Nipissing Indians and to act as an agent and interpreter. Nicolet stayed with them until 1633, when he returned to New France to take up exploring and mapping expeditions westward.

The following year he went to Huronia on the east coast of Lake Huron. There, he set out with seven Huron Indians in two large canoes and traveled northward. He passed through the Straits of Mackinac, entered Lake Michigan and reached Green Bay. He was sure he had reached the shore of Asia. To be in proper circumstances, he donned a Chinese robe of damask decorated with birds and flowers in many colors. His "Asians" turned out to be naked members of the Winnebago tribe who had never seen a white man.

Nicolet was the first European to see Lake Michigan and Green Bay, and to set foot on Wisconsin soil. He was understandably disappointed that he had not found Cathay (China). However, the Winnebago Indians told him of the great waters to the west. When he was only a day's journey from the Mississippi River, Nicolet returned to Trois Rivieres and reported that he had learned of a sure route to China. (Marquette and Jolliet would learn the truth in 1672.) In 1642, while on a mission of mercy on the St. Lawrence River, a sudden storm capsized Nicolet's boat and he drowned.

A Canadian lake, river and county were called Nicolet in honor of the explorer. Nicolet is also commemorated with the 1934 Wisconsin Tercentenary issue, which shows him landing on the shores of Green Bay.

Chester William Nimitz

Scott 1869
Born: February 24, 1885, Fredericksburg, Texas
Died: February 20, 1966, San Francisco, California

Chester Nimitz was only 15 when he entered the U.S. Naval Academy, where he graduated in 1905. His first overseas assignment was a tour of duty on the *China Station*, where he gained experience as a submarine commander. He then commanded the Atlantic Submarine Flotilla as a lieutenant. In 1913 Nimitz studied diesel engines in Germany and Belgium. When the first diesel ship was constructed for the U.S. Navy, he supervised the program. During World War I, he was promoted to lieutenant commander and served as chief of staff to the commander of the submarine division of the Atlantic Fleet. He attended the Naval War College from 1922 to 1923. Upon completion, he was assigned as chief of staff to the commander of the U.S. fleet.

Nimitz organized the first training division for officers in the naval reserve at the University of California, where he served from 1926 to 1929. By 1938, he had reached the rank of rear admiral. In 1939 he was made chief of the Bureau of Navigation.

Following the Japanese attack on Pearl Harbor, Nimitz was named commander in chief of the Pacific Fleet. He directed sea battles and island landing, including such historic events as Midway, Solomon Islands, Gilbert Islands, the Marshalls, Marianas, Palau, the Philippines, Iwo Jima and Okinawa. These operations, in coordination with General Douglas MacArthur's island-hopping strategy, won the war of the Pacific for the United States.

In 1944 Nimitz was promoted to admiral of the fleet. On September 2, 1945, he was aboard the *Missouri* to receive and sign the surrender of Japan with General MacArthur. During the post-war period, Nimitz served as Chief of Naval Operations. He served later as United Nations commissioner for India and Pakistan. He also was the special assistant to the secretary of the navy. He had not retired at the time of this death.

Chester Nimitz is honored on a 1985 50¢ Great Americans stamp.

George William Norris

Scott 1184
Born: July 11, 1861, Sandusky County, Ohio
Died: September 3, 1944, McCook, Nebraska

When George William Norris was still a child, he had to work to help support the family. Therefore, he was unable to attend school and had to learn on his own. He attended Northern Indiana Normal School and Business Institute in Valparaiso, Indiana. Norris obtained a law degree in 1882. At age 24, he moved to Beaver City, Nebraska, the county seat of Furnas County. Almost directly, Norris went into local politics. He was the Furnas County prosecuting attorney for three terms and district judge from 1895 to 1902. In 1902 he campaigned successfully for the House of Representatives as a Republican. He represented his district until 1912, when he began a 30-year career as a senator from Nebraska. Although he was Republican, he was staunchly independent.

In the House of Representatives, Norris fought to strip the speaker, then "Uncle Joe" Cannon, of his autocratic prerogatives. In the Senate, Norris opposed United States entry into World War I, and afterward, he opposed United States entry into the League of Nations. Norris denounced the Versailles Treaty. He sponsored the Norris-La Guardia Anti-Injunction Act in 1932. He also wrote the 20th Amendment to the Constitution, which is known as the Lame Duck Amendment.

He directed most of his political efforts toward public ownership and operation of hydroelectric resources. After two presidential vetos, these efforts finally resulted in the Tennessee Valley Authority (TVA). Norris did not always follow party lines in support of candidates. He fully supported Franklin D. Roosevelt, a Democrat.

In 1943 Norris ran for re-election as an Independent, but was defeated by the Republican candidate. He retired to McCook, Nebraska, where he died the following year. He is depicted as a "gentle knight of progressive ideals" on the 1961 4¢ Senator Norris issue. The Norris Dam in Tennessee is shown, as well.

269

Adolph Simon Ochs

Scott 1700
Born: March 12, 1858, Cincinnati, Ohio
Died: April 8, 1935, Chattanooga, Tennessee

In 1865 the Ochs family moved from Cincinnati to Knoxville, Tennessee, where Adolph Simon Ochs went to elementary school until he was 11 years old. From his German immigrant parents, Ochs learned the value of a diligent occupation. He worked as an office boy at the local newspaper, the *Knoxville Chronicle*.

When he was 13, Ochs worked as a grocer's clerk in Providence, Rhode Island, and attended night school. He returned to Knoxville and apprenticed with a druggist for a year. By the time he was 18, he was back in the printing business working as the assistant to the foreman in the composing room of the *Knoxville Tribune*. Ochs went to Chattanooga and worked on the *Dispatch* until it failed. He then borrowed money and bought the *Chattanooga Times*, which also was on the verge of bankruptcy. Ochs improved the quality of the paper, and by 1891 it was one of the South's leading newspapers. In that same year, he founded the Southern Associated Press and served as its chairman for three years. He also established the *Tradesman* for southern businessmen.

In 1900, he gained control of the *New York Times*, which at that time was on the verge of collapse. It was Ochs' credo to print "All the News That's Fit to Print." He avoided sensationalism and insisted on accurate, complete coverage of the news directed to the intelligent reader. He did not allow advertisers to dictate editorial content. The *Times* sold for a penny in 1898.

He acquired the *Philadelphia Times* in 1901 and the Philadelphia *Public Ledger* in 1902, then merged the two. His brother, George, managed the paper as the *Philadelphia Public Ledger* until it was sold in 1913. In 1913, Ochs began to publish the *New York Times Index*. He donated generously toward the publication of the *Dictionary of American Biography*.

The Adolph Ochs stamp, which pictures the publisher, was released as a 13¢ value in 1976.

James Edward Oglethorpe

Scott 726
Born: December 22, 1696, London, England
Died: July 1, 1785, Cranham Hall, Essex, England

James Oglethorpe joined the army at age 14 after he had studied at Eton and Corpus Christi College, Oxford, England. Two years later, he joined the Austrian army of Prince Eugene of Savoy and served with distinction in the battles against the Turks between 1716 and 1717. In 1719 Oglethorpe returned to England to be master of the family estate. In 1722 he represented Haslemere in the House of Commons.

Oglethorpe was an adamant humanitarian. He spoke against the injustices of forced public service of seamen and against the penal conditions, especially of debtors. In 1732 he secured a charter to colonize Georgia to provide a residence for newly freed and unemployed debtors. In 1733 he and 114 colonists traveled what is now the United States and founded Savannah, Georgia. He returned to England the next year, since Georgia was growing with new settlers who included German Lutherans, Scottish Presbyterians and German Moravians.

In 1735 Oglethorpe made a second journey to Georgia, and brought with him the Methodist missionaries John and Charles Wesley. John Wesley remained for two years and established Methodism in the colony.

Oglethorpe built Fort Frederica on St. Simon Island to defend against the Florida Spaniards. He experienced trade conflicts with North and South Carolina and had to return to England to settle matters. He then returned to Georgia in 1738 with a British regiment.

In 1739 hostilities broke out between England and Spain. Oglethorpe defended Georgia. He failed to capture St. Augustine at the Battle of Jenkin's Ear, but repulsed the Spanish in the Battle of Bloody Marsh in 1742. He won favor from his troops and colonists.

He returned to England in 1743. He was made a major general in 1745 and a full general in 1765. He and his trustees surrendered their charter in 1752 so Georgia could become a royal province.

James Oglethorpe appears on a 1933 3¢ Georgia Bicentennial stamp.

271

Eugene Gladstone O'Neill

Scott 1294
Born: October 16, 1888, New York, New York
Died: November 27, 1953, Boston, Massachusetts

Eugene O'Neill was born in a New York City hotel near Manhattan's Times Square. He was the second surviving son of Ellen Quinlan and noted actor James O'Neill. Eugene O'Neill attended Princeton University in 1906, but was dismissed after the first year when he threw a bottle through Woodrow Wilson's study window. For the next five years, he worked as a common seaman on voyages to Europe and Latin America. He also worked as a laborer in Argentina.

In 1909 O'Neill married Kathleen Jenkins. They had one son, Eugene Jr. The marriage lasted until 1912, when O'Neill contracted tuberculosis while working in New London, Connecticut, as a reporter. While recovering at Gaylor Farm Sanitarium, he worked on 11 one-act plays and two full-length dramas. In 1914 he attended a playwriting workshop at Harvard. Four of his plays earned him Pulitzer Prizes. These were *Beyond the Horizon* in 1920, *Anna Christie* in 1922, *Strange Interlude* in 1928 and *Long Day's Journey into Night* in 1957. O'Neill received the Nobel prize for literature in 1936. He was the first American dramatist to write tragedy consistently.

O'Neill was married three times, in 1909, 1918 and 1928. His second marriage to Agnes Boulton ended in divorce in 1929. They had two children, Shane and Oona.

O'Neill suffered from Parkinson's disease, a form of palsy, in his later years. Lying in Shelton Hotel in Boston, he spoke his last words to his third wife, Carlotta Monterey O'Neill, "Born in a hotel, died in a hotel."

Eugene O'Neill appears on a 1967 $1 Prominent Americans stamp.

Francis Ouimet

Scott 2377
Born: May 8, 1893, Brookline, Massachusetts
Died: September 2, 1967, Newton, Massachusetts

Francis Ouimet began as a golf caddy and eventually became captain of the Royal and Ancient Golf Club of Saint Andrews, Scotland. By ancient it is meant that historians believe golf originated in Holland. As early as 1457, the Scottish Parliament became alarmed because young men were not practicing archery for defense but were playing football and golf instead. King James II prevailed upon parliament to issue a proclamation stating that "futeball and golf be utterly cryit down and noct usit." In the royal line of Stuarts, James I and Charles I were enthusiatic golfers so tht golf became known as an ancient and royal game. Today, golf is dominated by the United States, although it is played in nearly every country of the world. The rules of golf are determined by the joint decisions of the United States Golf Association and the Royal and Ancient Golf Club of Saint Andrews, of which Ouimet was elected captain.

Ouimet's notoriety began at age 20 when he was an amateur golfer. In 1913, at the United States Open Tournament at Brookline, Massachusetts, he was matched against two of England's best professional golfers, Ted Ray and Harry Vardon. At the end of the match play, he was the winner in a playoff and declared the champion.

At that time, Ouimet was a relatively unknown golfer, and golf was a rather aristocratic and sedate pastime. When Ouimet's feat reached the newspapers and newsreels, the event stirred interest in golf among young men and women.

In 1914 Ouimet won the United States Amateur championship. He won again in 1931, a year after Robert T. Jones Jr. performed the greatest feat in golf history by winning the British Open, the British Amateur, the U.S. Open and the U.S. Amateur titles in the same year.

Francis Ouimet is shown on a 1988 25¢ American Sports stamp.

James Cleveland 'Jesse' Owens

Scott 2496
Born: September 12, 1913, Oakville, Morgen County, Alabama
Died: March 31, 1980, Tucson, Arizona

When James Cleveland Owens was a boy growing up in Cleveland, he was called J.C., which he turned into Jesse. He was known by that name the rest of his life. On May 25, 1935, while attending Ohio State University, Owens set new records in the 220-yard dash, the 220-yard low hurdle and the running broad jump. He also tied the 100-yard dash record. Owens won four gold medals at the 1936 Olympic Games in Berlin, Germany. He nullified Adolph Hitler's dream of showing the world that the Aryan race was supreme.

Owens received his degree from Ohio State University in 1937. After graduation, he tried several business ventures. The Depression forced him to take a job as a playground attendant. He staged exhibitions racing against horses, dogs and cars, but because he accepted money, he lost his amateur standing. He tried other ventures with various successes.

In 1950 Owens was voted by sportswriters as the top track performer for the first half of the 20th century. This elevated his image. He became secretary of the Illinois Athletic Commission, but resigned in 1955 to undertake a goodwill tour to India for the U.S. Department of State.

Owens also headed a lucrative public relations firm and became recognized as the U.S. ambassador to sports. He traveled extensively, giving inspirational public speeches. He established a sports clinic for boys for the Illinois Youth Commission, which sponsors the junior Olympic games.

In his book, *Blackthink: My Life as Black Man and White Man*, Owens condemned blacks for any pro-Negro, anti-white bigotry. He said, "There is no difference between the races. If a black athlete has been better than his white counterpart, it's because he is hungrier; he wants it more."

In 1976 President Gerald Ford awarded Owens the Presidential Medal of Freedom. In 1979 President James Carter presented Owens with the Living Legacy Award. Owens died of lung cancer on March 31, 1980, in Tucson.

He is shown on a 1990 25¢ Olympians stamp.

Ignace Jan Paderewski

Scott 1159
Born: November 18, 1860, Podolia, Poland
Died: June 29, 1941, New York, New York

Ignace Paderewski was a concert pianist who gave recitals and perform-ances from 1891 to 1914 in Europe and America. He was also a pianoforte teacher, but his excellence as a performer took the greater part of his time. He studied at the Warsaw Conservatoire and made his debut in 1877 in Vienna.

When Poland became a newly constituted republic directly after World War I, Paderewski gave up his concert tours at the age of 60, returned to his home in Poland and joined the Nationalist Party. In 1919 he became Poland's first prime minister and foreign minister. He was a signer of the Treaty of Versailles for Poland. Paderewski instigated several needed reforms. How-ever, his Nationalist Party was soon defeated by Marshal Pilsudski. Pad-erewski returned to his piano and his concerts. In 1923 he returned to the concert tour. His free tempo and interpretation varied widely from what was considered customary. Nevertheless, his great reputation could not be shaken, and he was wildly accepted at all his performances.

Paderewski's long gray mane and exaggerated artistic bearing added to his theatrics. At age 75, he played the piano in the film *The Moonlight Sonata*.

After Poland was partitioned in 1939, the Polish government was reorganized at Angers, France. Paderewski was elected speaker of the exiled parliament. When Hitler overran France, Paderewski fled to the United States and died the next year at age 80.

Paderewski was a composer of opera, piano concertos and other large-scale works, but he is remembered most by his two little pieces, *Minuet in G Opus 14, No. 1* and *Crocovienne fantastique, Opus 14, No. 6*, and his interpretation of the romantics, especially Chopin.

He is commemorated by the 1960 4¢ Champion of Liberty issue.

Thomas Paine

Scott 1292
Born: January 29, 1737, Thetford, Norfork, England
Died: June 8, 1809, New York, New York

Thomas Paine's father, Joseph, was a poor Quaker corset maker. His Anglican mother, Frances Locke Paine, was a shrew. Fortunately, Thetford, England, had an excellent grammar school, and Paine's father scrimped to send him to the school. Thomas Paine worked for his father for five years. At age 16, he ran off and signed on as a seaman on the *Terrible*. His father tracked him down and brought him home. Two weeks later the *Terrible* had sunk.

At age 19, Paine signed on the privateer *King of Prussia* and served with distinction in 1756 during the Seven Years' War. From 1757 until 1774, he worked at numerous jobs in various towns.

He met Benjamin Franklin in London. Franklin wrote of him, in a letter of introduction, that he was an "ingenious, worthy young man." Paine separated from his wife, went to America and arrived in late November of 1774. He received employment with Robert Aitken, who appointed him editor of his *Pennsylvania Magazine*. Paine wrote blistering editorials on controversial subjects of the day. He coined the name United States of America and was an early advocator of American independence and a republican form of government.

In 1776 he published a pamphlet called *Common Sense*. In it, he demanded complete independence from England and the establishment of a strong federal union. He demanded many things, including the emancipation of slaves, safeguards to prevent a president from acquiring the powers of a king, the abolition of dueling, the prevention of cruelty to animals, equitable divorce laws, copyright laws and equal rights for women. In 1787 Paine returned to Europe. As a French Girondist, he was opposed to executing King Louis XVI. He wrote *The Age of Reason* while imprisoned in France.

In 1802 he returned to the United States. He died in 1809 in the tiny community of Greenwich Village in New York City. He was buried on his farm in New Rochelle, but 10 years later his body was removed to England.

Thomas Paine appears on a 1968 40¢ Prominent Americans stamp.

276

Nathaniel Brown Palmer

Scott 2386
Born: August 8, 1799, Stonington, Connecticut
Died: June 23, 1877, San Francisco, California

Nathaniel Brown Palmer and his crew on the little sloop, *Hero*, were probably the first white men to sight the Antarctica. Palmer was the first to officially document his discovery. He was 21 years old when he made the exploration on November 18, 1820. In 1907 his niece, Mrs. Richard Fanning Loper, published in the New London, Connecticut, *Globe*, an account of his meeting with the Russian ships commanded by Captain Baron Fabian Gottlieb von Bellingshausen on behalf of Czar Alexander I. Palmer was invited aboard Bellingshausen's ship, the *Vostok*. He related his sightings, as follows:

"I was ushered into the presence of the venerable commander, who was sitting at the table of his cabin, himself and a group of officers in full dress. The gray-headed mariner arose, took me by the hand, saying, through the medium of his interpreter, 'You are welcome, young man, be seated.' I gave him an account of my voyage, tonnage of sloop, number of men and general details, when he said, 'How far south have you been?' I gave him the latitude and the longitude of my lowest point and told what I had discovered.

"He rose much agitated, begging I would produce my logbook and chart, with which request I complied and a boat was sent for it. When the log book and chart were laid upon the table, he examined them carefully without comment, then rose from his seat saying, 'What do I see, and what do I hear from a boy in his teens — that he is commander of a tiny boat of the size of a launch of my frigate, has pushed his way to the pole through storm and ice and sought the point, I, in command of one of the best appointed fleets at the disposal of my august master, have for three, long, weary, anxious years searched day and night for.' "

The account ends by quoting Bellingshausen saying, "I name the land you have discovered in honor of yourself, noble boy, Palmer's land." This account was rather dramatic, embellished by a proud niece. This account was not confirmed in Bellingshausen's report.

Nathaniel Palmer appears on a 1988 25¢ Antarctic Explorers stamp.

277

Dr. George N. Papanicolaou

Scott 1754
Born: May 18, 1883, Coumi, Greece
Died: February 19, 1962, Miami, Florida

Dr. George N. Papanicolaou was the son of a Greek physician in Coumi, Greece. He graduated from the University of Athens with a degree in medicine in 1904. Papanicolaou made the United States his home in 1905 and studied in the pathology department at the New York Hospital. He was on the staff of the Cornell Medical College until 1961. He offered conclusive evidence that malignant tumors of the uterus and cervix could be diagnosed by the microscopic examination of desquamated single cells found in vaginal secretions.

This work has been widely accepted and expanded since that time. At present, exfoliated cells found in secretions from many other areas of the body, such as the respiratory tract, intestinal tract, urinary tract, prostate and breast, can be examined for evidence of anaplastic cell changes (early cancer), when indicated by clinical signs and symptoms. The diagnostic evaluation of cytologic smears for the presence or absence of anaplastic changes (cancer) requires considerable experience and knowledge. A thorough understanding of the normal cells is of primary importance, as is a familiarity with the alterations in cells encountered in malignant tumors. The final decision of these cytologic smears depends upon consideration given not only to normal cells, but also to all abnormal cellular changes or growth changes in cells (dysplasia) that may occur under the influence of inflammation or chronic irritation.

A Pap test can detect 90 percent of early cervical cancers, and its use has reduced deaths from cervical cancer by more than 50 percent through treatment before malignant cells spread, according to *The Merck Manual*.

Papanicolaou is honored on a 13¢ stamp issued in 1978.

Francis Parkman

Scott 1281
Born: September 16, 1823, Boston, Massachusetts
Died: November 8, 1893, Jamaica Plain, Massachusetts

Francis Parkman came from an old and wealthy Puritan family and was heir to a mercantile fortune.

While a sophomore at Harvard, he was influenced and inspired by Jared Sparks, a pioneer American historian, to write a concise and detailed history of the French and Indian conflicts. In 1892 the indomitable Parkman published the final panel of his great historical series on the struggle between the French and English for the control of North America. The series extended from the dawn of French colonization in America to the conquest of New France by the British in 1763. It was truly his life's work.

Parkman spent several months in Europe after his graduation from Harvard in 1844. He then entered Harvard Law School and received a degree in 1846. Parkman did not seek admission to the bar, but instead traveled west to Independence, Missouri, which was the staging point for most of the Western emigrants. He then went on to Westport, Kansas, and set out on the Oregon and Sante Fe trails to learn firsthand about the frontiersmen, the Indians and the early settlers along the newly unsettled territory.

Parkman returned to Boston in October 1846, exhausted from the trip. He described what he saw and heard in the serial called *The Oregon Trail* (1849). He turned to horticulture at one point in his life and was given a professorship of horticulture at Harvard in 1871.

This diversion seemed to improve his failing health and eyesight, and he was able to return to the extensive research and writing of the English and Indian conflicts in America. From 1865 until 1892 segments of his works appeared periodically.

Years before his historiographical tomes were even completed, he and his contemporary, George Bancroft (1800-1891), were established as America's foremost historians. When they died, the golden age of American historiographics came to an end.

Parkman is depicted on the 1967 3¢ Prominent Americans issue.

279

Alden Partridge

Scott 1854
Born: February 12, 1785, Norwich, Vermont
Died: January 17, 1854, Norwich, Vermont

Alden Partridge attended Dartmouth College in Hanover, New Hampshire, for three years. He also attended the United States Military Academy after accepting an appointment in 1805 and receiving a commission as first lieutenant of engineers in 1806. With his past education, Partridge was appointed an instructor at the academy. He remained there until 1817. He was superintendent for two years. When he returned from a leave of absence, he found Sylvanus Thayer, a junior officer, holding forth in his stead.

Partridge refused to relinquish his post, but Congress and the secretary of war claimed that Captain Partridge's administration was lax. He was cashiered for refusing to relinquish his post to Thayer. He was, however, allowed to resign (1818).

These events and his observation of the weakness of the militia system in the War of 1812 led to his founding a military academy. He founded the American Literary, Scientific, and Military Academy in 1819, which became Norwich University in 1834.

The academy served as a model for many military academies in New England and the Middle Atlantic states. These schools were the forerunners of the elementary and secondary military academies that developed throughout the United States to provide trained officers from civilian life as a reserve of military officers available on call. Norwich University was one of the first institutions to offer college-level instruction in engineering and agriculture.

Partridge was elected to the legislature four times. He was an unsuccessful candidate for the House of Representatives three times, and he served a year as surveyor general of Vermont.

A 1985 11¢ stamp from the Great Americans issue features Partridge.

George Smith Patton Jr.

Scott 1026
Born: November 11, 1885, San Gabriel, California
Died: December 21, 1945, Heidelberg, Germany

George Patton received his first military training at the Virginia Military Institute in 1903. He then was appointed to the United States Military Academy at West Point in 1904. He graduated in 1909. As a second lieutenant, Patton was assigned to the 15th Cavalry. He graduated from the Mounted Service School, Fort Riley, Kansas, in 1913 and from the Advanced Course at the Cavalry School, Fort Riley, in 1914.

Patton accompanied General John J. Pershing in the Mexican punitive expedition in 1916. The following year, he went with Pershing to France as commander of Pershing's headquarters troops. In November of that year, Patton established the tank corps and trained the 1st Tank Brigade near Langres, France. In mid-September 1918, he was wounded at the Meuse-Argonne offensive after his unit had completed the St. Mihiel drive. He was decorated and promoted to colonel.

Between the wars, Patton graduated in 1924 from Command and General Staff School and from the Army War College in 1932. In 1940 he commanded the 2nd Armored Division at Fort Benning, Georgia. Following that, he led the 1st Armored Corps training in Indio, California. In 1942 Patton led the Western Task Force ashore in Morocco. In July 1943, he took command of the Seventh Army for the allied invasion of Sicily.

In January 1944, he assumed command of the Third Army for the French campaign. In August his army swept through France to Metz and Nancy, where his extended supply lines and the stiffened enemy resistance stopped him. On December 16, 1944, with reinforcements, Patton attacked the German offensive on its southern flank in the Battle of the Bulge near Bastogne, Belgium.

At the end of 1945, the Third Army was ready to drive across Germany. During the first week of May that year, the Third Army troops were the first to enter Czechoslovakia and liberate Pilsen just prior to the armistice. Relieved of his command, Patton was assigned to the Fifteenth Army. Near the end of the year, he was fatally injured in an automobile accident near Mannheim, Germany.

George Smith Patton Jr. appears on a 1953 3¢ stamp.

Charles Willson Peale

Scott 1064
Born: April 15, 1741, Queen Anne County, Maryland
Died: February 22, 1827, Philadelphia, Pennsylvania

Charles Willson Peale was in the saddle business until he had to give up his trade in 1764. He was a talented young man and a jack-of-all-trades. Since the colonies were short of portrait painters and portrait painting was in demand, Peale devoted himself primarily to the study of this profession. In 1767 the people of Annapolis, Maryland, backed him on a trip to London, England, to study with Benjamin West. He did well and learned modeling, miniature painting and mezzotinto engraving as well. Peale returned to Annapolis in 1769 and stayed until 1776, when he moved to Philadelphia.

He served in the Continental Army primarily as a portrait painter and did portraits of many prominent leaders. George Washington granted him 14 sittings in several situations, from colonel of the Virginia militia to bust portraits. He also painted for John Hancock, Nathanael Greene and John Quincy Adams. In 1779 Peale was elected a representative in the Pennsylvania General Assembly. Natural history was one of his interests, and in 1802 he opened a museum in Philadelphia. Peale also founded the Pennsylvania Academy of the Fine Arts in 1805. He was enterprising and had the good luck of being one of the few portrait painters in the area. The well-publicized fact that Washington was one of his clients did not hinder his reputation.

Peale had 17 children and named many of them after famous artists. A few became artists of some note, especially his son Rembrandt Peale. Peale's brother, James (1749-1831), was an excellent miniature painter in Philadelphia. Two of James' daughters were fine portrait painters and counted Andrew Jackson and the Marquis de Lafayette as their clients.

Charles Peale is shown in his museum on the 1955 3¢ Pennsylvania Academy of Fine Arts issue, which was released to honor the 150th anniversary of the academy's founding.

282

Robert Edwin Peary

Robert E. Peary, Matthew Henson

Scott 2223
Born: May 6, 1856, Cresson, Pennsylvania
Died: February 20, 1920, Washington, D.C.

While working on surveys for a canal across Nicaragua from 1884 to 1885 and again from 1887 to 1888, Robert Peary became interested in polar exploration after reading about the inland ice of Greenland. In 1886 Peary sailed north on the whaler *Eagle*. With the help of Christian Maigaard from Denmark, he made it to the deepest charted penetration of Greenland and the highest recorded elevation upon an ice cap. Peary returned to the Nicaragua canal survey in 1887 and spent some time in Brooklyn, New York, and Philadelphia, before organizing his first expedition in 1891 to the northern reaches of Greenland.

Aboard the ship *Kite*, with his wife, the former Josephine Diebitsch; Matthew Henson, and Frederick A. Cook, the group left for Ingflefield Gulf in June 1891. Late in 1892, Peary and Eivind Astrup of Norway sledged northeast and proved that Greenland was an island.

Peary made trips to the Arctic in 1893, 1896, 1898 and 1905. In 1909 he reached the North Pole after more than 20 years of cultivating the Eskimo. He went as far as possible by ship, then by dog train. Peary established supply points for provisions upon his return. He also left some members of the beginning party every five days along the way.

Peary, Matthew Henson, four Eskimos, five sleds, and 40 dogs reached the pole on April 6, 1909. Three weeks later, they were back on the ship, *Roosevelt*. Peary sent a telegraph message of his discovery in September 1909, but soon learned that Cook had claimed the discovery. In the final analysis, Peary and his party were given credit as the true discoverers of the North Pole.

In 1911 Peary retired from the Navy as a rear admiral. In the same year, he was a delegate to the International Polar Commission in Rome. In 1917, during World War I, Peary was appointed chairman of the National Aerial Patrol Commission.

Robert Edwin Peary appears with Matthew Henson on a 1986 22¢ stamp.

William Penn

Scott 724
Born: October 14, 1644, London, England
Died: July 30, 1718, Berkshire, England

William Penn was the son of Admiral Sir William Penn. The younger Penn went to school at Chigwell, where he came under strong Puritan influences. At age 13, he had a deep religious experience. Although Penn never obtained an academic degree, he attended school at Oxford and Lincoln's Inn in England and at Saumur in France. His education gave him a foundation for the humanistic, theological and legal training that fashioned him as a copious writer, a fluent preacher and a pleader in the courts of law.

When the elder Penn died in 1670, young Penn inherited his father's estates in England and Ireland, as well as his father's standing at court with England's King Charles II and James, the Duke of York.

In 1672, Penn married Gulielma Maria Springett, the stepdaughter of Isaac Pennington. Pennington was a prolific writer of Quaker mystical tracts. Charles II canceled an old debt owed to Admiral Sir William Penn by granting young Penn a huge tract of land in North America. Thus, in 1681, Penn became proprietor of Pennsylvania.

In September 1682, Penn sailed in the *Welcome* to launch the new colony. Many people came to American colonies, such as Pennsylvania, for religious freedom. Penn planned the city of brotherly love, Philadelphia, on a checkerboard pattern. He traveled back and forth from Pennsylvania to England, managing his political and religious affairs.

In 1694, Gulielma died, and Penn married Hannah Callowhill. They had eight children, five of whom lived to adulthood. Penn's deputy, James Logan, and Hannah handled the Penn affairs well. Penn's steward, Philip Ford, swindled him so completely, though, that Penn spent nine months in debtors' prison. In 1712, he nearly surrendered his authority to the crown. He suffered a stroke, and his wife handled his affairs until his death in 1718.

Pennsylvania remained a proprietary colony until the adoption of the Declaration of Independence in 1776.

The 1932 U.S. 3¢ William Penn issue commemorated the 250th anniversary of his arrival in America.

Frances Perkins

Frances Perkins
USA15c

Scott 1821
Born: April 10, 1882, Boston, Massachusetts
Died: May 14, 1965, New York, New York

After graduating from Mount Holyoke College in 1902, Frances Perkins taught school and served as a social worker for the Episcopal church. For a time, she worked and studied at Hull House in Chicago with Jane Addams. Perkins returned to school at the Wharton School of Finance and Commerce at the University of Pennsylvania, then received her masters degree in social economics in 1910 at Columbia University.

After her graduation from Columbia, she held various positions in New York. She was executive secretary of the Consumer's League of New York, executive secretary of the New York Committee on Safety and executive secretary of the New York Council of Organization for War Service.

In 1919 she was appointed to New York's State Industrial Commission by Governor Alfred E. Smith. In 1923 Perkins was named to the State Industrial Board, which she chaired in 1926 for Governor Franklin Roosevelt. In 1929 Roosevelt appointed her the state industrial commissioner.

Roosevelt, as U.S. president, named Perkins the secretary of labor in 1933. She was the first woman to serve in a cabinet position. She was directly responsible for supervising New Deal labor legislation. Perkins left the cabinet in 1945 to serve as a member of the U.S. Civil Service Commission from 1946 to 1953.

For the next 10 years, she was much sought after as a lecturer on subjects concerning labor and industry. Her most popular book, *The Roosevelt I Knew*, was published in 1946.

She was a strong advocate of unemployment insurance after she witnessed the problems and pains of the Great Depression. She also advocated closer government supervision of fiscal policy and saw the period when labor was experiencing great problems in the area of organization.

Perkins is the subject of a 1980 15¢ denomination.

285

Matthew Calbraith Perry

Scott 1021
Born: April 10, 1794, South Kingstown, Rhode Island
Died: March 4, 1858, New York, New York

Matthew Perry was the younger brother of Commodore Oliver Hazard Perry, who died of yellow fever in Venezuela at age 34. The younger Perry entered the Navy in 1809 and served as a midshipman on the *Revenge*, which was commanded by his brother. In 1813 Matthew Perry was promoted to lieutenant. He received his first command in 1821. He cruised the West Indies, protecting commerce from pirates. In 1824 he became the executive officer of a Mediterranean squadron flagship.

From 1833 to 1843, Perry was stationed at the New York Navy Yard. He was made a commandant in 1841. During this stint of duty, he directed the operation of the *Fulton II* and proved the worth of the steam engine for naval purposes. He also was given the honorary lifetime title of commodore.

His next assignment was commanding the African squadron that helped wipe out the slave trade. In 1846, during the Mexican War, Perry captured Frontera, Tabasco and Laguna. He also gave naval support to General Winfield Scott in the siege and capture of Veracruz.

In late 1852, he sailed his squadron to Japan "to demand as a right, and not to solicit as a favor, those acts of courtesy which are due from one civilized country to another." Perry set anchor in Edo Bay in July 1853. By a show of force, he left President Millard Fillmore's message with the Tokugawa shogunate and left with a promise to return. In February 1854 he returned, distributed gifts and obtained a treaty providing hospitable reception of ships in duress, and fueling and supply privileges in Shimoda and Hakodate ports. Even so, it took Townsend Harris, the American consul, until 1858 to negotiate the treaty in full. Not until the Tokugawa rule was put to an end in January 1868 and the Meiji Restoration began did Perry's mission succeed.

Perry's negotiations with Japan were noted on the 1953 5¢ Opening of Japan Centennial issue.

286

Oliver Hazard Perry

Scott 218
Born: August 23, 1785, South Kingstown, Rhode Island
Died: August 23, 1819, off Port of Spain, Trinidad

Oliver Hazard Perry was the older brother of Matthew Calbraith Perry, who opened Japanese ports to world trade. Their father was a naval officer. Oliver Hazard Perry entered the navy as a midshipman in 1799. He served under his father in the West Indies during the naval war with France. During the war with Tripoli, Perry was stationed twice in the Mediterranean Sea.

Perry was commissioned a lieutenant in 1807 and given command of the *Revenge*, on which he trained his younger brother Matthew. In 1811 the *Revenge* was wrecked off the coast of Watch Hill, Rhode Island, but Perry was acquitted of blame by the courts. He commanded a division of gunboats at Newport, Rhode Island, at the outbreak of the War of 1812.

Perry then transferred to Lake Erie under the command of Commodore Isaac Chauncey, who ordered him to Sackets Harbor, New York, to superintend the construction and equipment of a fleet. During the summer of 1813, a fleet of nine vessels carrying 54 guns was equipped at Erie and placed under Commodore Perry's command. To oppose this, the English had a fleet of six vessels, carrying 63 guns, under the command of Commodore Barclay.

On September 10, the two squadrons met in the western part of Lake Erie, out from the mouths of the Maumee and Raisin Rivers. A fierce naval action ensued. Combat lasted three hours, and resulted in a victory for the Americans. Perry sent to Major General William H. Harrison, the military commander in the West, the famous message, "We have met the enemy, and they are ours." Harrison's troops embarked on Perry's ships, crossed to Canada, took Malden, and pursued the British up the Thames River in Canada.

In 1816 Perry took command of the *Java*. While sailing on the Orinoco River in Venezuela in 1819, he contracted yellow fever and died. Perry's Victory and International Peace Memorial stands at Put-in Bay on South Bass Island, Ohio, in Lake Erie. It commemorates the years of peace between Canada and the United States, as well as Perry's victory.

Oliver Hazard Perry is commemorated on an 1888 90¢ stamp.

287

John Joseph Pershing

Scott 1042A
Born: September 13, 1860, Laclede, Missouri
Died: July 15, 1948, Washington, D.C.

John Pershing worked on his father's farm and taught school in a local Negro college. He went to Kirksville Normal School in Missouri and graduated in 1880. He was accepted to West Point and graduated in 1886. His first active service came in a conflict against the Apache.

Pershing served as a military instructor at the University of Nebraska in Lincoln from 1891 to 1895. While there, he earned a law degree. He later returned to West Point and taught tactics from 1897 to 1898. When the Spanish-American War broke out in 1898, he fought as a first lieutenant with the 10th Cavalry in the Santiago campaign.

Afterward, Pershing organized the Insular Bureau for administration and was sent to the Philippine Islands as adjutant general of the Mindanao Department. He fought against the Moro insurgents in 1903. He was with the general staff in Washington, D.C., and served as U.S. military attache in Tokyo during the Russo-Japanese War.

Pershing was promoted in 1906 from captain to brigadier general by President Theodore Roosevelt. He returned to the Philippines to put down the Moro with finality in 1913.

As commander of the 8th Brigade in San Francisco, Pershing was sent to patrol the troubled Mexican border in 1915 in pursuit of Pancho Villa. Villa had raided and burned the town of Columbus, New Mexico.

By 1917, Pershing, a major general, was named to command the American Expeditionary Force destined for France. He refused to submit his troops as replacements for the French. Finally, Marshal Foch gave Pershing a combat assignment. The Americans were successful on the St. Mihiel salient and the Meuse-Argonne offensive, which wound up the war and resulted in the armistice. Pershing returned to the United States a hero and was made the first general of the armies. This rank was originally created for George Washington, but he never assumed it. From 1921 to 1924, Pershing served as Army chief of staff and maintained an office in the War Department.

John Joseph Pershing appears on a 1961 8¢ Liberty stamp.

Franklin Pierce

Scott 819
Born: November 23, 1804, Hillsborough, New Hampshire
Died: October 8, 1869, Concord, New Hampshire

Franklin Pierce was the son of Benjamin Pierce, a prominent New Hampshire Democrat. Pierce graduated from Bowdoin College, Brunswick, Maine, in 1824 and was admitted to the bar in 1827. In 1829 Pierce was elected to the state legislature. In 1833 he was elected to the House of Representatives. From 1837 until his resignation in 1842, he served in the Senate.

For the next decade he served as U.S. attorney general for his home state and practiced law in Concord. In May 1847, Pierce sailed for Veracruz. In July, under General Winfield Scott, Pierce led his volunteers to Mexico City. He suffered a crushed leg at the Battle of Churubusco but stayed with his troops until Mexico City was captured.

In 1852 the Democratic party nominated Pierce for the presidency. The inauguration on March 4, 1853, was a triumph of the Democratic party. The Whigs chose General Winfield Scott as their candidate. Scott carried only four states. The Whigs never recovered from this defeat.

Pierce settled the boundary question with Mexico known as the Gadsden Purchase. For $10 million, the purchase extended the Arizona-New Mexico boundary southward from the Guadeloupe Hidalgo treaty. In January 1854, Senator Stephen Douglas of Illinois proposed the Kansas-Nebraska bill. Despite opposition, the bill became a law in May 1854, and the controversy over slavery heated up.

Also during Pierce's administration, the ports of Japan were opened to trade. In 1856 the Democratic convention wrested the presidential nomination from Pierce, the first president to be denied a second term by his own party. Pierce retired to Concord.

Franklin Pierce appears on a 1938 14¢ Presidential stamp.

289

Pocahontas (Matoaka)

Scott 330
Born: circa 1595, Virginia
Died: March 1617, Gravesend, England

Pocahontas, the daughter of American Indian chief Powhatan, is probably best known for having saved the life of Captain John Smith, leader of the settlers of Jamestown, Virginia. Smith was brought before the chief and condemned to die. Pocahontas threw herself between the captain and her father, who was about to kill Smith with a club. In his book, *Generall Historie of Virginia*, published in 1624, Smith recounted this incident. Since he had not mentioned it in his first publication, *A True Relation*, published in 1608, many consider the story fiction, although controversy over its authenticity exists.

In 1613, while visiting the chief of the Potomac tribe, Pocahontas was captured and taken to Jamestown as a hostage to ensure the good behavior of the Indians. While in Jamestown, she was treated courteously, was converted to Christianity and was baptized with the English name of Rebecca. A healthy and attractive girl, she won the heart of one of the colonists, John Rolfe, who requested permission to marry her. It was hoped that this union would cement relations and friendship between the colonists and the natives. Sir Thomas Dale, then governor, agreed to the marriage, as did Powhatan, Pocahontas' father. The two were married in the Jamestown church in April 1614.

In 1616 John Rolfe took his new wife and several other Indians to England, where he presented them to King James I and Queen Anne. The Rolfe's were given a royal reception by the bishop of London, since Pocahontas was considered an Indian princess. Just prior to sailing back to America, Pocahontas died of smallpox. She was buried in the chancel of the church at Gravesend.

The couple had one son, Thomas, who was educated in England. He settled in Virginia, where a number of noted Virginia families who claim to be his descendants now live.

Pocahontas is featured on a 1907 5¢ Jamestown Exposition stamp.

290

Edgar Allan Poe

Scott 986
Born: January 19, 1809, Boston, Massachusetts
Died: October 7, 1849, Baltimore, Maryland

Edgar Allan Poe's parents were actors performing in Boston when he was born. By late 1811, before Poe was three years old, his father had left and his mother had died. Their three children were left destitute. Poe's older brother William died young, and his older sister Rosalie suffered from mental illness. Poe went to live in the home of John Allan, a prosperous tobacco merchant, in Richmond, Virginia. Poe lived with the Allans in England for five years and attended school near London.

In 1820 they returned to Richmond. Poe attended the University of Virginia, but was compelled to withdraw after he incurred gambling debts trying to win money for books and clothing. Poe left home after quarreling with John Allan about becoming a lawyer.

In 1827 Poe joined the army. In 1830 John Allan secured for Poe an appointment to West Point. Again he got into deep debt gambling. He was court-martialed and dishonorably discharged. Poe moved to Baltimore to live with his aunt, Maria Clemm, his father's widowed and poverty-stricken sister and her young daughter, Virginia. Poe won a $50 prize for a short story in the *Baltimore Saturday Visitor*. This launched his career as a staff member of various magazines from which he was either soon retired or soon discharged.

In 1836 Poe married his cousin, Virginia, after she and her mother had joined him in Richmond where he was working at *The Southern Literary Messenger*. John Allan had recently died, leaving Poe nothing. Poe's wife died of tuberculosis after they had been married 11 years. Poe turned to occasional drinking to ease his sorrow. However, he was neither an alcoholic nor a drug addict, as some people believed. In 1849 Poe became engaged to Sarah Royster Shelton. On October 3 of that year, he was found lying outside a voting place in Baltimore. Poe died in a hospital three days later, having never regained consciousness. The cause of his death was undetermined.

Edgar Allan Poe is pictured on a 1949 3¢ stamp.

James Knox Polk

Scott 2217b
Born: November 2, 1795, near Pineville, North Carolina
Died: June 15, 1849, Nashville, Tennessee

James Polk grew up on a farm but was better at book learning than farm chores because of his frail health. After graduation from the University of North Carolina in 1818, Polk moved to Tennessee, where he studied law under Felix Grundy. Polk was admitted to the bar in 1820 and practiced law in Columbia, Tennessee. In 1825 he was elected to the first of seven consecutive terms in the House of Representatives. In 1839 he was elected governor of Tennessee, but was defeated for re-election in 1841 and 1843.

Polk was expected to become Martin Van Buren's running mate in 1844, but Van Buren's stand on Texas alienated Southern support. On the ninth ballot the nomination went to Polk, with George M. Dallas of Pennsylvania as his running mate. Polk proceeded to win the election over Henry Clay and was inaugurated March 4, 1845. The election of Polk was a triumph for the Democratic party. The Whigs had put up Henry Clay, who opposed the annexation of Texas, which Polk had pledged to accomplish.

Polk achieved four major objectives during his term. These included the acquisition of California, the settlement of the Oregon question, the reduction of the tariff and the establishment of the independent treasury. He also expanded the Monroe Doctrine to exclude all non-American intervention in American affairs, whether forcible or not.

In addition, he forced Mexico into a war that was waged to a successful conclusion with the treaty of Guadeloupe Hidalgo on February 2, 1848. This treaty added territory now comprised of New Mexico, Utah and California. The northern half of Oregon was yielded to Great Britain, which resulted in the ultimate downfall of Polk and the Democratic party. Zachary Taylor, with Millard Fillmore of the Whig party, won the presidency in 1849. Polk retired to his home in Nashville and died in June of that year.

James Knox Polk appears on a 1986 22¢ Presidential stamp.

Juan Ponce de Leon

Scott 2024
Born: 1460, Santervas de Campos, Spain
Died: 1521, Havana, Cuba

Juan Ponce de Leon was born into a noble family in a part of the old kingdom of Leon in northwest Spain. As a young boy, Ponce de Leon served as a page and squire to Pedro Nunez de Guzman in the court of King Ferdinand V and Queen Isabella I. In 1492 he fought with Spanish troops that drove the Moors out of Grenada. In 1493, looking for adventure, he sailed with Columbus to the New World. In 1502 Ponce de Leon was in Santo Domingo, where he served as a captain, fighting against the Indians. Governor General Nicolas de Ovando appointed him acting provincial governor in the northeastern part of the island.

He received permission to colonize Boringquen, the native name for Puerto Rico. He landed on the island on August 12, 1508. On the island, Ponce de Leon built a settlement called Caparra, then returned to Santo Domingo to be declared Adelantado, or provincial governor, of Borinquen in 1509. Diego Columbus succeeded Ovando and appointed Juan Ceron in place of Ponce de Leon, who pleaded to stay on. The council, consejo de Indias, selected Ceron, and Ponce de Leon was told to seek new land.

On March 3, 1513, feeling debilitated at age 53 and having been told by the natives of a wonderful fountain on the island of Bimini that had extraordinary curative powers, Ponce de Leon sailed west in quest of restoring his youth. On March 27, he touched land 175 miles south of present-day St. Augustine, Florida. The place was lush with greenery and flowers. Since it was Eastertime, Pascua Florida in Spanish, Ponce de Leon named the island la Florida. He sailed around the keys and explored along the west coast of this so-called island.

He returned to Puerto Rico and then to Spain in 1514 to secure his title as adelantado of la Florida and Bimini. Ponce de Leon returned to his family affairs and to pacifying the Carib Indians who were causing trouble. By 1521, Ponce de Leon, who was 61 years old and in need of the waters of Bimini, sailed over to his island. He reached Sanibel Island, where he was wounded by poison arrows from the Indians who were defending their homeland. Ponce de Leon died soon afterward at Havana, Cuba.

He is commemorated on a 1982 20¢ stamp.

293

Salem Poor

Salem Poor   Gallant Soldier

Scott 1560
Born: between 1747-58, Andover, Massachusetts
Died: unknown

Salem Poor was a free Negro, having been born free. He had a wife, but left her in Andover, Massachusetts, when he went off to war to fight for the Revolution. He enlisted under Captain Benjamin Ames in Colonel Fryes' regiment. He fought at Bunker Hill, as did Peter Salem. As Salem was credited with shooting down Major John Pitcairn, Poor was credited with eliminating Lieutenant Colonel James Abercrombie. Poor's valor and intrepidness at the Battle of Bunker Hill caused 14 officers, including Colonel William Prescott, to cite him with heroism and thus petition the General Court of Massachusetts:

"The Reward due to so great and Distinguisht a Caracter. The Subscribers begg leave to Report to your Honble. House (Which Wee do in justice to the Caracter of so Brave a man) that under Our Own observation, Wee declare that A Negro Man Called Salem Poor of Col. Fryes Regiment, Capt. Ames. Company in the late Battle of Charleston, behaved like an Experienced Officer, as Well as an Excellent Soldier, to Set forth Particulars of his Conduct would be Tedious, Wee Would Only begg leave to say in the Person of this sd. Negro Centers a Brave & gallant Soldier."

Such brief accounts from revolutionary rolls, such as the Massachusetts Archives at the Statehouse in Boston, reflect the remarkable character of such men as Poor and Peter Salem. Like Peter Salem, Poor also enlisted and re-enlisted according to the mandates and remands of General Washington and Lord Dunmore.

Records show that Poor served at Valley Forge and White Plains. What became of him is unknown. The conduct of most Negroes was little recorded, and their later lives were completely ignored. Any rewards Poor may have received went unrecorded.

Poor is commemorated on a 1975 10¢ American Bicentennial issue as a contributor to the cause.

294

David Dixon Porter

Scott 792
Born: June 8, 1813, Chester, Pennsylvania
Died: February 13, 1891, Washington, D.C.

David Dixon Porter was the son of Captain David Porter (1780-1843). At age 10, the younger Porter first went to sea with his father. In 1826, Captain Porter became commander and chief of the Mexican navy, and young David joined him as a midshipman. Young David was taken prisoner by the Spanish, and upon his release in 1829, he received a commission in the U.S. Navy as a midshipman and did duty on the European station.

During the Civil War, David Dixon Porter commanded the *Powhatan* for relief of Fort Pickens. In March 1862 he joined his adopted brother, David Farragut, in blowing up forts Jackson and Saint Philip, enabling Farragut's fleet to take New Orleans. Porter also shelled Vicksburg. Then as a rear admiral he commanded the Mississippi squadron. He aided Sherman in the capture of the Arkansas Post and cooperated with General Grant in the siege of Vicksburg. Porter also aided General Banks in the Red River expedition. In 1864 he commanded the North Atlantic blockading squadron and assisted General Terry in the capture of Fort Fisher.

When James Farragut (1801-70) was nine years old, he was adopted by Captain David Porter. Farragut then changed his name from James to David in honor of his adopted father, but kept the Farragut name. He began his career with his new father as a midshipman on the Essex. Farragut received the rank of admiral in 1866, a title that was especially created for him. The younger Porter was given the same title after Farragut's death in 1870. Thus, both of Captain Porter's sons reached the highest rank in the U.S. Navy.

After the war, the younger Porter became superintendent of the U.S. Naval Academy and made many improvements. Despite his high rank, his later years were spent very quietly as a member of the Board of Inspection.

The 1937 3¢ stamp released in the Navy issue pictures Admiral Porter, as well as his adopted brother, Admiral Farragut.

Wiley Post

Scott C95
Born: November 22, 1899, near Grand Saline, Texas
Died: August 15, 1935, Walkpi, near Point Barrow, Alaska

When Wiley Post was eight years old, his parents moved to a farm near Maysville, Oklahoma, about 45 miles south of Oklahoma City. Post took his first automobile ride when he was 14. That same year, he saw an airplane at the county fair. He attended an automobile school in Kansas City, Missouri. In 1917 he was a radio student at an army training camp at Norman, Oklahoma. On the farm, Post kept the machinery in order and did odd jobs.

Following World War I, he went to work in the oil fields. He joined an airplane barnstorming circuit as a parachutist and stunt man and learned to pilot a plane.

Hard times in 1926 forced Post to return to the oil fields. In a drilling accident, he lost his left eye. With $1,800 in compensation money, Post bought an old airplane. In 1928 F.C. Hall, an Oklahoma oil man, hired Post as his private pilot. The plane he flew was the *Winnie Mae*. The *Winnie Mae*, a Lockheed Vega, was named after the daughter of its original owner, F.C. Hall. Post entered the Bendix Trophy race in 1930 and won. From June 23 to July 1 of that year, Post and his navigator, Harold Getty, flew around the world in a little more than 8 1/2 days.

Post bought the *Winnie Mae* and in 1933 left from Floyd Bennett Field to fly around the world alone, demonstrating new flying instruments. Fifty thousand people greeted him upon his return. He explored high-altitude flying using special equipment. He reached the unofficial height of 49,000 feet. In August 1935, Post set out in a new airplane with his friend Will Rogers to fly from the West Coast to the Orient via Alaska and Siberia. They landed 15 miles south of Point Barrow. On take-off the plane plummeted to earth, killing both men.

The *Winnie Mae* was purchased by Congress for preservation in the Smithsonian Institution.

Wiley Post is pictured with his plane on a 1979 25¢ airmail stamp.

John Wesley Powell

Scott 1374
Born: March 24, 1834, Mount Morris, New York
Died: September 23, 1902, Haven, Maine

John Powell's parents emigrated to the United States from England in 1830. His father was a minister and wanted his son to follow him but Powell had more interest in the natural sciences. Powell's parents moved around because of his father's profession. He lived in Ohio and Wisconsin before his family finally settled in Wheaton, Illinois. Powell went to three colleges, Wheaton, Illinois and Oberlin, but received no degree. He made long field trips through the eastern Great Plains and was secretary of the Illinois Society of Natural History.

At the beginning of the Civil War, he enlisted and served with the artillery. He was discharged as a major, but at the Battle of Shiloh, he lost his right arm at the elbow. Powell became professor of geology at Illinois Wesleyan College in Bloomington in 1865. He also held the positions of lecturer and museum curator at Illinois State Normal University, now Illinois State University, at nearby Normal, Illinois.

In 1867 Powell made a field trip into the Rocky Mountains. In 1869 Congress and the Smithsonian Institution sponsored Powell's dangerous and daring 900-mile trip down the Colorado River and through the Grand Canyon by boat. Powell made further explorations, and in 1875 was appointed director of the United States Geological and Geographical Survey of the Territories. In his 1895 report, *Canyons of Colorado*, Powell stated that the rivers cut into the rocks, which formed canyons. Powell made close observations of the Indian's language, establishing a classification.

In 1879 he was the first director of the Smithsonian's Bureau of American Ethnology. His survey group merged with the U.S. Geological Survey, of which he became director two years later and initiated the publication of its bulletins. Powell continued to direct the survey until 1894, and was active in the Bureau until his death.

Powell is shown exploring the Colorado River on a 1969 6¢ stamp.

Joseph Priestley

Scott 2038
Born: March 13, 1733, Fieldhead, West Riding of Yorkshire, England
Died: February 6, 1804, Northumberland, Pennsylvania

Before attending the Nonconformist Academy at Daventry, England, in 1752 at the age of 20, Joseph Priestley spent four years at Chaldee and Syriac studying Gravesande's *Natural Philosophy*. As a non-conformist minister, he served a small congregation at Needham Market in Suffolk from 1755 to 1758. He then moved to Nantwich to serve a congregation and open a school.

In 1761 Priestley moved to Warrington to tutor students in the classics in the new academy where M. Turner of Liverpool was lecturing on chemistry. He pursued the study of chemistry and electricity and was elected to membership in the Royal Society. In 1766 he was able to acquire material for his book *The History and Present State of Electricity*. In 1767 he was placed in charge of Mill Hill Chapel at Leeds, where he wrote critically of the government's policy toward the colonies in America.

Priestley invented soda water in 1772. That same year he was taken into the French Academy of Sciences in a position at Calne as a librarian and literary companion to Lord Shelburne. His most famous discovery was in 1774, when he obtained a colorless gas during an experiment and called it dephlogisticated air (oxygen). In 1774 he met the French chemist Antoine Lavoisier and told him about the new gas.

Priestley settled in Birmingham as a junior minister of the New Meeting Society in 1780. He met Matthew Boulton, James Keir, James Watt and Erasmus Darwin. While the Constitutional Society of Birmingham was entertaining Priestley, a mob burned his chapel and sacked his home, destroying years of his work. He was not well-received in London. He took a position at Gravel Pit Chapel in Hackney until 1794. He then emigrated to America, where he worked in Northumberland, Pennsylvania. The American Chemical Society was established in Northumberland in 1876 in his honor.

The Joseph Priestley 20¢ issue was released April 13, 1983.

General Kazimierz Pulaski

Scott 690
Born: March 4, 1748, Winiary, Mazovia, Poland
Died: October 11, 1779, Savannah Harbor, Georgia

Casimir Pulaski (common Anglicized spelling) was the oldest son of Count Jozef Pulaski, the organizer of the Confederation of Bar and an avid Polish patriot. Casimir and his two brothers fought for the confederation. He defended Czestochowa against the Russians in 1770-71, which brought him widespread fame. In 1772 the Russians were aided by the Austrians and Prussians, and Pulaski became overwhelmed and went into exile, first in Turkey and then in Paris. He was introduced to Silas Deane and Benjamin Franklin, who relieved him of his restlessness by sending him to America in 1777 to aid in the Revolution. He was assigned to General George Washington at Brandywine.

Congress made Pulaski a brigadier general in charge of the continental cavalry. He served at Germantown and was at Valley Forge during the winter campaign of 1777-78. He refused to serve under General Anthony Wayne and, in bitterness, resigned his commission. However, he was persuaded to reform a combination cavalry and light infantry called Pulaski's Legion. He waged a guerrilla-type warfare against the British, but to little avail.

Pulaski often disputed his fellow officers. Meanwhile, an amphibious operation captured Savannah from its weak continental garrison on December 29, 1778, then overran Georgia. The royal governor was reinstated, an assembly was summoned and the state was virtually restored to the British empire. In 1779 Pulaski marched his men to join General Benjamin Lincoln in South Carolina, where he performed effectual service. Pulaski led his cavalry in the siege of Savannah. The attack was under the command of the French fleet and Admiral Comte d'Estaing. But in the assault on October 9, 1779, Count Pulaski was mortally wounded and carried on board the brig *Wasp* in the Savannah harbor, where he died two days later. D'Estaing, twice wounded, re-embarked his landing force and sailed from France.

Pulaski is honored on a 1931 2¢ Pulaski stamp.

Joseph Pulitzer

Scott 946
Born: April 10, 1847, Mako, Hungary
Died: October 29, 1911, Charleston, South Carolina

Joseph Pulitzer came to the United States from Hungary, landing in Boston at age 17. He served in the Civil War with a cavalry regiment for a year. Educated in Budapest, Pulitzer held several minor jobs after the war until he became a reporter on a German-language daily paper owned in part by Carl Schurz. In addition to working on the *St. Louis Westliche Post*, Pulitzer was active in politics. In 1869 he was elected to the Missouri legislature as a liberal Republican.

Pulitzer worked for Horace Greeley's presidential campaign, but after Greeley's disastrous defeat, Pulitzer changed to the Democratic party. He purchased the defunct *Staats-Zietung* and sold its Associated Press subscriptions to the *St. Louis Globe*. In 1876 he was admitted to the District of Columbia bar, but instead of law practice, he chose journalism. In 1878 he purchased the bankrupt *St. Louis Dispatch*, which he combined in 1880 with the *Post*. It became the *Post-Dispatch*. Pulitzer's editorial targets were soft money, high tariffs and corrupt politicians.

He purchased the *New York World* from Jay Gould in 1883 and transformed it from a poor paper to one with the largest circulation in the nation. He was elected to Congress from New York in 1885, but resigned after several months. In 1887 he founded the *Evening World* of New York. Ill health and failing eyesight compelled him to relinquish management of his paper. After fierce competition between the *World* and William Randolph Hearst's *New York Morning Journal*, both of which were known as full of scandalous sensationalism (yellow journalism), Pulitzer resumed management and returned his paper to responsible reporting.

His will endowed the Columbia School of Journalism and the Pulitzer prizes for journalism, letters, and music. Pulitzer died in Charleston, South Carolina, in 1911. His eldest son, Joseph Pulitzer Jr., became the publisher and editor of the *St. Louis Post-Dispatch*.

Joseph Pulitzer appears on a 1947 3¢ stamp.

Rufus Putnam

Scott 795
Born: April 9, 1738, Sutton, Massachusetts
Died: May 4, 1824, Marietta, Ohio

Rufus Putnam, at age 16, was apprenticed to a millwright. At age 19, he enlisted for the French and Indian War. He re-enlisted until 1760 and saw action near Lake Champlain. Putnam engaged in farming, surveying and millwrighting until 1773. That year, he was appointed a member of a committee to inspect lands in Florida and along the Yazoo River that were granted by the crown to veterans of the French and Indian War.

After the Battles of Lexington and Concord, Putnam entered the Continental army as a lieutenant colonel. He organized the batteries on Dorchester Heights that caused the evacuation of the British from Boston. In 1776 Putnam was commissioned in the Massachusetts militia. He commanded the fifth regiment under General Gates and served at Saratoga. In 1778 Putnam worked at West Point. He served with General Anthony Wayne in 1779. Putnam settled on his farm near Rutland, Massachusetts, in 1783. He served in the Rutland legislature.

In 1785 Congress appointed him to survey the Western lands. With Benjamin Tupper, Manasseh Cutler and others, Putnam formed in Boston the Ohio Company of Associates to obtain land in Ohio for settlement by Revolutionary veterans. One and a half million acres were obtained at 9¢ an acre. The Northwest Ordinance of July 13, 1785, which was the most momentous act in the Confederation's history, bridged the gap between wilderness and statehood.

On April 7, 1788, Putnam settled in Marietta, Ohio. In 1790 George Washington appointed him judge of the Northwest Territory. After serving as brigadier general to conclude a treaty at Vincennes, Indiana, with eight Indian tribes, Putnam resigned his commission in 1793. In 1796 he was named United States surveyor general, but in 1803 Jefferson promptly dismissed him. In 1802 he became a member of the first Ohio constitutional convention.

Rufus Putnam appears with Manasseh Cutler and a map of the Northwest Territory on a 1937 3¢ stamp.

301

Ernest Taylor Pyle

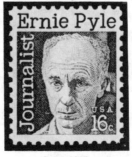

Scott 1398
Born: August 3, 1900, Dana, Indiana
Died: April 18, 1945, Ie Shima, Okinawa, Ryukyu Islands, Japan

Ernie Pyle won the Pulitzer prize in 1944 for stories he wrote about how World War II soldiers fought and lived. Pyle's syndicated columns were collected in three volumes *Ernie Pyle in England*, published in 1941; *Here is Your War*, published in 1943, and *Brave Men* published in 1944.

Pyle was a roving reporter. In 1935 he gave up his desk job and, with his wife, traveled some 200,000 miles throughout the Western Hemisphere, sending letters of human interest home.

Five years before his untimely death, Pyle reported on the Luftwaffe's bombing of London. He also sent back stories about the American troops stationed in England and Ireland. He went with the troops into North Africa and Italy, and described the scenes from the average soldier's point of view at the invasion of Normandy in June 1944.

In September 1944, Pyle returned to the United States, but left in January of the following year to go to the Pacific War theater. *His Last Chapter* was published posthumously in 1946.

Pyle attended Indiana University but left in 1923 before graduation to work on the *Herald* in La Porte, Indiana. He also worked on Washington, D.C., and New York City dailies, and from 1928 to 1932 covered aviation stories for the Scripps-Howard newspapers. From 1932 to 1935, he was managing editor of the magazine section of the *Daily News* in Washington.

In 1945 Pyle died instantly from a Japanese sniper's machine gun bullet on the island of Ie Shina, just off the main island of Okinawa in the Ryukyu Islands.

Ernest Taylor Pyle appears on a 1971 16¢ stamp.

Asa Philip Randolph

Scott 2402
Born: April 15, 1889, Crescent City, Florida
Died: May 16, 1979, New York, New York

Asa Randolph was the son of a Methodist minister. He studied at City College of New York. Randolph in 1917 founded the journal, *The Messenger*, and taught at the New York Rand School of Social Science. He was unsuccessful in his quest for the seat of New York secretary of state in 1921.

Randolph lectured across the country, urging blacks to join unions. In 1925 he organized the Brotherhood of Sleeping Car Porters, now part of the Brotherhood of Railway and Airline Clerks.

In June 1941 Randolph persuaded President Franklin Roosevelt to form the Fair Employment Practice Committee. This committee paved the way for equal employment of minority groups in war production and defense industries, and government employment. The following year, New York City Mayor Fiorello LaGuardia appointed Randolph to the New York Housing Authority. Randolph convinced President Harry Truman to curb discrimination in the armed forces. In 1947 Randolph founded the League for Nonviolent Civil Disobedience in the armed forces. This helped lead the way for blacks to attend West Point and Annapolis.

In 1955 the American Federation of Labor and the Congress of Industrial Organizations merged. Randolph was appointed to the executive council and became the union's vice president in 1957. In 1960 he founded the Negro-American Labor Council and was its president until 1966.

Within the AFL-CIO, Randolph struggled with George Meany for more support of civil rights. In 1963 Randolph helped organize the march on Washington, D.C. In 1966 Randolph was honorary chairman of the White House Conference on Civil Rights.

Randolph wrote for *Opportunity*, the journal of the Urban League, and founded the A. Philip Randolph Institute of New York City, an educational institute where minority youths could be trained for skilled jobs.

Asa Philip Randolph appears on a 1989 25¢ Black Heritage stamp.

Samuel Taliaferro Rayburn

Scott 1202
Born: January 6, 1882, Roane County, Tennessee
Died: November 16, 1961, Bonham, Texas

Samuel Rayburn grew up on a farm in north Texas, where he went to school in a one-room schoolhouse in Flag Springs. He continued his education at East Texas Normal School, now East Texas State University, graduating in the class of 1903. Early in his life, Rayburn decided that one day he would be speaker of the House of Representatives. He began by studying law at the University of Texas and was admitted to the bar in 1908. He set up law practice in Bonham, Texas. He had been elected to the Texas House of Representatives in 1907 and was its speaker in 1911.

Rayburn, a Democrat, was elected in 1912 to the U.S. House of Representatives. He was re-elected 24 times, for a total of 48 years and eight months, which was a record span up to that point. As a Democrat, Rayburn helped materially in molding the New Deal legislation in the 1931-1937 period. He was instrumental in passing the Federal Securities Act of 1933, the Securities Exchange Act of 1934 and the Wheeler-Rayburn Holding-Company Act of 1935.

In 1937 Rayburn was elected leader of the Democratic party. In 1940 his dream was realized when he was made speaker of the House. Rayburn held that position from 1940 until his death in 1961, except when the Republicans controlled the House from 1947 to 1949 and again from 1953 to 1955. During these periods, he served as minority leader.

Rayburn's devotion to his country and to his party was "without prefix, without suffix, and without apology." He was a close confidant and trusted adviser to Franklin D. Roosevelt, Harry S Truman, Dwight D. Eisenhower and John F. Kennedy. He was considered one of the most powerful speakers of the House in the history of the country, even though he was a master of the legislative process.

Samuel Taliaferro Rayburn appears on a 1962 4¢ stamp.

304

Red Cloud (Makhpiya Luta)

Scott 2176
Born: 1822, near where the North and South Platte Rivers join in Nebraska
Died: December 10, 1909, Pine Ridge Reservation, South Dakota

Red Cloud was a young Indian warrior and leader of his people, the Bad Face band of Oglala Sioux. By age 40, Red Cloud was the chief of the entire Oglala Sioux nation. He spent most of his middle years fighting the westward advance of the white man and harassing his advances in the prairies and into the Rocky Mountains along the emigrant route through Nebraska and Wyoming into Montana.

Red Cloud won a series of battles in the 1860s defending the Powder River country from the encroaching white men. When the government decided to open a road along the Bozeman Trail northwest of Cheyenne to central Rosebud County, Montana, Red Cloud began his attacks. The Arapaho and Cheyenne Indians had taken brutal beatings from the United States Army, and the mining activities in Montana were usurping the Indian's sacred land. Red Cloud left Laramie and joined the attack on Fort Phil Kearny in Wyoming. Scholars do not believe Red Cloud was solely responsible for this massacre, even though many whites thought he planned the 1866 attack on the soldiers commanded by Captain W.J. Fetterman.

Red Cloud fought a standoff battle at the Wagon Box Fight on August 2, 1867. He held off signing the final Fort Laramie Treaty until 1869 when he forced the burning and disbanding of the forts along the Bozeman Trail. Red Cloud was later removed as head of the Oglala because he threatened a government agent. He then attempted to aid the peace with the whites.

Red Cloud made frequent trips to Washington, D.C. He left the further hostilities up to Crazy Horse and Sitting Bull. He even made personal appearances on William Cody's Wild West show. His prestige began to wane within the Sioux nation. In 1878 Red Cloud and his people left Nebraska for the Pine Ridge Reservation in South Dakota. He remained there until he died.

Red Cloud is depicted on a 1987 10¢ Great Americans stamp.

Walter Reed

Scott 877
Born: September 13, 1851, Gloucester County, Virginia
Died: November 23, 1902, Washington, D.C.

Walter Reed is best remembered for proving the mode of infection of yellow fever. Reed studied at the University of Virginia and at Bellevue Hospital Medical College in New York City. He received a degree from both places. He served on the New York City and Brooklyn board of health for several years. In June 1875, he gained a commission in the Army Medical Corps, serving in New York, Arizona and Baltimore.

Reed was a professor at the Army Medical School and curator of the Army Medical Museum in Washington, D.C. In 1895 he studied typhoid fever at Johns Hopkins University. He was detailed as the head of a group to study yellow fever in Cuba.The group included James Carroll, Aristoide Argamonte and Jesse Lazear.

Carlos Finley had advanced the theory that yellow fever was transmitted by a mosquito. Henry Carter, of the United States Public Health Service, had shown that a lapse of two weeks was necessary before the disease became dangerous to others. Reed immediately identified mosquitoes as the culprits in the transmission of the disease. Twenty-two cases of yellow fever were produced experimentally, 14 by infected mosquito-bites, six by injection of blood, and two by injection of filtered blood serum. In the experiment, Carroll survived the infection, but Lazear died. Clara Maass, a nurse who volunteered, also died. (See Clara Maass biography.)

Major William C. Gorgas, army sanitary engineer, freed Havana of the mosquito and the disease in three months. Reed returned to Washington, D.C., to resume teaching. He died of appendicitis in November 1902.

He is depicted on a 1940 5¢ Famous American Scientists stamp.

Frederic Remington

Scott 888
Born: October 4, 1861, Canton, New York
Died: December 26, 1909, near Ridgefield, Connecticut

Frederic Remington attended private schools before entering the Fine Arts College of Yale. He played varsity football and also was a heavyweight boxer. Although Remington participated at the Art Student's League of New York City, he was mostly self-taught.

At age 19, he went west in search of frontier adventure and began documenting scenes of the Old West. He was a stickler for authenticity and made detailed sketches. Remington worked as a cowboy and on sheep ranches to make enough money to travel and buy art supplies. He was a correspondent for Hearst newspapers during the Spanish-American War in Cuba and also traveled to Germany, Russia, and North Africa.

Remington depicted cowboys, frontiersmen and Indians in real-life situations and realistic action. He collected military uniforms and equipment, Indian garb and cowboy clothes so he could copy them to the minutest detail. His paintings, such as *Smoke signals*, and his bronze sculptures, such as *Coming through the Rye*, represented animals and people in authentic detail and life-like action. His works, especially his paintings and drawings, number in the thousands and are extensively reproduced in prints.

Remington illustrated for leading magazines, and his books are profusely illustrated and well-written. Some examples of his work include *Pony Tracks*, *Men with the Bark On* and *The Way of the Indian*. Remington illustrated Francis Parkman's *Oregon Trail*, Henry Wadsworth Longfellow's *Son of Hiawatha* in 1890, and books by Owen Wister. Remington's nickname, Sackrider, originated from the way he traveled around on horseback.

He is commemorated on a 1940 10¢ Famous American Artists stamps.

307

Ernst Reuter

Scott 1137
Born: July 29, 1889, Apenrade, Germany
Died: September 29, 1953, West Berlin, West Germany

When Ernst Reuter was 23 years old, his father disowned him because of his avid leftist tendencies. The younger Reuter was attending school at the University of Marburg at the time and had to discontinue his studies for lack of support. In 1913 he entered politics as the secretary of the Social Democratic Party's adult school in Berlin. He was conscripted into the German army in 1915, supposedly because of his pacifist writings.

The next year he was taken prisoner by Russia. The Russian Revolution began in 1917, and Reuter organized a prisoners soviet. Bolshevik Lenin appointed him commissar of the German Volga Republic.

Reuter was returned to Germany in 1918. He edited the left-wing periodical *Die rote Fahne* (*The Red Banner*) under the name Ernst Freisland. He was also general secretary of the German Communist Party for a short period, but he soon rebelled and again joined the Social Democrats. Reuter was elected to the Berlin City Assembly, was in the Reichstag and became mayor of Magdeburg.

When Adolph Hitler came to power, Reuter was confined to concentration camps from 1933 to 1935. He was then exiled to England and Turkey, where he served in the Economic and Transport Ministry and taught in the University of Ankara until 1946. He was elected mayor of Berlin in 1947, but the Russians prevented him from taking office. In 1948-49, he resisted the Soviet's Berlin blockade and organized the airlift. In 1948, Reuter was again elected mayor of Berlin, and he took office in the Western sector of the city. He was re-elected in 1951. He worked diligently to make West Berlin a part of West Germany, and he prompted the Allies to give all-out assistance and support to Western Germany, which they did.

Reuter lived to see Berlin rebuilt into a new and modern city, and the economic miracle that followed. Mercifully, he did not live to see Russia hurriedly construct the Berlin Wall in August 1961.

He is remembered with the 1959 8¢ Champion of Liberty issue.

Bernard Revel

Scott 2194
Born: September 17, 1885, Pren, Lithuania
Died: December 2, 1940, New York, New York

Bernard Revel was the son of Rabbi Nachum and Leah Revel of Pren, near Kovno (Kaunas), Lithuania. Revel had the ability to quickly memorize difficult Talmudic subjects. He was associated with the maskilim, who engaged in Haskala, or enlightenment. Revel's father taught him until he needed the guidance of teachers of the famous Yeshivah Tels. He also mastered mathematics, science, history and literature.

As a Jew, he had a difficult life in Russian Lithuania, as social unrest spread throughout Eastern Europe. In 1906, with a half million European Jews, Revel immigrated to New York City. He enrolled at the Rabbi Isaac Elhanan Theological Seminary. He studied under Rabbi Bernard Levinthal of Philadelphia, who was a leader of the Orthodox American rabbinate.

Revel entered Temple University and the University of Pennsylvania to study law, philosophy, Oriental languages and economics. In 1909 he received his master's degree from New York University. Also in that year, Revel married Sarah Travis, daughter of Solomon Travis, who founded the Oklahoma Petroleum and Gasoline Company.

In 1912 Revel became a United States citizen and was awarded the first doctorate degree at the new Dropsie College of Philadelphia. He moved to Tulsa, Oklahoma, where he managed the family oil business.

In 1915 the Jewish community of New York invited him to assume the presidency of the newly merged Etz Chaim Yeshiva and Rabbi Isaac Elhanan Theological Seminary. Yeshiva College was added in 1928, forming Yeshiva University. Revel combined a liberal arts program with Jewish studies and a graduate school for training rabbinical leaders and teachers. Today, the university has branches in Los Angeles and Israel.

Bernard Revel appears on a $1 Great Americans definitive.

Paul Revere

Scott 1059A
Born: January 1, 1735, Boston, Massachusetts
Died: May 10, 1818, Boston, Massachusetts

Paul Revere learned silversmithing, his father's trade, while growing up in Boston. When he was 21, Revere joined the Army and was involved in the Crown Point fighting during the French and Indian War. He returned to the family shop in 1757 and married Sara Orne. They had eight children.

Revere participated in the Boston Tea Party in December 1773 and also served as a mounted messenger for the Whig patriots of Boston. In September 1774, he rode from Boston to Carpenter's Hall in Philadelphia, carrying in his saddlebags the radical *Suffolk Resolves*, an important message to the First Continental Congress.

On April 18, 1775, British General Thomas Gage sent a strong detail to destroy military stores being collected at Concord. Revere, William Dawes and Samuel Prescott rode out ahead of the British and aroused the whole countryside, warning them about the impending arrival of the British. At Lexington, the Minutemen were lined up to meet the enemy. A battle ensued. The British moved on the Concord where, on North Bridge, the volunteers repulsed the Redcoats back to Boston.

During and after the war, Revere made fine silverware, as well as gunpowder, copper bells and cannons. He also made the copper fittings for the USS *Constitution* known as "Old Ironsides," and worked with Robert Fulton to develop copper boilers for steamboats. Revere became the first American to discover the process of rolling sheet copper. He built the first copper rolling mill in the United States. Until he did this, all sheet copper had to be imported.

Paul Revere's picture appears on a 1965 25¢ Liberty stamp.

James Whitcomb Riley

Scott 868
Born: October 7, 1849, Greenfield, Indiana
Died: July 22, 1916, Indianapolis, Indiana

James Whitcomb Riley was the son of Reuben Riley, a prominent lawyer in Greenfield, Indiana. The young Riley left school at age 16 and earned money by painting signs, fences, and barns up and down the Ohio Valley.

He also joined a medicine show as an actor. He wrote songs for the medicine show company.

When he was 21, Riley worked for an Indiana newspaper, the *Anderson Democrat*. Under the name Benj. F. Johnson of Boone, Riley submitted poems to several newspapers. He gained notoriety with these verses. He traveled around the United States with Bill Nye, reading his poems.

In 1877 Riley was hired by the *Indianapolis Journal*. In his newspaper articles, he wrote in the rustic Hoosier dialect he had acquired on his painting jobs and medicine show travels.

Some of Riley's most popular works include *The Old Swimmin' Hole* and *'Leven More Poems*, published in 1883, *Rhymes of Childhood*, published in 1890, *Poems Here at Home*, published in 1893, and *Book of Joyous Children*, published in 1902.

Although he is most famous for his works written in dialect, he also wrote verse in pure English.

James Whitcomb Riley appears on a 1940 10¢ Famous Americans Authors stamp.

Jack Roosevelt Robinson

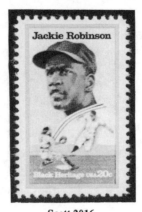

Scott 2016
Born: January 31, 1919, near Cairo, Georgia
Died: October 24, 1972, Stamford, Connecticut

Jackie Robinson was the son of a Georgia sharecropper. He moved with his family to California when he was an infant and grew up in Pasadena. A born athlete, Robinson excelled in all major sports at John Muir Technical High School and Pasadena Junior College. He was a star in track, football, basketball and baseball at the University of California at Los Angeles.

During World War II, Robinson served in the Army as a morale officer. He was medically discharged in 1945 as a first lieutenant.

Robinson went from the Army to the Kansas City Monarchs baseball club. The Brooklyn Dodgers' president, Branch Rickey, persuaded Robinson to break the color line in major league baseball. With the Montreal Royals in 1946, Robinson led the league in batting and was the best fielding second baseman. He went with the Brooklyn Dodgers in 1947 and was voted rookie of the year. In 1949 he won the National League batting title with an average of .342. He led the league in stolen bases with 37, and was voted its most valuable player. A right-handed hitter, Robinson played all three bases and the outfield. Between 1949 and 1954, he was chosen for six National League All-Star teams. He had a lifetime batting average of .311, with 734 runs batted in and 137 homeruns. He helped his team win six National League pennants and one World Series.

Robinson retired after the 1956 season and achieved prominence as a leader in business, politics and civil rights. He was elected to the National Baseball Hall of Fame in 1962. Robinson's autobiography, *I Never Had it Made*, appeared in 1972.

Jack Roosevelt Robinson is pictured on a 1982 20¢ stamp.

Comte de Rochambeau

Scott 703
Born: July 1, 1725, Vendome, France
Died: May 10, 1807, Thore (Loir-et-Cher), Framce

In 1742, at age 17, Jean Baptiste Donatien de Vimeur, Comte de Rochambeau left his theological studies and entered the army. He saw action in the War of the Austrian Succession, and was promoted to colonel at age 22. He fought in the Seven Years' War and advanced to brigadier general.

In 1780 the French Government allied with the American colonies for the United States' struggle for independence. Lieutenant General Rochambeau was given command of 6,000 French soldiers and sent to America, where he landed in Rhode Island in July. For one year, the troops waited at Newport for French naval ships to arrive and give them support.

Generals Washington and Rochambeau joined forces and marched to White Plains, New York, then south in the direction of Yorktown, Virginia, to join, on September 14, 1781, other Continental forces and Marquis de Lafayette's forces at Williamsburg. Admiral Grasse added 4,000 troops brought from Haiti. The siege on Major General Charles Cornwallis was laid. A second French fleet blocked the escape of Cornwallis by sea.

On October 19, 1781, the British surrendered, which virtually ended the War for Independence. Some foreign generals serving the American cause were not willing to submit to directives from the American commanders, but Rochambeau was always a noble gentleman and was distinguished by the grace with which he accepted Washington's authority as commander in chief. For his service to the colonies, Rochambeau received the thanks of Congress. He remained in Virginia until 1783 and returned to France, where he was appointed a military commander.

During the French Revolution, Rochambeau was made a marshal of France. He narrowly escaped execution after being imprisoned during the Reign of Terror. Comte de Rochambeau appears with George Washington and Comte Grasse on a 1931 2¢ stamp.

313

Knute Kenneth Rockne

Scott 2376
Born: March 4, 1888, Voss, Norway
Died: March 31, 1931, near Bazaar, Kansas

Knute Rockne came to the United States in 1893 when he was five years old with his parents who immigrated to Chicago. He grew up and attended school in Chicago. After graduation, he worked at various jobs. When he was 22, he entered Notre Dame University. Rockne studied chemistry and played on the Notre Dame football team. In 1913 he was the team captain. That year, he put into play what, until then, was the little-used, but legal, forward pass. This helped his team upset the heavily favored Army team. The pass became a major play in football games.

Rockne graduated in 1914. He began teaching chemistry at Notre Dame, and was an assistant to the football coach. In 1918 he became head coach. During the ensuing 13 years, he demonstrated that football teams could win by using their brains and speed as well as their brawn and by using trick plays against brute strength.

Rockne developed the shift. He substituted an entire team at once, called his shock troops. His teams won 105 games, took 12 losses, and tied five times. His 1930 team was undefeated. He made the game exciting by emphasizing the offensive.

One of Rockne's players, George Gipp, died in mid-career. Rockne pepped up his team up with the line, "Win one for the Gipper," which became a catch phrase, re-established by President Ronald Reagan.

On his way to California in 1931, Rockne died in an airplane crash near the village of Bazaar, Kansas. His autobiography appeared later that year.

Knute Rockne appears on a 22¢ stamp issued in 1989.

James Charles Rodgers

Scott 1755
Born: September 8, 1897, Meridian, Mississippi
Died: May 26, 1933, New York, New York

Jimmie Rodgers is a name known by most country music lovers and those who indulge in folk songs of the railroad and the South. Rodgers grew up near Meridian, Mississippi, and quit school at age 13 or 14 to work as a water carrier for the Mississippi and Ohio Railroad. In 1924, he learned that he was ill with tuberculosis. He had always been interested in singing and playing the guitar, so he decided to quit the railroad and take up music.

By 1927 he was fortunate to play for Ralph Peer, a recording company executive who was touring the South to record folk music. Rodgers recorded two songs for Peer, *Sleep Baby Sleep* and *The Soldier's Sweetheart*. Under Peer's supervision, he recorded more than 100 songs during the next six years. The songs included *T. for Texas*, *TB Blues*, *Mule Skinner Blues*, and *Waitin' for a Train*. Rodgers was a favorite among country music performers and fans. He had picked up the music from black workers who knew and sang folk songs of the South, and he leaned toward any tunes that were connected with railroading. Rodgers became known as the Singing Brakeman. He wrote and sang numerous songs about trains and was one of the first to bring the music of the rural South to the attention of the nation.

By the end of the 1920s, he was a national figure, and his records sold in great quantities. Today the originals are highly valued. It was tuberculosis that turned Rodgers to music as a career and spurred him on to greatness, but it also ended his life at the young age of 35.

His wife, Carrie Rodgers, wrote *My Husband Jimmie Rodgers*, published in 1975. A 1978 Performing Arts stamp pictures the country music singer with a guitar and a brakeman's cap, with a locomotive in the background.

William Penn Adair Rogers

Scott 975
Born: November 4, 1879, Oologah, Indian Territory (Oklahoma)
Died: August 15, 1935, near Point Barrow, Alaska

Wil Rogers, an actor, writer, humorist and rope twirler, was born on a ranch near Oologah in the Indian Territory, which is now Oklahoma.

Rogers attended several schools but quit in 1898 to be a Texas cowboy. He joined Texas Jack's touring Wild West Circus in 1902 as a rope artist in South Africa. After touring Australia and New Zealand with the Wirth Brothers' Circus, Rogers returned to the United States in 1904 and performed in various Wild West and vaudeville shows. In 1905 he was in New York with Oscar Hammerstein's *Roof Garden*. He performed on Broadway. In 1916 he became a regular in the Ziegfield Follies. Rogers added humorous patter to his act, which was full of humorous satire directed toward the political scene and elite society.

In 1922 Rogers began a weekly column for the *New York Times*. In 1926 he toured Europe as President Coolidge's unofficial goodwill ambassador.

Rogers wrote six books, was a popular radio broadcaster, and was in motion pictures as early as 1918. His last appearance was in 1934 in *David Harum*. He was killed in Alaska with Wiley Post, a pioneer American aviator, when the two were attempting to fly from California to the Orient by way of Alaska and Siberia. Their plane crashed a few moments after take-off from a point 15 miles south of Point Barrow, Alaska.

Rogers is best known for his quote, "I never met a man I didn't like." He is shown on a 1948 3¢ stamp.

Anna Eleanor Roosevelt

Scott 1236
Born: October 11, 1884, New York, New York
Died: November 7, 1962, New York, New York

Eleanor Roosevelt was the niece of President Theodore Roosevelt. Her father was Elliott Roosevelt, Theodore's younger brother; her mother was Anna Hall Roosevelt. At age nine, Eleanor Roosevelt became an orphan and was thereafter raised by her maternal grandmother. She attended private schools in the United States and abroad. In 1905 she made her formal debut in New York City. That same year, she married her fifth cousin, Franklin Delano Roosevelt.

The young couple lived at her husband's birthplace and family estate in Hyde Park, New York. In the next 10 years, they had six children. Roosevelt was much involved in raising her children, but after her husband was stricken with polio and paralyzed, she began participating in political affairs. In 1928 Roosevelt persuaded her husband to run for governor of New York.

She taught civics at Todhunter School for Girls in New York City until the family moved to the White House in Washington, D.C. Even when her husband was president of the United States, Roosevelt was involved in many social causes, including world peace, race relations, education and women's rights. In 1936 she wrote a syndicated column, "My Day." She joined the American Newspaper Guild, a labor union.

In 1941 she was appointed assistant director of defense. During World War II, she made numerous goodwill tours to European and Pacific military bases. After the death of her husband in 1945, Roosevelt was appointed by President Harry Truman as a delegate to the United Nations General Assembly. In 1946 she was elected chairman of the U.N.'s Human Rights Commission, part of the Economic and Social Council. Roosevelt also headed the American Association for the United Nations, a private supportive group.

In 1961 President John F. Kennedy named her the United States representative to the 15th session of the U.N. General Assembly.

Roosevelt wrote four books: *This is My Story*, *This I Remember*, *On My Own* and *Tomorrow is Now*.

Anna Eleanor Roosevelt appears on a 1963 5¢ stamp.

Franklin Delano Roosevelt

Scott 1284
Born: January 30, 1882, Hyde Park, New York
Died: April 12, 1945, Warm Springs, Georgia

Franklin Delano Roosevelt received his basic education at Groton School for Boys in Massachusetts and Harvard University, where he graduated in 1903. In 1905 he married his distant cousin, Anna Eleanor Roosevelt. He attended Columbia University Law School and was admitted to the New York bar in 1907. He was elected to the New York State Senate in 1910 and was re-elected two years later.

President Woodrow Wilson appointed Roosevelt as assistant secretary of the Navy in 1913. In 1920 Roosevelt was nominated for vice president as James M. Cox's running mate. After their defeat, Roosevelt became a vice president of the Fidelity and Deposit Company of Maryland, a surety-bonding firm. In 1921 he was stricken by polio and was crippled from the waist down.

He aided Alfred E. Smith in his bid for governor of New York in 1924 and again in 1928 for the Democratic nomination for president. Roosevelt followed Smith as governor of New York in 1928. In 1932 he defeated Herbert Hoover by a wide margin for the presidency of the United States. In his acceptance speech, Roosevelt unfolded a New Deal program to combat the depression. He also focused attention on the war in Europe.

He was re-elected in 1936 over Alfred M. Landon. The crisis in Europe prompted him to run for an unprecedented third term, which he won over Wendell L. Willkie in 1940. Roosevelt instigated maximum aid to Great Britain and Russia and was severely opposed for this until the attack on Pearl Harbor on December 7, 1941. Shelving the New Deal, Roosevelt declared war on Germany and Italy. Conferences with Winston Churchill and Joseph Stalin laid the groundwork for the postwar world.

In 1944 Roosevelt was elected to a fourth term, running against Governor Thomas E. Dewey of New York. Soon after his return from Yalta, Roosevelt died of a cerebral hemorrhage at his retreat in Warm Springs, Georgia.

Franklin D. Roosevelt's portrait appears on a 6¢ denomination of the 1965-78 Prominent Americans definitive series.

318

Theodore Roosevelt

Scott 2218g
Born: October 27, 1858, New York, New York
Died: January 6, 1919, Sagamore Hill, Oyster Bay, New York

Theodore Roosevelt's father was of the wealthy old Dutch New York mercantile Roosevelt family. His mother was of the Bulloch family of Georgia. In 1880 Roosevelt graduated from Harvard University, entered Columbia University School of Law, and married Alice Hathaway Lee of Massachusetts. He withdrew from law school when he was elected to the New York state assembly in 1881 as a Republican. In 1884 Roosevelt's wife died two days after the birth of their daughter Alice. The same day his mother died.

He returned to a ranch in the Dakota Territory. Two years later, he went to New York and ran for mayor, but lost. In 1886 he married Edith Kermit Carow. From 1889 to 1895, he served as U.S. civil service commissioner.

In 1895 Roosevelt was elected president of the New York City's Board of Police Commissioners. In May 1898, with Colonel Leonard Wood, Roosevelt organized the first United States Volunteer Cavalry Regiment to serve in Cuba during the Spanish-American War. In 1899 he became governor of New York. In 1900 he was elected vice president with William McKinley as president. On September 14, 1901, at age 42, Roosevelt became president of the United States when McKinley died from an assassin's bullet.

As president, Roosevelt guided the completion of the Panama Canal. In 1902 he instigated several reclamation projects, the Department of Commerce and Labor, and the Interstate Commerce Commission. In 1904 he won the election by a large plurality. He received the Nobel Peace Prize for negotiating the 1905 Russo-Japanese treaty of Portsmouth, New Hampshire. He also controlled the conflicts in Cuba.

In 1912 Roosevelt lost his bid for re-election to Woodrow Wilson. He returned home to write. A lingering illness he had contracted during a South American exploration proved fatal, and he died in 1919.

Theodore Roosevelt's portrait appears on a 1986 22¢ Presidential stamp.

Elizabeth 'Betsy' Griscom Ross

Scott 1004
Born: January 1, 1752, Philadelphia, Pennsylvania
Died: January 30, 1836, Philadelphia, Pennsylvania

Betsy Ross came from a family of strict Quakers. Her grandfather, Andrew Griscom, built the first brick house in Philadelphia, and in Carpenter's Hall is listed with the names of Tobias and Samuel Griscom, who were carpenters. Ross' mother was Rebecca James, sister of Abel James, who was the head of the importing firm of James and Drinker, which was involved in the tea incident with the British brig, *Polly*. Ross and her seven sisters and a brother were educated in Society of Friends' schools.

In Gloucester, New Jersey, on November 4, 1773, Betsy married John Ross, son of an Episcopalian clergyman. She was disowned by the Society of Friends for "marrying out of meeting." The couple became members of Christ Church where John's uncle, Colonel George Ross, regularly attended. Colonel Ross was a member of the Continental Congress and a signer of the Declaration of Independence.

John Ross, a patriot, joined the militia, and while guarding supplies was injured in a gun-powder explosion. He died on January 21, 1776. John had established an upholstering business, and Betsy continued with the business.

In May and June of 1776, while George Washington was in Philadelphia, he contacted Colonel George Ross. With Robert Morris, the three talked in secret committee to Betsy about making a flag for the new country. According to a story that has never been proven, Ross suggested a design, and Washington made a rough pencil sketch. Supposedly, Washington wanted six-pointed stars for the flag, but Ross convinced him to make them five-pointed.

Ross made the first flag with a circle of white stars in a blue square and a field of red and white stripes. Congress adopted the design on June 14, 1777. Only stars for new states have been added since.

Elizabeth Griscom Ross appears with George Washington, Robert Morris and George Ross on a 1952 3¢ stamp.

George Ross

Scott 1004
Born: May 10, 1730, New Castle, Delaware
Died: July 14, 1779, Philadelphia, Pennsylvania

George Ross was born in New Castle, Delaware. He practiced law in Lancaster, Pennsylvania, after he was admitted to the bar in 1750 at age 20.

Ross served as prosecutor for the English crown in Cumberland County for 12 years.

He took an avid interest in the affairs of the Indians as a member of the provincial assembly between 1768 and 1774.

Ross served in the Pennsylvania assembly, where he opposed the governor. He assisted in the preparation in 1776 of Pennsylvania's declaration of rights.

He also was a delegate of the Continental Congress from 1774 to 1777 and a signer of the Declaration of Independence.

In 1779 he became judge of the state of Pennsylvania. He served in that position until his death that year.

Ross' brother was an Episcopalian clergyman whose son, John Ross, married Betsy Griscom.

Betsy Ross is believed by some to have been the seamstress who made the first flag of the United States.

George Ross appears with Betsy Ross, George Washington and Robert Morris on a 1952 3¢ stamp commemorating the 200th anniversary of the birth of Betsy Ross.

Richard Brevard Russell

Scott 1853
Born: November 2, 1897, Winder, Georgia
Died: January 21, 1971, Washington, D.C.

Richard B. Russell's father was the chief justice of the Georgia Supreme Court. The younger Russell graduated from the University of Georgia and practiced law in Winder, Georgia. He soon became involved in state politics and served as the speaker of the Georgia Assembly from 1927 until 1931. At age 31, Russell was elected governor of Georgia. He was the youngest person ever to hold that office at that time. He became popular as a governor essentially by reducing state expenditures. In 1932 he was elected to the United States Senate. He was the youngest member of the Senate at that time. Russell was re-elected each time he sought the office. He was the chief strategist of the southern senators in their fight against civil rights legislation. Except when the Democrats were in direct opposition to southern interests, Russell was a strong supporting Democrat of President Franklin D. Roosevelt's foreign and domestic policies. He exerted tremendous influence on legislation while in the Senate, perhaps more than any other senator.

At the 1948 and 1952 Democratic national conventions, he was a major contender for the presidential nomination. Because of his stand against civil rights, he lost out on any possible chance for the presidential nomination in 1948 and 1952. Should he have been nominated, his negative position on civil rights legislation would have assured his defeat. He was chairman and a member of the powerful Armed Services Committee (1951-69). He was also chairman of the Appropriations Committee in 1969. Russell was chosen president pro tem of the Senate that same year.

The Civil Rights Act of 1964 came about when President Johnson dislodged the bill from the House Rules Committee and broke the southern filibuster in the Senate. It won Johnson 90 percent of the black vote and a huge presidential election victory.

Russell is included in the Great American issue on a 1984 10¢ stamp.

George Herman 'Babe' Ruth

Scott 2046
Born: February 6, 1895, Baltimore, Maryland
Died: August 16, 1948, New York, New York

When George Herman Ruth was seven years old, he was sent to St. Mary's Industrial School in Baltimore, where he learned, among other things, to play baseball. Ruth began his professional career in 1914 with the Baltimore Orioles, then a minor league team, under the management of Jack Dunn. According to a story, Ruth got his nickname "Babe" when he reported to the team and someone said, "Well, here's Jack's newest babe now."

A powerful man, Ruth hit 714 home runs with his 44-ounce bat, "Black Betsy." He became known as the "Sultan of Swat." Before the end of his season with Jack Dunn, Ruth was traded to the Boston Red Sox, an American League team. He started as a pitcher, but his hitting was better, so he began playing regularly in the outfield. A left-handed hitter, Ruth hit 15 home runs in 10 World Series games. In four different seasons he hit more than 50 home runs and in 1927 he hit 60. He set or tied 76 batting or pitching records. His lifetime average was .342.

In 1920 Ruth was sold to the New York Yankees of the American league for $125,000. He stayed with the Yankees until after the 1934 season, when he played briefly with the Boston Braves in 1936. In 1938 Ruth became a coach with the Brooklyn Dodgers. A few years before his death from cancer he established the Babe Ruth Foundation for underprivileged children.

Ruth's home run career total of 714 held until 1974 when Henry Aaron of the Atlanta Braves hit his 715th home run.

Ruth was one of the first five players chosen for the National Baseball Hall of Fame. George Herman Ruth is commemorated on a 1983 20¢ stamp.

Jean Baptiste Pointe du Sable

Scott 2249
Born: circa 1750, Santo Domingo (now Haiti)
Died: 1818, St. Charles, Missouri

Jean Baptiste Pointe du Sable's father was a French mariner and his mother was a free black woman. Jean was once the wealthiest man in Eschecagou (Chicago). He established a trading post on the north bank of the Chicago River. His business became the center of a permanent Chicago settlement. He owned a building that by all standards of his day and its location (what is today the corner of Wacker Street and Michigan Avenue) was quite large. It was said to be 40-foot long and 20-foot wide and well-furnished. He had several outbuildings, with chickens and livestock. He lived with a Potawatomi woman, Catherine (Indian, Kittiwaha).

Du Sable was described by Colonel de Peyster, British commander at Mackinaw, as a "well-educated and handsome negro" who favored the French interests. He had been taken into custody by Lieutenant Thomas Bennett of the King's Regiment from St. Joseph in August 1779, so the lieutenant had reported to Colonel de Peyster. A few weeks later the lieutenant reported that Du Sable was a man of good character. The following summer a delegation of Indians from the British settlement on the St. Clair River south of Port Huron demanded that Governor Sinclair fire the French overseer and appoint Du Sable in his place. Sinclair freed Du Sable and sent him to replace the Frenchman.

When the war was over, Du Sable returned to Eschecagou to be with his Potawatomi woman. In 1784 Du Sable was described as a big man, well-to-do, but inclined to drinking. In 1788 he and Catherine were married by a priest at Cahokia. They had two children, Suzanne and Jean Baptiste Jr.

In 1800 Jean Baptiste Sr. sold his property to a French trader, Jean Lalime, for $1,200. He moved to St. Charles, Missouri, to live with his son. His son died in 1814. Jean Baptiste Sr. died four years later, in poverty.

He was honored with a 22¢ Black Heritage stamp issued in 1987.

324

Sacagawea

Scott 1063
Born: 1787? near headwaters of Missouri River
Died: November 7, 1884, Shoshoni Agency, Wyoming

The exact year of Sacagawea's birth is not known. Her birthplace was somewhere in the area of the headwaters of the great rivers Missouri, Snake and Salmon in western Montana and eastern Idaho. Born among the Shoshoni Indians, she was betrothed as an infant, then captured by the Minnetaree (Hidatsa of the Mandan) Indians, a Siouan people of the Missouri River Valley in North Dakota. She was later gambled away to a Frenchman named Toussaint Charbonneau. She became his wife and was living in the Dakotas when Lewis and Clark came along on their expedition to the West.

Charbonneau and Sacagawea were engaged by the expedition to act as guides and interpreters on the journey. She and her husband spent the winter with Lewis and Clark at Fort Mandan, where Sacagawea's son, Baptiste Charbonneau, was born on February 11, 1805. Sacagawea eventually led the party to her home grounds, where she found a brother and a sister's daughter living. All else were gone, so she adopted the little girl as her own child and took her along.

Sacagawea had remarkable knowledge of the country, and by following the directions given to her by the tribes she encountered along the way, she led Lewis and Clark to the Pacific, arriving November 7, 1805. She returned with Clark by way of the Yellowstone. Lewis went by way of the Marias River, the north tributary of the Missouri, and was shot in the leg by a one-eyed member of the party who mistook him for an elk. Lewis also had a skirmish with the Blackfoot Indians. When Lewis rejoined Clark at the Yellowstone, Sacagawea nursed his wound.

Sacagawea returned to Minnetaree country, and Lewis and Clark returned to St. Louis. She was not heard from again until she was found at the Shoshoni Agency in Wyoming. She lived to be almost 100 years old.

Sacagawea can be seen on the 1954 Lewis and Clark Expedition issue. She is standing behind and to the left of the two explorers.

325

Augustus Saint-Gaudens

Scott 886
Born: March 1, 1848, Dublin, Ireland
Died: August 3, 1907, Cornish, New Hampshire

Augustus Saint-Gaudens came to the United States with his parents when he was less than one year old. The family settled in New York City. In 1861, when he was 13 years old, he was apprenticed to a cameo cutter. Saint-Gaudens continued this work until he was 17. He spent his evenings studying art at Cooper Union. In 1866, he attended the National Academy of Design. After traveling around Europe for a few months in 1867, he enrolled in the Ecole des Beaux-Arts in Paris for three years.

Saint-Gaudens moved to Rome to perfect his skills in sculpture, and paid for his expenses by cameo cutting. He made Rome his home until 1875, when he returned to New York to establish himself with a number of leading architects and artists. In 1877 he carved the relief reredos for St. Thomas Church, and in 1880 he became famous with his memorial statue of David G. Farragut in Madison Square Garden, New York City.

Saint-Gaudens accomplished *The Puritan*, (Deacon Samuel Chapin) in Springfield, Massachusetts, in 1885; *The Standing Lincoln* in Lincoln Park in Chicago, in 1887; and *Diana* for Madison Square Garden in New York City in 1892. His draped meditating figure of the Adams Memorial for Mrs. Henry Adams in the Rock Creek Cemetery, Washington, D.C., is especially moving. The equestrian statue of General William T. Sherman at 5th Avenue and 59th Street in New York City, is one of his most notable accomplishments.

Saint-Gaudens was an active member of the Society of American Artists from its founding in 1877. He taught sculpture at the Art Students League in New York City from 1888 to 1897. He was also helpful in establishing the American Academy of Rome. From 1885 he worked from his studio near his home in Cornish, New Hampshire. He designed the United States $20 gold piece of 1907 and the head on the $10 gold piece, which capped his career.

Augustus Saint-Gaudens is honored and pictured on a 3¢ stamp in the 1940 Famous Americans issue.

326

Peter Salem

Scott 1361
Born: 1750, Framingham, Massachusetts
Died: August 16, 1816, Framingham, Massachusetts

Peter Salem was a slave whose owner, Jeremiah Belknap, named him for Belknap's former hometown of Salem, Massachusetts. In 1656, Massachusetts, fearing an insurrection by blacks, made it illegal for blacks to serve in the military. When the need for soldiers arose during the French and Indian Wars, however, blacks were pressed into military duty. In mid-1775, the Massachusetts Committee of Safety recruited free blacks, but not slaves. This resulted in the freeing of many slaves so they could be soldiers and sailors.

Salem had been sold by Belknap to Major Lawson Buckminster, who freed Salem. Salem became one of the Minutemen heroes of the American Revolutionary War. On April 19, 1775, he fought at Concord, Massachusetts. A week later, he enlisted in Colonel Nixon's Fifth Massachusetts Regiment. He served in Captain Drury's company and fought with Drury at the Battle of Bunker Hill. At dawn on June 17, 1775, General William Howe ordered fire on the Americans' fortifications, but this did not end in victory. Howe struck again at the central redoubt and was again repulsed. With reinforcements, he struck the third time and drove the Americans northward across Bunker Hill. The Colonials had 400 dead and wounded men; the British lost more than 1,000. Salem was credited with the shot that killed Major John Pitcairn.

Salem re-enlisted in 1776 and fought at Saratoga and Stony Point. General George Washington forbade blacks from soldiering. After Virginia's governor, Lord Dunmore, freed slaves to serve the British, Washington reversed his own orders, and in January 1776, Salem re-enlisted.

After the war, Salem built a cabin near Leicester, Massachusetts, and worked as a cane weaver. He died in the Framingham poorhouse.

In 1882 Framingham erected a monument in his honor. Peter Salem appears with Lieutenant Thomas Grosvenor on a 1968 6¢ stamp.

Haym Salomon

Scott 1561
Born: 1740? Lissa, Poland
Died: January 6, 1785, Philadelphia, Pennsylvania

Haym Salomon was well-educated and traveled extensively around Europe. He was of Jewish-Portuguese background. In Poland he was considered an unwanted revolutionary. He fled to America in 1772 and opened a dry-goods business in New York City. He took up the patriot's cause and was responsible for outfitting the Continental troops in upper New York state.

Salomon traveled with the troops for a time, then returned to New York City just before the British captured the city on September 15, 1776. He was captured and put in prison, accused of being one of the spies plotting to blow up the harbor. The British used him as an interpreter, however, because he understood and could speak several languages. He was released, only to be arrested again in 1778 and condemned to death. But he cleverly bribed his jailer and escaped.

Salomon fled to Philadelphia and reported to the Second Continental Congress for service. Robert Morris of the Bank of North America put him to work selling government bonds to help finance the war. He did so well he was called the most successful of the war brokers. He loaned Washington $400,000 in 1779 (much of it his own money). Between 1778 and 1782, he provided thousands of dollars to finance the Revolution. No exact figure has ever been established.

After the war, he established himself as a successful banker, but the recession of 1783 set him back.

Salomon spent much time and effort toward gaining equal and just treatment of the Jews in America. The public oath that was required for civil service employment demanded belief in both the New and the Old Testament. Salomon fought to have this revised. Later, the constitution of the state was so amended. Tuberculosis, contracted while in prison, led to his early death. Ironically, he died penniless.

For his efforts to help finance the Revolutionary War, Haym Salomon is pictured on a 1975 10¢ American Bicentennial issue depicting contributors to the cause.

328

William Thomas Sampson

Scott 793
Born: February 9, 1840, Palmyra, New York
Died: May 6, 1902, Washington, D.C.

William Thomas Sampson graduated at the top of his class in 1861 from the U.S. Military Academy. Wherever he served, he made improvements in the U.S. naval force. In 1880 the Navy ranked 12th in the world. By 1900, it ranked third.

During the night of February 15, 1898, the battleship *Maine* was blown up in Havana Harbor, and 260 lives were lost. Admiral Montgomery Sicard and Captain Charles Sigsbee survived the blast. Cuba wanted independence from Spain, but Madrid would not grant it. President William McKinley worked for neutrality in the conflict.

The sinking of the *Maine* resulted in an inquiry headed by Sampson. It was determined that it was an external explosion caused by a floating mine. The cry, "Remember the Maine," became the fight slogan for war.

On May 19, 1898, Spanish admiral Pascual Cervera y Topete slipped into Santiago Bay with four armed cruisers and three destroyers, but was bottled up by the American navy force under Admiral Sampson and Commodore Winfield Schley. On July 3, Cervera tried to escape, but it was disastrous.

Admiral Sampson cabled that the fleet under his command won the victory, but a controversy arose between him and Commodore Schley as to who owned the victory. A court of inquiry censured Schley, but Congress failed to give Sampson recognition.

William Thomas Sampson appears with George Dewey and Winfield Schley on a 1937 4¢ Navy stamp.

Jose de San Martin

Scott 1125
Born: February 25, 1778, Yapeyu, Argentina
Died: August 17, 1850, Boulogne, France

Born to a prominent Spanish official in Argentina, Jose de San Martin was sent to Madrid, Spain, to military school at age nine. At age 15, he was commissioned a second lieutenant. San Martin served with Spanish forces in the struggle against Napoleon. By 1808, he was a lieutenant colonel.

In 1812 he offered his services to Buenos Aires in its war for independence from Spain. He was placed in command of an army of revolutionaries in upper Peru. He noted that the Spaniards must first be routed from Chile, as well as Peru. He enlisted help from Buenos Aires and, with Bernardo O'Higgins, equipped an army at Mendoza. He took his army of 4,000 over the Andes through the Upsallata pass and routed a large force of Spanish royalists at Casas de Chacabuco on February 12, 1817.

Northern Chile, including Santiago, was occupied, with O'Higgins as governor. San Martin chose to head out to reconquer southern Chile. He freed the south from the Spanish on April 5, 1818, with his decisive victory at the Maipu River, thus completing the independence of Chile. He then reorganized his army and secured the aid of Lord Cochrane's fleet. In July 1821, rather than face the land and sea force that San Martin had gathered, the Royalists retired into the Andes.

San Martin proclaimed Lima independent and set himself up as protector. Meanwhile, Simon Bolivar was at the northern borders of Peru, intent on extending southward. San Martin and Bolivar met secretly at Guyaquil on July 26, 1822. What transpired at that meeting is not known. At any rate, San Martin relinquished his protectorship and his military command to the new Peruvian congress in September 1822. He returned to Argentina. Simon Bolivar was proclaimed emperor of Peru in 1824. San Martin sailed for Europe in self-exile and poverty.

Today, Argentina regards San Martin as its greatest revolutionary hero. He is the subject of a 1959 4¢ Champion of Liberty stamp.

Carl Sandburg

USA 13c

Scott 1731
Born: January 6, 1878, Galesburg, Illinois
Died: July 22, 1967, Flat Rock, North Carolina

Carl Sandburg grew up in Galesburg, Illinois, a trade center for livestock and grain, and also the home of Knox College where, in 1858, the year after the town was incorporated, Abraham Lincoln and Stephen A. Douglas had one of their historic debates. The town abounded in stories of Lincoln, who became young Sandburg's hero.

When Sandburg was 13, he had finished the eighth grade and had to seek work. He drove a milk wagon and kept himself occupied by quoting to himself Bible verses and Thomas Gray's *Elegy*. At age 20, Sandburg enlisted in the Army for the Spanish-American War. He landed in Puerto Rico and served as a correspondent for the Galesburg *Evening Mail*. He recorded the events leading up to the surrender of Santiago. After the war, in September 1898, Sandburg went to Lombard College but left just before graduation and traveled through out the Midwest as a hobo. In 1902 his first, book, *In Reckless Ecstasy*, was published.

In Chicago, Sandburg was associate editor of the *Lyceumnite* and met Winfield R. Gaylor, who had organized the Social-Democratic party in Wisconsin. Sandburg then went to Milwaukee to work. He married Lillian Steichen in 1908, and wrote for the Milwaukee *Journal and Daily News*.

He returned to Chicago, wrote prize-winning poetry, was a correspondent in Sweden and Norway during World War I, then worked for the Chicago *Daily News*. He published his four-volume *Abraham Lincoln: The War Years* in 1939. The work won him the Pulitzer Prize for history in 1940.

A portrait of Sandburg, by William Smith, appears on a 1978 13¢ stamp.

Santa Claus (St. Nicholas)

Scott 2064
Born: latter 3rd century A.D., Patara, Lycia, Asiana (now Turkey)
Died: early 4th century A.D., Myra, Lycia

On the south shore of eastern Turkey in Lycia, Asia Minor, was the city of Myra. Once a seaport, it is now ruins and rock tombs. By the year 325, Myra was strongly Christianized. Theodosius II made Myra the Byzantine capital of Lycia. In 808, the city was besieged by Harun al-Rashid and fell into decay. The church of St. Nicholas is located in the plain at the western edge of a small village. Its floor is far below the present level of the plain.

Late in the 3rd century, Sacrificulus Nicholas of Patara was the church's bishop. Elected bishop while still a boy, he was imprisoned during the reign of Emperor Diocletianus, who persecuted the Christians. Bishop Nicholas was said to have tossed a small bag of gold through a window one night. It landed in the stocking of the daughter of a poor merchant. She hung it by the chimney to dry. Stockings now are hung by the fireplace at Christmas time.

St. Nicholas was popular among Eastern Christians. The Byzantine princess, Theophano, introduced him into Germany when she became Emperor Otto II's wife. According to legend, Bishop Nicholas also had restored the life of three children who had been cut to pieces and pickled in brine.

During the middle ages, St. Nicholas became the patron saint of schoolboys. Schoolboys celebrated his feast day on December 6 in England and Germany. A small boy was selected to represent bishop and paraded through the town in complete episcopal regalia. The English in colonial New York City moved the feast of St. Nicholas from December 6 to the English gift day, Christmas. They also changed St. Nicholas' name to Santa Claus.

About 1881, cartoonist Thomas Nast depicted Santa Claus in *Harper's Weekly* as we know him today, a rudy-complexioned man, somewhat elderly, obese, bearded and jolly. Somehow, Santa Claus' home was moved to the North Pole, where he reigns as the patron saint of children, sailors, merchants, bankers, thieves, scholars, Greece, Sicily, Russia and New York City.

Santa Claus is pictured here on a 1983 20¢ Christmas stamp.

Winthrop Sargent

Scott 955
Born: May 1, 1753, Gloucester, Massachusetts
Died: January 3, 1820, New Orleans, Louisiana

Winthrop Sargent was a graduate of Harvard College in 1771. He served as a major in the American Revolution. When the Ohio Territory was organized in 1787, he became its secretary. That same year, he was appointed by Congress as secretary of the Northwest Territory. When Governor General Arthur St. Clair was absent, Sargent served in his place. When St. Clair was defeated by Shawnee Chief Tecumseh, Sargent took over as governor.

With the Treaty of Paris in 1783, Great Britain relinquished its claims north of latitude 31 degrees, but Spain objected. Georgia laid claim to the land, calling it Bourbon County and selling parcels of it in 1795. The government had to redeem the corrupt claims, resulting in what was called the Yazoo fraud. Finally, Spain relinquished its claim in March 1798, and on April 7, 1798, the federal government created the Territory of Mississippi. Winthrop Sargent was the territory's first governor. He inherited a chaotic land problem with conflicting claims based on French, British, Spanish and Georgian grants.

Sargent left the governorship in 1801, and the problem in the territory continued. The intrigues of Aaron Burr and James Wilkinson multiplied the confusion. Andrew Jackson, had to corner Indian troubles by defeating the Indians at Econochaca (Holy Ground) in 1813 and at Horseshoe Bend in 1814. America was at war with Britain in 1812-15, which ended with Jackson's Battle of New Orleans. The western half of the territory became a state on December 10, 1817, and the eastern part became the Territory of Alabama.

During this time, Sargent pursued many of his scientific and historical interests. He published papers on American antiquities and on the natural sciences. He lived to see Ohio become a state in 1803, the Louisiana Purchase the same year and Indiana statehood in 1816.

As the Territory of Mississippi's first governor, Sargent is commemorated on the 1948 3¢ Mississippi Territory issue.

Winfield Scott Schley

Scott 793
Born: October 9, 1839, Frederick County, Maryland
Died: October 2, 1911, New York, New York

Winfield Scott Schley, who was named for the great American General Winfield Scott, began his military career at the U.S. Naval Academy. Schley graduated in 1860 and was a classmate of William Thomas Sampson, who later became a rear admiral in the Spanish-American War. Schley saw active duty as a lieutenant in the Civil War until July 1863. He taught modern languages at the Naval Academy from 1872 to 1875. He was promoted to commander in 1874.

From 1876 to 1879, Schley commanded the *Essex* mostly in the area of the South Atlantic. Until October 1883, he was inspector of the second lighthouse district. When the Arctic explorer Lieutenant Adolphus Washington Greely and six other survivors reached Cape Sabin, 250 miles south of their base, in June 1884, it was Schley who steamed to their rescue.

In 1891 he was in command of the *Baltimore* off the coast of Chile in Rear Admiral George Brown's squadron. In February 1898, Schley was commissioned commodore and put in command of the "flying squadron."

Aboard his flagship *Brooklyn*, Schley was sent to serve in the war against Spain. Off Santiago, Cuba, the command of the fleet went to acting Rear Admiral W.T. Sampson. In Sampson's absence, on July 3, 1898, in the battle of Santiago harbor, Schley was the senior officer. The question of whether the credit for the victory belonged to Sampson, whose flagship reached the scene of action only as the last Spanish ship was beached, or Schley, who had been on hand all the while, but whose orders to the captains of the squadron had been mainly unnoticed or ignored, was finally argued in court. Admiral George Dewey, chairman of the inquiry in 1901, held that Schley had been in command at Santiago, but he was reprimanded for his actions. Sampson was given no credit.

In 1899 Schley was commissioned rear admiral. *Cosmopolitan* in 1912 featured "Admiral Schley's Own Story," an article in Schley's defense. Schley wrote *Forty-five Years under the Flag* in 1901 and, with James Russell Soley, *The Rescue of Greely* in 1885.

Winfield Scott Schley is shown with Admirals William Sampson and George Dewey on a 1937 4¢ Navy stamp.

Carl Schurz

Scott 1847
Born: March 2, 1829, Liblar, Prussia
Died: May 14, 1906, New York, New York

Carl Schurz attended the University of Bonn and became involved in the revolutionary movement of 1848-49 in Germany. He promoted an insurrection, which failed. Schurz fled to France, then Switzerland. He returned to Germany in 1850 just long enough to rescue an imprisoned comrade.

After a year in London, England, as a correspondent for the German press, he emigrated to Philadelphia. He went to Watertown, Wisconsin, and was admitted to the Wisconsin bar in 1859.

Schurz embraced the abolitionist cause. He joined the Republican Party, and campaigned for John C. Fremont for president and Abraham Lincoln for senator. Later, Schurz supported Lincoln for president. After the election, Lincoln appointed him minister to Spain. He returned in January 1862 to join the Union Army. He was commissioned a brigadier general and saw action in several major battles. In 1863, he was promoted to major general.

He was the Washington correspondent for Horace Greeley's *New York Tribune*. He became editor of the *Detroit Post* in 1866. In 1867 he became a co-editor, with Joseph Pulitzer, of the *St. Louis Westliche Post*.

In 1868 Schurz was elected as a senator from Missouri for one term. As a liberal Republican, he campaigned for Horace Greeley. He also campaigned for Rutherford B. Hayes, who appointed him secretary of the interior.

From 1881 to 1883, Schurz was editor of the *New York Evening Post* and the *Nation*. He changed politcal parties twice, once as a Mugwump against James G. Blaine's nomination and again to support William J. Bryan against William McKinley.

From 1892 to 1901, he was president of the National Civil Service Reform League and wrote editorials for *Harpers Weekly*. He wrote the two-volume *Life of Henry Clay* and the three-volume *Reminiscences*, published after his death.

Schurz is featured on a 4¢ denomination released in 1983 as part of the Great Americans issue.

Blanche Stuart Scott

Scott C99
Born: 1886
Died: January 12, 1970, Rochester, New York

Blanche Scott made her first solo flight in September 1910, barnstorming with a daredevil troupe, making 3,000-foot death-dives. She was a special consultant for many years for the Air Force Museum at Wright-Patterson Air Force Base, located near Dayton, Ohio. Scott flew planes in the days when aircraft were built of wooden frameworks, covered with canvas and braced by wires and turnbuckles. Those flimsy planes were relatively cheap to build and repair, with the engines being the most expensive item. Pilots like Scott did not wear safety belts and were exposed to the wind. Many pilots were killed when they were pitched out of their plane upon an upsetting landing. Goggles, a cap worn backwards, a checkered Norfolk-style jacket and a long flowing silk scarf became the uniform of the pilots during those early days.

Fierce competition at the air meets and air shows encouraged improved performances and more substantial equipment. Scott and other pilots made their way by stunt flying at county and state fairs and small town celebrations. The fact that one of the daredevils was a woman made it all the more attractive. Such feats as that in 1911 of Cal P. Rodgers, who flew a Wright biplane in the first transcontinental flight from New York City to Pasadena, California, in about 49 days, encouraged young pilots. Rodgers survived 15 crashes in the record-breaking flight.

Scott and other heroes of the air, such as Glenn Curtiss, and later Charles Lindbergh, were as well-known as astronauts are today. Later, air racing became an exciting sport, although crashes were frequent. By World War I, few racing-era pilots had survived. Having lived with these experiences, Scott could provide otherwise forgotten details for the U.S. Air Force Museum and the early history of aviation. She retired in 1956.

She is portrayed on a 28¢ airmail stamp issued in 1980.

336

Winfield Scott

Scott 786
Born: June 13, 1786, Petersburg, Virginia
Died: May 29, 1866, West Point, New York

Winfield Scott gave up a law career in 1808 to spend the next 53 years in the Army. He rose to the rank of lieutenant general in 1855, the highest ranking officer since George Washington. Because he demanded strict military discipline, he was nicknamed Old Fuss and Feathers.

Scott was court-martialed by General James Wilkinson and suspended for one year from 1810 to 1811. In the War of 1812, he was made lieutenant colonel. He saw action at Niagara and was captured by the British at Queenston Heights. He was released to General Henry Dearborn as adjutant, then took part in the attack on Fort George. He took command in 1813 and secured the stronghold.

In 1814 he was promoted to brigadier general. Scott fought at Chippewa and Lundy's Lane, where he was wounded twice. He was made department commander in New York City, and was sent to Europe to study war and update Army field manuals.

Scott saw active duty in the Black Hawk War in 1832. Later, Andrew Jackson commissioned him to observe the activities of the Nullifiers in South Carolina. In 1835-37, Scott commanded the war against the Indians in Florida. Jackson relieved him, charging him with laxity. In 1838, he was in charge of removing the Cherokee Indians to reservations in the West. Van Buren sent him to the far Northeast to settle the conflict with Canada, known as the Aroostook War.

In 1841 Scott succeeded to the command of the entire Army. He sent Zachary Taylor to the Mexican War, but had to go himself to finally settle it. After several notable battles, he entered and occupied Mexico City. Eight months later, he returned home a hero.

Nominated for U.S. president by the Whigs, he was soundly defeated by Franklin Pierce in 1852. In 1859, at age 73, he served as mediator between Great Britain and the United States. He was still commander in chief of the Army when the Civil War began in 1861, but he retired that fall. Winfield Scott appeared on a 2¢ stamp issued as part of the 1936-37 Army series. He is shown with Andrew Jackson and the Hermitage.

Sequoyah

Scott 1859
Born: 1769/70? in Taskigi Village on the Tennessee River
Died: August 1843, San Fernando, Tamaulipas, Mexico

Sequoyah is remembered by a statue placed by the state of Oklahoma in the Statuary Hall of the United States Capitol. Even grander is Sequoia National Park in California. It was named for him, as were the giant redwood trees, *Sequoiadendron giganteum* and *Sequoiadendron sempervirens.*

Sequoyah's father was probably the English trader Nathaniel Gist. His mother was part Cherokee. Sequoyah was raised by his mother and learned to speak only Cherokee. A wound received in the 1813-14 Creek War left him with a lame leg. He worked as a silversmith, hunter and fur trader. When he was grown up, he took the English name, George Guess, the name of the man whom he thought to be his father. Sequoyah was fascinated by the white man's printed books, which he called "talking leaves."

About 1809, Sequoyah began to work out an alphabet for the Cherokee language. He used the English, Greek, and Hebrew alphabets to assign an alphabetical symbol to the sounds of the Cherokee language, 86 symbols in all. His syllabary was approved by the Cherokee general council in 1821 and was taught to the Cherokee nation. The new, written version of the language enabled thousands of Cherokee tribesmen to read and write. The missionaries used it. In 1824 parts of the Bible were printed in Cherokee, and in 1828 the first weekly issue of the *Cherokee Phoenix and Indian Advocate* newspaper appeared. It was printed in both English and Cherokee.

That same year, Sequoyah joined with the western Cherokee who were moved to Indian Territory, later Oklahoma. He taught in their schools and later traveled to Washington, D.C., as their political envoy.

In 1843 he set out to locate a tribe of Cherokee thought to have crossed the Mississippi River. He probably was more than 70 years old. He died while on that journey.

The first Great Americans definitive, the 19¢ value issued in 1980, pictures Sequoyah.

Father Junipero Serra

Scott C116
Born: November 24, 1713, Petra, Spanish Majorca Island
Died: August 28, 1784, Carmel Mission, Carmel, California

Miguel Jose Serra grew up among the peasants of his home, Majorca, and earned his early education in the cathedral schools at the island's nearby capital city of Palma. His investiture of the Franciscan habit was on September 14, 1730. Exactly one year later he received his sacred orders and took the name of St. Francis of Assisi's friend and counselor, Junipero. He was ordained in 1738 and taught philosophy at Majorca's Lullian University. Serra earned his doctorate in theology in 1743.

After 17 years in Palma, he took the opportunity to be a missionary by joining several lifelong friends and going to Mexico. The group arrived in Veracruz on December 9, 1749, and Junipero walked the entire distance to the College of San Fernando in Mexico City, nearly 200 miles away. He was bitten during his trip. The bite became infected, and for the rest of the "walking friar's" life, the healed wound caused him pain. He arrived in Mexico City on January 1, 1750.

Six months later he was in the village of Jalpan, Queretaro, administering to the Pame Indians in the Sierra Gorda until 1758. Serra returned to Mexico City for nine more years. Charles II expelled all Jesuits from the New World, and the Franciscans were to take their place in Baja (lower) California. Instead, they arrived at Loreto on April 1, 1768.

The visitador general of New Spain, Jose Galvez, formulated a plan to conquer Alta (upper) California to fend against the Russians and the British. With troops under Gaspar de Portola, Serra and his friars went north to found Mission San Diego de Alcala on July 1, 1769. After that time, 21 California missions were founded by the Franciscans. Father Serra directed the building of San Carlos Borromeo on Mission Bay on June 3, 1770, with Portola's help. From 1771 to 1782 he saw seven more major missions built. He died at and is buried by the altar of Mission San Carlos Borromeo del Rio Carmelo.

Serra is remembered on a 1985 44¢ airmail stamp.

339

John Sevier

Scott 941
Born: September 23, 1745, Rockingham County (New Market), Virginia
Died: September 24, 1815, near Fort Decatur, Alabama

John Sevier had only a little schooling at the academy in Fredericksburg, Virginia. He moved from place to place, finally settling in 1773 in eastern Tennessee. He was a captain of the militia in the Lord Dunmore's War (1773-74), then served in the provincial legislature of North Carolina. From 1777 to 1780, Sevier was a county clerk and district judge. In 1780 he participated in the Battle of Kings Mountain. After a victory over the Loyalists, he emerged as a war hero.

For the next two years he conducted raids against the Cherokee Indians, forcing them to cede more tribal land. After North Carolina gave up its land claims to the federal government, numerous frontiersmen met at Jonesboro in 1784 to plan for an independent state. They named it the state of Franklin, and Sevier was its governor. However, Congress refused to recognize the state of Franklin, and by 1788, it was defunct.

Sevier, in disfavor with many, became involved in the Spanish conspiracy plots. A number of Americans cooperated secretly with Spanish colonial officials to detach the West from the United States and to protect Florida and Louisiana from American encroachment. Nothing ever came of the plot, and Sevier lost interest. He then turned to respectability, was pardoned and elected to the North Carolina senate in 1789. After the new national government began to function, Sevier was elected to the House of Representatives. He was a representative from the western district.

When the Southwest Territory was created in 1790, Sevier was made a brigadier general of militia. He became the first governor of Tennessee when it was made a state in 1796. He served three consecutive terms. Sevier held several appointed and elected positions thereafter. In 1815 he was commissioned to survey the boundary between Georgia and the Alabama Indian territory. He died on that expedition, near Fort Decatur.

A statue of Sevier represents Tennessee in the Statuary Hall collection in the U.S. Capitol in Washington, D.C. The Tennessee Statehood issue of 1946 features Andrew Jackson, Sevier and the state capitol in Nashville.

340

William Henry Seward

Scott 370
Born: May 16, 1801, Florida, New York
Died: October 10, 1872, Auburn, New York

William Seward practiced law in Auburn, New York, after being admitted to the bar two years after he graduated from Union College in Schenectady, New York, in 1820. Ten years later, he was elected to the state senate on the Anti-Masonic ticket. He was a close associate of Thurlow Weed, a journalist who had published the *Anti-Masonic Enquirer* and the Albany *Evening Journal.* The Anti-Masonic party subsided into the National Republican party, whose name later changed to Whigs. Seward became governor of New York in 1836. He was re-elected in 1840. He backed the William Henry Harrison-John Tyler ticket in 1840. He took bold stands in his governorship, especially advising resistance to the extradition of fugitive slaves.

In 1843 he returned to his law practice. He was elected to the U.S. Senate in 1849, along with the Whig Zachary Taylor-Millard Fillmore ticket. Seward opposed the Compromise of 1850, which was a series of acts designed to settle the conflict between opponents of slavery and southern slave owners. He also opposed the Kansas-Nebraska Bill in 1854, which provided that two new territories be made from Indian land west of the Missouri River bend. He supported Kansas as a free state and opposed the Dread Scott decision made in 1857 that declared that no black could claim U.S. citizenship and slavery could not be prohibited in U.S. territories.

Seward served through the Pierce and Buchanan administrations. In 1856 and 1860 he was considered for a presidential nomination. He supported Lincoln on the Republican ticket. Lincoln chose him for his secretary of state.

Seward kept Europe out of the American Civil War and negotiated the French withdrawal from Mexico. On April 14, 1865, when Lincoln was shot, Seward suffered injuries from an accomplice of Lincoln's assassin. Seward recovered and continued as secretary of state under Andrew Johnson. In 1865 he negotiated the purchase of Alaska from Russia. This event was known as "Seward's Folly" or "Seward's Ice Box." He left office in 1869 when Ulysses S. Grant took office.

He is depicted on a 1909 2¢ Alaska-Yukon Pacific Exposition stamp.

Chief Shadoo

Scott 683
Born: circa: 1660, Kiawah Island (South Carolina)
Died: circa 1700, Charleston, South Carolina

Shadoo was chief of the Kiawah Indian tribe, a small tribe that lived on Kiawah Island, south of Charleston, South Carolina. The tribe is now extinct.

Twenty-year-old colonist Henry Woodward was a surgeon on a ship sailing south in search of a new port. Two hundred fifty miles south of Cape Fear the ship's crew discovered a place on Port Royal. They encountered friendly Indians. Woodward stayed to study the Indians until his captain returned. However, Woodward was taken prisoner by the Spanish. They took him to St. Augustine. He escaped to the Leeward Islands. A year later he boarded a ship to London but only made it to Nevis, where his ship was wrecked. An English ship rescued him. He soon was bound for Port Royal.

When he arrived in Port Royal, he found the Indian village had been burned to the ground. Kiawah Chief Shadoo told him that the Westo Indians had pillaged the camp and had taken the people into slavery. Chief Shadoo advised Woodward to sail north to the Kiawah River. The chief guided them 16 miles upstream in April 1670. They built a log palisade and plank houses located between a creek and the Indian village.

The town was called Albermarle Point. It was later renamed Charles Town. Chief Shadoo's Kiawah River was renamed the Ashley River for Sir Anthony Ashley Cooper.

The settlement of 148 people was hundreds of miles from other English settlements. Spaniards, with the help of inland Indians, attempted an attack from the sea. It was thwarted by a severe storm. The absentee proprietors demanded that the settlers load the English ships with saleable goods to fill their depleted purses. Acting Governor Joseph West refused. Lord Ashley sided with the settlers. Chief Shadoo and his Kiawahs shared rich beds of oysters, wild turkey hunting grounds and fresh meat with the colonists.

In 1674 Woodward opened trade to the west, finding rich sources of income. The settlement prospered to become Charleston.

Chief Shadoo is shown with Governor Joseph West on a 1930 2¢ stamp.

William Shakespeare

Scott 1250
Born: April 23, 1564, Stratford-upon-Avon, England
Died: April 23, 1616, Stratford-upon-Avon, England

William Shakespeare was the eldest son of a prominent Stratford-upon-Avon family. His father, John, was a glove maker. His mother, Mary Arden, was from a family of high social standing. Shakespeare received his formal education at the Stratford-upon-Avon grammar school. His strict schooling trained his mind for acting and writing plays. When he was 18, Shakespeare married Anne Hathaway, who was 26. They had a child, Susanna, within the first year of their marriage. Two years later, they had twins, Hammet and Judith. Two years after that, Shakespeare moved to London to act. Shakespeare's wife, who was a Puritan, objected to the acting profession and stayed behind in Stratford-upon-Avon.

In 1594, Shakespeare became a member of the Chamberlain's Men, an acting group that, in 1603, became known as the King's Men when James I came to the throne. Shakespeare remained with the group while he wrote and directed plays.

Only 18 of his plays appeared in small books called quartos. Three-fourths of his works has vanished. His manuscripts were collected by Hemminges and Condell, who published his plays in 1628.

Shakespeare owned shares in the Globe Theater, invested wisely in real estate, and became quite wealthy. He bought New Place in Stratford-upon-Avon in 1597, then came home in 1611. Five years later, he died and was buried in Holy Trinity Church, where he had been baptized.

William Shakespeare appears on a 1964 5¢ stamp.

Philip Henry Sheridan

Scott 787
Born: March 6, 1831, Albany, New York
Died: August 5, 1888, Nonquitt, Massachusetts

Philip Sheridan grew up in Somerset, Ohio. He entered West Point in 1848 and graduated in 1853. He got his baptism of fire in western Indian campaigns, then served as captain and quartermaster officer in Missouri.

In May 1862, Sheridan was appointed colonel in command of the 2nd Michigan Cavalry. He saw action at Booneville on July 1 of that year. He was promoted to brigadier general at the head of the 11th Division of the Army of the Ohio. He fought at Perryville and Stones River.

Sheridan advanced to major general in charge of the 20th Corps, Army of the Cumberland, in 1863. He fought at Chickamouga, and under General George H. Thomas, charged up Missionary Ridge, which assured the victory for General Ulysses S. Grant. Grant took over the Army of the Potomac, and Sheridan went along, playing an active role in the Wilderness Campaign around Richmond, Virginia, in 1864.

In August, Sheridan took command of the Army of the Shenandoah. He defeated Jubal Early at Winchester, Fisher's Hill and Cedar Creek. In 1864, he was promoted to major general in the Regular Army. In March 1865, he began cavalry actions around Petersburg, Virginia. His victories at Dinwiddie Courthouse and Five Forks led to the fall of Petersburg, which cut off General Lee's retreat from Appomattox and forced Lee to surrender to Grant.

After the Civil War Sheridan was sent to command the Division of the Gulf on the Mexican border, where he worked to force the French out of Mexico. During the South's Reconstruction, Sheridan was assigned the Fifth Military District of Louisiana and Texas. Relieved of that duty, he was to serve again in Indian campaigns in the West. In 1869 he was promoted to lieutenant general in command of the Department of the Missouri.

Between 1870 and 1871, he was sent to Prussia to observe the Franco-Prussian war. In 1884 he became commander in chief of the army, succeeding General William Tecumseh Sherman. On June 1, 1888, an act of Congress promoted him to full general, a position he enjoyed only two months and four days. He died August 5 of that year.

Philip Henry Sheridan appears with Generals Sherman and Grant on a 1937 3¢ Army stmap.

William Tecumseh Sherman

Scott 787
Born: February 8, 1820, Lancaster, Ohio
Died: February 14, 1891, New York, New York

When William Sherman was nine years old, his father died. He grew up in the home of Thomas Ewing, an Ohio politician, who secured for him an appointment to West Point in 1836. After he graduated in 1840, Sherman served at various posts in the South until the outbreak of the Mexican War.

As commander of the Division of the Pacific, Sherman served until California organized for statehood in 1848. He quit the army to manage the San Francisco branch of a St. Louis bank, which failed in 1857. Sherman then practiced law in Leavenworth, Kansas. From 1859 to 1861, he was superintendent of the new military college in Alexandria, Louisiana.

In May 1861, Sherman was appointed colonel of the 13th Infantry and led a brigade at the first Battle of Bull Run. He was made brigadier general of volunteers and sent to Kentucky to keep the state in the Union. He then was sent to join General Ulysses S. Grant at the Battle of Shiloh and Corinth.

Sherman was promoted to major general and assigned to Memphis, Tennessee, for the Vicksburg Campaign in 1863. After the fall of Vicksburg in July 1863, he received the rank of brigadier general in the Regular Army. He succeeded Grant in command of the Army of the Tennessee and took part in the Chattanooga Campaign. Grant appointed Sherman commander of the Division of the Mississippi in 1864.

In July of that year, Sherman forced General Joseph Johnston back to Atlanta. Sherman burned the city to the ground, then left for the famous march to the sea, burning and blasting his way to Savannah. He turned north, and Johnston surrendered at Durham Station, North Carolina, on April 26, 1865, 17 days after General Robert E. Lee surrendered to Grant at Appomattox.

Sherman returned to restraining the Indians in Mississippi. After a mission in Mexico, he was given command of the entire army by President Grant. Sherman retired in 1886.

William Tecumseh Sherman is commemorated on a 1937 3¢ stamp.

345

Igor Ivanovich Sikorsky

Scott C119
Born: May 25, 1889, Kiev, Russia
Died: October 26, 1972, Easton, Connecticut

As a young boy, Igor Sikorsky was interested in the drawings of Leonardo da Vinci's flying machines. When he was about 12 years old, he made a toy propeller powered by a twisted rubber band, which, when released, flew upwards into the air. Sikorsky saw more than a mere toy in his little invention. He saw a machine that someday would take man off the ground and up into the air, then gracefully back down again. He was educated at the Petrograd Naval College and at engineering schools in Paris and Kiev.

In 1909, at age 20, Sikorsky attempted to build his first helicopter, but failed because he did not have suitable engines. In two more years, he had produced five successful airplanes and was an experienced pilot. His S-5 flew three men aboard for a distance of 30 miles at 70 miles an hour, a new record. From 1912 until the Russian revolution in 1918, Sikorsky was the aeronautics engineer of the Russo-Baltic Railroad Car Works. As early as 1913, he built a multi-engined airplane. One plane he called the *Le Grand* had four engines. His *Ilia Mourometz* was used as a bomber during World War I.

To flee the revolution, Sikorsky went to New York, where he taught Russian immigrants. In 1923 he founded the Sikorsky Aero Engineering Corporation. His twin-engined S-29 carried up to 14 passengers at a speed of two miles a minute. In 1925 he formed the Sikorsky Manufacturing Corporation on Long Island, New York, where he designed and built the S-38 flying boat. In 1928, the year he became a naturalized citizen, he organized the Sikorsky Aviation Corporation, in Stratford, Connecticut, that became part of the United Aircraft Corporation, now United Technologies Corporation.

In 1931 he introduced the *American Clipper*, an S-40. The four-engined *Clipper* amphibian crafts that followed were transoceanic commercial planes. In 1939 Sikorsky produced a successful single-rotor helicopter with high load-carrying capacity per horsepower.

He retired from United Aircraft in 1957. He was elected to the International Aerospace Hall of Fame in 1966. He wrote *The Winged S* and *The Invisible Encounter*. He won the National Medal of Science in 1966.

Igor Ivanovich Sikorsky appears on a 1988 36¢ airmail stamp.

Sitting Bull (Tatanka Yotanka)

Scott 2184
Born: circa 1834, on Grand River
Died: December 15, 1890, Standing Rock Reservation, North Dakota

Sitting Bull received his name after showing great bravery in a fight against the Crow Indians. He fought with his father in that battle in 1849. Sitting Bull was a well-known medicine man and leader of the Hunkpapa Sioux Indians. His stubbornness to yield to the U.S. government moving to the reservation, along with his remarkable prophetic visions, unified the Sioux, Cheyenne and Arapaho Indians into a force of nearly 4,000 men and boys in 1876. That year, Sitting Bull led a sun dance at which he told the Indians to change their way of fighting. They should fight to kill, instead of showing off to prove their bravery. Otherwise, they would lose all their land to the whites. The year before, Sitting Bull had a vision of the coming of many soldiers. He saw dead soldiers "falling right and left into our camp." On June 25, 1876, Sitting Bull's apparition came true when General George A. Custer and his soldiers fell upon the Indians and were slaughtered to the last man. Contrary to popular belief, Sitting Bull did not lead this attack on Custer. He acted only as the leading medicine man in preparation for the battle.

After the Battle of the Little Bighorn, Sitting Bull and his followers were driven into Canada. With only 187 dejected people, Sitting Bull surrendered to Fort Buford in July 1881. He was taken to Fort Randall and then to Standing Rock Reservation.

Sitting Bull took an active part in the Ghost Dance agitation. Fearing his influence, agent McLaughlin and Lieutenant Colonel Drum conspired to take Sitting Bull away from the dancers. His cabin was surrounded by the agent's Indian policemen. Sitting Bull was brought out of his cabin. Shooting began. Sitting Bull was shot three times. A fight broke out. Sitting Bull, his son Crow Foot and six others were dead. Four policemen were dead and three wounded. Two died later.

In 1953 Sitting Bull's remains were reinterred near Mobridge, South Dakota, across from where the Grand River runs into the Missouri.

Sitting Bull is depicted on a 1989 28¢ Great Americans stamp.

Alfred Emanuel Smith

Scott 937
Born: December 30, 1873, New York, New York
Died: October 4, 1944, New York, New York

Born and raised in New York City's Lower East Side, Alfred Smith had little formal education. He worked at the Fulton Street Fish Market until, at age 22, he was taken into the fold of Tammany Hall. Smith was given minor political jobs in the city's Democratic politics. He married Catherine Dunn in 1900. In 1903 Smith was elected to the state legislature with support from Tammany Hall. Smith remained until 1915, when he became sheriff of New York County. In 1917 he became president of the New York City board of aldermen. In 1918 he ran for governor and won a narrow but upsetting victory over the Republican candidate.

Smith was a popular governor. His Lower East Side accent held him in good stead with the commoner, whom he championed. The 1920 national shift to the Republican party lost him his bid for re-election in 1920 to Nathan L. Miller. Smith spent the next two years heading the United States Trucking Corporation, but in 1922 he was back in the race and won the governorship, holding that office from 1923 to 1928. He was a contender for the presidential nomination in 1924, but lost to John W. Davis over William G. McAdoo on the 103rd ballot.

In 1928 Smith won the nomination on the first ballot. His protege, Franklin D. Roosevelt, dubbed him the Happy Warrior. Smith lost to Herbert Hoover, however, because of his stand on Prohibition, his big-city political background and his Roman Catholic religion. Roosevelt won Smith's place as governor of New York.

When Roosevelt became president, Smith did not agree with the New Deal policies. He also had some major setbacks in his financial dealings, which made life unhappy for him.

Smith also is remembered as the president of the corporation that built the Empire State Building, the skyscraper landmark at 34th Street and Fifth Avenue in Manhattan.

Alfred Emanual Smith is shown on a 1945 3¢ stamp.

John Smith

Scott 328
Born: January 6, 1580, Willoughby, Lincolnshire, England
Died: June 21, 1631, London, England

John Smith attended school until age 15, then apprenticed himself to a wealthy merchant. He traveled around Europe and became a soldier in Transylvania at age 22. Smith won bloody duels and was wounded and taken prisoner by the Turks and made a slave in South Russia. He managed to escape by killing his guard, then made his way through Russia and Europe. After more adventures in Europe and Africa, he finally returned to England in 1604.

At age 26, Smith was a mature man. He joined the London Company enterprise for more adventure. With Captain Newport and three ships, an emigration party numbering 105 men headed for Virginia for gold trade with the Indians on Roanoke Island, but storms drove them north into Chesapeake Bay. They sailed up the river and in May 1607 founded Jamestown, which was named in honor of James I, who awarded the company their patent. A seven-man council was appointed and the first charter of Virginia was established. Bad management obliged the colonist to ward off starvation and disease by appointing Smith as their leader. Despite being almost killed by the Indians, Smith bartered for life-saving supplies and food.

In various voyages during the ensuing summer of 1608, Smith explored Chesapeake Bay and mapped it. He also sailed for considerable distances up the Susquahanna, the Potomac and the James rivers. The early geography of the Atlantic seaboard was largely founded on the sketches made by this intrepid and restless explorer.

Smith also gave New England its name. Due to severe burns from a gunpowder explosion, Smith had to return to England in 1609. He came back to America in 1614 for more exploration. In 1615 he was captured by pirates on a trip to what is now the United States. After his release, he remained in England to write of his explorations and to encourage colonization.

John Smith is shown on a 1907 Jamestown Exposition 1¢ stamp.

John Philip Sousa

Scott 880
Born: November 6, 1854, Washington, D.C.
Died: March 6, 1932, Reading, Pennsylvania

John Philip Sousa's father, a Spanish musician who emigrated to the United States, taught his son to play wind instruments. John Philip received a good musical education. In his youth, he played in various theater orchestras in Washington, D.C. He joined the U.S. Marines in 1868 as a Marine Band apprentice. At age 26, he became conductor of the Marine Band.

Helen Kaufman wrote of Sousa: "For him the corps was a guinea-pig which he dissected in the interest of music. When he finally retired after 12 years, he had made the corps into something more than one worth listening to. He had learned through his experiments how to produce beautiful tones instead of the clangorous and blaring noises of the normal brass band."

When Sousa formed his own touring band in 1892, he entirely changed the normal composition of the brass band. He decreased the number of brass and percussion instruments and increased the number of wood winds. He also introduced a harp. Sousa's musicians were capable of executing programs almost as varied as those of a symphony orchestra. His compositions earned him the title "March King."

Sousa also wrote symphonic poems, suites, operas and operettas. Although it was his marches that won him fame, he preferred to be known as an operatic composer.

In all, Sousa composed more than 2,000 works. He wrote a book on military band instruments and an autobiography, *Marching Along*. His best-known marches are: *El Capitan* (1896), *King Cotton* (1895), *Stars and Stripes Forever* (1897) and *Washington Post* (1889). A compilation of his occasional writings was issued in 1910 as *Through the Years with Sousa*.

The familiar marching band's bass tuba helicon, with its two-foot-diameter detachable bell and its tubing wrapped around the body of the musician and resting on the player's shoulder, was designed by Sousa. It is commonly known as the sousaphone.

Between 1917 and 1919, he was bandmaster for the U.S. Navy. Sousa is pictured in uniform on a 2¢ stamp in the Famous Americans.

350

Elmer Ambrose Sperry

Scott C114
Born: October 12, 1860, Cortland, New York
Died: June 16, 1930, Brooklyn, New York

Elmer Sperry attended the State Normal and Training School at his hometown in Cortland, New York, then spent one year at Cornell University, at nearby Ithaca. Sperry visited the Philadelphia Centennial Exposition in 1876, which spurred his enthusiasm in electronics and engineering. He worked to improve the dynamics of lighting systems. He manufactured appliances, dynamos and an updated arc lamp in his own company, which he founded in Chicago in 1880 at age 19. For the next 20 years, Sperry also manufactured mining machinery, streetcar equipment, locomotives, storage batteries and electric automobiles. In 1900, in partnership with C.P. Townsend, Sperry established an electrochemical research laboratory in Washington, D.C. This kept him busy for the next 10 years.

Sperry formed the Sperry Gyroscope Company in Brooklyn, New York, in 1910, and headed that firm until 1929. As early as 1890, Sperry experimented with the gyroscope and other devices by applying the principles of basic electronics and mechanics. Through this he invented several instruments used to improve the safety of air and sea travel.

In 1911 Sperry's non-magnetic gyrocompass was installed on the battleship *Delaware* and was soon adapted as standard equipment in the Navy and several steamship lines. Sperry invented the arc searchlight and a gyro-controlled aerial torpedo that was used in World War I.

During his lifetime, Sperry established eight different companies to manufacture and market his inventions. In all, he obtained more than 400 separate patents.

For his numerous and useful contributions to technology, Sperry received many honors and awards in the United States and abroad. He was decorated for his work by Japan, Russia and France. Sperry shared his knowledge by founding the American Institute of Electrical Engineers and the American Electrochemical Society. His base company was in Brooklyn, where he made his home.

Sperry appears with his son Lawrence on a 1985 39¢ airmail stamp.

Lawrence Burst Sperry

Scott C114
Born: December 21, 1892, Chicago, Illinois
Died: December 13, 1923, English Channel, between England and France

Lawrence Sperry was the son of Elmer Ambrose Sperry. Like his father, he had an inquisitive mind and a natural adaptation to mechanical apparatuses. He, too, began to work with machinery at an early age. Sperry was especially interested in aviation and flying machines. He built his own airplane while he was in high school and developed into an excellent pilot.

Sperry successfully adapted his father's work with gyroscopes and gyrostabilizers, especially for airplanes. He worked with Glenn Curtiss in Europe on the gyrostablizer, showing its usefulness in the Curtiss flying boat. He also developed an automatic pilot and a turn-and-bank indicator to be used in planes that fly at night. Sperry made the first blind flight at night to show that instrument flying was feasible, practical and possible. He pioneered what is now standard procedure, since instruments are more dependable and accurate than a pilot's judgment when flying, as a flyer would say, "by the seat of my pants."

As the head of his own aircraft company, Sperry developed a small plane called the *Messenger*, which was for personal use. He would fly his *Messenger* from his airplane factory at Farmingdale, Long Island, to his Garden City, Long Island, home, and park it in his two-stall garage.

Sperry went to England to demonstrate his little *Messenger*. On December 13, 1923, he took off to fly across the English Channel to France. His engine sputtered and conked out not too far from the beach. He made a perfect landing on the surface of the water, stripped off his flying suit and started to swim for shore, but was lost in the fog and icy water.

The world lost a 31-year-old genius to what was a rather foolish adventure and a heroic attempt to save himself. Had he stayed with his craft he may have been saved.

Both Lawrence Sperry and his father are commemorated on the 3¢ Aviation Pioneers airmail stamp of 1985.

Edwin McMasters Stanton

Scott 138
Born: December 19, 1814, Steubenville, Ohio
Died: December 24, 1869, Washington, D.C.

Edwin Stanton attended Kenyon College in central Ohio. For financial reasons, he was unable to finish school and turned to law. He was admitted to the bar in 1836 and entered practice in Cadiz, Ohio. In 1847 Stanton moved to Pittsburgh and gained national recognition in the early 1850s by representing Pennsylvania in a case argued before the Supreme Court. Stanton moved to Washington, D.C., in 1856, where he represented the United States in cases involving fraudulent Mexican land titles in California.

In December 1860, President James Buchanan named Stanton his attorney general. As a Democrat, Stanton left his Cabinet post when Abraham Lincoln was inaugurated president in March 1861. He became legal adviser to Secretary of War Simon Cameron. When Cameron was dismissed by Lincoln in 1862, Stanton took over the position in the midst of the Civil War.

Stanton was abrasive and brusque and often in conflict with other civil leaders and military generals. He was most unpopular. He had little regard for Andrew Johnson, even though Johnson retained him as his secretary of war. Stanton and Johnson were in conflict over Reconstruction policies, and Stanton collaborated with others against Johnson.

In August 1867, Johnson requested Stanton's resignation. Stanton refused, claiming the recently passed Tenure of Office Act. The Senate refused to confirm Stanton's suspension, so Stanton stayed on as secretary of war. A month later, Johnson dismissed Stanton outright. Stanton defiantly remained.

In May 1868, impeachment charges against Johnson, based on the dismissal of Stanton, failed. Johnson remained president, and Stanton had no choice but to resign.

In 1869 President Ulysses S. Grant nominated Stanton to the Supreme Court. He was duly confirmed by the Senate, but died four days later.

Edwin McMasters Stanton appears on an 1871 7¢ stamp.

Elizabeth Cady Stanton

Scott 959
Born: November 12, 1815, Johnstown, New York
Died: October 26, 1902, New York, New York

Elizabeth Cady Stanton, the daughter of an eminent lawyer, was well-educated at Troy Female Seminary and by her father in his law office. Stanton observed her father counseling tearful women. The law did not protect these women from drunken and abusive husbands. It also deprived them of their property and their children. She was so hurt by this that she resolved early in life to bring women up to their proper level in the state, the church and society.

In 1840 Elizabeth married Henry Brewster Stanton, a prominent abolitionist. Later that year, they went to London to attend the World's Anti-Slavery Convention. At the convention, she was refused official recognition because she was a woman.

Stanton and Lucretia C. Mott organized the first women's rights convention at Seneca Falls, New York, in 1848. This convention launched the women's rights movement in earnest. Stanton's suffrage proposals and her proposal that abusive and drunken husbands were grounds for divorce pegged her as a radical. She worked closely with Susan B. Anthony for the next 40 years. Their movement was encouraged in 1860, when New York amended laws granting women joint guardianship of their children, the right to sue in court, the right to receive and keep wages earned, and the right to own personal property.

Stanton wrote stinging articles for the *Revolution*, a women's rights newspaper, in 1868-70. She also served as chairwoman of the National Woman Suffrage Association from its inception in 1869 until 1890. At that time, it merged with the American Woman Suffrage Association and changed its name to the National American Woman Suffrage Association. She was elected its first president and held that position until 1892.

Stanton contributed considerably to the first three volumes of the six-volume *The History of Woman Suffrage* (1881-1922). She published *Eighty Years and More*, an autobiography, four years before her death.

Stanton is depicted, along with Lucretia Mott and Carrie Chapman Catt, on a 1948 3¢ stamp. The issue commemorates a century of progress of American women.

354

Vilhjalmur Stefansson

Scott 2222
Born: November 3, 1879, Arnes, Manitoba, Canada
Died: August 26, 1962, Hanover, New Hampshire

Vilhjalmur Stefansson's parents came to America from Iceland. After he graduated from the University of Iowa, he made two trips back to his parent's native land. With a heritage of ice water in his veins, Stefansson chose to make Arctic exploration and research his life's work. He first visited the Arctic in 1906-07 with an expedition studying the Mackenzie River delta. He traveled overland to meet a ship at a designated place, but the ship was iced in and failed to reach him. Thus, he was forced to live with the Eskimos of the Mackenzie delta for a year. He learned their language and ate their food — raw meat and blubber. Stefansson concluded that anyone could live in the Arctic if he lived as the Eskimos had lived for many centuries.

From 1908 to 1912, he led an expedition north of the Northwest Territories of Canada for the American Museum of Natural History and the Canadian government. From 1913 to 1918, Stefansson was the leader of the Canadian Arctic Expedition. Upon his return, he delivered a lecture at the Mayo Clinic in Rochester, Minnesota, concerning his belief that a five-year diet of high protein and animal fat had not impaired his health in any way. Stefansson continued on a similar diet and submitted to blood analyses and other physical examinations to prove his conclusions. He remained in excellent health, and his blood chemistry remained within normal levels.

Stefansson argued the merits of a high-protein diet and wrote *Cancer: Disease of Civilization* in 1960. He served as a consultant to the Pan American World Airways in planning Arctic routes. He was also an adviser to the government on Arctic survival during World War II. He donated his extensive library to the Northern Studies program at Dartmouth College.

Stefansson's valuable contributions were noted on the 1986 22¢ Arctic Explorers issue.

John Ernst Steinbeck

Scott 1773
Born: February 27, 1902, Salinas, California
Died: December 20, 1968, New York, New York

John Steinbeck grew up around Monterey, California, and attended Stanford University irregularly from 1920 to 1925. He moved to New York City, where he worked as a bricklayer and newspaper writer. Steinbeck returned to California in 1926, when he was hired to work as a caretaker on an estate in the High Sierra. He spent the next two winters writing his first novel, *Cup of Gold*, which was published in 1929. In 1935 Steinbeck published *Tortilla Flat*, which became a best-seller.

In 1937 Steinbeck published *Of Mice and Men*, which was both a novel and a stage play. It won for him the New York Critic's Circle Award. It was a tragic story of two itinerants who fantasized about owning a ranch. Steinbeck's collection of short stories, *The Long Valley*, was well-received.

While accompanying migrants on their way west, Steinbeck gathered first-hand material for *The Grapes of Wrath*. This was a shocking expose of the poor "Okies" of the Tom Joad family. The family escaped the bankrupting drought of the sun-baked prairie states to resettle in fertile but hostile California. The book and the movie created a wide and shocking reaction. The book won the Pulitzer Prize.

During World War II, Steinbeck was a correspondent for the *New York Herald Tribune*, and his collected dispatches resulted in *Once There Was a War*, which appeared in 1958.

The culmination of Steinbeck's works was in 1962 with his amusing and somewhat autobiographical *Travels with Charley*, an account of his trip across the United States with his dog. For all his contributions to literature, which included short stories, newspaper dispatches, novels and movie scripts, the Nobel Prize for Literature was awarded to him in 1962.

John Ernst Steinbeck is shown on a 1979 15¢ stamp.

Charles Proteus Steinmetz

Scott 2055
Born: April 9, 1865, Breslau, Germany (now Wroclaw, Poland)
Died: October 26, 1923, Schenectady, New York

His original name was Karl August Rudolf Steinmetz, but when he applied for citizenship papers, he changed his name to Charles and used his college day's nickname, Proteus, instead of August Rudolf. At age 18, he entered the University of Breslau and studied mathematics, electrical engineering and the physical sciences. He also studied in Berlin.

Steinmetz was a ghost writer and editor for *The People's Voice*, a Socialist paper in Breslau. The job got him into trouble with the law, and without taking his doctorate, which he had just earned, he fled to Switzerland. He attended the University of Zurich for a year, then emigrated to New York City in 1889. He obtained a job as draftsman with an electrical-engineering company in Yonkers, but his vast knowledge of electricity and mathematics soon promoted him to doing independent research.

He solved the problem of residual magnetism in electrical generators and motors that caused lagging power loss, and he made an improved design. He presented a paper on this phenomenon of hysteresis in 1892. That same year his firm merged with the General Electric Company located in Schenectady, New York. He was its consulting engineer.

In 1893 he announced the results of his theoretical studies of alternating currents and helped make the use of alternating current (AC) commercially feasible. Steinmetz' studies of lightning resulted in the development of lightning arresters for the protection of electric power lines.

From 1897 to 1917, he wrote several technical texts that became standard works. While Thomas A. Edison was committed to the development of direct-current (DC) power systems, Steinmetz, as well as Nikola Tesla (Scott 2057), held out for the use of AC. Alternating current became the standard of electrical power systems in America.

In addition to his position at the General Electric Company, Steinmetz was professor of electrophysics at Union College in Schenectady.

Steinmetz is commemorated on the 20¢ 1983 American Inventors issue.

Friedrich Wilhelm von Steuben

Scott 689
Born: September 17, 1730, Magdeburg, Germany
Died: September 28, 1794, Remsen, New York

Friedrich von Steuben spent his early childhood in Russia, where his father was a lieutenant of engineers. At age 14, he entered the rigorous military school of Frederick the Great. At age 16, Steuben entered the Prussian army. Having reached the rank of captain, he was discharged in 1763, when the Peace of Paris ended the Seven Year's War. Steuben spent the next 14 years as chamberlain in the court of Hohenzollern-Hechingen, since no military assignments were available.

In the ensuing 10 years, he acquired the title of Baron Steuben. While in Paris in 1777, Steuben's old friend, the Count of St. Germain, persuaded him to contact the American agents in Paris, including Benjamin Franklin. Franklin wrote a letter of introduction with glowing credentials to George Washington, stating that Steuben was a highly qualified military officer and a lieutenant general in the service of the King of Prussia's army.

Steuben sailed for the United States and reported to the Continental Congress at York, Pennsylvania. He was well-received, along with his aide-de-camp, and his private secretary. He reported directly to General Washington at Valley Forge on February 23, 1778. Washington, impressed by his credentials, appointed him inspector general of the Continental Army in charge of training men.

By May 5, 1778, Steuben was a major general. He applied his Prussian military learning to the raw troops. In 1780 he prepared the standard army drill manual. In 1781 he served under the young Marquis de Lafayette and commanded one of the three divisions of Washington's army at the siege of Yorktown, which ended the war. He was granted American citizenship by Congress and was given an estate at Remsen, New York, and an annual pension. He was the founder of the prestigious Society of the Cincinnati of former Continental officers.

Friedrich Wilhelm von Steuben is depicted on a 1930 2¢ stamp.

Adlai Ewing Stevenson

Scott 1275
Born: February 5, 1900, Los Angeles, California
Died: July 14, 1965, London, England

Adlai Stevenson was the son of Lewis Green Stevenson, a newspaper executive and secretary of state of Illinois between 1914 and 1916. Stevenson's grandfather, Adlai Ewing Stevenson, was vice president during William McKinley's second term as president of the United States and was William Jennings Bryan's running mate in 1900.

The youngest Stevenson attended Choate Preparatory School, graduated from Princeton in 1922 and entered Harvard Law School. After two years, he joined the family newspaper, the *Bloomington Daily Pantagraph*, as assistant managing editor.

Stevenson returned to his law studies at Northwestern University and graduated in 1926. He was admitted to the bar that same year and opened practice in Chicago. Franklin D. Roosevelt called Stevenson to Washington in 1933 to assist in the Agriculture Adjustment Administration. In 1935 he returned to his law practice. Stevenson was appointed a special assistant to Secretary of the Navy Frank Knox. In 1943 he served on the foreign-aid mission to Italy. In 1945 he served in San Francisco as senior adviser to the United Nations.

Between 1946 and 1947, he was the U.S. adviser to the United Nations General Assembly in London. In 1948 Stevenson was elected Illinois governor on the reform Democratic ticket by a large margin. He was the Democratic candidate for the presidency in 1952 but lost to Dwight D. Eisenhower. He ran again in 1956 and again lost to Eisenhower. In 1961 John F. Kennedy appointed him U.S. ambassador to the United Nations.

Stevenson also was a director of the *Encyclopedia Britannica*. On July 14, 1965, he was in London to cut a tape for the British Broadcasting Corporation. He died that day of a heart attack.

Adlai Ewing Stevenson is commemorated on a 1965 5¢ stamp.

Harlan Fiske Stone

Scott 965
Born: October 11, 1872, Chesterfield, New Hampshire
Died: April 22, 1946, Washington, D.C.

Harlan Fiske Stone began his education at the Massachusetts Agricultural School with all intentions of becoming an educated farmer using the latest in scientific technology. However, he transferred to Amherst College to study medicine. He then switched to law and graduated in 1894. Stone continued his law studies at Columbia University, received his law degree in 1898 and was admitted to the New York bar. He practiced law in New York City and taught at Columbia University after being appointed a professor in 1902. In 1910 he became the dean of the Columbia Law School. Stone worked to extend the requirements for a law degree to five years and to simplify the statutes, which he believed were a hindrance to progress.

In 1924 President Calvin Coolidge appointed Stone attorney general. Stone began to overhaul the Federal Bureau of Investigation (FBI) following the scandalous Harding administration.

In 1925 Stone was named to the Supreme Court. He stood with the minority supporting the Agricultural Adjustment Act of 1933 that provided farmers with government subsidies. As a Supreme Court justice, he chose to disregard his own personal philosophies. If a Jehovah's Witness did not salute the flag because his religion opposed it, the Jehovah's Witness did not have to salute the flag, according to Stone.

He wrote more than 600 opinions, many on important constitutional questions. For Stone, the law was "a human institution for human needs." It was "not an end, but a means to an end."

In 1941 President Franklin D. Roosevelt appointed Stone chief justice. The trio of Oliver Wendell Holmes, Louis D. Brandeis and Stone upheld the far-reaching reforms instituted by many legislative acts of the New Deal. Stone administered the oath of office to Harry S Truman on the eve of Roosevelt's death, April 12, 1945.

The Harlan F. Stone issue was released as a 3¢ denomination in 1948. The stamp honors Stone's career as associate justice and chief justice of the United States Supreme Court.

Lucy Blackwell Stone

Scott 1293
Born: August 13, 1818, West Brookfield, Massachusetts
Died: October 18, 1893, Dorchester, Massachusetts

Lucy Stone was determined to obtain a higher education, although her parents considered it unthinkable for a girl to attend college. With no support, Stone worked her way through school. She entered Oberlin College. She attended the college for more than 12 years and graduated in 1847.

While at college, she joined the abolitionist and temperance movements. She was a gifted speaker. Stone helped organize the first national women's rights convention, at Worcester, Massachusetts, in 1850 and the annual conventions that followed.

At age 40, she married an abolitionist from Ohio, Henry Brown Blackwell, and took his name only as her middle name. The couple lived in New Jersey for 10 years.

In 1868 they moved to Boston, where Stone participated in the New England Woman Suffrage Association. She chartered the American Woman Suffrage Association, which worked for women's right to vote, and founded the *Woman's Journal*, which continued publication until 1917.

In November 1869, the American Woman Suffrage Association was established to obtain woman suffrage through amendment of state constitutions. Its principal leaders were Stone and Julia Ward Howe. Other women who greatly added their support were Susan B. Anthony, Elizabeth Cady Stanton and Lucretia Mott. Suffragette Carrie Lane Chapman Catt lived to see Tennessee become a state on August 18, 1920, and to ratify the amendment that eight days later was proclaimed as part of the U.S. Constitution as the 19th Amendment.

Stone's last lecture was delivered in Chicago at the World's Columbian Exposition in 1893, the year of her death at age 75.

Lucy Blackwell Stone is depicted on a 1968 50¢ Prominent Americans definitive stamp.

Igor Fyodorovich Stravinsky

Scott 1845
Born: June 17, 1882, Oranienbaum (near St. Petersburg), Russia
Died: April 6, 1971, New York, New York

Igor Stravinsky was the son of the first bass singer of the Imperial Opera. His mother was also a musician. At age nine, he began studying the piano. At age 20, he showed some of his compositions to the great composer Nicholas Rimsky-Korsakov, who was a professor in the St. Petersburg Conservatoire. Rimsky-Korsakov encouraged Stravinsky, his student. Stravinsky composed *Fireworks*, an orchestral fantasia, as a greeting to Rimsky-Korsakov's daughter on her wedding day. After Rimsky-Korsakov's death in 1908, Stravinsky composed a *Chant funebre*, in which each instrument is introduced into the piece as if in a funeral procession.

About this time, Stravinsky met Sergei Pavlovich Diaghilev, the great Russian ballet master, who invited Stravinsky to orchestrate two of Frederic Chopin's pieces for the ballet *Les Syphides*. Stravinsky did so well that Diaghilev commissioned him to do *The Firebird* for the Russian ballet's 1910 spring Paris presentation. In 1911 Stravinsky produced *Petrouchka,* and in 1913 his *The Rite of Spring* premiered in Paris.

In 1914 Stravinsky went home to Russia for the last time. He spent the war years in Switzerland, where he composed *The Soldier's Tale* in 1918. After the war, he resumed his collaboration with Diaghilev until Diaghilev's death on August 19, 1929.

In 1930 Stravinsky composed *Symphony of Psalms* for the 50th anniversary of the Boston Symphony Orchestra. He became a French citizen in 1934, then left France in 1940 to settle in the United States. He became an American citizen in 1945. He died in 1971 and is buried in the Russian corner of San Michele cemetery in Venice, near Diaghilev's grave.

Igor Stravinsky is shown on a 1982 2¢ Great Americans stamp.

Gilbert Charles Stuart

Scott 884
Born: December 3, 1755, North Kingstown, Rhode Island
Died: July 9, 1828, Boston, Massachusetts

Gilbert Charles Stuart was raised and schooled in Newport, Rhode Island. Having shown an interest in painting, he was tutored by Cosmos Alexander, a Scottish painter living in Rhode Island. Stuart went with Alexander to Edinburgh in 1771. Alexander soon died, and Stuart tried to make a living painting in Edinburgh, but had to return home in 1772. He then went to England in 1775 and lived in poverty until 1778, when he approached Benjamin West. West took him in as a student, and Stuart remained with him for six years. In 1777 he exhibited in the Royal Academy. His painting titled *The Skater* boosted his acceptance, and he received several commissions.

Stuart was quite successful as a portrait painter, but not in matters of money. To avoid creditors, he went to Ireland in 1787, but again had the same money problems. He then went to New York City in 1793, and in late 1794 he moved to Philadelphia, where he met with his greatest success.

He completed a series of portraits of prominent women, then completed two paintings of President George Washington. Stuart had executed paintings of George III, the future George IV in England, Louis XVI and other notables, but only in the presence of George Washington did he find himself embarrassed. His first portrait of Washington (1795), a profile, was in his estimation a failure. Today it is in the National Gallery of Art, Washington, D.C. Stuart then painted a full-length portrait of Washington in 1796, which is now in the Pennsylvania Academy of Fine Arts. Later that year he painted the famous unfinished Athenaeum head of Washington, which remains the most accepted likeness of Washington and the most popular.

He moved to Washington, D.C., where he also painted John Quincy Adams, Jefferson, Madison, Monroe and many distinguished public figures such as John Jay, Generals Gates and Knox, and many others. Stuart even painted his former teacher Benjamin West, but West did not influence his style. After 1805, Stuart lived in Boston, always in debt but well-liked.

The artists series of the 1940 Famous Americans issue features Stuart on a 1¢ denomination.

363

Peter Stuyvesant

Scott 971
Born: between 1592 and 1610, Scherpenzeel, Friesland, the Netherlands
Died: February 1672, Manhattan Island, New York

If Peter Stuyvesant had remained in Scherpenzeel in the Netherlands after studying at Franeker and had become a clergyman in the Dutch Reformed Church, he may well have led a less turbulent life. Instead, Stuyvesant chose a military career, entered the service of the Dutch West India Company in 1635 and, by 1643, became governor of several Caribbean islands, including Curacao.

In 1644 Stuyvesant attacked the Portuguese island of St. Martin and was wounded. He returned to the Netherlands. His right leg was amputated, and he replaced it with a silver ornamented peg leg.

In 1646 Stuyvesant became governor of New Netherland. New Netherlands had been ruled with a rod of iron by a series of petty autocrats. Governor Kieft killed a number of the Wecquaesgeek Indian tribe at Pavonia in 1643, provoking war that forced all the white inhabitants to seek refuge behind the wall at Wall Street. Stuyvesant arrived in New Amsterdam on May 11, 1647 and found the colony a motley bunch speaking 18 different languages. He restored order and business and made friends with the Indians. His stringent regulations and high customs duties kept traders away. New Amsterdam, now New York City, stagnated.

In 1655 Stuyvesant annexed weak New Sweden, which included lands in what are now New Jersey, Delaware and Pennsylvania. In 1664 an English fleet ordered the surrender of the city, Stuyvesant was forced to give in after the citizens refused to support him.

He was sent to the Netherlands in disgrace, but he returned to New York after a few years and settled on his farm, part of which later became the Bowery of New York.

Peter Stuyvesant is depicted on a 1948 3¢ Volunteer Firemen stamp.

364

Anne Mansfield Sullivan

Scott 1824
Born: April 14, 1866, Feeding Hills, Massachusetts
Died: October 20, 1936, Forest Hills, New York

Anne Sullivan's eyesight was seriously weakened by an infection during her early childhood. She was treated at the state infirmary at Tewksbury, Massachusetts, at age 10. When she was 14, she entered the Perkins School for the Blind in Boston, where she learned the manual alphabet. She graduated with a brilliant scholastic record in 1886. She had had several minor eye operations that considerably improved her eyesight.

On March 2, 1887, when she was 20, she became the teacher and companion of seven-year-old Helen Keller, after Keller's parents appealed to Alexander Graham Bell for help. A severe fever had left Keller, at 19 months old, blind, deaf and mute. Within months, Sullivan taught Keller to feel objects and associate them with words spelled out by finger signals on her palm. Keller also learned to read sentences by feeling raised words on cardboard and to make her own sentences by arranging words in a frame.

Sullivan assisted Keller's education at the Perkins Institute, Boston's Horace Mann School for the Deaf, New York City's Wright-Humason Oral School, Cambridge School for Young Ladies and Radcliffe College, where Keller graduated cum laude in 1904. Sullivan communicated the lectures and reading material to her pupil by means of the touch alphabet. Keller not only learned to read, write and talk, but became exceptionally proficient in the ordinary educational curriculum.

In 1905, the year after Keller graduated from Radcliffe, Sullivan married John Albert Macy, but her relationship with Keller continued until her own death in 1936. Sullivan's eyesight began to fail rapidly, and by 1935, she too was nearly totally blind. Polly Thompson, Keller's secretary since 1914, took Sullivan's place as Keller's constant companion in 1936.

Anne Sullivan Macy appears with Helen Keller on a 1980 15¢ stamp.

John Sullivan

Scott 657
Born: February 17, 1740, Somersworth (now Rollinsford), New Hampshire
Died: January 23, 1795, Durham, New Hampshire

John Sullivan studied law privately and began practice at Berwick, Maine, and Durham, New Hampshire. In 1772 he was commissioned a major in the colonial militia. As a member of the New Hampshire provincial assembly in 1774, he was a delegate to the first and second Continental Congresses. Late in 1774, with New Hampshire troops, Sullivan captured ordnance stored at the Portsmouth Harbor forts.

When the Revolutionary War began, Sullivan came under the command of George Washington and served through the siege of Boston. He was commissioned brigadier general in 1775. In 1776 he was promoted to major general. He served mostly in New York, New Jersey and Pennsylvania. In August 1776, Sullivan was captured by the British in the Battle of Long Island. His high rank caused him to be traded for a British general.

Between 1777 and 1778, he was involved in the New Jersey battles at Trenton and Princeton. He tried in August 1777 to rout the British from Staten Island but met with stubborn resistance. He spent the winter of 1777 with General Washington at Valley Forge, planning his assignment to capture Newport, Rhode Island. The French navy failed to appear for his needed support and the venture failed.

In 1779 Sullivan spent most of the year routing the British and their Indian allies out of western New York State and Pennsylvania. On November 30, 1779, he resigned from the Army, tired and in poor health.

He served in the Congress of the Confederation between 1780 and 1781, and participated in the New Hampshire constitutional convention. He also was the state's attorney general and a member of the state's legislature.

In 1788 Sullivan was the chairman of the New Hampshire constitutional ratification convention. Between 1786 and 1788, and again from 1789 to 1790, he was the governor of New Hampshire. In 1789 he was appointed a federal district judge, for which he served continually until his death in Durham, New Hampshire, at age 54.

John Sullivan appears on a 1929 2¢ Sullivan Expedition stamp.

Sun Yat-sen

Scott 1188
Born: November 12, 1866, Hsiang Shan, Kwangtun, China
Died: March 12, 1925, Peking, China

Sun Yat-sen was the son of a poor farmer, who was paying the Manchus for protection. Sun grew up in the village not far from the Portuguese island of Macao. At age 14, he left China to work for his brothers in Honolulu. He attended a Christian school and assimilated the religion. He learned the English language and western ways, including democracy. His brothers sent him back to China, but he was banished from his village. He entered the Alice Memorial Hospital in Hong Kong to study medicine.

Five years later, Sun graduated with honors. However, his mind teemed with revolution, not medical practice. He joined a group sworn to overthrow the Manchu dynasty and replace it with socialistic Kuomintang. In China a price was put on Sun's head. He went to Macao to practice medicine, but being non-Portuguese, he was not licensed. He went out into the world to preach revolution and raise funds.

In Honolulu, he met Dr. Cantlie, the founder of the Alice Memorial Hospital, who advised him to go to London. In London, the Chinese Legation imprisoned him. Cantlie forced Lord Salisbury to intervene, and Sun was freed. Following the downfall of the Manchu dynasty and the ousting of the regent of the new infant emperor, archrevolutionist Sun was recalled to be president of the new republic. He turned it over to Yuan Shih-k'ai, who declared himself emperor of China and then died the next year. In May 1919, Sun turned to Russia for help. This move resulted in the early Chinese Communist party.

In 1922 Sun went to Shanghai and was expelled by Chen Chiun-Ming. General Chiang Kai-shek defeated Chen, and Sun came back to govern southern China. Sun died of cancer in March 1925. Chiang Kai-shek became generalissimo of Kuomintang China.

Sun Yat-sen is depicted on the 1961 4¢ issue.

Robert Alphonso Taft

Scott 1161
Born: September 8, 1889, Cincinnati, Ohio
Died: July 31, 1953, New York, New York

After elementary school, Robert Taft entered Taft School at Watertown, Connecticut, the school founded by his uncle, Horace D. Taft. This education prepared him for Yale University, where he graduated in 1910, and Harvard Law School, where he graduated in 1913. Taft was admitted to the Ohio bar that same year. He began law practice in Cincinnati.

Taft was the son of President William Howard Taft. A substantial inheritance, wise business investments and an Ivy League education made Robert Taft a man of wealth and a fiercely conservative Republican, which later in his career earned him the title "Mr. Republican." In 1920 Taft was elected to the Ohio legislature and served six years. From 1930 to 1932, he served as Ohio state senator.

In 1938 Taft entered the U.S. Senate and became an outspoken critic of President Franklin D. Roosevelt's foreign and domestic policies. Taft was a staunch isolationist until the attack on Pearl Harbor by the Japanese in December 1941, but still he opposed Roosevelt's international involvements.

Taft was re-elected to the Senate in 1944 and 1950 and served until his death in 1953. He was a stone in the Democratic shoe under President Harry S Truman and opposed many of Truman's Fair Deal measures.

Taft was the chairman of the powerful Republican Policy Committee and was the party's floor leader in the Senate. In 1947 he was instrumental in the passing of the Taft-Hartley Act, which set controls over labor unions. He opposed U.S. membership in the North Atlantic Treaty Organization and lent support to Joseph R. McCarthy's investigations of Communists in the government and the military.

Taft was considered strongly as a presidential candidate in 1940 and 1948. In 1952 he lost to General Dwight D. Eisenhower after a long and determined struggle that nearly split the party. As an ever-faithful Republican, however, Taft supported Eisenhower and became Senate majority leader in the new Congress in 1953. He lived only a few months thereafter.

Robert Alphonso Taft appears on a 1960 4¢ stamp.

William Howard Taft

Scott 2218h
Born: September 15, 1857, Cincinnati, Ohio
Died: March 8, 1930, Washington, D.C.

William Howard Taft was educated at Yale College and the Cincinnati Law School, where he earned a law degree in 1880. Taft became involved in Republican politics. In 1887 he filled an unexpired seat on the Cincinnati Superior Court. The following year he was elected to a full five-year term.

President Benjamin Harrison interrupted his judgeship by appointing him U.S. solicitor general in 1890. In 1892 Taft became presiding judge of the sixth federal Circuit Court of Appeals and served until 1900, when President William McKinley appointed him president of the Philippine commission. The next year Taft was the country's civil governor.

Although he wanted to be a U.S. Supreme Court justice, he rejected President Theodore Roosevelt's offer for the seat because he wanted to complete his Philippine assignment. He accepted the position of secretary of war because it kept him in contact with his Philippine accomplishments. Taft became Roosevelt's most trusted adviser. He helped negotiate the Treaty of Portsmouth, which ended the Russo-Japanese War, and organized the construction of the Panama Canal. He was Roosevelt's hand-picked successor for the presidency and was elected easily over William Jennings Bryan in 1908.

Taft found the office of the presidency disappointing. He was the inevitable but reluctant nominee at the 1912 Republican national convention. He ran third behind Woodrow Wilson and Theodore Roosevelt, gathering only eight electoral votes. He became professor of constitutional law at Yale University in 1913. During World War I, he served as joint chairman of the National War Labor Board and was an advocate of the League of Nations.

In 1921 President Warren G. Harding appointed Taft to succeed Edward D. White as chief justice of the U.S. Supreme Court. He presided over the court until a month before his death.

William Howard Taft appears on a 1986 22¢ Presidential stamp.

369

Henry Ossawa Tanner

Scott 1486
Born: June 21, 1859, Pittsburgh, Pennsylvania
Died: May 25, 1937, Paris, France

Henry Tanner's father, Benjamin Tucker Tanner (1835-1923), was a graduate of Avery College, licensed as a Methodist minister and appointed bishop of the African Methodist Episcopal Church in 1888. Henry Tanner had a sound religious education at home and in his church, but in his childhood he showed artistic ability and chose to follow art as his career. At age 21 he began several years of intensive study under Thomas Eakins at the Pennsylvania Academy of Fine Arts. He lived for a time in Atlanta, making his way in photography but continuing to develop his painting technique.

He later had a showing in Cincinnati, Ohio, and from this he raised enough money to go to Europe for study. He arrived in Paris in 1891 and made the city his home. Tanner received instructions under the guiding hands of Benjamin Constant and Jean-Paul Laurens at the Academie Julien. In 1895 the Paris Salon accepted one of his paintings. He finished a large biblical scene, *Daniel in the Lions' Den*, which gained considerable recognition and inspired him to do more religious painting.

Louis R. Wanamaker of Philadelphia, provided generously for him to go to the Holy Land and paint. By 1900 Tanner had earned an international reputation for his paintings of biblical subjects and landscapes. He won several awards abroad and in the United States during his most prolific period between 1896 and 1915. At the American Art Galleries in New York City in 1908 he had his first one-man show. Others followed in Buffalo; St. Louis; Washington, D.C.; Chicago; and San Francisco. His *Destruction of Sodom and Gomorrah* is in the Metropolitan Museum of Art in New York City, and his *Disciples at the Tomb* hangs in the Art Institute in Chicago.

During the 1920s, he encouraged other black artists, and his success as a painter gave impetus to the Universal Negro Improvement Association (UNIA) led by such men as Marcus Mosiah Garvey.

Tanner is portrayed on an 8¢ value in the 1973 American Arts issue.

Zachary Taylor

Scott 817
Born: November 24, 1784, near Barboursville, Virginia
Died: July 9, 1850, Washington, D.C.

Although Zachary Taylor was born in Virginia, he grew up near Louisville, Kentucky, when his parents moved there in 1785. With little education, Taylor volunteered in 1806 for a short time in the militia. In 1808 he received a commission in the regular army as a lieutenant. He served under General William Henry Harrison in the War of 1812 and was promoted to captain. In 1816 President James Madison commissioned Taylor a major. For the next 21 years, Taylor saw garrison duty from Louisiana to Wisconsin and was advanced to colonel.

In 1832 Taylor saw action in the Black Hawk War. He went to Florida to subdue the Seminole Indians. His victory in December 1837 brought him the rank of brigadier general. He was nicknamed "Old Rough and Ready."

In 1840, at his own request, Taylor left the Seminole campaign and transferred to Fort Smith, Arkansas. In 1845 he was ordered to be ready for trouble with Mexico. In 1846 he advanced to the Rio Grande with 4,000 troops. Even before war was declared, he claimed minor victories at Palo Alto and Resaca de la Palma. He was promoted to major general as commander of the Rio Grande. Taylor became a popular hero, and political infighting began. General Winfield Scott was prepared for a Veracruz invasion, but Taylor advanced south and forced General Santa Anna's army back. This ended the war on the northern front.

Taylor was chosen as the Whigs' candidate for the presidency, and in 1848 was nominated over Henry Clay, Daniel Webster and Taylor's own commander, Winfield Scott. With the Democratic party split, Taylor, with running mate Millard Fillmore, was elected over Lewis Cass and Martin Van Buren. As president, he saw 16 months of turbulence. The slavery controversy was revived, which resulted in the Compromise of 1850. Taylor took a firm position against appeasing the South, but died five days after becoming ill at a July 4th celebration, just when the national crisis was acute.

Zachary Taylor appears on a 1938 12¢ Presidential stamp.

Nikola Tesla

Scott 2057
Born: July 10, 1856, Smiljan, Austria-Hungary (now in Yugoslavia)
Died: January 7, 1943, New York, New York

Nikola Tesla's mother was an expert needleworker and had invented some useful gadgets. His father was a clergyman of the Serbian Orthodox Church. Tesla grew up surrounded by creativity and philosophy. For four years, he studied mathematics, physics and engineering in Graz, Austria. He then attended the University of Prague from 1870 to 1880 and concentrated on philosophy. In 1881 Tesla was in Budapest with a newly founded telephone company, where he worked as an electrical engineer. In late 1882 he was in Paris, where he was associated with the Continental Edison Company. He later worked with George Westinghouse, to whom he sold his patent for the rotating field motor.

He left Europe in 1884 for the United States, where he hoped his alternating-current (AC) concepts would be accepted. Europe preferred direct-current (DC) electricity. Tesla formed the Tesla Electric Company but without success. He went into independent research in his laboratory after 1900. He devised about 700 inventions, which included the telephone repeater in 1881 and in 1888 a rotating magnetic field applied to an induction motor fed by an alternating current.

Tesla independently devised the split-phase, induction and synchronous motors. From 1890, he worked on high-frequency current and oscillators and developed the Tesla coil. In 1893 he was able to transmit messages by wireless telegraphy. At Colorado Springs, he constructed a gigantic Tesla coil that generated 12 million volts. The construction of a power transmission tower on Long Island fell through when Tesla's financial backer, J.P. Morgan, died. The Niagara Falls power plant owes much of its existence to the expertise of Tesla.

In 1898 he began developing wireless guidance systems for ships. Tesla also predicted the possible practical use of solar energy, and attempted wireless communication with outer worlds.

Nikola Tesla is shown on a 1983 20¢ American Inventors stamp.

Sylvanus Thayer

Scott 1852
Born: June 9, 1785, Braintree, Massachusetts
Died: September 7, 1872, South Braintree, Massachusetts

Sylvanus Thayer graduated from Dartmouth College, in Hanover, New Hampshire, in 1807, and then entered the United States Military Academy at West Point, New York. He was permitted to graduate the following year. Thayer worked with the Army's Corps of Engineers on fortifications until the War of 1812, when he served at Norfolk, Virginia, and along the Canadian border in garrison duty. He was advanced to major, and was sent to Europe to study defense systems and military education curriculums.

Thayer was appointed superintendent of the Military Academy in 1817 with the rank of major. During the next 16 years, he began to overhaul West Point from a second-rate military diploma mill to an excellent four-year college. In engineering, it was the best. Thayer increased the faculty, restructured the student body, made the requirements for entrance more stringent, examinations tougher, and above all, military discipline became stricter. Discipline became so strict, in fact, that the student body of 200 revolted in 1818. Five revolt leaders were court-martialed and dismissed. Thayer's action was upheld by President James Monroe and Secretary of War John Calhoun.

A riot occurred again on Christmas 1826, and President Andrew Jackson reinstated the cadets Thayer had dismissed. Disgusted for being overridden, Thayer requested to be released on July 1, 1833. He spent the next 30 years as the Army's chief engineer in charge of New England's coastal fortifications and harbor improvements. In 1863 he retired from the Army with the rank of brigadier general. He did not serve in the Civil War, being too old.

He is generally called the "Father of the Military Academy," at least the "modern" Military Academy. In 1867 he established the Thayer School of Engineering at Dartmouth College, his alma mater, and spent the remaining years of his life at Braintree, Massachusetts. He was 87 when he died.

Thayer was honored on a 1985 9¢ Great Americans stamp.

Henry David Thoreau

Scott 1327
Born: July 12, 1817, Concord, Massachusetts
Died: May 6, 1862, Concord, Massachusetts

Henry Thoreau and his family were nature lovers and spent many happy jaunts together in the lush woodlands of Concord, Massachusetts. Thoreau's father was a poor pencil maker but was able to send his son to Harvard College in 1833. Thoreau had attended Concord Academy, where he indulged himself in the classics. He graduated with honors from Harvard. Thoreau began teaching but soon resigned and went to work in the family's pencil business. In 1839 he and his brother opened a school, at which he remained only two years. In 1841 he went to live with Ralph Waldo Emerson, a writer who encouraged Thoreau to write, gave him useful criticism and later employed him as a gardener and handyman. Emerson also introduced Thoreau to the philosophy of transcendentalism, with its emphasis on mysticism and individualism. For years Thoreau read much European literature, mystical poetry and oriental philosophy. He was hired as a tutor by Emerson's brother William, who lived in Staten Island, New York. Thoreau disliked urban society, especially what he saw of it in New York City. In 1844 he returned to Concord. The following year, he moved to the shore of Walden Pond, near Concord. On land provided by Emerson, he spent two years living in a little hut he built and subsisting on a little garden he planted. He wrote about his experience in *Walden, or Life in the Woods*.

In 1849 he published the essay "On the Duty of Civil Disobedience," which stemmed from his refusal to pay a poll tax to support the Mexican War.

Thoreau returned to live with Emerson from 1847 to 1849, then returned to the family's pencil business. He also did some surveying and took long walks on trips in Maine, Canada and Cape Cod. In "A Plea for John Brown" in 1859, he defended abolitionist John Brown after the Harpers Ferry raid.

Thoreau died of tuberculosis at age 44. He is depicted on a 1967 5¢ stamp.

James Francis Thorpe

Scott 2089
Born: May 28, 1888, Prague, Oklahoma
Died: March 28, 1953, Lomita, California

James Thorpe, an Indian, grew up in the small town of Prague, about 50 miles east of Oklahoma City. He had little education but, because of his outstanding athletic ability, he was sent to the Carlisle Indian Industrial School in Pennsylvania in 1907. At Carlisle, Thorpe played football under the coaching of Glenn S. "Pop" Warner. In 1908 he left school to play baseball with the Fayetteville and Rocky Mount teams of the Eastern Carolina League for $15 a week. He returned in 1911 to Carlisle, where he was an outstanding runner, place kicker and tackler. He was named to Walter Camp's All-American football team in 1911 and 1912.

In 1911 he went to Stockholm, Sweden, to participate in track and field events at the Olympic Games. He became the first athlete to win gold medals in both the decathlon and pentathlon. Sweden's King Gustav V referred to Thorpe as the world's greatest athlete. However, because Thorpe had been paid to play baseball in the Eastern Carolina League, he was deprived of his gold medals. His name was erased from the record books by the Amateur Athletic Union (AAU).

Thorpe turned professional, playing outfield for the New York Giants, Cincinnati Reds and the Boston Braves from 1913 through 1919. His batting average for 289 games was .252. He also played professional football for teams in Canton, Cleveland, Marion, Toledo, Rock Island and New York.

In 1929 Thorpe made his last professional appearance with the Chicago Cardinals. He was the first president of the American Professional Football Association, now the National Football League, in 1920. In 1950 he was voted the best athlete of the first half of the 20th century by an Associated Press Poll. In 1973 the AAU voted to recognize his amateur status posthumously, and his gold medals and his name were restored in the records books.

James Francis Thorpe is commemorated on a 1984 20¢ stamp.

375

Arturo Toscanini

Scott 2411
Born: May 25, 1867, Parma, Italy
Died: January 16, 1957, New York, New York

Arturo Toscanini was the youngest child and only son of a poor Italian tailor. Having demonstrated obvious musical talent, he became a pupil at age nine, at the Parma Conservatory, where he studied cello and piano. Toscanini was a small, sinewy, square-built man, not much more than five feet tall.

Toscanini began his musical career in 1885 as a cellist with a traveling opera troupe. In Rio de Janeiro, in 1886, while on a South American tour with this company, he had his first experience as a conductor. Toscanini married in 1897. He and his wife had a son and two daughters, one of whom married the pianist Vladimir Horowitz.

Toscanini became artistic director of La Scala in Milan, the most important opera house in Italy. There, he inaugurated a new epoch by including German, French and Russian operas in the repertoire. In 1908 he traveled to the United States and astonished the audience at the Metropolitan Opera by conducting Richard Wagner's *Gotterdammerung* entirely from memory.

Toscanini left the Metropolitan in 1915 and returned to Italy, where, during World War I, he conducted mainly at concerts for the wounded. He made a tour of the United States in 1920, giving 124 symphony concerts, with the La Scala orchestra. He remained at La Scala for eight years until 1929, when he was appointed conductor of the New York Philharmonic Orchestra.

A staunch Democrat, Toscanini refused to conduct the Italian Fascist anthem in 1922 and again in 1931. He conducted at the Bayreuth Festival in 1930 and 1931, but refused to appear in Germany after the rise of Hitler, as a protest against the treatment of the Jewish musicians.

From 1937 to 1954, Toscanini directed the National Broadcasting Company Symphony Orchestra, which NBC formed especially for him.

Arturo Toscanini is shown on a 1989 25¢ Performing Arts stamp.

Harry S Truman

Scott 1499
Born: May 8, 1884, Lamar, Missouri
Died: December 26, 1972, Kansas City, Missouri

Harry Truman was the oldest of three children of John Anderson Truman and Martha Ellen Young Truman. He graduated from high school but did not attend college. In his early 30s, when World War I broke out, Truman served in the National Guard in France as a captain with the 35th Division. In 1919 he married Bess Wallace. He entered local politics under the sponsorship of Thomas Pendergast, the Missouri Democratic leader.

In 1934 Truman was elected to the U.S. Senate and was re-elected in 1940. Truman was a faithful but non-aggressive supporter of Franklin Roosevelt's New Deal. His assignments in the Senate brought out his qualities of hard work, honesty and good judgment.

In 1944 Truman was elected vice president of the United States. When Roosevelt died in 1945, he became president in time to face the problems of ending World War II. His decision to use the atomic bomb against Japan was at the time a welcome expedient to avoid the estimated million casualties that would result with an invasion on the Japanese mainland.

The years between 1947 and 1948 were distinguished by civil-rights proposals, the Truman Doctrine, which contained the spread of Communism, and the Marshall Plan, which the proposed to aid economic reconstruction of war ravaged nations. In 1948 Truman won re-election over New York Governor Thomas E. Dewey in an unexpected victory. Truman's second term was harassed by the cold war with the Soviet Union, the implementing of the North Atlantic Treaty, the United Nations police action in Korea, and economic stabilization in the face of rearmament programs.

In 1952 Truman announced he would not run for re-election. He returned to Independence, Missouri, where he established the Harry S. Truman Library and wrote his memoirs.

Harry S Truman appears on a 1973 8¢ stamp.

Sojourner Truth

Scott 2203
Born: circa 1797, Hurley, Ulster County, New York
Died: November 26, 1883, Battle Creek, Michigan

Sojourner Truth's real name was Isabella Baumfree. Her legal surname became Van Wagener, the name of the last of a series of masters. Truth was born a slave. She was emancipated on July 4, 1828, as a result of a New York law that banned slavery. John Dumont, who owned her, refused to free her. Truth took her infant daughter and ran away to a family named Van Wagener. Truth's five-year-old son had been sold into slavery to an Alabama plantation. This was illegal under New York law. Truth took it to court and won the child's recovery in a precedent-setting suit.

Early in her life, Truth was involved with religion. Although she never learned to read or write, she could quote extensively from the Bible and was an eloquent speaker. After her emancipation, she worked as a servant in New York City, became involved in evangelism, and adopted the name of Sojourner Truth. In 1843 she became an itinerant preacher, speaking out for women suffrage and against slavery. She joined the abolitionist crusade, opening her orations with, "Children, I talks to God and God talks to me!"

Truth traveled across Connecticut, Massachusetts, Ohio, Indiana, Illinois and Kansas. Truth sold her story in the form of a book written by Olive Gilbert, titled, *The Narrative of Sojourner Truth*, prefaced by William Lloyd Garrison. After the Civil War, Harriet Beecher Stowe also prefaced the book.

Abraham Lincoln appointed Truth counselor to his freedmen in the Capitol, and she continued to work for the Freedmen's Bureau on behalf of former slaves. Truth forced a Washington streetcar company to allow blacks to ride and sued them when she received a shoulder injury.

After 1850, she made her home in Battle Creek, Michigan. During the 1870s, she promoted a plan under which the federal government was to set aside undeveloped lands in the west as farms for blacks.

Sojourner Truth is pictured on a 1986 22¢ Black Heritage stamp.

Harriet Tubman

Scott 1744
Born: 1820 or 1821, Bucktown, Maryland
Died: March 19, 1913, Auburn, New York

Harriet Tubman's real name was Araminta Ross, but as a child, she became known by her mother's name, Harriet. She was born into slavery on a Maryland plantation. Her mother was Harriet Green and her father was Benjamin Ross. In her early 20s, Tubman was forced to marry a freed slave, John Tubman. When she was nearly 30 years old, she escaped from her plantation master and headed into the North along the Underground Railroad. This was a system of cooperation among the active antislavery people who hid the runaway slaves, fed them, and gave them shelter and clothes, then directed them to the next protector. For the next 10 years, Tubman helped direct escaping slaves, many of whom called her Mosco, after the Biblical figure who led the Jews from Egypt. Tubman made 19 trips into the South to aid escaping slaves and brought more than 300 to the free North and Canada. In 1857, she managed to rescue her own aged parents.

Although a big price was offered for her, she always managed to escape capture. She was well-known by such abolitionists as Ralph Waldo Emerson, William H. Seward and Wendell Phillips. John Brown, the radical abolitionist, consulted with Tubman before he made his daring raid on Harpers Ferry.

During the Civil War, Tubman worked tirelessly for the North in the battlefields as a cook, laundress and nurse. She guided spies into the South and helped free more than 750 slaves during one military campaign. After the war, she helped establish schools in North Carolina for freedmen.

The book, *Harriet, the Moses of Her People*, by Sarah H. Blackford, which was rewritten from an earlier book, *Scenes in the Life of Harriet Tubman*, was sold to help defray her expenses.

Tubman finally settled down in Auburn, New York, where she established the Harriet Tubman Home for Aged Negroes.

Harriet Tubman appears on a 1978 13¢ Black Heritage stamp.

John Tyler

Scott 2217a
Born: March 29, 1790, Greenway, Charles City County, Virginia
Died: January 18, 1862, Richmond, Virginia

John Tyler was the second son of John Tyler, who served as governor of Virginia and as U.S. district judge. The younger Tyler was educated at the grammar school of the College of William and Mary, at Williamsburg, Virginia. He graduated from the college in 1807. Tyler studied law under his father's tutelage and two years later was admitted to the bar. He served in the Virginia House of Delegates from 1811 to 1816. In 1816 he was elected to the U.S. House of Representatives. He opposed the Bank of the United States, Henry Clay's nationalistic program of internal improvements and tariffs, and objected to the Missouri Compromise of 1820. Poor health forced him to resign in 1821. In 1828 he returned to the Virginia legislature. He served as governor of the state from 1825 to 1827. He was elected to the U.S. Senate in 1827. He opposed the tariff bills of 1828 and 1832, and initiated the Compromise Tariff of 1833, which ended the tariff crisis.

He resigned from the Senate and withdrew from the Democratic party when the Virginia legislature instructed him to support Andrew Jackson. In 1840 Tyler was elected vice president with William Henry Harrison. Harrison died a month into his term of office, and Tyler became the first vice president to succeed to the presidency. As president, he vetoed a legislative program that called for a new Bank of the United States and for higher tariffs. Every cabinet member, except Secretary of State Daniel Webster, resigned.

In 1842 Tyler settled the boundary of Maine by the Webster-Ashburton Treaty between the United States and England. He also sent troops to Rhode Island to settle the Dorr Rebellion, which erupted over that state's constitution.

Though nominated for re-election, Tyler withdrew in favor of James K. Polk and retired to his plantation. In 1861 he endorsed secession, but died before he could serve on the Confederate Congress.

John Tyler is depicted on a 1986 22¢ stamp.

Martin Van Buren

Scott 813
Born: December 5, 1782, Kinderhook, New York
Died: July 24, 1862, Kinderhook, New York

Martin Van Buren had very little education aside from local schools. He studied law and set up practice in Kinderhook, New York. As a Democratic Republican, Van Buren was elected to the state senate in 1812. He opposed the Bank of the United States. He served two four-year terms and concurrently was state attorney general.

In 1821 Van Buren was elected to the U.S. Senate. He was a staunch foe of John Quincy Adams and a supporter of William H. Crawford. He drew closer in support to Andrew Jackson and was re-elected to the senate in 1827. When Henry Clinton died, Van Buren resigned from the Senate to become governor of New York. After a few months, he resigned the governorship to become Jackson's secretary of state.

He stood firm with Jackson on all issues. Jackson appointed Van Buren as U.S. minister to Great Britain. The Senate refused to confirm the appointment by one vote. Van Buren clearly became Jackson's designated successor and was elected president in 1836, with Richard M. Johnson as his vice president. During his first year in office, Van Buren faced the Panic of 1837, which was a financial crash that came about due to loans made without security. Next came the Canadian rebellion, along the Maine-Canadian border, known as the Aroostook War.

Nominated in 1840 for the presidency, Van Buren lost to William Henry Harrison and John Tyler in a campaign that was marked with great emotion. Van Buren was the leading candidate in 1844, but lost. Again in 1847 he was nominated by the Free Soil Party, but lost to James K. Polk.

Martin Van Buren is pictured on a 1938 8¢ Presidential stamp.

Alfred V. Verville

Scott C113
Born: 1890, Atlantic, Michigan
Died: 1970

When Alfred Verville was 13 years old, Wilbur and Orville Wright flew a heavier-than-air machine off the ground on December 17, 1903, at Kitty Hawk, North Carolina, when Verville was 16, a box kite flying machine built by Alberto Santos-Dumont, a Brazilian aeronaut working in Paris, flew 220 meters in 21 seconds in November 1906. In 1909, Santos-Dumont built his famous grasshopper monoplane, the forerunner of the modern light plane.

The 1906 flight prompted the English newspaper publisher, Baron Northcliffe, to write, "The news is not that man can fly, but that England is no longer an island." The 1909 flight prompted Major Gouhet to write, "The sky, too, is about to become another battlefield."

By 1918, Verville had been sent by the Army to Paris to study fighter-plane design. He returned and designed a fast new pursuit plane, the VCP (Verville Chasse Plane). In 1921 he was back in Europe with Brigadier General William Mitchell for another survey.

In 1917 Alexander Graham Bell foresaw that ". . . land power and sea power will ultimately be secondary in importance to air power." In 1922 Mitchell gave Verville an order, "Build tomorrow's plane today . . . I don't want any birdcage!" Verville followed orders and, with Lawrence Sperry, built the Verville-Sperry R-3, with streamlining and retractable landing wheels to increase efficiency and speed.

When Sperry died in 1923, problems developed in the Verville-Sperry plane, and it failed to make the Pulitzer race of 1922. The Army shelved the project, not recognizing its advanced technology until years later.

Verville set up his own aircraft company, and spent his final 20 years in the National Bureau of Aeronautics.

Alfred V. Verville is shown on a 1985 33¢ stamp.

Mary Edwards Walker

Scott 2013
Born: November 26, 1832, Oswego, New York
Died: February 21, 1919, Oswego, New York

Mary Edwards Walker studied medicine at the Syracuse Medical College and in 1855 received a physician's certificate to practice medicine. She began her practice in Columbus, Ohio, then moved back to her home state to set up practice in Rome, New York. When the Civil War broke out, she volunteered her services, but was accepted only as a nurse. In 1864 she was finally recognized as a qualified doctor of medicine and was given a commission, but was allowed to serve only as an assistant surgeon.

She was remembered for her exemplary service with the Medal of Honor in 1865. However, a federal review board revoked her medal in 1917, claiming that she had never actually served in the Army. The Army restored her award in 1977. She performed her duties as well as any male surgeon, and to emphasize her position, she wore a male officer's uniform, the same as any other military medical officer. As a matter of fact, even when she was a young girl, Walker wore trousers partly concealed with a skirt.

After the war, in 1865, she worked briefly as a journalist in New York City, then moved to Washington, D.C., and took up the practice of medicine again. In the daytime, while working as a doctor, Walker wore men's attire: shirt, coat, trousers and shoes. But in the evening, she bloomed like a cactus flower and wore an evening dress, put her hair up in ringlets of curls and was a lady all the way. Indeed, she was quite advanced for her times in advocating women's rights and equality with men. She took up the stand and lectured on the subject (dressed as a lady when she did so) and demonstrated that she was capable of performing the same as any man with equal qualifications.

Walker spent her retiring years in the home of her birth, Oswego, New York. She died at the age of 86. She is depicted on the 1982 20¢ Women's Rights issue. The words "Army Surgeon" and "Medal of Honor" also appear on the stamp.

Booker Taliaferro Washington

Scott 873
Born: April 5, 1856, Hales Ford, Virginia
Died: November 14, 1915, Tuskegee, Alabama

Booker Washington's mother, Jane Ferguson, was a slave on a Virginia plantation. His father is believed to have been a white man. Upon emancipation, Washington's mother took him and two other children to Malden, West Virginia, at the southeast edge of Charleston, where she lived in poverty. At age nine, Washington went to work in a salt furnace, then a coal mine. He attended a school for blacks and gave his name as Booker Washington. He knew his name was Booker but only later did he learn his mother had named him Taliaferro. He used all three names as his official name.

When he was 16, Washington entered the Hampton Normal and Agricultural Institute. He worked as a janitor to pay his keep and graduated in three years. Returning to Malden, he taught children during the day and adults in the evening. Between 1878 and 1879, Washington attended the Wayland Seminary in Washington, D.C.

He returned to Hampton upon request for an experimental education program for American Indians. This may not have succeeded, for he was soon in Tuskegee, Alabama. There, in 1881, he founded and became principal of Tuskegee Institute.

The institute began in an old abandoned church and a shanty. Its students learned specific trades such as carpentry, farming and mechanics. The school also taught teachers. Years later, the school was nationally recognized, and had more than 100 well-equipped buildings, an enrollment of more than 1,500 students, a faculty of 200, and an endowment of $2 million.

Although many people opposed his beliefs, Washington believed blacks could benefit more from industrial training than liberal arts. His philosophy led to his establishment of the National Negro Business League in 1900.

Washington's *Up From Slavery* is a classic. His birthplace was established as a national monument in 1957.

Washington appears on a 1940 10¢ Famous American Educators stamp.

George Washington

Scott 1031
Born: February 22, 1732, Pope's Creek Farm, Westmoreland County, Virginia
Died: December 14, 1799, Mount Vernon, Virginia

George Washington's early education came mainly from the local church sexton and later with a schoolmaster named Williams. He learned the elements of surveying at age 15. Washington's father died when he was 11, and he came under the guardianship of his half-brother, Lawrence, at Mount Vernon, Virginia. Washington went on frequent surveying trips and was soon appointed public surveyor of Culpeper County, Virginia. He learned from this occupation the importance of developing the lands to the West.

In 1752 Washington's brother, Lawrence, died at Mount Vernon. At age 20, Washington became the manager of the large plantation. In 1753 he was commissioned a major and put in charge of training militia in Southern Virginia. In 1757 he extended his plantation to more than 4,000 acres of land. He was ahead of his time in using such farm methods as crop rotation and prevention of soil erosion.

Washington was appointed lieutenant-colonel in 1754 and was launched into war against the French. He was sent to Ohio in the French and Indian War, where he received his initiation into battle and the humiliation of defeat. Washington returned to Virginia and was assigned in 1755 to General Edward Braddock as aide-de-camp with the rank of colonel.

In 1759 he married Martha Dandridge Custis. He was a good plantation manager, participated in local politics and attended the Episcopal Church. In 1774 he was elected to the Virginia provincial convention. In July 1773, he took command of the military forces of all the colonies. The first phase was from July 1775 to the British evacuation of Boston in 1776. The second phase ended with the surrender of Cornwallis in October 1781 at Yorktown.

Washington served as the president of the Federal Convention in Philadelphia in May 1787. In 1789 the electors cast their unanimous vote for Washington as the first president of the United States. He served eight years. In 1797 he returned to Mount Vernon in quiet retirement.

Washington is shown here on a 1¢ definitive of the 1954-68 series.

385

Martha Custis Washington

Scott 805
Born: June 2, 1731, New Kent County, Virginia
Died: May 22, 1802, Mount Vernon, Virginia

Martha Dandridge was a nice-looking capable young girl, the daughter of the well-to-do and well-respected John and Frances Jones Dandridge. At age 17, Martha married Daniel Parke Custis, who was the son of the wealthy plantation owner, John Custis. The young couple lived on Pamunkey River Plantation, called the White House. Two of their four children, John Parke Custis and Martha, lived past infancy. In 1757 Daniel Parke Custis died, leaving his widow, at age 26, one of the richest women in Virginia.

Of her several ardent suitors, Martha chose George Washington, the promising young plantation owner of Mount Vernon, Virginia. The couple was married on January 6, 1759. Within a few months, they moved into the Mount Vernon home, where together they refurbished the home, which had been neglected while George was off to war against the French and Indians. They lived modestly but had the best of what was available. The couple had no children of their own, but raised Martha's two children, who died before Washington became president.

During the Revolutionary War, Martha joined her husband at his camp at Valley Forge, Pennsylvania, during the winter of 1777-78. She spent the winters of 1778-79 and 1779-80 with him in camp at Morristown, New Jersey. She organized a women's sewing circle and mended clothes for the troops.

After the war, she served as a gracious hostess, although she did not enjoy being first lady. Following George's death in 1799, Martha lived in seclusion at Mount Vernon. She is shown on a 1938 1 1/2¢ stamp.

Anthony Wayne

Scott 680
Born: January 1, 1745, Waynesborough, Pennsylvania
Died: December 15, 1796, Presque Isle (now Erie), Pennsylvania

Wayne spent two years at the Pennsylvania Academy, then quit to help his father on the farm and to work as a surveyor. Between 1774 and 1775, he served on the Pennsylvania assembly. He led the Fourth Pennsylvania Battalion when the Revolutionary War broke out. By 1777, Wayne had advanced from colonel to brigadier general and saw duty throughout the entire war in both the northern and southern departments. He saw action in the battle of Three Rivers in Quebec, Canada. He also helped defend Philadelphia and participated in the battles of Brandywine and Germantown. He spent the winter of 1777-78 with George Washington at Valley Forge.

In the spring of 1778, Wayne led the attack in the battle of Monmouth. In 1779 he stormed Stoney Point, New York, on the Hudson River, and received the congratulations of Washington and the Continental Congress. For his courage, he was awarded a gold medal. In September 1780, Wayne forestalled the British at West Point after Benedict Arnold's betrayal. In 1781, he served under the Marquis de Lafayette against General Cornwallis and took part in the siege of Yorktown.

Wayne retired in 1783, the same year he became a brevet major general. He moved south and represented Georgia in the House of Representatives in 1791. The seat was declared vacant because of election irregularities. George Washington called Wayne back to duty in 1792 to quell the Indian trouble in the Ohio Valley. Wayne won Fort Recovery in June 1794, then built Fort Defiance along the Maumee River, and decided the battle with the Indians at Fallen Timbers.

Steadily, Wayne pacified the whole region and built Fort Wayne in present-day Indiana. He made the Treaty of Greenville with the Indians in 1795. This opened part of the Northwest for settlement. Wayne was busy settling the abandoned British forts vacated in accordance with the Jay Treaty when he died in 1796 in Presque Isle, now Erie, Pennsylvania. Anthony Wayne is shown on a 1929 2¢ Battle of Fallen Timbers stamp.

John Wayne

Scott 2448
Born: May 26, 1907, Winterset, Iowa
Died: June 11, 1979, Los Angeles, California

Marion Michael Morrison hardly seemed a fit name for a tall, tough cowboy and soldier intent on fighting bands of holdout Indians, boomtown outlaws and enemies of his country. Thus, in true Hollywood fashion, Morrison was renamed John Wayne. He began his motion picture career as a prop boy in 1927, at age 20. For 10 years, he made 40 second- and third-rate cowboy pictures. These prepared him for *Stagecoach*, John Ford's paradigmatic Western, filmed in 1939. In the movie, Wayne portrayed the Ringo Kid.

Wayne's acting career spanned 50 years. It took those 50 years to film more than 200 titles, most of which were directed by John Ford and Howard Hawks, who escalated Wayne to superstardom. Wayne, who was affectionately called the Duke, dominated every scene.

During the presidency of Richard M. Nixon in the 1970s, Wayne supported the U.S. involvement in Vietnam.

Not all of his films were Westerns. He symbolized American heroism in such films as *The Sands of Iwo Jima* in 1949 and *The Green Berets* in 1968. His Westerns included *Stagecoach, The Long Voyage Home* in 1940, *Reap the Wild Wind* in 1942, *Red River* in 1948 and in 1949, *She Wore a Yellow Ribbon,* followed by *Quiet Man* in 1952.

In 1962 Wayne made three notable movies: *The Man Who Shot Liberty Valance, Hatari* and *The Longest Day. The Cowboys* was released in 1972, when Wayne was 65. In 1964, he developed lung cancer. In 1969 he played Marshall Rooster Cogburn in *True Grit,* which won an Academy Award. Wayne's last movie was *The Shootist.* In this 1976 movie, he portrayed the life of a terminally ill gunfighter. It was truly an epitaph for him. In January 1979, Wayne had major surgery. In April, he presented the award for best picture at the Academy Awards ceremony. It was his final public appearance.

On June 4, 1979, President Jimmy Carter and Congress authorized a special gold medallion in Wayne's honor. One week later he died.

John Wayne appears on a 1990 25¢ Classic Films stamp.

Daniel Webster

Scott 1380
Born: January 18, 1782, Salisbury, New Hampshire
Died: October 24, 1852, Marshfield, Massachusetts

Daniel Webster's early schooling was only rudimentary but his father saved enough to send him to Phillips Exeter Academy and Dartmouth College. Webster graduated from Dartmouth in 1801. He studied law in Boston and taught in Maine at the Fryeburg Academy. He was admitted to the bar in Boston in 1805 and start a law practice in Portsmouth, New Hampshire.

He won a seat in the House of Representatives. He objected to war taxes and helped defeat a bill for drafting soldiers. In 1816 he moved to Boston. He appeared before the Supreme Court in the Dartmouth College Case, arguing for the trustees of the college. Chief Justice John Marshall delivered the court's opinion in 1819, establishing the authority of the college.

Webster gained a reputation as a great orator. In 1823 he was elected to the House of Representatives from Massachusetts. In 1827 he was elected to the Senate. In a speech known as the "Reply to Hayne," Webster told Senator Robert Hayne that the Constitution had created a single, unified nation.

Although Webster became a supporter of Andrew Jackson for president in 1832, he had some disagreements with Jackson. In 1836 Webster was the presidential candidate for the new Whig party but won only Massachusetts. He returned to the Senate until 1841, when William Henry Harrison appointed him secretary of state. When Harrison died, Tyler became president. All Whig cabinet members, resigned except Webster, who wanted to finish the 1842 Maine border dispute known as the Webster-Ashburton Treaty.

Webster finally resigned in 1843. He returned to the Senate in 1845. He opposed the annexation of Texas and the war with Mexico but supported the Compromise of 1850. He was passed over by war hero Zachary Taylor for the presidential nomination in 1848. However, he again became secretary of state in 1850. In 1852 poor health forced him to retire.

Daniel Webster is depicted on a 1969 6¢ stamp.

Noah Webster

Scott 1121
Born: October 16, 1758, West Hartford, Connecticut
Died: May 28, 1843, New Haven, Connecticut

Noah Webster was the son of a Connecticut farmer and a descendant of John Webster, who served as governor of Connecticut in 1656. Webster attended Yale College from 1774 to 1778, during which time he served briefly in the Revolutionary War. While doing clerical work and teaching school, Webster studied law and was admitted to the bar in 1781. In 1882 he taught school in Goshen, New York, where he wrote *The American Spelling Book*, because of his dissatisfaction with the old books. He then compiled a grammar book in 1783 and a reader in 1785.

With these books, he instituted spelling reforms between American and British spelling. He experienced difficulties in obtaining copyrights, so he lobbied until 1790, when the first national copyright law was enacted.

Webster founded the *American Magazine* in 1787 in New York City. The magazine did not last, so he went to practicing law in Hartford, Connecticut. Webster returned to New York City in 1793 and founded the *American Minerva*, a daily newspaper, and the *Herald*, a weekly newspaper. Both were Federalist publications.

With the success of his books, Webster disposed of his newspapers in 1803. He had already moved to New Haven in 1798, and in 1806 bought the *Compendious Dictionary of the English Language*, and published it in 1828. It contained 70,000 words, 12,000 of which had not been listed previously. In 1833 he published a revised edition of the authorized version of the English Bible. He also wrote about a variety of subjects, including medicine, physical sciences, economics and agriculture.

In 1809 he wrote *Experiments Respecting Dew*, which anticipated the weather bureau. He moved to Amherst, Massachusetts, in 1812 and served in the state legislature from 1815 to 1819. In 1821 he helped found Amherst College. He also established the Connecticut Academy of Arts and Sciences in 1822. From then until 1843, he lived in New Haven, Connecticut.

Noah Webster is commemorated on a 1958 4¢ stamp.

Ida Bell Wells

Scott 2442
Born: July 16, 1862, Holly Springs, Mississippi
Died: March 25, 1931, Chicago, Illinois

The 13th Amendment to the Constitution was proclaimed on December 18, 1865, when Ida Bell Wells was three years old. Born of slaves, she too had been a slave, but now she was free. The 14th Amendment was proclaimed on July 28, 1868. Ida Bell Wells was just six years old. The amendment proclaimed her a citizen of the United States.

Wells believed in freedom and fought for it. On a train, she once sat in a seat marked "whites only." This resulted in a lawsuit, which led in 1891 to her dismissal as a schoolteacher by the Memphis school board. The lawsuit ultimately went to the state supreme court. Wells lost.

She had been a country schoolteacher since she was 14 years old and had taught in Memphis since she was 22. She was educated at the Holly Springs freedmen's school and continued her schooling at Fisk University. In 1889, she became part-owner and a reporter for *Free Speech*, a Memphis newspaper. She used the paper to speak out against the lynching of blacks, after three of her friends had been hanged. The next year her office was ransacked.

She moved to New York and began as a staff writer for the *New York Age*. She lectured across the country and organized societies against lynching.

In 1895, at age 33, she married Ferdinand L. Barnett, a lawyer, editor and public officer in Chicago. She worked mostly in Chicago, adding the women's suffrage movement to her campaigns. In 1909 she helped found the National Association for the Advancement of Colored People. She also served as secretary to the National Afro-American Council in 1910 and served on the Chicago municipal court as a probation officer.

After 1925, her tireless effort resulted in the 14th Amendment becoming the cornerstone of the growing Bill of Rights against state infringement. It also became the core of the civil rights movement of the 1950s and 1960s.

Wells is depicted on a 1990 25¢ Black Heritage commemorative stamp.

Benjamin West

Scott 1553
Born: October 10, 1738, Springfield, Pennsylvania
Died: March 11, 1820, London, England

Like many artists, Benjamin West began drawing and painting when he was a child. He graduated from the College of Philadelphia and opened an art studio, where he received a number of commissions, especially for portraits. West also solicited work from New York City.

In 1760 his friends financed a trip for him to Italy. He was the first American to study art in Italy. Italian artists Titian and Raphael impressed West greatly. The Baroque and Renaissance paintings influenced his style.

West went to London in 1763, and settled there permanently. He soon became one of the foremost artists of the day. His paintings impressed King George III, who appointed him to the Royal Academy of Arts. His compositions pointed toward a growing realism and added impetus to a new movement that placed contemporary figures in classical compositions. West was appointed as painter to the king and executed portraits of the royal family and other works suggested by his royal patrons. He became president of the Royal Academy in 1792.

West taught and assisted many American painters who went to England with the sole objective of studying under him. He instructed and encouraged such men as John Singleton Copley, Gilbert Stuart, John Trumbull, Robert Fulton, Samuel F.B. Morse and Charles Wilson Peale.

In 1801, with his position in court waning, West left for France to paint. He exhibited some of his works in Paris.

His career was most dominant in both England and the United States. He painted about 400 canvasses during his life. He never returned to the United States but stayed loyal to his Quaker heritage. West refused the knighthood offered to him. When he died in London, his body lay in state in the Royal Academy before it was buried with great ceremony in St. Paul's Cathedral.

Benjamin West is portrayed on a 1975 10¢ American Arts stamp.

Joseph West

Scott 683
Born: England
Died: 1692, New York

Joseph West was an agent and storekeeper for the proprietor deputy of the duke of Albemarle. In 1663 the Carolina Charter gave eight Englishmen everything from sea to sea between the present southern boundary of Virginia and the latitude of Daytona Beach, Florida. The charter expressed the policy of religious toleration, guaranteeing liberty of conscience to all settlers demeaning themselves, hoping that people from older colonies would move into the area. It afforded a haven for persecuted Protestants from Europe.

Lord Ashley took hold and made himself the real founder. He moved his secretary, John Locke, to draft a document called The Fundamental Constitutions of Carolina. It was the longest and most reactionary of all colonial frames of government. It did not work in pioneer society. In the summer of 1669, three ships were fitted out in England and put under the command of Joseph West. Two ships were wrecked. The third, the *Barbados*, picked up a few hundred emigrants and reached Carolina in the spring of 1670.

West passed by Port Royal, because it was too near St. Augustine, "in the very chops of the Spaniards." He sailed until he reached a bay at the mouths of two rivers, which he named the Ashley and the Cooper. He settled at Albemarle Point on the west bank of the Ashley River.

West was elected colonial governor of South Carolina by the council in 1671. He directed the colony from 1671 to 1672, from 1674 to 1682, and from 1684 to 1685. West also made regulations respecting the militia, roads and status of slaves. In 1680 he moved the location from Albermarle Point to a place across the river and called it New Charles Town. In 1682 he changed the name to Charlestown, then in 1683 to Charleston. Today, it is a center of Southern wealth and culture.

Chief Shadoo of the local Kiawah, Catawba tribe, peacefully cooperated with Captain West. The area under West was a fur-trading outpost and became a rice-growing region.

West is pictured on the 1930 2¢ Carolina-Charleston stamp.

393

Edith Newbold Wharton

Scott 1832
Born: January 24, 1862, New York, New York
Died: August 11, 1937, St. Brice-sous-Foret, France

Edith Newbold Wharton spent her lifetime studying, writing and reading. When she was 16 years old her writings were published in *Scribner's Magazine*. Her early schooling was with private tutors and governesses at home and in Europe. Despite her sheltered upbringing, she had a worldly insight into people and their situations.

Wharton saw the complex social problems against a background of fashionable New York City. Civil War profiteers and the nouveaux riches were crashing the gates of society, shattering old standards of elegance and taste, and calling in question old moralities. She was fascinated by the moral implications of the clash of cultures. Though she began as a rebel against the traditional social standards, she ended as something of an apologist for them.

While she was in her early 20s, she married Edward Wharton, a wealthy Boston banker. Twenty years went by before she published her first really popular work, *The House of Mirth* (1905), which analyzed the society she knew and its reaction to social change. Wharton poured out a constant stream of books for the next 30 years, writing and publishing more than 50 in all. Half into her prolific career, she wrote *The Age of Innocence* (1920), which won a Pulitzer Prize and was considered her best novel. In it she explored hypocrisy and convention infused with ironical observations on social foolishness and affectation.

The other two intrepid women of this time, Ellen Glasgow and Willa Cather, also carried the theme of the superiority of the moral values of the past over the material interests of the present. Wharton is often compared to Henry James, with whose work her own has much in common. James and Wharton were very close friends. Her last best book was probably *Hudson River Bracketed* in 1929. She wrote the sequel, *The Gods Arrive*, in 1932.

The 15¢ Edith Wharton stamp was issued in 1980.

394

Joseph Wharton

Scott 1920
Born: March 3, 1826, Philadelphia, Pennsylvania
Died: 1909, Milestown, Pennsylvania

Joseph Wharton was educated by private tutors. He received honorary degrees from the University of Pennsylvania and from Swarthmore College in Swarthmore, Pennsylvania. From 1845 to 1847, Wharton was a clerk in a mercantile house, then went into the manufacturing of white lead and other manufacturing enterprises. Wharton built the first successful spelter works in the United States while he was at the Lehigh Zinc Company between 1853 and 1863. In 1873 he purchased the Gap Nickel Mines in Lancaster County, Pennsylvania. He established the first successful nickel and cobalt works in the United States in Camden, New Jersey.

Wharton was a director of the Bethlehem Iron Company, later the Bethlehem Steel Works, which was the first armor plant in the United States. He was the sole owner of three blast furnaces at Wharton, New Jersey, and owner of the Andover Iron Company, in Phillipsburg, New Jersey.

He was president of the board of managers of Swarthmore College and endowed its chair of history and economics. He also gave $500,000 to the University of Pennsylvania for the creation of the Wharton School of Finance and Commerce. About 1890, Wharton became the pioneer manufacturer of armor plate for the U.S. Navy.

Originally a Whig, Wharton followed the Whigs into the Republican party. It was a certainty that he could be elected to Congress, but he declined the offer when it was proposed to him. For the state of Pennsylvania, Wharton headed the electoral ticket for Ohio Governor William McKinley at the Republican National Convention, which was held in St. Louis in 1896.

Joseph Wharton appears on a 1981 18¢ Professional Management stamp.

James Abbott McNeill Whistler

Scott 885
Born: July 10, 1834, Lowell, Massachusetts
Died: July 17, 1903, London, England

While James Whistler was in St. Petersburg, now Leningrad, Russia, with his father, who was an Army engineer for the United States, he took drawing lessons in the St. Petersburg Academy of Fine Arts. The Whistler family moved to England to be with their daughter, who had married Seymour Haden, an etcher. In 1849, when Whistler was 15, his father died and the family returned to the United States.

Whistler entered school in the summer resort town of Pomfret, Connecticut. In 1851 he received an appointment to enter West Point Military Academy but was expelled. Whistler left the academy in his third year and joined the U.S. Coast and Geodetic Survey as a draftsman.

By 1855, he was in Paris, where he became an expatriate. He studied art with Charles Gabriel Gleyre, who was in the school of Jean August Dominique Ingres. Whistler's friends and acquaintances in Paris included Eduard Manet, Henri Fantin-Latour and Claude Monet. He exhibited one of his paintings, *The White Girl* in the Royal Academy but was refused at the Salon. This opened the way for him to exhibit his painting at the Salon des Rufuses in 1863. It was well accepted. Whistler's painting *Arrangement in Gray and Black: Portrait of the Artist's Mother* (better known as *Whistler's Mother*) now hangs in the Louvre Museum in Paris.

When Whistler moved to London in 1859, where he maintained a studio, he traveled in the society of Algernon Swinburne, Oscar Wilde and the pre-Raphaelites. He was more noted for his witticisms, elegant and eccentric attire and his flamboyant personality. Whistler became a member of the Royal Society of British Artists in 1884, and in 1886 became its president.

Whistler appears on a 1940 2¢ Famous American Artists stamp.

Paul Dudley White

Scott 2170
Born: June 6, 1886, Boston, Massachusetts
Died: October 31, 1973, Boston, Massachusetts

Paul White's early education was at the Roxbury Latin School in his hometown where his father was a physician. White entered Harvard University, where he obtained his degree in 1908. He earned his medical degree from Harvard in 1911. White accepted an internship at Massachusetts General Hospital, where he worked from 1911 to 1913. He continued his studies at the University College Hospital Medical School in London, England, from 1913 to 1914. White returned to the Massachusetts General Hospital as a resident physician with a teaching fellowship at the Harvard Medical School, where he taught until 1956. He served with the American Expeditionary Forces in 1916 and again from 1917 to 1919. He then returned to his residency and his long association with the Massachusetts General Hospital, where he was to become a pioneer in the diagnosis, treatment and prevention of diseases of the heart and circulatory system. White laid the foundation for modern cardiology as head of the hospital's cardiac clinic and laboratory. While in London, he larned the particulars of the electrocardiograph and introduced its use to the Massachusetts clinic. A staunch advocate of weight control, proper diet and regular exercise, White served as president of the American Heart Association from 1942 to 1944 and became president in 1954 of the International Society of Cardiology. His 1931 text on heart disease is a standard work. He used as many as 21,000 cardiograms for the basis of his many books. In 1955, White's book, *Clues in the Diagnosis and Treatment of Heart Disease*, was published. He was the consulting cardiologist when President Dwight D. Eisenhower suffered a coronary thrombosis while in office.

White received the American Medical Association's distinguished service award and the Lasker award for distinguished achievement in the field of cardiovascular disease.

Paul Dudley White is depicted on a 1986 3¢ Great Americans stamp.

William Allen White

Scott 960
Born: February 10, 1868, Emporia, Kansas
Died: January 29, 1944, Emporia, Kansas

William Allen White grew up in El Dorado, Kansas, 60 miles southwest of his birthplace in Emporia. White attended the University of Kansas from 1886 to 1890 but quit without graduating to work on the El Dorado *Republican* as its business manager. From 1892 to 1895 he worked as an editorialist on the *Kansas City Star*. In 1895 he acquired the *Emporia Gazette* which he edited and published the rest of his life. Although the *Gazette* had a relatively small readership, the articles White wrote were widely reprinted. They soon earned him the nickname Sage of Emporia.

White spoke for liberalism in the Republican party and in the nation. He attacked the Populist party and boosted William McKinley's campaign for the presidency in the August 1896 article, "What's the Matter with Kansas?" White usually did not sway from the Republican party, but in 1912 he actively wrote in favor of Theodore Roosevelt's Bull Moose Progressive Party.

In 1906 he joined with four other journalists, who took over the *American Magazine*. He entered into investigative journalism, at times associating himself with the so-called muckraker movement. In addition to journalism, White wrote several books and some novels between 1901 and 1924. He then turned to biographical works on Woodrow Wilson and Calvin Coolidge. White wrote his autobiography, which was published in 1946, two years after his death. It won a Pulitzer Prize and was reissued in 1951.

White's essay, *Mary White*, written about the death of his 17-year-old daughter who died in a riding accident in 1921, is a classic. His editorials were collected in 1924 and published under the title *The Editor and His People*. Another collection was published in 1937, *Forty Years on Main Street*.

A genial and warm, humane person, White epitomized the middle-class wheat and prairie people of Mid-America. He appears on a 1948 3¢ stamp.

Walter Whitman

Scott 867
Born: May 13, 1819, West Hills, New York
Died: March 26, 1892, Camden, New Jersey

Walter Whitman grew up in West Hills and Brooklyn, New York. In Brooklyn, he went to school until he was 12, then became a printer in various places in New York City and Long Island. He taught school and wrote for leading magazines, including *Brother Jonathan, American Review* and *Democratic Review.* From 1846 to 1848, he was editor of the Brooklyn Eagle. Political differences lost him his job.

Whitman went to New Orleans to work for the *New Orleans Crescent* but soon returned to New York City. He wrote and worked as a carpenter. Not a poetaster, Whitman developed a rhythmically rambling verse form, which was somewhat mystical and lost all trace of convention. A radical poet, Whitman fell under the influence of Thomas Carlyle and Ralph Waldo Emerson. He published his own poems, a dozen in all, called *Leaves of Grass.* He sent a copy to Emerson, who, contrary to others who read Whitman's poems, said it was "the most extraordinary piece of wit and wisdom that America has yet contributed . . . I greet you at the beginning of a great career."

Whitman enlarged his edition in 1856 and on the cover quoted Emerson's encouraging remarks. It wasn't until another enlarged edition was published in 1860 that Whitman became recognized.

In 1862 he went to Virginia to seek a wounded brother. He returned to Washington, D.C., to care for wounded soldiers. His image was slowly transformed from that of a barbaric young man to that of a "good gray poet."

Whitman lost a job with the Department of the Interior in 1865 because of *Leaves of Grass.* However, the attorney general's office hired him. He stayed in Washington until he suffered a paralytic stroke in 1873. He then moved to Camden, New Jersey. Europe accepted his poetry more than the United States. His genius was not universally recognized until after his death.

Whitman is honored on a 1940 5¢ Famous American Authors stamp.

Eli Whitney

Scott 889
Born: December 8, 1765, Westborough, Massachusetts
Died: January 8, 1825, New Haven, Connecticut

Eli Whitney was too young to bear arms in the Revolutionary War but old enough to proffer his aid by working in his father's workshop on the farm making nails and wire that were difficult to buy during the war. After the war, when he was nearly 20, he decided to seek an education. He graduated from Yale College in 1792 and went to Savannah, Georgia, as a tutor.

On the plantations, one of the most tedious jobs for slaves was to remove green seeds from the short-staple cotton. The widow of General Nathanael Greene, whom Whitney had met, recognized his inventive genius and persuaded him to work on a cotton "gin" (Southern Americanism for engine) to do the work by machine.

In April 1793 he had produced a machine that was easy to build, easy to operate and effective. It was also easy to copy, and he initiated many lawsuits to protect his patent.

When the war with France threatened in the late 1790s, Whitney obtain a contract to furnish the U.S. government 10,000 muskets. He fabricated parts by power-driven machine tools. These parts were produced so exact that any part could be replaced with a newly fabricated part in stock. He personally demonstrated to President John Adams how to assemble and disassemble a musket and how the parts were interchangeable. He called this his uniformity system. He was the innovator of the modern assembly line in manufacturing. This put the United States ahead as a leading industrial nation.

The cotton gin rejuvenated slavery and promoted the South to go to war rather than give up slavery. Many historians say the Civil War would not have occurred had it not been for Whitney's cotton gin.

He is portrayed on a 1¢ stamp in the Famous Americans series of 1940.

John Greenleaf Whittier

Scott 865
Born: December 17, 1807, Haverhill, Massachusetts
Died: September 7, 1892, Hampton Falls, New Hampshire

John Greenleaf Whittier grew up on his father's farm. With the little schooling he had, he learned to read. His further education was based on his avid reading habits. He loved poetry. Whittier's parents were devout Quakers, as he was throughout his lifetime. When he was about 20, his sister sent his poem, *The Exile's Departure*, to William Lloyd Garrison. It was printed in the Newburyport *Free Press*.

In 1827 and 1828, Whittier attended Haverhill Academy, writing poetry and studying journalism. He was an editor of the *New England Weekly Review* from 1830 to 1832. Whittier's book, *Legends of New England in Prose and Verse*, was published in 1831. He wrote *Molly Pitcher* the next year.

Interested in politics, Whittier entered into the abolitionist movement in 1833. In 1835 he sat in the Massachusetts legislature as a Whig. He and Garrison split over political policies. In 1840 Whittier became active in the American and Foreign Anti-Slavery Society. In 1842 he ran for a seat in the House of Representatives on the Liberal party ballot.

He edited the *Pennsylvania Freeman* from 1838 to 1840, contributed to the *National Era* and helped establish the *Atlantic Monthly* in 1857.

Much of Whittier's poetry against slavery was printed in *Voices of Freedom* in 1846. His contributions in the next 15 years brought him into the ranks with William Bryant and Henry Wadsworth Longfellow. "Ichabod," a criticism of Daniel Webster for his role in the Compromise of 1850, and "Laus Deo!," in celebration of the ratification of the Thirteenth Amendment abolishing slavery, were notable pieces.

After the Civil War, Whittier lived quietly in Amesbury and later Danvers, Massachusetts, enjoying increasing popularity and acceptance as a poet of homely faith and joy. In 1866, *Snowbound*, reminiscent of Whittier's childhood days on his father's farm, became his most famous work.

Whittier appears on a 1940 2¢ Famous American Authors stamp.

Hazel Virginia Hotchkiss Wightman

Scott 2498
Born: December 20, 1886, Healdsburg, California
Died: December 5, 1974, Chesnut Hill, Massachusetts

Hazel Hotchkiss Wightman's name is synonymous with the game of tennis. Her name is in the International Tennis Hall of Fame in Newport, Rhode Island. She instigated the Wightman Cup matches when, in 1919, she presented the cup to the United States Lawn Tennis Association. British and American women's teams vie for it annually.

Wightman won 44 national titles. Her father, William Joseph, and mother, Emma Lucretia (Grove) Hotchkiss, were well-to-do ranchers and cannery owners. In 1900, when she was 14, the family moved to Berkeley, California. At 16, she began playing tennis. She graduated from the University of California at Berkeley in 1911. In 1909, 1910 and 1911 she won the U.S. Women's Singles, as well as the National Doubles and Mixed.

The year after graduation she married George William Wightman, a former Harvard tennis player, member of a prominent Boston family and a successful lawyer. Over the next several years, Wightman managed to combine motherhood and playing tennis. In 1913 at the Longwood Cricket Club in Chestnut Hill, Massachusetts, she defeated the national champion. Her first child, George, was an infant at the time. After the births of her two daughters, Virginia and Hazel, she won the National Women's Singles again in 1919. In 1922 Dorothy was born, and William in 1925. In 1924 she won Olympic gold medals in Doubles and Mixed, and won the Wimbledon Doubles. In 1927 she captured the National Squash Championship, and was the runner-up in the National Badminton Mixed.

In 1928, despite the responsibility of five children, her name again went in the record books as winner of the National Women's Doubles, with Helen Wills as her partner. Her last national title came in 1954 at age 68. In 1960, at age 73, she made her last appearance in a national tournament.

In 1973, on the 50th anniversary of the Wightman Cup, she was made an honorary commander of the British empire by Queen Elizabeth II.

Wightman is featured on a 1990 25¢ Olympic commemorative stamp.

Harvey Washington Wiley

Scott 1080
Born: October 18, 1844, Kent, Indiana
Died: June 30, 1930, Washington, D.C.

Harvey Wiley graduated in 1867 from Hanover College in Hanover, Indiana. He then received his doctor of medicine degree from Indiana Medical College in 1871. He did his post-graduate work at Harvard in 1873 and studied in Germany in 1878. He taught chemistry at Purdue University and served as Indiana's state chemist from 1881 to 1883.

In 1883 Wiley received an appointment as chief chemist for the United States Department of Agriculture in Washington, D.C., where he served for the next 30 years. During his tenure of duty, he expanded the department from a small force of five persons to more than 500. He thoroughly analyzed many agricultural and food products, which resulted in knowing where best to grow and process specific food and forage crops. His staff made extensive analyses of commercial food products for adulteration of additives and preservatives. Since many additives were harmful or merely added for cheap bulk, he campaigned for congressional action to correct such atrocities.

The muckrakers were behind his efforts in the early 1900s. Upton Sinclair's widely read and inspiring novel, *The Jungle*, exposed bad practices in the Chicago stockyards and boosted Wiley's cause. The book created public awareness and evoked responses to the evils displayed on the grocery store shelves. These evils included sodium nitrate in meat, rat excreta in peanut butter, cockroach carcasses in raisin bread, and dirt in breakfast food.

In 1906 Congress passed the Pure Food and Drug Act. Wiley administered the act until 1912, then resigned to work for *Good Housekeeping* magazine. He also served as professor of agricultural chemistry at George Washington University. He wrote *History of Crime Against the Food Law*, as well as several other books. In 1930, Wiley published his autobiography.

A 3¢ stamp depicting Wiley was released in 1956 on the 50th anniversary of the Pure Food and Drug Laws.

Charles Wilkes

Scott 2387
Born: April 3, 1798, New York, New York
Died: February 8, 1877, Washington, D.C.

Charles Wilkes worked his way up to an appointment in Washington, D.C., as head of the depot of charts and instruments, now known as the U.S. Naval Observatory. Wilkes began as a naval midshipman in 1818, with duty in the Mediterranean and Pacific areas and Narraganset Bay. In 1838 he made some scientific explorations in the South Pacific, Australia and the Antarctic coastal area. He was the first person to recognize Antarctica as a separate continent and not just a field of ice.

Wilkes also sailed to the Hawaiian Islands, the northwest coast of the United States and the Oceania Islands, thereby circumnavigating the globe when he returned to New York Harbor in 1842.

Until the outbreak of the Civil War, Wilkes wrote many books, articles and reports. In 1861 he was placed in command of the *USS San Jacinto* and ordered to search for Confederate vessels. He overhauled the British steamer, *Trent*, in November 1861, and removed two Confederate envoys, James Mason and John Slidell, from the ship. Difficulties with the Navy Department resulted in a court-martial, a reprimand, and suspension from duty. He was later reinstated as a rear admiral.

Wilkes' expedition to Antarctica was authorized by an Act of Congress on May 18, 1836. With six vessels, 345 men, 83 officers and 12 civilian scientists and attaches, the expedition set out from Norfolk, Virginia, on August 18, 1838. South of the Shetlands, Wilkes was unsuccessful, so he based at Sidney Harbor. On December 26, 1939, the squadron sailed to the south ice pack. With ill-equipped ships, Wilkes fought his way to the rim of Antarctica in 1849, and claimed discovery of an immense extent of continental land. The period of actual discovery of the Antarctic continent found three men, a Frenchman, D'Urville, an American, Wilkes, and an Englishman, Ross, on the very edge of the continent within a year. Fifty-three years passed before anyone set foot on the land surrounding the South Pole.

Charles Wilkes is portrayed on a 1988 25¢ Antarctic Explorers stamp.

404

Frances E.C. Willard

Scott 872
Born: Sepember 28, 1839, Churchville, New York
Died: February 18, 1898, New York, New York

Frances Elizabeth Caroline Willard grew up in Ohio and Wisconsin. Her parents were religious teachers, and when Frances was 17, her parents sent her to the Milwaukee Female College. A year later she transferred to the North-Western Female College in Evanston, Illinois. She graduated in 1859, went out to teach schools in Illinois, Pennsylvania and New York successively for 10 years and then toured Europe in 1868-70. Soon after her return, Willard was appointed president of the Evanston College for Ladies in 1871. When Evanston College joined Northwestern University in 1873, she became dean of women at Northwestern. A year later she resigned to follow her calling to join the growing national crusade against liquor. She became the corresponding secretary of the National Woman's Christian Temperance Union (WCTU). In 1879 she was its president and remained so until her death.

Willard worked tirelessly establishing departments for home protection, temperance, better schools, politics, lobbying, labor reform, prison reform, police matrons, peace, nutrition and kindergarten — 39 departments in all. Willard raised the membership to 250,000 paying members in 10,000 local units. She was an excellent orator, organizer and lobbyist, and soon became one of the insiders of the Prohibition party in 1882. She took part in the Industrial Conference in St. Louis that became part of the Populist party in 1892. Four years before that, in 1888, she had been elected president of the National Council of Women.

By 1900, Willard had established a temperance hospital, a publishing association, a lecture bureau, an office building in Chicago and a world WCTU organization with a membership of more than two million. Congress voted to erect a statue in her honor in the rotunda of the Capitol in Washington, D.C., proclaiming her "the first woman of the 19th century, the most beloved character of her time."

Willard is honored on a 5¢ stamp in the issue for educators of the Famous Americans series in 1940.

Roger Williams

Scott 777
Born: circa 1603, London, England
Died: between January and April 1683, Providence, Rhode Island

Roger Williams' father was James Williams, of London, England, a merchant taylor. Roger Williams was employed by the English judge, Sir Edward Coke, and served briefly as a chaplain to a wealthy family. Two years later, in 1622, he was admitted to Pembroke College in Cambridge. In 1627 he was awarded a bachelor of arts degree. He was ordained in 1628 and became chaplain to Sir William Masham in Otes, Essex County. In 1629 he attended a meeting at Sempringham called by Puritans John Cotton and Thomas Hooker. They proposed immigrating to what is now the United States. On December 15, 1629, Williams married Mary Bernard, the daughter of the Reverend Richard Bernard, who was an author and a Puritan. The next year, on December 10, 1630, the couple sailed from Bristol on the *Lyon*, landing at Boston on February 5, 1631.

Williams declined to serve at the Salem church because he believed the church was dishonest in not publicly acknowledging its separation from the Church of England. He went to Plymouth, where he aroused controversy and was sent back to Salem. He demanded that all New England churches must separate from the Church of England.

On October 9, 1635, Williams was convicted of venting "new and dangerous opinions" and was banished from the Massachusetts colony. He and a few companions reached the shores of Narraganset Bay and purchased land from the Indians. He compiled a dictionary of their language.

With prophetess Anne Hutchinson of Boston, the settlements were federated as Rhode Island and Providence Plantation in 1644. Under Williams, Rhode Island became a haven for the persecuted. In the King Philip's War, he bore arms in New England's defense. In 1663 he saw his colony and the Providence Plantation joined by a charter from King Charles II.

Williams is honored on a 1936 3¢ Rhode Island Tercentennial stamp.

Thomas Woodrow Wilson

Scott 2218i
Born: December 28, 1856, Staunton, Virginia
Died: February 3, 1924, Washington, D.C.

Thomas Woodrow Wilson was the son of the Reverend Joseph R. Wilson, a Presbyterian minister. Wilson studied at Davidson College in North Carolina. He also was a student at the College of New Jersey, now Princeton University, and pursued law at the University of Virginia. Wilson opened a law office in Atlanta in June 1882 and was admitted to the bar. He entered Johns Hopkins University in Baltimore in September 1883 to prepare himself for a teaching career in political science. He married Ellen Louise Axson on 24 June, 1885. The next year he received his doctorate. He accepted a professorship in history at Bryn Mawr College near Philadelphia in 1885, then changed to Wesleyan University in Connecticut in 1888. In 1890 Wilson accepted a professorship at Princeton, where he remained for 12 years. In 1902 he followed Francis L. Patton as president of the university.

In 1910 he was elected governor of New Jersey. The Democratic national convention nominated him on the 46th ballot in 1912. He was elected president of the United States and was inaugurated on March 4, 1913. In 1916 he sent General John J. Pershing to Mexico to pursue Pancho Villa. War was miraculously averted, troops were withdrawn and Mexican dictator Victoriano Huerta resigned.

In 1914 two tragedies shattered the president. One was his wife's death and the other was the outbreak of war in Europe. Wilson married Edith Galt in 1915. In 1916 he was re-elected over Charles Evans Hughes.

Wilson broke diplomatic relations with Germany on February 3, 1917, and war was declared in April. Victory was won in 1918, and the armistice was signed November 11. He reiterated his call for a League of Nations in his Fourteen Points Address of January 1918. The Versailles Treaty was signed on June 28, 1919. On October 2, he suffered a paralytic stroke.

Wilson appears on a 22¢ Presidential stamp issued in 1986.

Carter Godwin Woodson

Scott 2073
Born: December 19, 1875, New Canton, Virginia
Died: April 4, 1950, Washington, D.C.

Born to abject poverty, Carter Godwin Woodson was unable to get much schooling when he was young. He was 21 years old when he finally received a high school diploma. Woodson spent the next 15 years working for his higher education, which included graduating from Berea College in 1903, obtaining his bachelor's and master's degrees from the University of Chicago in 1907 and 1908, and graduating from Harvard in 1912 with his doctorate.

To support his education, Woodson taught school. From 1909 to 1918, he taught at a high school in Washington, D.C. He was dean of the liberal arts college at Howard University in Washington, D.C., from 1919 to 1920, and dean at West Virginia State College for two years.

Woodson's goal in education was to free black studies from traditional biases and interpretations often recorded by white historians. He made black studies a respectable academic pursuit. Woodson founded the Association for the Study of Negro Life and History in 1915, and the following year supplemented it with the regular issue of the *Journal of Negro History*. He organized the Associated Publishers Inc. to provide black writers and educators with an outlet for their works, which other publishers were reluctant to accept. He was the foremost author on the history of black people in America and their African background. He was known as the father of black history.

Woodson wrote several books about blacks. In 1922 he published *The Negro in Our History*. He also wrote on rural Negro life, the African background of blacks, and African heroes. In 1937 he began publication of the *Negro History Bulletin*, which was to double as a teaching reference.

Woodson was awarded the Springarn medal of the National Association for the Advancement of Colored People (NAACP) in 1926. He spent his latter years editing the six-volume *Encyclopedia Africana*.

He is depicted on the 1984 20¢ Black Heritage issue.

Frank Lloyd Wright

Scott 1280
Born: June 8, 1867, Richland Center, Wisconsin
Died: April 9, 1959, Phoenix, Arizona

Frank Lloyd Wright attended the University of Wisconsin briefly in the mid-1880s, where he studied civil engineering. After college, he apprenticed with Louis H. Sullivan, Chicago's leading architect of large commercial buildings. He then opened his own office in Oak Park, Illinois, in 1893. Wright's architectural concepts were somewhat unorthodox and might be called Shintoistic elegance. His houses and buildings were intended to adapt to their environment in color, form and texture, conform to the lifestyle of the people who occupied them, and blend with the terrain. Wright made use of the pre-formed concrete block, which he said could be put up quickly, and done by workers who were not especially skilled in the fine art of masonry.

Before completing a house plan, Wright's intention was to know the people who were to live in it and build the house that suited them in every way. His prairie style was to blend with the Western landscapes with long, low proportions, wide windows, overhanging roofs and open terraces. His rooms flowed from one to the next to give the entire house unity.

He showed great innovation in his Imperial Hotel in Tokyo by using floating footings so that it was the only major building to survive the earthquake of 1923.

Wright adapted his structures to the existing grounds. Such examples are Fallingwater, a house in Bear Run, near Uniontown, Pennsylvania; Taliesin in Spring Green, Wisconsin; and Taliesin West in Scottsdale, Arizona. He patterned the Solomon R. Guggenheim Art Museum after a snail, and structured a concert hall after an oyster. He also controlled acoustics and lighting to their best effect.

Although he was a genius in design, Wright was lax with his finances, and often in arrears with his creditors.

Frank Lloyd Wright appears on a 1966 2¢ Prominent Americans stamp.

409

Orville Wright

Scott C91
Born: August 19, 1871, Dayton, Ohio
Died: January 30, 1948, Dayton, Ohio

Orville Wright was the son of Milton and Susan Catherine Koerner Wright. The Reverend Milton Wright was bishop of the Church of the United Brethren Church of Christ. While in high school, Orville built a large printing press and began publishing a local newspaper, *The West Side* News. His older brother, Wilbur, joined him in 1890. Two years later, the brothers opened a bicycle shop, where they made, sold and repaired bicycle parts. After a few years, they became interested in glider planes. They read pioneer glider Otto Lilienthal's books on soaring and Octave Chanute's book on flying machines.

Kitty Hawk, North Carolina, was chosen for their experiments from 1900 to 1903, during which time they made more than one thousand test flights by glider. They developed warping, or twisting, of the wings, the forerunner of the movable aileron, to guide it in flight. They built a box-kite type of glider to carry one person in a powered flight, using a screwlike propeller driven by a four-cylinder motor. On December 17, 1903, Orville flew the glider for 120 feet in 12 seconds.

By 1906, they had the machine patented. In 1908, they had a U.S. War Department contract to build a machine that went 125 miles at a speed of 40 miles per hour. In 1909 they formed the American Wright Company to manufacture planes and train pilots. After Wilbur's death in 1912, Orville continued with the company for two years. In 1913 he won the Collier Trophy for a device to balance airplanes automatically.

In 1915 he retired, having sold his interests to the Wright Company. He continued to work on the development of aviation, and received the first Daniel Guggenheim Medal for his and Wilbur's contributions to the advancement of aeronautics.

Wright appears with his brother Wilbur on two 1978 31¢ airmail stamps.

410

Wilbur Wright

Scott C91
Born: April 16, 1867, near New Castle, Indiana
Died: May 30, 1912, Dayton, Ohio

Wilbur Wright was the son of a bishop of the United Brethren Church of Christ in Dayton, Ohio, and the older brother of Orville, with whom he had a close association in business, manufacturing and flying. Before joining his brother Orville in 1890 in the printing business, Wilbur received his education in Dayton; Richmond, Indiana; and Cedar Rapids, Iowa. He was about to enter college when an ice hockey accident disabled him from physical work.

Wilbur devoted his time to caring for his ailing mother and his father, who was having legal problems concerning the church. He and Orville opened a bicycle sales and repair shop in 1892 and soon were manufacturing bicycles. They studied the writings of Otto Lilienthal in Germany and Octave Chanute in the United States.

Their ingenious inventive minds were soon making gliders, which led to putting together a heavier-than-air flying machine that looked like a box kite with a small but powerful four-cylinder engine. The engine was designed with an efficient air screw that worked in air like a ship's propeller works in water. Their original plane was flown on the sand hills at Kitty Hawk, North Carolina. On December 17, 1903, after Orville had flown a distance of 120 feet in 12 seconds, Wilbur, later that day, flew for 59 seconds, spanning 852 feet. The brothers, in 1906, were granted a U.S. patent for a flying machine. In 1908 the U.S. War Department awarded them a contract for a machine capable of flying 40 miles per hour for a distance of 125 miles carrying a pilot and one passenger. In the next few years, the brothers were busy demonstrating their plane to the government and the public. Wilbur went to Europe, and Orville stayed in the United States.

In 1909 the American Wright Company was incorporated. It was devoted to manufacturing and improving the flying machine and training pilots. Wilbur served as president of the company until 1912, when he contracted typhoid fever and died at age 45.

Wright is shown with his brother Orville on two 1978 airmail stamps.

Whitney Moore Young Jr.

Scott 1875
Born: July 31, 1921, Lincoln Ridge, Kentucky
Died: March 11, 1971, Lagos, Nigeria

In 1941 Whitney Moore Young Jr. received his bachelor of science degree from Kentucky State College in Frankfurt, Kentucky. He taught school for a year, then entered the Army. He studied engineering at the Massachusetts Institute of Technology (MIT) for two years. He then served in Europe until the end of World War II, when he was discharged from the Army. Young enrolled in the University of Minnesota for graduate studies in social work, earning his masters degree in 1947.

He worked for the St. Paul Urban League for three years. From 1950 to 1954, he served as the executive secretary of the Omaha Urban League and as an instructor at the Nebraska School of Social Work at Creighton University in Omaha. From 1954 to 1961, he was the dean of social work at Atlanta University. He became executive director of the National Urban League, which had offices in New York City.

While with the Urban League, Young served on various commissions under Presidents John F. Kennedy and Lyndon B. Johnson. The Urban League helped blacks find housing and jobs.

In the 1960s, with the upsurge of the civil rights movement, Young called for a domestic Marshall Plan for all the nation's blacks. He broadened the plan of the Urban League to include all blacks who needed help and to take advantage of any legal or activist victories to improve housing, employment and education for blacks. Young's programs were incorporated into President Lyndon Johnson's anti-poverty program in the mid-1960s. He lectured on civil rights and wrote two books, *To Be Equal* and *Beyond Racism*.

Young drowned in a swimming accident at age 50 while on a trip to Lagos, Nigeria. A 1981 15¢ Black Heritage stamp features Young.

Mildred Didrikson Zaharias

Scott 1932
Born: June 26, 1914, Port Arthur, Texas
Died: September 27, 1956, Galveston, Texas

Babe Didrikson was the daughter of Norwegian immigrants and was reared in Beaumont, Texas. While still in high school, she played basketball for an insurance company team and was named All-American for three years running. She entered eight of the 10 events in the women's national track and field tournament held by the Amateur Athletic Union (AAU) in 1932. She won five of them, and Babe Didrikson was soon a name known to all sports fans. That same year Didrikson entered the 1932 Olympic Games held in Los Angeles and won two gold medals, setting a new record in the javelin throw and the 80-meter hurdles. She also won the high jump, but was disqualified because of a technicality.

Didrikson took advantage of her new fame and turned professional to travel around the country giving exhibitions. She pitched for the House of David, a baseball troupe of bearded men. She also excelled in billiards, swimming and diving. In 1938 she married George Zaharias, a professional wrestler of some note, and from then on she was known as Babe Zaharias.

She turned to golf with an amateur standing, since she had never played golf professionally. Zaharias soon became the leading amateur golfer in the nation, winning 17 straight titles in 1947, including the British Women's Amateur. She turned professional and continued to win. In 1949 the Associated Press poll voted her the outstanding woman athlete of the century.

In 1952, at age 38 and at the peak of her professional career, her health began to fail. In 1953 Zaharias underwent surgery for cancer. She made a good recovery and went on to win the Women's U.S. Open and the All-American Open in 1954. In 1956 her health was failing again, and she underwent surgery, but it was too late. In her last year, Babe wrote about her plight with cancer in a story of faith and courage titled *The Life I've Led*.

A 1981 18¢ stamp depicts Zaharias holding a trophy.

Scott catalog numbers

The following is a listing of all persons whose biographies appear in this book along with the Scott catalog numbers of all United States stamps honoring these persons.

Adams, Abigail Smith 2146
Adams, John 806, 841, 850, 2216b
Adams, John Quincy 811, 846, 2216f
Addams, Jane 878
Alcott, Louisa May 862
Allen, Ethan 1071
Anthony, Susan Brownell 784, 1051
Armstrong, Edwin Howard 2056
Arnold, Henry Harley 2192
Arthur, Chester Alan 826, 2218c
Audubon, John James 874, 1241, 1863, C71
Austin, Stephen Fuller 776
Balboa, Vasco Nunez de 397, 401
Baldwin, Abraham 1850
Banneker, Benjamin 1804
Barbe-Marbois, Francois de 1020
Barry, John 790
Barrymore, Ethel 2012
Barrymore, John 2012
Barrymore, Lionel 2012
Bartholdi, Frederic Auguste 2147
Barton, Clarrissa Harlowe 967
Bell, Alexander Graham 893
Bethune, Mary McLeod 2137
Bissell, Emily P. 1823
Black, Hugo LaFayette 2172
Blackwell, Elizabeth 1399
Blair, Montgomery C66
Bolivar, Simon 1110-1111
Boone, Daniel 1357
Bryan, William Jennings 2195
Buchanan, James 820, 2217f
Buck, Pearl S. 1848
Bunche, Ralph Johnson 1860
Burbank, Luther 876
Burgoyne, John 644, 1728
Byrd, Richard 2388
Cadillac, Antoine de le Mothe 1000
Carlson, Chester Floyd 2180

Carnegie, Andrew	1171
Carson, Rachel Louise	1857
Carteret, Philip	1247
Caruso, Enrico	2250
Carver, George Washington	953
Cassatt, Mary	1322, 2182
Cather, Willa Sibert	1487
Catt, Carrie Lane Chapman	959
Chanute, Octave	C93, C94
Chapman, John	1317
Chennault, Claire	2186
Churchill, Winston	1264
Clark, George Rogers	651
Clark, Grenville	1867
Clark, William	1063
Clay, Henry	140, 151, 162, 173, 198, 227, 259, 274, 284, 309, 1846
Clemens, Samuel Langhorne	863
Clemente, Roberto	2097
Cleveland, Steven Grover	564, 693, 827, 2218d
Cody, William F.	2178
Cohan, George Michael	1756
Columbus, Christopher	230-245, 2426, 2512, C121, C127
Comstock, Henry T.P.	1130
Cook, James	1723, 1724
Coolidge, John Calvin	834, 2219b
Cooper, Gary	2447
Cooper, James Fenimore	860
Copernicus, Nicolaus	1488
Copley, Elizabeth	1273
Coronado, Francisco Vasquez de	898
Crazy Horse	1855
Crockett, David	1330
Curtiss, Glenn Hammond	C100
Cushing, Harvey Williams	2188
Cutler, Manasseh	795
Dante, Alighieri	1268
Dare, Virginia	796
Davis, Jefferson	1408
Decatur, Stephen	791
Dewey, George	793
Dewey, John	1291
Dickinson, Emily Elizabeth	1436
Dirksen, Everett McKinley	1874
Disney, Walter Elias	1355
Dix, Dorothea Lynde	1844

Douglas, Stephen Arnold 1115
Douglass, Frederick 1290
Drew, Charles Richard 1865
Dulles, John Foster 1172
Dunbar, Paul Laurence 1554
Eagan, Edward Patrick Francis 2499
Earhart, Amelia C68
Eastman, George 1062
Edison, Thomas 654-656, 945
Einstein, Albert 1285, 1774
Eisenhower, Dwight David 1383, 1393-1395, 1401-1402, 2219g, 2513
Eliot, Charles William 871
Eliot, Thomas Stearns 2239
Ellington, Edward Kennedy 2211
Ellsworth, Lincoln 2389
Emerson, Ralph Waldo 861
Ericsson, John 628
Erikson, Leif 1359
Ewry, Ray C. 2497
Fairbanks, Douglas 2088
Farnsworth, Philo Taylor 2058
Farragut, David Glasgow 311, 792
Faulkner, William 2350
Fields, W.C. 1803
Fillmore, Millard 818, 2217d
Flanagan, Edward Joseph 2171
Ford, Henry 1286A
Foster, Stephen Collins 879
Fox, George L. 956
Francis of Assisi 2023
Francisco, Peter 1562
Franklin, Benjamin 1, 3, 5-5A, 6-8A, 9, 18-24, 38, 40, 46,
        55, 61, 63, 71, 81, 85-86, 92, 100, 102, 110, 112, 123,133-134, 145,
        156, 167, 182, 192, 206, 212, 219, 246-247, 264, 279, 300, 314, 316,
        318, 331, 343, 348, 352, 357, 374, 383, 385, 387, 390, 392, 414-423,
        431-440, 460, 470-478, 497, 508-518, 523-524, 547, 552, 575, 578, 581,
        594, 596-597, 604, 632, 658, 669, 803, 1030, 1073, 1393D, 1690, 1753
Fremont, John Charles 288
French, Daniel Chester 619, 887, 1116
Frost, Robert Lee 1526
Fulton, Robert 1270
Gable, Clark 2446
Gallatin, Abraham A.A. 1279
Gallaudet, Thomas Hopkins 1861
Galvez, Bernardo de 1826

Gandhi, Mohandas K. 1174-1175
Garfield, James Abram 205, 205C, 216, 224, 256,
        271, 282, 305, 558, 587, 638, 664, 675, 723, 825, 2218b
Garibaldi, Giuseppe 1168-1169
Garland, Judy 2445
Gates, Horatio 1728
Gehrig, Henry Louis 2417
George, Walter F. 1170
Gershwin, George 1484
Giannini, Amadeo Peter 1400
Gilbreth, Lillian Evelyn Moller 1868
Goddard, Robert Hutchings C69
Goethals, George Washington 856
Gompers, Samuel 988
Goode, Alexander D. 956
Grant, Ulysses Simpson 223, 255, 270, 281, 303,
        314, 560, 589, 640, 666, 677, 823, 2217i
Grasse, Francois Joseph Paul 703
Greeley, Horace 1177
Greely, Adolphus Washington 2221
Greene, Nathanael 785
Griffith, David Wark 1555
Hale, Nathan 551, 653
Hamilton, Alexander .. 143, 154, 165, 176, 190, 201, 217, 629, 1053, 1086
Hammarskjold, Dag Hjalmar Agne Carl 1203-1204
Handy, William Christopher 1372
Hanson, John 1941
Harding, Warren Gameliel 553, 576, 582, 598, 605,
        610-613, 631, 633, 659, 670, 684, 686, 833, 2219a
Harris, Joel Chandler 980
Harrison, Benjamin 308, 622, 694, 828, 1045, 2218e
Harrison, William Henry 814, 996, 2216i
Harte, Bret 2196
Hartley, David 2052
Harvard, John 2191
Hawthorne, Nathaniel 2047
Hayes, Rutherford Birchard 563, 692, 824, 2218a
Hemingway, Ernest Miller 2418
Henry, Patrick 1052, 1144
Henson, Matthew 2223
Herbert, Victor 881
Herkimer, Nicholas 1722
Hoban, James 1935-1936
Hollow Horn Bear 565
Holmes, Oliver Wendell Jr. 1288, 1288B, 1305E

Hoover, Herbert Clark 1269, 2219c
Hopkins, Johns 2194A
Hopkins, Mark 870
Houston, Samuel 776, 1242
Howe, Elias 892
Howe, Julia Ward 2177
Hughes, Charles Evans 1195
Hull, Cordell 1235
Irving, Washington 859
Isabella I 234, 241, 244
Jackson, Andrew 73, 84-85, 87, 93, 103, 135, 146,
            157, 168, 178, 180, 183, 193, 203, 211, 211D,
         215, 221, 253, 268, 302, 812, 941, 1209, 1225, 1286, 2216g
Jackson, Thomas Jonathan 788, 1408
Jay, John 1046
Jeffers, John Robinson 1485
Jefferson, Thomas 12, 27-30A, 42, 57, 67,
            75-76, 80, 95, 105, 139, 150, 161, 172,
       187-188, 197, 209, 228, 260, 275, 310, 324, 561, 590,
     641, 667, 678, 807, 842, 851, 1033, 1055, 1278, 1299, 2216c
Johnson, Andrew 822, 2217h
Johnson, James Weldon 2371
Johnson, Lyndon Baines 1503, 2219i
Jolliet, Louis 1356
Jones, Casey 993
Jones, John Paul 790, 1789
Jones, Robert Tyre Jr. 1933
Joplin, Scott 2044
Joseph 1364
Kamehameha I 799
Kane, Elisha Kent 2220
Kearny, Stephen Watts 944
Keller, Helen Adams 1824
Kennedy, John Fitzgerald 1246, 1287, 2219h
Kennedy, Robert Francis 1770
Kern, Jerome David 2110
Key, Francis Scott 962, 1142
King, Martin Luther Jr. 1771
Knox, Henry 1851
Kosciuszko, Tadeusz 734-735
Kossuth, Lajos 1117-1118
Lafayette, Marquis de 1010, 1097, 1716
LaGuardia, Fiorello Henry 1397
Langley, Samuel Pierpont C118
Lanier, Sidney 1446

Laubach, Frank Charles 1864
Lee, Jason 964
Lee, Robert Edward 788, 982, 1049
Leigh, Vivien 2446
Lewis, Harry Sinclair 1856
Lewis, Meriwether 1063
Lincoln, Abraham 77, 85F, 91, 98, 108,
        122, 132, 137, 148, 159, 170, 186, 195, 208, 222, 254, 280,
        289, 304, 315, 317, 367-369, 555, 584, 600, 635, 661, 672, 821,
        906, 978, 1036, 1058, 1113-1116, 1282, 1303, 2106, 2217g, 2433, C59
Lincoln, Thomas 2106
Lippmann, Walter 1849
Livingston, Robert R. 323
Lockwood, Belva Ann Bennett 2179
London, John Griffith 2183, 2197
Long, Crawford Williamson 875
Longfellow, Henry Wadsworth 864
Louis XVI 1753
Low, Juliette Gordon 974
Lowell, James Russell 866
Ludington, Sybil 1559
Luther, Martin 2065
Lyon, Mary 2169
Maass, Clara 1699
MacArthur, Douglas 1424
McCormack, John 2090
McCormick, Cyrus Hall 891
Macdonough, Thomas 791
MacDowell, Edward Alexander 882
McDowell, Ephraim 1138
McKinley, William 326, 559, 588, 639, 665, 676, 829, 2218f
McLoughlin, John 964
McMahon, James O'Brien 1200
Madison, Dolley 1822
Madison, Helene 2500
Madison, James 262, 277, 312, 479, 808, 843, 2216d
Magsaysay, Ramon 1096
Mann, Horace 869
Mannerheim, Carl Gustaf Emil 1165-1166
Marquette, Jacques 285, 1356
Marshall, George Cartlett 1289
Marshall, John 263, 278, 313, 480, 1050, 2415
Masaryk, Tomas Garrigue 1148
Mason, George 1858
Masters, Edgar Lee 1405

Mayo, Charles Horace 1251
Mayo, William James 1251
Mazzei, Philip C98
Mellon, Andrew William 1072
Melville, Herman 2094
Michael, Moina Bell 977
Millay, Edna St. Vincent 1926
Millikan, Robert Andrews 1866
Mitchell, Margaret 2168
Monroe, James 325, 562, 591, 603,
               642, 668, 679, 810, 845, 1038, 1105, 2216e
Moore, John Bassett 1295
Moore, Marianne Craig 2449
Morris, Robert 1004
Morse, Samuel Finley Breese 890
Moses, Horace 2095
Mott, Lucretia Coffin 959
Muir, John 1245
Munoz Marin, Luis 2173
Nevin, Ethelbert Woodbridge 883
Nicolet, Jean 739
Nimitz, Chester William 1869
Norris, George William 1184
Ochs, Adolph Simon 1700
Oglethorpe, James Edward 726
O'Neill, Eugene Gladstone 1294, 1305C
Ouimet, Francis 2377
Owens, James Cleveland (Jesse) 2496
Paderewski, Ignacy Jan 1159-1160
Paine, Thomas 1292
Palmer, Nathanial Brown 2386
Papanicolaou, George N. 1754
Parkman, Francis 1281, 1297
Partridge, Alden 1854
Patton, George Smith Jr. 1026
Peale, Charles Wilson 1064
Peary, Robert Edwin 2223
Penn, William 724
Perkins, Frances 1821
Perry, Matthew Calbraith 1021
Perry, Oliver Hazard 144, 155, 166, 177,
           191, 202, 218, 229, 261-261A, 276-276A
Pershing, John Joseph 1042A
Pierce, Franklin 819, 2217e
Pocahontas 330

Poe, Edgar Allan 986
Poling, Clark V. 956
Polk, James Knox 816, 2217b
Ponce de Leon, Juan 2024
Poor, Salem 1560
Porter, David Dixon 792
Post, Wiley C95-C96
Powell, John Wesley 1374
Priestley, Joseph 2038
Pulaski, Casimir 690
Pulitzer, Joseph 946
Putnam, Rufus 795
Pyle, Ernest Taylor 1398
Randolph, Asa Philip 2402
Rayburn, Samuel Taliaferro 1202
Red Cloud 2176
Reed, Walter 877
Remington, Frederic 888, 1187, 1934
Reuter, Ernst 1136-1137
Revel, Barnard 2194
Revere, Paul 1048, 1059A
Riley, James Whitcomb 868
Robinson, Jack Roosevelt 2016
Rochambeau, Comte de 703
Rockne, Knute Kenneth 2376
Rodgers, James Charles 1755
Rogers, William Penn Adair 975, 1801
Roosevelt, Anna Eleanor 1236, 2105
Roosevelt, Franklin Delano 930-933, 1284, 1298, 1305, 1950, 2219d
Roosevelt, Theodore 557, 586, 602, 637, 663, 674, 830, 1039, 2218g
Ross, Elizabeth Griscom 1004
Ross, George 1004
Russell, Richard Brevard 1853
Ruth, George Herman 2046
Du Sable, Jean Baptiste Pointe 2249
Sacagawea 1063
Saint-Gaudens, Augustus 886
Salem, Peter 1361
Salomon, Haym 1561
Sampson, William Thomas 793
San Martin, Jose de 1125-1126
Sandburg, Carl 1731
Santa Claus 1472, 2064
Sargent, Winthrop 955
Schley, Winfield Scott 793

Schurz, Carl 1847
Scott, Blanche Stuart C99
Scott, Winfield 142, 153, 175, 200
Sequoyah 1859
Serra, Miguel Jose Junipero C116
Sevier, John 941
Seward, William Henry 370-371
Shadoo 683
Shakespeare, William 1250
Sheridan, Philip Henry 787
Sherman, William Tecumseh 225, 257, 272
Sikorsky, Igor Ivanovich C119
Sitting Bull.. 2184
Smith, Alfred Emanuel... 937
Smith, John 328
Sousa, John Philip 880
Sperry, Elmer Ambrose C114
Sperry, Lawrence B.. C114
Stanton, Edwin McMasters................ 138, 149, 160, 171, 196
Stanton, Elizabeth Cady 959
Stefansson, Vilhjalmur 2222
Steinbeck, John Ernst 1773
Steinmetz, Charles Proteus 2055
Steuben, Baron Friedrich von 689
Stevenson, Adlai Ewing 1275
Stone, Harlan Fiske 965
Stone, Lucy Blackwell 1293
Stravinsky, Igor Fyodorovich 1845
Stuart, Gilbert Charles 884
Stuyvesant, Peter 971
Sullivan, Anne 1824
Sullivan, John 657
Sun Yat Sen 906, 1188
Taft, Robert Alphonso 1161
Taft, William Howard 685, 687, 831, 2218h
Tanner, Henry Ossawa 1486
Taylor, Zachary 179, 181, 185, 204, 817, 2217c
Tesla, Nicola 2057
Thayer, Sylvanus 1852
Thoreau, Henry David 1327
Thorpe, James Francis 2089
Toscanini, Arturo 2411
Truman, Harry S 1499, 1862, 2219f
Truth, Sojourner 2203
Tubman, Harriet.. 1744

Twain, Mark 863
Tyler, John 815, 847, 2217a
Van Buren, Martin 813, 2216h
Verville, Alfred V. C113
Walker, Mary E. 2013
Washington, Booker Taliaferro 873, 1074
Washington, George 2, 4, 10-11, 13-17, 25-26,
    31-37, 39, 41, 43-45, 47, 56, 58-60, 62, 62B, 64-66, 68-70, 72,
    74, 78-79, 82-83, 85, 85C-85E, 88-90, 94, 96-97, 99, 101, 104,
    106-107, 109, 111, 115, 126, 136, 147, 158, 169, 184, 194, 207,
    210-211, 213-214, 219D, 220, 248-252, 265-267, 279, 301, 319-322,
    332-342, 344-347, 349-351, 353-356, 358-366, 375-382, 384, 386,
    388-389, 391, 393-396, 405-413, 424-430, 427-430, 441-450, 452-459,
    461-469, 481-496, 498-507, 519, 525-528, 530-536, 538-546, 554, 577,
    579, 583, 595, 599-599A, 606, 617, 634-634A, 660, 671, 704-715,
    720-722, 804, 829, 839, 848, 854, 947-948, 1003, 1031,
    1054, 1139, 1213, 1229, 1283, 1283B, 1304, 1304C,
    1686, 1688-1689, 1704, 1729, 1952, 2149, 2216a
Washington, John P. 956
Washington, Martha Custis 306, 556, 585, 601,
    636, 662, 673, 805, 840, 849
Wayne, Anthony 680
Wayne, John 2448
Webster, Daniel.............................. 141, 152, 163, 174, 189,
    199, 226, 258, 273, 282C, 283, 307, 725, 1380
Webster, Noah.. 1121
Wells, Ida Bell 2442
West, Benjamin... 1553
West, Joseph 683
Wharton, Edith Newbold Jones 1832
Wharton, Joseph 1920
Whistler, James Abbott McNeill 885
White, Paul Dudley 2170
White, William Allen 960
Whitman, Walter.. 867
Whitney, Eli 889
Whittier, John Greenleaf 865
Wightman, Hazel Virginia Hotchkiss 2498
Wiley, Harvey Washington 1080
Wilkes, Charles... 2387
Willard, Frances Elizabeth Caroline 872
Williams, Roger 777
Wilson, Thomas Woodrow 623, 697, 832, 1040, 2218i
Woodson, Carter Godwin 2073
Wright, Frank Lloyd 1280, 2019

Wright, Orville C45, C91-C92
Wright, Wilbur C45, C91-C92
Young, Whitney Moore Jr. 1875
Zaharias, Mildred Didrikson 1932

Topical Index

Agriculture:
Carver, George Washington
McCormick, Cyrus Hall

Architects:
Hoban, James
Wright, Frank Lloyd

Art and Artists:
Audubon, John James
Bartholdi, Frederic Auguste
Cassatt, Mary
Copley, Elizabeth
French, Daniel Chester
Morse, Samuel F.B.
Peale, Charles Willson
Remington, Frederic
Saint-Gaudens, Augustus
Stuart, Gilbert Charles
Tanner, Henry Ossawa
West, Benjamin
Whistler, James Abbott McNeill

Astronomers:
Banneker, Benjamin
Copernicus, Nicolaus

Automotives:
Ford, Henry

Aviation:
Chanute, Octave
Curtiss, Glenn Hammond
Earhart, Amelia
Goddard, Robert Hutchings
Langley, Samuel Pierpont
Post, Wiley
Scott, Blanche Stuart
Sikorsky, Igor Ivanovich
Sperry, Lawrence Burst
Sperry, Elmer Ambrose
Verville, Alfred V.
Wright, Orville

Wright, Wilbur

Banking and Economics:
Carnegie, Andrew
Giannini, Amadeo Peter
Harvard, John
Hopkins, Johns
Mellon, Andrew William

Blacks:
Banneker, Benjamin
Bethune, Mary McLeod
Bunche, Ralph Johnson
Carver, George Washington
Douglass, Frederick
Drew, Charles Richard
Dunbar, Paul Laurence
Handy, William Christopher
Henson, Matthew Alexander
Joplin, Scott
King, Martin Luther Jr.
Owens, James Cleveland
Poor, Salem
Randolph, Asa Philip
Robinson, Jack Roosevelt
du Sable, Jean Baptiste Pointe
Tanner, Henry Ossawa
Truth, Sojourner
Tubman, Harriet
Washington, Booker Taliaferro
Wells, Ida
Woodson, Carter Godwin
Young., Whitney Moore Jr.

Botany:
Burbank, Luther

Children:
Elizabeth Clarke Copley
Virginia Dare
Lincoln, Thomas

Educators:
Bethune, Mary McLeod

Dewey, John
Eliot, Charles William
Gallaudet, Thomas Hopkins
Hopkins, Mark
Lockwood, Belva Ann Bennett
Lyon, Mary
Mann, Horace
Sullivan, Anne
Washington, Booker Taliaferro
Webster, Noah
Willard, Frances E.C.

Energy and conservation:
Carson, Rachel Louise
Chapman, John
Muir, John
Sequoyah

Engineers:
Armstrong, Edwin H.
Ericsson, John
Gilbreth, Lillian Evelyn Moller
Goethals, George Washington

Entertainers:
Barrymore, Ethel
Barrymore, John
Barrymore, Lionel
Caruso, Enrico
Cooper, Gary
Fairbanks, Douglas
Fields, W.C.
Gable, Clark
Garland, Judy
Leigh, Vivien
McCormack, John
Rogers, William Penn Adair
Wayne, John

Explorers:
Balboa, Vasco Nunez de
Boone, Daniel
Byrd, Richard Evelyn
Clark, William
Cody, William Frederick

Columbus, Christopher
Cook, James
Coronado, Francisco Vasquez de
Crockett, David
Du Sable, Jean Baptiste Pointe
Ellsworth, Lincoln
Erikson, Leif
Fremont, John Charles
Greely, Adolphus Washington
Henson, Matthew Alexander
Jolliet, Louis
Kane, Elisha Kent
Lewis, Meriwether
Marquette, Jacques
Nicolet, Jean
Palmer, Nathaniel Brown
Peary, Robert Edwin
Ponce de Leon, Juan
Stefansson, Vilhjalmur
Wilkes, Charles

Folklore, culture & fairy tales:
Chapman, John
Santa Claus

Geology:
Powell, John Wesley

Government & diplomacy:
Adams, Abigail
Adams, John
Adams, John Quincy
Arthur, Chester Alan
Barbe-Marbois, Francois de
Buchanan, James
Carteret, Philip
Churchill, Sir Winston
Cleveland, Stephen Grover
Dirksen, Everett McKinley
Douglas, Stephen Arnold
Dulles, John Foster
Eisenhower, Dwight David
Fillmore, Millard
Gandhi, Mohandas Karamchand
Garfield, James Abram

George, Walter Franklin
Grant, Ulysses Simpson
Grasse, Francois Joseph Paul
Hamilton, Alexander
Hammarskjold, Dag
Harding, Warren Gameliel
Harrison, Benjamin
Harrison, William Henry
Hartley, David
Hayes, Rutherford Birchard
Hoover, Herbert Clark
Jackson, Andrew
Jefferson, Thomas
Johnson, Andrew
Johnson, Lyndon Baines
Kennedy, John Fitzgerald
Kennedy, Robert Francis
La Guardia, Fiorello Henry
Lincoln, Abraham
Madison, Dolley
Madison, James
Magsaysay, Ramon
Marin, Luis Munoz
McKinley, William
McMahon, Brien
Monroe, James
Moore, John Bassett
Morris, Robert
Paine, Thomas
Perkins, Frances
Pierce, Franklin
Polk, James Knox
Rayburn, Samuel Taliaferro
Reuter, Ernst
Roosevelt, Anna Eleanor
Roosevelt, Franklin Delano
Roosevelt, Theodore
Ross, George
Russell, Richard Brevard
Sargent, Winthrop
Seward, William Henry
Smith, Alfred Emanuel
Stevenson, Adlai Ewing
Stuyvesant, Peter
Sun Yat-sen

Taft, Robert Alphonso
Taft, William Howard
Taylor, Zachary
Truman, Harry S
Tyler, John
Van Buren, Martin
Washington, George
Washington, Martha Custis
Wilson, Thomas Woodrow

History:
Parkman, Francis
Woodson, Carter Godwin

Human rights:
Douglass, Frederick
Gompers, Samuel
King, Martin Luther Jr.
Randolph, Asa Philip
Stone, Lucy Blackwell
Truth, Sojourner
Tubman, Harriet
Wells, Ida
Young, Whitney Moore Jr.

Indians:
Crazy Horse
Hollow Horn Bear
Joseph
Pocahantas
Red Cloud
Sacagawea
Sequoyah
Shadoo
Sitting Bull

Inventors:
Carlson, Chester Floyd
Edwin Armstrong
Bell, Alexander Graham
George Eastman
Edison, Thomas Alva
Farnsworth, Philo
Fulton, Robert
Howe, Elias

McCormick, Cyrus Hall
Morse, Samuel F.B.
Priestly, Joseph
Steinmetz, Charles
Tesla, Nikola
Whitney, Eli

Judaica:
Revel, Bernard

Law and Order:
Black, Hugo LaFayette
Holmes, Oliver Wendell Jr.
Marshall, John
Stone, Harlan Fiske

Medicine:
Barton, Clara
Cushing, Harvey Williams
Maass, Clara
McDowell, Ephraim
Papanicolaou, George N.

Military, hunting & arms:
Allen, Ethan
Arnold, Henry Harley "Hap"
Barry, John
Bolivar, Simon
Burgoyne, John
Chennault, Claire Lee
Churchill, Sir Winston
Clark, George Rogers
Decatur, Stephen
Dewey, George
Francisco, Peter
Galvez, Bernardo de
Garibaldi, Giuseppe
Gates, Horatio
Greene, Nathanael
Hale, Nathan
Hanson, John
Herkimer, Nicholas
Houston, Samuel
Jackson, Thomas Jonathan
Jones, John Paul

Kearny, Stephen Watts
Knox, Henry
Kosciusko, Thaddeus
Kossuth, Lajos
Lee, Robert Edward
Ludington, Sybil
MacArthur, Douglas
Macdonough, Thomas
Mannerheim, Carl Gustaf Emil
Mazzei, Philip
Nimitz, Chester William
Patton, George Smith Jr.
Perry, Matthew Calbraith
Perry, Oliver Hazard
Pershing, John Joseph
Pitcher, Molly
Poor, Salem
Porter, David Dixon
Pulaski, Kazimierz
Revere, Paul
Rochambeau, Jean Baptiste
Salem, Peter
Salomon, Haym
Sampson, William Thomas
San Martin, Jose de
Schley, Winfield Scott
Scott, Winfield
Sevier, John
Sheridan, Philip Henry
Sherman, William Tecumseh
Smith, John
Steuben, Friedrich Wilhelm von
Sullivan, John
Thayer, Sylvanus
Wayne, Anthony

Musicians:
Cohen, George Michael
Ellington, Edward "Duke"
Foster, Stephen
Gershwin, George
Handy, William Christopher
Herbert, Victor
Joplin, Scott
Kern, Jerome David

Key, Francis Scott
MacDowell, Edward Alexander
Nevin, Ethelbert Woodbridge
Paderewski, Ignace Jan
Rodgers, James Charles
Sousa, John Philip
Stravinsky, Igor Fyodorovich
Toscanini, Arturo

Nobel Prize & international awards:
Addams, Jane
Buck, Pearl
Bunche, Ralph J.
Churchill, Winston
Einstein, Albert
Eliot, Thomas Stearns
Faulkner, William
Hammarskjold, Dag
Hemingway, Ernest
Hull, Cordell
King, Martin Luther Jr.
Lewis, Sinclair Harry
Marshall, George C.
Millikan, Robert
O'Neill, Eugene Gladstone
Roosevelt, Theodore
Steinbeck, John
Wilson, Woodrow

Olympics:
Eagan, Edward Patrick Francis
Ewry, Ray C.
Madison, Helene Emma
Owens, James Cleveland
Thorpe, James Francis
Wightman, Hazel Virginia
Zaharias, Mildred Didrikson

Photography:
Eastman, George

Physicians:
Blackwell, Elizabeth
Drew, Charles Richard
Long, Crawford

Mayo, Charles Horace
Mayo, William James
Reed, Walter
Walker, Mary Edwards
White, Paul Dudley

Presidents:
Adams, John
Adams, John Quincy
Arthur, Chester Alan
Buchanan, James
Cleveland, Stephen Grover
Coolidge, John Calvin
Eisenhower, Dwight David
Fillmore, Millard
Garfield, James Abram
Grant, Ulysses Simpson
Hamilton, Alexander
Harding, Warren Gameliel
Harrison, Benjamin
Harrison, William Henry
Hayes, Rutherford Birchard
Hoover, Herbert Clark
Jackson, Andrew
Jefferson, Thomas
Johnson, Andrew
Johnson, Lyndon Baines
Kennedy, John Fitzgerald
Lincoln, Abraham
Madison, James
McKinley, William
Monroe, James
Pierce, Franklin
Polk, James Knox
Roosevelt, Franklin Delano
Roosevelt, Theodore
Taft, William Howard
Taylor, Zachary

Railroads:
Jones, John (Casey)

Red Cross:
Barton, Clara

Religion and philosophy:
Fox, George L.
Francis of Assisi
Goode, Alexander D.
Laubach, Frank Charles
Lee, Jason
Luther, Martin
Pohling, Clark V.
Priestly, Joseph
Revel, Bernard
Serra, Junipero
Washington, John P.
Williams, Roger

Royalty:
Isabella I
Louis XVI

Saints:
Francis of Assisi

Science & technology:
Bell, Alexander Graham
Carlson, Chester Floyd
Edison, Thomas Alva
Einstein, Albert
Farnsworth, Philo T.
Franklin, Benjamin
Fulton, Robert
Millikan, Robert Andrews
Morse, Samuel Finley Breese
Priestley, Joseph
Steinmetz, Charles Proteus
Tesla, Nikola
Wiley, Harvey Washington

Scouts:
Low, Juliette Magill Kinzie Gordon

Sports:
Clemente, Roberto
Eagan, Edward Patrick Francis
Ewry, Ray C.
Gehrig, Henry Louis
Jones, Robert Tyre Jr.

Madison, Helene Emma
Naismith, James A.
Ouimet, Francis
Owens, James Cleveland "Jesse"
Robinson, Jack Roosevelt
Rockne, Knute Kenneth
Ruth, George Herman
Thorpe, James Francis
Zaharias, Mildred Didrikson

Statesmen:
Baldwin, Abraham
Blair, Montgomery
Bolivar, Simon
Bryan, William Jennings
Bunche, Ralph Johnson
Clay, Henry
Davis, Jefferson
Gallatin, Albert
Gandhi, Mohandas Karamchand
Henry, Patrick
Hughes, Charles Evans
Hull, Cordell
Jay, John
LaFayette, Marquis de
Livingston, Robert R.
Marshall, George Cartlett
Masaryk, Tomas Garrigue
Mason, George
Norris, George W.
Schurz, Carl
Stanton, Edwin McMasters
Webster, Daniel

Suffrage:
Anthony, Susan Brownell
Catt, Carrie Chapman
Lockwood, Belva Ann Bennett
Mott, Lucretia Coffin
Stanton, Elizabeth Cady
Stone, Lucy Blackwell

Theater & film:
Barrymore, Ethel

Barrymore, John
Barrymore, Lionel
Cohen, George Michael
Cooper, Gary
Disney, Walter Elias
Fairbanks, Douglas
Fields, W.C.
Gable, Clark
Garland, Judy
Gershwin, George
Griffith, David Wark
Kern, Jerome David
Leigh, Vivien
Wayne, John

United Nations:
Hammarskjold, Dag

Women:
Adams, Abigail
Addams, Jane
Alcott, Louisa May
Anthony, Susan Brownell
Barrymore, Ethel
Barton, Clara
Bethune, Mary McLeod
Bissell, Emily P.
Buck, Pearl S.
Carson, Rachel Louise
Cassatt, Mary
Cather, Willa S.
Catt, Carrie Chapman
Dare, Virginia
Dickinson, Emily
Dix, Dorothea Lynde
Earhart, Amelia
Garland, Judy
Gilbreth, Lillian Evelyn Moller
Howe, Julia Ward
Isabella I
Keller, Helen
Leigh, Vivien
Lockwood, Belva Ann Bennett
Low, Juliette Magill Kinzie Gordon
Ludington, Sybil

Lyon, Mary
Maas, Clara
Madison, Dolley
Madison, Helene Emma
Michael, Moina Belle
Millay, Edna St. Vincent
Mitchell, Margaret
Moore, Marianne Craig
Mott, Lucretia Coffin
Perkins, Frances
Pitcher, Molly
Pocahontas
Roosevelt, Anna Eleanor
Ross, Elizabeth Griscom
Sacagawea
Scott, Blanche Stuart
Stanton, Elizabeth Cady
Stone, Lucy Blackwell
Sullivan, Anne
Truth, Sojourner
Tubman, Harriet
Washington, Martha Custis
Wells, Ida
Wharton, Edith Newbold
Wightman, Hazel Virginia
Zaharias, Mildred Didrikson

Writers & journalism:
Alcott, Louisa May
Buck, Pearl S.
Cather, Willa S.
Cooper, James Fenimore
Dante Alighieri
Dickinson, Emily
Dunbar, Paul Laurence
Eliot, Thomas Stearns
Emerson, Ralph Waldo
Frost, Robert Lee
Greeley, Horace
Harris, Joel Chandler
Harte, Bret
Hawthorne, Nathaniel
Hemingway, Ernest Miller
Irving, Washington
Jeffers, John Robinson

Johnson, James Weldon
Keller, Helen
Lanier, Sidney
Lewis, Harry Sinclair
Lippmann, Walter
London, John Griffith "Jack"
Longfellow, Henry Wadsworth
Lowell, James Russell
Masters, Edgar Lee
Melville, Herman
Millay, Edna St. Vincent
Mitchell, Margaret
Moore, Marianne Craig
O'Neill, Eugene Gladstone

Ochs, Adolph
Poe, Edgar Allan
Pulitzer, Joseph
Pyle, Ernest Taylor
Riley, James Whitcomb
Sandburg, Carl
Shakespeare, William
Steinbeck, John Ernst
Thoreau, Henry David
Twain, Mark
Wharton, Edith Newbold
White, William Allen
Whitman, Walter
Whittier, John Greenleaf

Tony C. ✓
Norman
Joe S.
Murph ✓
Artie A. ✓
Joe G. ✓
Tony G. ✓
Rocky
Cass.
Jerry B.
Gene E. ✓
Paddy R.
Elliot C.
Henry V.
Tony Connell
Alex M.
Wesley F.
Lester
Duffy
Tommy D.
John N.
Billy R. ✓
Willy M.
Billy Netthavot ✓
Bill B.
Jerry O. ✓
Harold B.
Brend W.
Nettie L.
Milly
929-5682 ✓

Jit
Gert
Brian
Peg
Johnny 2
Bob Q.
Jay B. ✓
Paddy O. ✓
Nancy G. ✓
Bobby G. ✓
Joe Pench ✓
Roddy G. ✓
Al the Cat ✓
Joe Lynch ✓
Al Watson ✓
Buddy S. ✓
Eddie R. ✓
Wally ✓

Gen. Flan.
Walton Serge